Stolen Childhood

A Saga of Polish War Children

Kochanej Janeczce
i Stefankowi
na pamiątkę naszej
wielkiej przyjaźni.
Teresa Kiśmowska

Toronto, June 24, 1984

Stolen Childhood

A Saga of Polish War Children

LUCJAN KROLIKOWSKI
O.F.M. Conv.

Translated by KAZIMIERZ J. ROZNIATOWSKI

FATHER JUSTIN ROSARY HOUR
Buffalo, New York

STOLEN CHILDHOOD
A Saga of Polish War Children
Lucjan Krolikowski, O.F.M. Conv.

ISBN: 0-9691588-0-7

Printed in Canada by John Deyell Company

To the Memory of
the late Archbishop of Montreal
Joseph Charbonneau
through whose radiant charity
the Canadian Government
welcomed into La Belle Province of Quebec
a Group of Polish Orphans
Remnants of the Thousands
deported during World War II
to Soviet Russia
and
in grateful appreciation to
numerous French Canadians, Religious and Lay People,
whose cordial response to the appeal of their Pastor
helped the young Exiles find in Canada
a haven-home

Contents

Foreword

Forewords to books are, as a rule, written by prominent people at least theoretically well acquainted with the subject but otherwise not connected with it in any way. My case is different. I think Fr. Lucjan chose me to preface his saga of Polish war children because I witnessed and participated in every aspect of it.

Poland lost 2,200,000 children in World War II; all other countries 11,000,000. Of my family of eight—parents, four girls, and two boys—only three survived the Gehenna in Soviet Russia. We live now in Canada—my older sister a nurse, the younger one a hairdresser, and I a doctor of medicine, all married with children of our own. But we cannot forget what we went through, and today it is like a tangle of nightmares. As a consequence, we are sensitive to the fate of all children throughout the world.

In 1959, ten years after our group of Polish orphans arrived safely on the hospitable shores of Canada, the United Nations drew up a Declaration of Children's Rights, obliging mankind to give each child whatever is most valuable in its cultures. Now the world even celebrates International Children's Day. But millions of children still suffer without respite. Behind the Iron, Bamboo, and other curtains, they are tortured, rejected, abandoned; here in America thousands are exploited and manipulated for greedy purposes. Ours is a century of inhumanity and children are the easiest and most plentiful victims.

I weep for them. I join in spirit Adam Mickiewicz, the brilliant Polish poet, who, in "Dziady," speaks of himself as the incarnation of the Polish nation, as having swallowed its soul. He loves the suffering millions and suffers with them. That is why he gave himself a new name, Million.

But with all its sadness, *Stolen Childhood* is a dear reminder of the deep concern that prompted many persons to sacrifice themselves on a thousand occasions to alleviate our miseries and save us. It is written with love, compassion, and optimism. I agree with the notable secular Catholic who wrote to Archbishop Joseph Gawlina, Chief Chaplain of the Polish Army and Refugees,

"Its pages of advice are so good that I would like to have my children memorize them and accept them as Life's guideposts."

Jan Mazur, M.D.

Montreal, Canada

Introduction

A beautiful young lady, bored at a family reception, picked up an album portraying the Hitler-contrived holocaust of Poland. "Who needs it today?" she exclaimed indignantly. "Shouldn't there be a stop to it? Shouldn't we forget those atrocities of the past and look to the future?"

I knew the parents of the young lady. They had survived the concentration camp, and she had come into this world ten years after the holocaust. She is representative of millions in the free world who for many years have voiced the same opinion, and some of whom even deny that a holocaust occurred.

A former deportee to a forced-labor camp in Soviet Russia, I too have been tempted to forget the past that haunted me for years as a horrible nightmare. When in 1960 I wrote *Stolen Childhood* in Polish, I did it, as a witness, for the records of Polish history at the request of Polish orphans whose parents had died in Russian captivity. But I was ready to forgive and forget the past. As a priest I saw Communists as disoriented people who did not know what they were doing to their innocent neighbors.

I was wrong. The holocaust is still going on behind the Iron Curtain, the cries of its victims drowned in the blare of peace propaganda. Die-hard Communists are still working toward world revolution and to that end are spreading terrorism all over the world, like the drum roll before a battle to paralyze the foe with fear.

Now I see the free world more ready to face this reality than it was when Soviet Russia enjoyed the privileged place of an ally in the community of nations. The free world must learn the stark truth, that Communism is the old Russian imperialism in disguise. Even Karl Marx would have condemned it in its present form.

Stolen Childhood describes the plight of thousands of Polish children deported to Soviet Russia and thereafter left virtually homeless. I hope it may draw attention to the parallel fate of the children of other races and nationalities who, as often in free societies as in the Communist world, are ravaged by the uncontrolled passion for power, wealth, success, and ill-understood independence. Their psychological and spiritual sufferings are likely to ruin the rest of their lives, even if they are allowed to live. We have learned that from the past. We dare not forget it.

Lucjan Krolikowski, O.F.M. Conv.

Father Justin Rosary Hour
Buffalo, New York

August 15, 1983

Acknowledgements

My heartfelt thanks are due to my friend, Mr. Kazimierz Rozniatowski of Winnipeg, Manitoba, for his faithful translation of my book, *Skradzione Dziecinstwo*, into English.

I owe a debt of gratitude to Mrs. Janina (Fulmyk) Lorenc, one of the many young victims of deportation to Soviet Russia, who participated in their long odyssey and, on their behalf, inspired and encouraged the translation; to Mrs. John O'Sullivan of Baie Comeau, Quebec, for her enduring interest in its publication; and to Miss Catherine Morrissey of Dunkirk, New York, for her editorial and secretarial assistance.

I wish to make grateful acknowledgement of the work of Professor Anthony Rozak, Art Department, University of Buffalo, who coordinated the production of the book, planned the layout for maps and photographs, and designed the jacket cover.

I am particularly indebted to Dr. Calvin Smith, Professor of English, State University College at Fredonia, New York, for his meticulous editing and invaluable suggestions for the improvement of the manuscript.

PART ONE

Deportation to Russia

1

Siberia Is for Children Also

The invasion of the Red Army into the eastern territories of Poland on September 17, 1939, magnified beyond all measure the panic and the fear among the inhabitants, who already lived under the threat of the rapidly spreading war, unleashed only seventeen days earlier by Hitler on the western borders of our country.

The Eastern aggressor started with smiles, and their "moloytsy" (youngsters) in the armoured columns invading our territories did not forget to wave their caps toward the local people just as they had been told to do as a sign of their friendly intentions. At that time nobody knew, or could even guess, that on August 23, a week before the German attack, the secret Ribbentrop-Molotov Treaty had been signed, clearly specifying the partition of all Polish territory between the two temporary allies. However, the population of the border areas had their own judgment upon these matters. They knew their nearest neighbor only too well to be deluded as to his plans and intentions. Soon, indeed, the smiles disappeared, and the rule of the bloody NKVD (now KGB) commenced in earnest.

By a quirk of fate, although I was a permanent resident of Greater Poland (the Western part of the country), I happened to be in Lwow in 1939, where I was studying philosophy in the monastery of the Franciscan Friars. Here, caught by the outbreak of the war, I witnessed all the horrors of the Soviet occupation from the outset. Not only was I an eyewitness, and a compassionate observer; but as fate would have it, I was also subjected to the terror, which, alas, soon began in those Eastern territories.

The situation deteriorated from day to day. The invader cut off the occupied territories from the rest of the world and rapidly reinforced security along the borders. A tight "iron curtain" fell upon everything happening there. These events were not at all encouraging.

The arrests and round-ups soon began, often more extensive than those of the German occupation. Lacking accommodation in prisons, the Russians crowded arrested people into cloisters requisitioned for the purpose or into derelict public buildings. The activity was aimed primarily against the intellectual elite, for the Kremlin intended here, as well as in other countries it dominated, to "obiezgalovit" (deprive of its head) the terrorized population. The jails were crammed with Polish working "intelligentsia," people employed in many professions having nothing to do with politics: respected university professors, high school and elementary teachers, judges, lawyers, physicians, state employees, and members of the police force. Landowners were especially persecuted. And army officers and priests, regarded as enemies of the "new order", were hounded by the NKVD.

But the matter did not end with these "higher-echelon" arrests. Beginning in February 1940, no less relentless terror was unleashed on peasants and laborers, as well as borderline poverty victims—the healthy and the sick, adults and children. Terror spread everywhere. Thousands of youngsters experienced it along with the others, at the very outset of their lives, and would bear forever after an indelible psychological stigma.

No one was safe, day or night. Some people hid like frightened animals, changing their shelters every night; some slept with a coiled rope under their heads, to escape through a window in case the Communist militia knocked. Others, still believing that arrest was inevitable, had their belongings ready in a bundle, with family mementos, a rosary, a prayer book, or a Bible. Every once in a while round-ups took place in towns. It was not easy to hide, because the militia and the Soviet soldiers would instantly block off the streets and check the identities of the people herded into a crowd, loading "suspects" onto heavy trucks. Most often arrests were carried out at night, during city blackouts, or while the air-raid alarm system was being tested. Cars would zoom through the streets and pick the victims from their homes—not only young people or men in their prime who had not managed to escape, but also their old parents, wives, and children; the families of those the police could not find, those taken into the army, or those who had hidden just in time.

Despite the intensified vigilance of the people, their relatives, acquaintances, and friends were disappearing from the streets even in daylight. Every once in a while someone would be summoned to the police commissariat, never to return.

All that affected the city was experienced in the villages also. The militia would raid the homesteads suddenly, usually in the middle of the night or at dawn. Militiamen or soldiers would surround a home while the commandant arrested the head of the family, placed him under guard facing the wall, then ordered the mother to pack their belongings, usually within an hour. It was in vain to ask about the cause of arrest or to inquire about the family's fate, because the militiamen would always reply with the lie that they would return in a few days and that was why they should take only a few of their belongings. They were assured that their property would be safe under the protection of the Soviet authorities. The deceived people wanted to believe these lies, although they should have known that they were losing their home, their belongings, and their land forever.

After an hour the bewildered people were herded onto trucks or sleds with their bundles, packages, and cases. From among the pillows, comforters, and quilts emerged the heads of terrified children. They were all afraid, but only the older ones guessed that something horrible was happening. Even the grown-ups did not perceive, as yet, all that was awaiting them. But their horror would increase as they encountered on the roads whole columns of trucks and sleds, in them their neighbors and strangers from distant areas.

After a while, Polish citizens were ordered to accept Soviet citizenship. Though they rejected the idea instinctively, all their attempts to resist only set off new rounds of police chicanery and arrests.

In our monastery the superiors left the matter of accepting Soviet citizenship to our own discretion. Three of us declined because our families were living under German occupation and that was where we wanted to go officially. Thousands of other people were in the same position, willing to join their closest ones at any price. We were all registered as those seeking departure. The consequences were soon apparent. The Red militia began to appear at the monastery time after time, allegedly searching for firearms. We had just completed the course in philosophy; taking advantage of a two-week vacation prior to commencing the study of theology, I left, together with my friend Richard Gruza, for a small grange owned by our Franciscan province on the outskirts of Lwow. Immediately on our return we were summoned to the commissariat for the documents permitting us to live temporarily in Lwow, with a warning, of course, that our not picking up the documents might result in our arrest.

The next day, long before dawn, in order to save ourselves a long wait in line, we took our places along the walls of the commissariat on Kurkowa Street; but quite a few people were there already, among them a young nun in disguise. The line grew rapidly, the sun began to blaze, but we were not called in. Then, exactly at noon, when we were swaying with fatigue, from the commissariat gate came a militiaman who swore at us and accused us of impeding traffic. Shortly afterward he kindly suggested that we enter the yard of the commissariat where there was shade and much more room.

Even a person who has already been cheated several times clings to a certain trust in the human heart. Not suspecting anything evil, we entered the yard. Just then the militiaman bolted the gate and locked it. There followed a kind of selection from a prepared list. A very small group of people were released, among them the nun, who, however, did not want to go. She offered to stay with those of us who were detained and perform any kind of service for us, but we declined her offer.

As we were being shifted in the halls and rooms of the commissariat, Wiesiek Kotarski, one of the three seminarians, taking advantage of the turmoil, jumped through a window and disappeared into the garden before the militiaman understood what was happening. That evening, however, he returned and surrendered himself, not willing to desert us in misfortune.

Since the commissariat was becoming packed with additional victims of the round-ups, we were led back into the yard. We lay down near a high wall, thoroughly exhausted and famished. In the last rays of the sunset our glances met, blank, expressionless, dulled by torment. From time to time the silence was broken by the grumblings of the militiamen still bringing in the human "svoloch" (scum). A woman, having obviously lost her senses, whispered something to herself and, smiling all the while, paced the yard in circles. The children tried to play in the sand but, discouraged by the general silence or by the sight of despair-ridden grown-ups, just ran to their mothers asking when they would be going home and was there going to be supper soon. These impatient questions awakened us from our torpor. It is not easy to bear the complaint of a hungry child. We were beginning to realize that nothing would save us from deportation, and were steeling ourselves to face cold, hunger, and slave labor. But those children? Would they have to endure all this too? And could they?

2

Boys and Girls in Prison

The laments of the Polish people rose to heaven throughout Eastern Poland, its 600 miles from north to south, its 250-mile breadth. My group at the Kurkowa Street Police Station should have felt lucky. At least we were spared the horror of weeks or months in prison before being thrown into a concentration camp. The very day after our arrest we were sentenced *in absentia* to ten years of hard labor.

Some less fortunate were transported by cattle train to Minsk, a Russian city not far from the pre-war Polish-Russian border, one of many deportation areas in Soviet Russia. There, early in the autumn of 1940, they entered a sort of transient prison that had been a monastery before the Bolshevik Revolution, to join hundreds of other captives, hungry and bewildered.

It was impossible to estimate how many prisoners had gone through this place. While thousands were being transported from here to the labor camps in Vorkuta, within the Arctic Circle, Siberia and Kazakhstan, other thousands were taking their place. The building was bursting with masses of prisoners overflowing the cells. Into a cell of eight metres (about twenty-five feet) square, the militiamen would jam 120 people. There they squatted on the concrete floor, in summer half-naked because of the terrible heat unrelieved by two tiny windows with broken panes and a ventilator that hardly ever worked. Close to the door a "parasha," a large container generally with no lid, served as a toilet. The prisoners were taken out of the cell only once a day. Their ages ranged from ten to eighty-five years; among them were some with active tuberculosis and many with open wounds. The prisoners, besides Poles, were of the many other nationalities that form the mosaic of the Russian population; some were Soviet Communists.

In one cell two young boys were dying, an eighteen-year-old Soviet "komsomolets" (member of the Soviet youth organization, equivalent to the Boy Scouts of America) and a Polish student from Brzesc. The "komsomolets" swore as only Bolsheviks can swear. His father, who was also in the cell, did not even look at his dying son. The Polish boy lay silent on his light overcoat spread on the floor. All the prisoners' rattlings and calls for a doctor were repeatedly answered by one word, "zavtra" (tomorrow).

When the "komsomolets" quieted down, tired out by his vain cries, the Polish boy said, "I would like to confess . . . I want a priest, now . . ." Silence fell upon the cell; the prisoners looked at each other helplessly. They were positive that there was no priest among them. The boy called out again, "I want a priest." Just then, somewhere near the wall, a man stirred. He approached the boy, knelt beside him, and crossed himself. All the prisoners watched in silence. The confession began. It was very brief. The priest granted the absolution, said the "Our Father" and the "Hail Mary" together with the boy, then returned to his spot by the wall. A few minutes later, in the silence, the boy stretched out his arms, smiled happily, whispered "Mama!" and died. Nobody knew the priest's name. At dawn he was taken out of the cell and never seen again.

And the "komsomolets"? He started swearing again and died early in the morning. The prisoners dragged the father to his son's corpse, but he only touched it with his foot and mumbled, "Noo, yevo k'chortu!" ("To hell with him!").

* * *

Sixteen-year-old Anthony Dabrowski had not been at home when his mother, sister, and brother were arrested. Lonely without them, he wandered over Eastern Poland and finally settled on Third of May Street in Lwow.

On August 25, 1940, when he had just returned from a visit with some acquaintances, there was a knock at his door. Anthony opened it and a man in civilian clothes came in and ordered him "to go along with him to the militia." Anthony refused until the visitor produced an NKVD identification card. When Anthony asked whether he should take his suitcase with his belongings, the agent replied that there was no need for that; it was only a matter of checking his passport, and he would be returning shortly after this formality.

Outside was a large police truck loaded with other Poles who had been seized in the same manner. On the way the truck picked up a few more people, randomly arrested, and took them to a prison. On the night of August 26, they were loaded into cattle cars for a three-day trip to the prison in Homel, in Byelo-Russia. "Here," as Anthony recalls the experience,

> they told me to undress completely. A very thorough search followed, although they had taken all my documents away from me while still in Lwow. They cut off all the buttons of my suit and my belt buckle, and took all belts and shoelaces. We were divided into groups. For some inexplicable reason I remained all by myself.
>
> They put me into cell No. 31 where twenty-eight other prisoners were held already: Russians, Jews, Ukrainians, but not a single Pole. The cell was about two metres wide and six long. The "parasha" was right in the corner. When the guard that brought me had closed the door behind him I could not move even one step further, the cell was so crowded.
>
> I stood motionless for a few minutes. Someone asked me who I was and what I was in for. Knowing Russian only vaguely, I answered that I was Polish. This was met by jeers and scorn. They pointed to the "parasha" as the only place suitable for a Pole. In this hopeless situation I took my place on top of the "parasha."
>
> Now I looked at my new abode more thoroughly. There, under the little window stood a small table for bread. The people lay on the floor, undressed, almost naked. Some were playing cards; others were telling how they happened to land in prison. One, for instance, boasted about having murdered his sister. The description of her agonies evoked outbursts of laughter. I had never in my life witnessed such depravity, so I sat there depressed and did not utter a word.
>
> The most puzzling thing to me was the spreading odor of rotten fish. After a few hours, the rattling of pots and tins was heard. They were bringing something to eat, I thought. I had eaten almost nothing for three days, since leaving Lwow. The door opened. They brought in the soup. I knew then where the sickening fishy odor had come from. The soup was of fish-heads, after the oil had been extracted. The prisoners, who over a period of months or even years had been eating the stuff, were so impregnated with its odor that the sweat of their bodies smelled of fish.
>
> I sniffed what was given to me, but despite my hunger, could not put it into my mouth. At that moment a vision of my own home came before my eyes. I broke out crying. . . .
>
> Night came. I was tired. I began to doze off. But my cell-mates, intent on having fun at my expense, poured urine over my head, and that caused bursts of laughter again. At dawn, near four o'clock, the door opened. The guard ordered that the "parasha"

be taken out and emptied. Together with one of the Russians I gladly performed this task in order to get a whiff at least of fresh air. At seven in the morning they brought in bread, boiling water instead of tea, and some salt. Each prisoner received 600 grams (about 21 ounces) of bread, half a litre of water, and a pinch of salt. This and the stinking soup constituted our daily diet.

Three days passed. My cell-mates offered me a spot under the table when two prisoners were taken away, and I could now sleep more comfortably. One evening around six o'clock I was led out of the cell. There in the corridor were five other Poles. We were all handcuffed. Not one of us knew what awaited us. We were loaded into an enclosed truck and carted away in an unknown direction.

We naturally assumed that we were to be shot. I began to cry and pray simultaneously. After fifteen minutes, the truck stopped. We were ordered to get down and were led under escort into some kind of building. We sat down on the floor in a corridor and waited. Half an hour or so passed. Each minute seemed like eternity. One of us was called into the office. After some time, from behind the door of the office, we heard a shot. The door opened and a body covered with a blanket was carried out on a stretcher. The next one was called in. Nobody doubted then that we had been brought here to be murdered one by one after they had obtained the confessions they wanted. One of the prisoners fainted.

I asked the guard for some water. He answered that drinking would be a waste because very soon none of us would ever again be in need of anything. We heard another shot from behind the door, and another body was carried out. The routine was followed with the others until my turn came. They led me into a large room and put me in front of a large table, behind which the NKVD officers were sitting. The glare of the spotlights behind them blinded me. My documents were there on the table. The officers asked me whether I understood Russian, and I said no. An interpreter was found, but I had difficulty understanding him. They asked me whether I was a Pole and where my mother was. "You have taken my mother away, so now you, yourselves, tell me where she is," I replied. "And where is your father? Maybe he was an officer and fought against our men?" "Maybe, I do not know," I said.

Examining my documents, they declared that I was accused of belonging to some secret organization about which I knew nothing, of spying on behalf of the capitalist powers, and so on. There followed names of people and places totally unknown to me. They ordered me to admit my guilt and to reveal the names of those with whom I had allegedly worked in the secret organization; having done this, I should be free. My answer was, "Even if I knew something, I would not tell you, so there is all the more reason I cannot tell you anything because I know nothing." This courage earned me a few blows on my head, back, wherever—all administered with a rifle butt. After each reply, "I do not know," I was hit again.

I felt blood running from my nose and mouth, but I stood firmly wanting to show them that I was not going to give in. Again a series of blows, and then one of the tormentors got up and said, "Wait! He is going to speak!" He pulled a handgun from the holster and held it against my head with a warning, "Speak, you Polish dog, or I shall clobber you right here!" At that moment I thought I was going to die the same way as my unfortunate companions had. My nerves gave in; I burst out crying. My tormentor yelled, "Do not cry, you Polish dog. Moscow does not trust tears," and hit me so hard with the butt of the gun that I lost consciousness.

I came to in a cell, the same one I had been taken from. Above me stood my cell-mates, Russians, trying to bring me to. The time was four in the morning. My hands were black from the prolonged handcuffing, my whole face bloody, the left cheek swollen and cut, two teeth loosened, one knocked out completely. My back and legs were blue. When I told my cell-mates where I had got this kind of treatment, they began banging on the door and demanding that I be taken to the little hospital, or they would go on a hunger strike. The threat worked. I was carried to the prison hospital where, to my amazement, I met all the five fellows with whom I had been interrogated during the night and who I thought had been shot. They had been handled the same way as I. The interrogators had been firing blanks, and the body on the stretcher had been a mannequin covered with a blanket; the prisoners had been led out through another door. Five times more I was interrogated, and each time was submitted to new tortures, such as having my fingers crushed in the door jamb.

A month and a half passed. I got used to the hard floor, the prison soup, even the interrogations.

* * *

Young Polish girls were being imprisoned also and often encountered in their cells Soviet girls, age twelve and older. The Soviet penal code charges children of twelve with legal responsibility for common breaches of the law, such as "hooliganism" and theft, and children fourteen years and older for political offenses. The young Soviet girls were so debauched physically and psychologically that often it was difficult to distinguish them from mature women.

Marysia, a Polish girl, arrested along with her mother for refusing to accept a Soviet passport, was thrown from one jail to another until finally, separated from her mother, she was sent to a penal colony for juveniles. At the time of her arrest she was fourteen. Her father, a physician in Lwow, was lost without trace at the time of the September upheaval. In her diary (recorded by Irene Wasilewska in *For Uncommitted Crimes* Rome 1945. p. 28) Marysia says:

> *The first prison:* My mother, with a cardiac problem, had a heart attack in jail. No help was given, and when I asked for water, the warden cursed me. After two days we were transported to Halicz, where we landed in the well known "pogreb" (cellar), a primitive prison in the cellar of a dwelling house. There was a corridor in the centre and at both sides tiny cells, 2½ by 2 metres, with no windows. In a horrible stench, and in darkness barely dispelled by the meager light of a lamp burning all day, eleven of us sat there, all women. . . .
>
> *Prison in Stanislawow* (about 100 miles south-east of Lwow): This was also a temporary prison, hastily arranged. Eighteen women slept in a tiny cell wherever there was space, on a plank bed, or underneath, or in the passage on the floor. Some light filtered in through the curtained window, but not a whiff of fresh air. The lamp burned all night—the inmates' enemy. Through the long months in jails and in the penal colony, I dreamed about sleeping through just one night in darkness. I tied a handkerchief over my tired eyes, but even so I felt the glare of the light.
>
> For a whole month we were not allowed out for a walk, as they thought it was enough to be let out once a day at any odd time (five in the morning or twelve noon) to use an outhouse in the back yard. We all competed for the privilege of taking out the "parasha." Those who have never spent time in a Soviet prison in this horrible inactivity will never know what happiness one can experience in performing this otherwise repulsive task. To see the sky, the sun, a bit of greenery; to fill the lungs with fresh air from the neighboring gardens—these were the dreams of each of us. We established a list, and for that brief interval of two or three minutes we waited the whole day. When we returned, the cell appeared even gloomier and the stench gave us a headache. Our food consisted of 600 grams of bread, actually clay, and boiling water without sugar for breakfast; for dinner, half a litre of stinking soup made of offal and cattle heads. I often found in my bowl an eye, teeth or tufts of hair. In the evening we were given the same soup.
>
> In our cell were "borderers" [people arrested for trying to cross the "border" into the German occupation zone] and a few women charged with counter-revolution and inciting unrest. The Soviets forced admissions of guilt from these latter by promising that they could return to their children, who otherwise would be deported to Russia.

In Kharkov jail [some 400 miles south of Moscow]: On the 22nd of September 1940, I was separated from my mother. A "stryelok" (soldier) called me out with the familiar "sobierajsia z wieszczami" (get ready with your belongings). I looked at my mother, who paled but sent me a smile as the door closed behind me. It took all my willpower to hold back my tears.

I was taken to another prison in Kharkov, one converted from an old monastery. It looked gloomy, with its great iron door, dark cells, thick walls with moisture running down them. There wasn't enough room even to stand in the cell I was pushed into. Seventy women, almost naked because of the unbearable heat, shrieked and milled around in the small space. Because of the lack of room in the cell, I spent my first night in the corridor near the "interrogation cells." From one of them emanated wild shrieks of a Russian female. In the morning a man was led out from the other. His clothes were wet and torn, his face swollen, with recent traces of blood. He was swaying, and from under his swollen eyelids stared crazed eyes. The guard pushing him urged him to pass by me quickly.

One day in our cell we heard the cry, "Don't hit me, you scoundrel!" and then groans and sounds as of kicking, then the bang of a door being shut. I began to pound on the door and cry because it seemed to me that I recognized the voice of my brother, who had been arrested in Lwow. . . .

In the penal colony for juveniles: While we were being moved from a camp in Starodub in the Orel province [about 300 miles southwest of Moscow], five of us underage Polish girls met for the first time free Soviet females. A woman going by asked us in a whisper, "Zakluczonnyje?" ("Sentenced?") "Do not be afraid, sisters; you go today, we go tomorrow." I got acquainted then with Soviet reality. "Żavtra my" (Our turn tomorrow) still sticks in my memory. . . .

At long last we arrived in Starodub. It was October 6, 1940, and autumn was in full swing. We went along a path in a neglected park, golden leaves rustling under our feet and fierce nostalgia gripping our hearts. Somehow my family home came to mind. A tall fence with barbed wire and broken glass, and the "storks" (elevated lookout posts) with the guards all told us that we had arrived at our destination. We stopped at a gate with a huge sign: "Starodubskaja trudowaja isprawitielnaja kolonia" (Starodub Correctional Colony). At the sentry post we were received by the manager of the "chozczast" (husbandry department) named Wladimir Chankiewicz. He consoled us by telling us that we would be not too bad off if we worked well.

The colony was located in what used to be a theological seminary, a large two-story building situated in an old park. In the center of a flower bed in front of the main entrance stood a statue of Stalin, the benevolent protector of juvenile female lawbreakers, cuddling a child in his arms. Above the entrance hung a very large portrait of him.

The colony had five hundred inmates from thirteen to eighteen years old; twenty-six of us were Polish girls, aged fourteen to eighteen. One of them was Zosia. She had tried to escape to Poland from Northern Kazakhstan, where she had been deported with her family. She had been arrested when she got stuck in the snow, though her family had managed to hide.

Kasia and Wanda had been arrested for having been members of the Polish Scouts. Each was sentenced to eight years. Applying all kinds of methods, the Soviets had tried to make them admit to other felonies they had not committed. Dressed only in shirts, they had been placed in "carcers" filled with water, and Wanda had been beaten.

There was a sewing factory in the colony and a knitting mill. Initially the work was organized into three eight-hour shifts, but from May, 1941, we worked in two shifts of ten hours each. The work was difficult and tedious, all the more so because we had to operate machines that were totally unfamiliar to us.

In the spinning section, working conditions were very bad. The cotton dust flew in clouds, getting into our eyes and lungs. One day Jadzia got sick and spat blood. . . .

Little Basia worked with molten lead, which she had to pour over the needles on the machines. Her complexion became yellow like a lemon, and in her little face the large eyes shone with a feverish light. She hemorrhaged a lot. I took her place once when she did not have enough strength to get up to work and, despite the threat of the "carcer," remained on her plank bed. The odor and the fumes of the lead were so awful that by evening I was totally unconscious.

Among the Soviet girls were only a few "political" ones: Bielowa Klawa, sentenced to ten years for scattering anti-Communist leaflets in Rostov at the instigation of her lover, a film actor; Anna Wozniesienskaya, sentenced to eight years because her grandfather had been a "pomyeshchick" (landowner). Her father, an engineer, was also in a camp somewhere; others had been sentenced to three or five years for counter-revolutionary utterances. About fifty were so-called "pyerebyezhcheets" (persons attempting to cross the border illegally) from Latvia, Estonia, Bessarabia, and Hungary, in the years 1939-1944. In Russia, to which they had been running with enthusiasm, they got sentences of three, five, or eight years of labor. Most of them had lost their former zeal, longed for their homes, and cried constantly, especially at the time of festivities.

The rest came from the underworld of Leningrad and Moscow: prostitutes, murderesses, thieves and female hooligans. These people, almost all of them infected by syphilis, we slept, bathed, and ate with; some of them, only fifteen years old, were serving the third year of their sentences. While they were still children they had worked in the penal "dyet-colony" (penal colony for children), four-hour shifts of light work. All of them were covered with tattoos like a Chinese screen. On their hands and legs they had tatooed some unprintable words, on their cheeks the initials of their lovers. One of them had "Stalin" on her left arm, "Lenin" on her right arm, and on her breasts a complicated design of pigeons. On the faces of some were scars made with a knife shaped like a fan. "The lover signed," they used to say; that is, they had been taken as the lover's property. They looked horrible, covered with ulcers, puffed up; one had no brows at all. They painted their faces in a horrible manner. Makeup, eau de cologne, and hair lotion they could buy in the shop on the grounds. They liked to drink the eau de cologne and hair lotion, and afterwards behaved like objectionable drunks. Their rude words and their conversation, their most extraordinary swearing, surrounded us all day long. Many of them were lesbians; many became lovers of the "vospitatiels" (educators), who spoke to them in their own lingo, using the foulest words from their vocabulary. All this drove us to tears, emotional upset, and utter despair. The most horrible one was Anna Gusieva, aged seventeen, the lover of the leader of a gang of thieves, sentenced for choking children to death.

They stole our belongings and our food, but this was less of a problem than their general behavior. They were loyally disposed towards the Soviet Union. The commandants emphasized for our benefit that, with regard to the "national-patriotic" aspect, they were very healthy. Maybe they were not so totally evil, but when they found victims among us, they persecuted us sadistically. They had a mob psychology, following whatever slogans they heard.

In May, 1941, a daughter of some former Soviet dignitary arrived in the colony. Her true identity was disguised, and she herself was rigorously forbidden to reveal it. In the colony she was called Gawronskaya Lola. Raised in the Kremlin, she spoke fluent English and French and used to go abroad with her parents. Her father had been shot, her mother had been sentenced to fifteen years, and she had got eight. She was nervous, or more properly, terrified. She was treated more cruelly than the others, often put into the "carcer" for no reason, thrown out of the dining hall, and treated unfairly at work. When I got better acquainted with her, she told me about her interrogation. For three days she had been locked up in the "carcer" without food or water. She had been under terrific mental stress; was told to be ready for interrogation at all times; and was beaten. I saw the unhealed wounds on her back myself. I believed everything she told me, and even if I had not wanted to, her completely grey hair would have convinced me.

There was a school at the colony, with lessons three hours a day. We were assigned to grade four because we did not know Russian and were lectured on the history of the "Soyuz" (Union) and the Party. We were forbidden to speak Polish.

Our lives were poisoned by the "obschestvyennaya rabota" (social-conscience development). The large crew of "vospitatiels" (educators) and "politrooks" (political officers) decided to "pyerevospitat" (re-educate) us to become "chestniye grazhdani Sovyetskavo Soyuza" (noble citizens of the Soviet Union).

3

The Exile and Settlement Called Free

The Siberian taiga, stretching from the Ural Mountains all the way to the Pacific Ocean, is a huge, unbroken forest, covering an area larger than the United States or Canada. Since Tsarist Russia annexed Siberia in the 17th century, the taiga has served almost solely as a gigantic political prison. Here the cruelest tormentors are hunger, cold, and all sorts of privation. In Tsarist days the most large-scale deportation took place after the uprising in January, 1863, when over 50,000 Poles were exiled to the areas of Tomsk (some 2100 miles due east of Moscow) and the Irkutsk (far north in central Siberia).

In both Tsarist and Soviet terminology, the labor camps, the Siberian settlements, those in Kazakhstan, and others go under the name of corrective camps. Here, as well as in jails, men and women of the highest intellect were detained together with the most hardened criminals; according to the historian Van Loon, "their only sin was based on the fact that they loved their neighbors more than they deserved." In such corrective camps, besides mature adults, landed large groups of Polish children and young people. Such was Soviet justice.

To the west of the Urals in inaccessible forests, in tundra, and in marshlands are located the ill-famed camps of Vorkuta, Pechora, and Ukhta. A third group of camps are on the steppes of Kazakhstan, home of the famous Cossacks, "Kazaks," a Central Asian republic of the Soviet Union covering an area larger than the whole of India and populated mostly by Kirghizians, commonly called Kazakhs.

It was to these huge Asiatic areas that the civilian population of Eastern Poland was deported; as if in mockery, they were called "free deportees." The obvious intention of the Soviet government was, by deporting and dispersing the Poles over these vast territories, to accelerate their assimilation into the local element and thereby make it impossible for them to organize; also, and above all, the Russians hoped to do away once and for all with the whole Polish question by incorporating the Eastern Polish territories into Russia. These territories, annexed by Russia in September, 1939, were inhabited by 13,000,000 people and constituted more than one half of Poland's territory.

Including the relatively small percentage of Ukrainians, Byelo-Russians, and Jews, the total number of Polish citizens deported by the Soviet government during its "eternal friendship" with Germany between 1939 and 1941 amounted to approximately 1,680,000 people, not including prisoners of war. The deportation of civilians was massive during four periods: in February, 1940, during the severe cold, 110 trains, each carrying 2,000 persons, transported a total of 220,000; in April, 1940, 160 trains transported 320,000; between June and July of the same year, 240,000 were deported; the fourth wave accounted for approximately 200,000 more. The total, in excess of 1,000,000, includes 500,000 women, 380,000 children, and a large number of the elderly and sick.

The deportations have never totally ceased. They were only suspended when Eastern Poland was invaded by German armies during the German-Russian war which broke out in June, 1941. The deportations were renewed in 1944-45, after the Germans were driven back and the Soviet occupation resumed.

Sanitary conditions in the transports mocked even the most elementary human requirements. Two and three-week treks were completed in unheated cattle cars through the severe cold of February, 1940. Hunger, disease, dirt, and exhaustion decimated the exiles along the way. Most of the victims, of course, were among the weakest, the elderly, but little children also died en masse during the journey. Even if they survived the trip, many died from hunger and cold upon arriving at their destination. The death harvest among these Poles was terrifying. By 1942, almost one half of them were dead. Every year, twenty percent of these people who did not go through prisons or camps but were deported to the taiga or the steppes died; and around thirty percent of those in prisons and camps, where housing conditions, nutrition, and hygiene were the worst.

In the so-called "free resettlement," the people were housed and fed so poorly that no one living in the West in normal conditions could imagine such a life at all. The local population, suffering extreme poverty, did not have much to offer even in barter for a suit, a pillow, or some other item that the exiles had to give up in order to stay alive. Because most of the stores were empty, money had little value. It could not buy much, even if one was "making the norm" and earning more than the average. Only the higher "norm" or greater productivity brought the most precious thing, a larger allocation of bread. It is true that to reach the norm required the last ounce of human strength, but the increased ration often saved the whole family from starvation. The worst off were the people incapable of hard labor, particularly mothers with small children. The family's conditions could improve when one of the children was able to start working; little waifs were set to work. Quite often twelve-year-old boys were the only supporters of the family, especially if the mother was sick. Of course, conditions were not the same in all "settlements" or collective farms. There were places where the natives lived in less misery and where the conditions of the deportees capable of work were therefore less difficult. On the average, however, the exiles were literally near death from hunger and exhaustion.

I was an exile myself and know of these matters at first hand. I know also that in some "settlements" conditions were worse than in ours, in others not quite so bad. But our settlement was the most common type. Being young and reasonably strong, I was able to bear a few hardships, and that is why I looked upon the weak and frail with all the greater compassion. There were, alas, many of them in our group. It could not have been otherwise because we had many women and children. I had an opportunity to observe them very closely during our two-week journey.

We covered approximately 2,000 miles by train during that August of 1940. The Lord be praised that we were not deported in winter, as was the earlier group; otherwise many people would not have made it. It is always easier to bear even the worst conditions in summer.

We traveled first towards Kiev, then towards Penza (about 400 miles southeast of Moscow); it seemed that we were being directed towards Asiatic Russia behind the Urals. Meanwhile, during a two-day stop-over in Penza after further directives from Moscow, we were routed northwest towards Moscow. The change of direction raised a certain hope: maybe we were being returned to Poland. That was a delusion.

We were held up in Moscow for a full day, shunted to a side-track, locked up in the freight cars like hens in coops. Nearby stood another transport jammed with Russian civilians and cattle. When our transport finally moved on, we tried to find our bearings by the sun, later the stars, to see what direction we were traveling in. There was no point in asking the guards, and even the commander of the convoy more than likely did not know our destination. We finally figured out that we were heading north towards the White Sea. The very thought of it brought a chill to the body.

We were released, half alive and fatigued almost beyond endurance, at a small, empty railway station—Tarza, in the Niandomsk region of the Archangelsk "oblast" (district). We knew that we would have no rest at this new location. Of this we were certain. Apart from that, we knew nothing, nor was anyone willing to tell us anything. Without a word we were loaded onto sleds—very odd because winter was still far off and the day was clear and almost summery. The convoy of huge sleds, pulled by tractors, moved slowly through the forest. The machines, their tracks clanking, groaned at every major obstacle and belched black smoke which gradually permeated the wall of the forest. Above the dust and smoke hung a high ceiling of fleecy clouds.

The expanse of greenery on both sides of the road was motionless as the engines roared into it. Even severely exhausted and afraid, we found it hard to resist the charm of this forest with its heavy scent of resins, its lichens and bracken, its candle-straight spruce, its pines with golden trunks, its white birches. It was difficult to believe that exiles could still admire such sights. The road itself was unevenly cleared, apparently in a hurry. Against the forest walls lay the star-shaped roots of trees carelessly scooped out, encrusted with mud and dust. In many spots we rode over marshes layered with tree trunks, the tractors working hard to avoid slipping off the wet, lichen-covered roadway.

As we wondered how far we were to go into the forest, and what we would encounter there, one of the more "optimistic" deportees jumped up on the side of the sled, broke off a willow twig, and fastened a large red handkerchief to it. He hoisted the handkerchief above the sled and held it up until we stopped in a large clearing torn from the forest in which were groups of barracks. We looked around, curious. Among the buildings one stood out because of its size, the headquarters of the Soviet management. Here, we were to learn, were the offices and private residences of officials of the NKVD and of the lumber company. Some distance away was a hut housing the supply supervisor, and the one store in the whole settlement. In a lean-to was the indispensable "Krasnyi Ugolok" (Red Corner) or culture centre where the workers held meetings and evening gatherings.

In the area in front of the main building, very obviously awaiting our arrival, stood the tall, lean commandant of the NKVD detachment, wearing an elegant, tight-fitting uniform and a tall hat with a purple band. He stood self-assured, feet wide apart, thumbs stuck under his belt, eyes half closed. He observed us without a word.

This silent inspection was interrupted by the "optimist" with the red flag, who stepped forward and offered his services to the new authority. In Poland, he said, he was the owner of a steam-powered mill and employed a large number of people; he knew how to handle workers to get the greatest productivity out of them. "Tovarisch" (Comrade), he went on, allowing himself to use the Soviet title created to emphasize equality, "Tovarisch! There are all sorts of people in this transport—Poles, Ukrainians, and Jews. Some of the Jews speak jargon, others speak German, others Polish. I know all these languages, also Russian. A man like myself will always be indispensable to tovarisch."

The representative of authority narrowed his eyes. They had the expression of a cat staring with malevolent attention at a frolicsome mouse unaware of the danger. Suddenly, his lips compressed with contempt, he quietly hissed, "Kakoy ya tyebye tovarisch?" ("What kind of a comrade am I to you?").

Not waiting for anything else, the optimist dived back into the crowd. We had learned that we were not the comrades of free Soviet citizens, and that we were to refer to them as "grazhdyanin," (citizen).

The people were reluctant to occupy the barracks assigned them because the ones who had entered first returned with discouraging reports: each board, each plank bed, each crack in the walls was full of bedbugs—dry as husks, true, but capable of reviving immediately when they sensed us.

The day after we arrived, we were organized into working brigades. The young men were sent to the forest as woodcutters or drivers of sleds pulled by half-starved nags; some were assigned to gathering logs in the old clearing, getting them ready to be picked up by a tractor. The elderly, the sick, and the children were ordered to cut wood for fuel with a handsaw.

We all left for work around seven in the morning to the accompaniment of a clanking on a piece of steel rail. We returned at six or seven in the evening. At lunchtime, the guards brought us our meal in a large, defective thermos sliding on wooden runners. Nobody ever had enough to satisfy his hunger. A ladleful of porridge at noon; in the evening a watery soup with some cabbage leaves floating in it, rarely a few grits, and 600 grams of bread—that was our food for the day. No fats, never any meat, no potatoes, nothing else, ever, throughout the year. The work was hard, all the harder since very few of us had had any experience at it. In addition, we could not rest at night because of the bedbugs.

Thus we toiled day after day on empty stomachs, even during high holy days such as Christmas and Easter. At first we could rest awhile on Sundays, but later on they too became ordinary working days. There was no respite, and each of us grew weaker at a terrifying rate. Such a life could quickly fell even the strongest, most resistant, and even worse, depress and derange. The religion deep-rooted in the Polish people suggested that we seek succor and endurance in prayer. Unable to do so during the day, we celebrated our holy days in the evenings; these religious services supplied us with many touching emotions and fortified our waning hope. Yet because of a steady loss of strength and the seeming hopelessness of the situation, some of the less resistant fell into a deep despair.

In these conditions, certain moods and reactions stood out as particularly notable. One of our youngest female workers, twelve-year-old Theresa, outdid her elders in many respects, especially in fortitude and self-control. We found it hard to understand whence this frail, delicate girl drew so much stamina, so much composure, so much buoyancy; possibly it came from her great love for her mother.

Theresa cut wood for fuel during working hours, but whenever she could she cared most tenderly for her mother, who fell into a more and more serious nervous disorder because of her misfortunes thus far and because of her increasing anxiety about the fate of her husband, a Polish army officer. Constant fear that she might be separated from her adored child also preyed on the nerves of this sick woman.

Theresa, worried about her father and her mother simultaneously, was capable of telling herself that as her mother's guardian she had to stay strong. Thus she forced herself to take everything calmly, despite her tender age. Within herself she managed to remain heroically composed and calm, whether at her woodcutting or afterwards, in cold or rain, waiting in line along the wall of the collective kitchen, sometimes for hours, among tired and hungry and often rude laborers who seldom had even a kind word for her.

She admitted that at times when someone tried by force or trickery or swearing to get into the dining hall ahead of her, she could hardly hold back her tears. But she did not step aside until she got the soup, sometimes a few oat cakes, for herself and her mother. After taking the pot to her quarters, she would run to join the bread line. Here, there was not so much swearing because people had had a few mouthfuls of soup by this time.

The storekeeper did not hurry at all to issue the bread, aware that he was master of the situation and knowing that the hungry souls waiting in line would clam up at his nod sooner than at an order from the NKVD. It would not do—God forbid!—to offend him in any way, even with an impatient gesture, because he would without a second thought cut the bread ration. He was a known scoundrel, stealing the supplies meant for us defenseless slaves.

Having bought her six hundred grams of bread—clay-like, moist, heavy, and therefore looking miserly even in Theresa's small hands—the little girl would smile gracefully at the storekeeper before running back to her mother. It was impossible to watch all this with indifference. Her smile had some quality that cheered us all and caused prisoners of every calibre to become fond of her.

Theresa was often seen with Sarah, an eighteen-year-old Jewish girl who had worn her summer dress and light shoes to tatters at work in the camp. She could not count on buying anything at the local store, for if any shabby clothing ever appeared there, it was not nearly enough to meet the needs of even five percent of the inhabitants and was always grabbed by the Russians and the few supervisors. But that was not the reason for Sarah's going about as if petrified with pain. Her stormy soul had been caught with the bait of beautiful Communist slogans before the war and she had given herself completely to the work of a Communist organization in Cracow. When the Russians invaded Poland, she had run to them blindly, going from Cracow cross-country toward the river San. Received with amazement, she had been sent to the industrial Black Sea area, where in a military garment factory she slaved beyond endurance. Her pure, ardent readiness for sacrifice had been met with chicanery and humiliation. Eventually she had been allowed to go back to Poland under Soviet occupation, but had been arrested at the railway station in Lwow and eventually deported to this camp.

Theresa, through some means known only to herself, managed to alleviate Sarah's sufferings. She got the poor creature not to run away from people so much, and even start talking to them. This was one of Theresa's small miracles.

Only one thing Theresa could not bear, the thought that she might be separated from her mother. She had heard about such separations arranged by the NKVD, even in this "free exile," yet most of what she had heard seemed much too inhuman to be believed. She trembled when she heard vivid reports of such things. She could bear everything but this! Besides, it could not happen to her because everybody knew that without her, her mother would perish.

Everybody knew, but it happened nonetheless. One day the cruel blow struck. It is impossible to imagine their despair. In vain they pleaded, and in vain their friends tried to intervene. The order had originated from above. And the commandant? Conceivably he himself had made a report about Theresa's extraordinary intelligence, and things being as they were, it seemed best to take the girl and educate her as a Marxist. Separated from her mother, she would be more willing to accept the Party as her family. Theresa had to go.

A severe winter came on. The snow was waist high, and it was so cold that trees split in two, sometimes half their length or more, as they fell. The hungry horses would push aside the snow with their nostrils to get at the rotting grass and moss underneath. The hungry workers picked frozen wild berries and congregated around the fire to thaw their numbed limbs and dry out their clothing.

Theresa's mother was assigned the job of collecting the strips of bark torn off as the trees were felled. Her dress, which had long since lost its color, hung on her like a grey rag. From under her matted, windblown hair stared a pair of eyes like the broken windows of a deserted home. The woodcutters had to be constantly careful to make sure she was not hit by falling trees, which every few minutes "flew like the angels, and hit the ground like 'chorti' (devils)," as the Soviet brigadier put it.

The lonely mother's senses returned only when she had a letter from her daughter. The letters were written in Polish at first, and brought words of tender consolation and hope. Even after the authorities allowed only letters written in Russian, Theresa continued faithfully to write.

We were terrified that we might not get out of this place at all. This fear was all the greater because of the passive resignation of the local people, who were convinced that no one was ever permitted to leave the taiga.

This conviction seemed to be confirmed by the story of a young forest official who trusted us. As a sixteen-year-old boy, working in Archangelsk, he had been caught stealing from the food store and sentenced *in absentia* to ten years of slave labor. When he had completed the sentence and asked permission to leave, the NKVD agreed but merely sent him to a different camp. Once there, he demanded his rights and was transferred to still another camp. It was then that he realized there was no way out for him. He was permitted to reach the mediocre position of a forestry official, but he knew that he would never again be a free man as long as he lived. Telling us his story, he would always add, "It does not happen any other way in the Soviet Union."

It was impossible to listen to such stories without a cold fear in one's heart. Were we meant never to enjoy freedom again? We were not, after all, criminals; we had never stolen from anybody. In fact, our own possessions had been stolen from us.

In the meantime, something absolutely unexpected happened. In June, 1941, Hitler struck out against Russia. The suppressed Soviet people nourished secret hopes linked to the outbreak of this war.

One of these "free" Soviet citizens, a Russian peasant, Malenkov, unable to earn enough to feed his wife and seven children, begged our brigadier's permission to work with us, the deportees. The brigadier consented and gave him the job of felling trees. Malenkov was not a good tree-feller; he cut down pines and spruce indiscriminately, thus making it difficult for the others to dress the lumber. As a "free" person, he was paid twice as much as the deportees. But even this doubled income was so inadequate that often Malenkov did not have a kopeck to his name and could not afford to buy his porridge at lunch time. There was always somebody merciful enough to buy it for him. In time he grew attached to us as his brothers. When the brigadier was not too near, his tongue would loosen and he would speak to us sincerely. He would strain his ears whenever the silence of dinner was shattered by the sound of a shot or an explosion (none could have come from the front line). The Press was allegedly reporting that the Germans were nearing Moscow. Malenkov, although not too bright, was capable of some strategic calculations. He maintained that if even one German army thrust northwards and cut off communications between Moscow and Archangelsk, of the thousands of slaves in the labor camps there would rise whole armies, armed with axes, to cut their way out to freedom.

As a result of the war, conditions in our settlement deteriorated even further. Now we had only two days off per year, the 1st of May and the anniversary of the October Revolution. But even during these two holidays, personal freedom was restricted, because in order to brace our morale and shore up our faith in the invincibility of the Red Army, we had to stand for long hours in the yard around the Marxist pulpit. Whenever the propagandist brought in for the occasion would ostentatiously pause in his speech, the "prompters" hidden among the crowd would make us applaud. Anyone who did not fancy being put on a starvation diet of bread and porridge took part in the tempest of "spontaneous" applause.

In the forest sectors, a new emphasis was placed on selecting trees suitable for aircraft, pontoons, masts, and railway ties. During the aurora borealis, some of the brigades were assigned to a night shift to expedite the delivery of urgently needed lumber to the railway stations. In the morning those teams returned from the forest covered with mosquito bites.

Wages were paid very irregularly, often only "on account." The cashier from the forestry combine, arriving on a black horse with a bag slung across his shoulder, came to be more and more eagerly awaited, and when he came, a long line would form immediately. Even the "on account" payments were small, because the "combines" were too deep in debt to the State, which would refuse further credits; the combines, in turn, to save themselves from bankruptcy, would not pay their workers all they had earned. Bankruptcy, however, led quite a few authorities to jail for "sabotage" and for defrauding the State.

Because of the changing war situation, the camp authorities

began to prepare us for the worst, in other words, for being completely cut off from food supplies. To save ourselves from starvation, we were advised to plant our own potatoes. There were no other vegetables.

The soil, however, was not suitable for cultivation. The clearing we lived in was covered with the thick roots and stumps of felled trees. The first task would be to dig out all the stumps, then dig the infertile soil again and again. But how were we to prepare the ground when the authorities forbade the use of tractors or horses for pulling out roots? Nor was even one hour of working time allocated for the job of making gardens. Nevertheless we started the job at night, in the light of the aurora borealis, using for tools only a pick, an axe and a shovel. To grub out the thick, forked roots required superhuman effort.

The final results of these murderous forays against the unrelenting earth were sparse, feeble clusters of small, greenish-blue, bitter little potatoes. These were our small defense against total hunger. The Russian people had died of hunger more than once before, and it could happen to us too. All we could do was trust in God's providence. It did not fail us.

In August, 1941, incredible news reached our isolated camp. We learned that on the 30th day of July the Polish Government-in-Exile had signed a treaty with the Soviet government, and this treaty was to rescue us. It provided that all Polish citizens in Russian prisons and camps, and in "exile," were to regain their freedom. "All!" That meant us too! It was not easy to believe.

Stalin liked to call this act—the act of freeing innocently suffering, terrorized people, among them hundreds of thousands of little children—an amnesty. A strange amnesty indeed when there had been no crime! We suspected that this word was meant to be Moscow's way of deluding the West, to camouflage the outrage that had been committed. But the meaning of this or any other word did not matter to us then, as long as it meant an end to our slavery.

This good news was brought to the forest sectors by the Russians, who had thus far remained aloof, reserved, and distrustful. It was obvious that our imminent release electrified everybody as without precedent in the history of the Soviet penal system. It may even have sparked some hope in the many Soviet citizens, such as that forestry official who had been deprived of freedom for years. Some of those wretches shared our jubilation, and sincerely so; we were sorry to think that they might remain there forever.

In the press there were allegedly stories about the formation of an army of freed Poles on Russian soil to fight the Germans. Thus we younger men knew what to do when we were set free. But what about the women and children, the old and the infirm and the sick? Where would they go? We did not know. In all the rumors there was not a word about the possibility of their regaining their stolen heritage.

We began preparing feverishly for a trip into the unknown. As we left the camp in small groups along the forest path, Sarah and Theresa's mother moved slowly side by side. They had no joy without Theresa. She had not been returned to her mother despite the "amnesty," just as hundreds of other children had not been restored to their families, having been sentenced to the "benefit" of a Soviet education designed to make them forget their past and become children of the Komsomol.

4

The Greenhorns Want to Fight

It would be difficult to recreate that staggering moment when all at once, throughout the length and breadth of Russia, Polish national songs began to reverberate among the hundreds of thousands of wretched people in camps and prisons as they thrilled to the news that a Polish Army was going to be formed. The NKVD, having received instructions from the Kremlin about how to treat these freed people, tried to direct the men "temporarily" into the Red Army, until the Polish Army was organized, with the proviso that the Poles would, at the proper time, be handed over to the Polish command. But Soviet "temporariness" was by now too well known to fool the Poles. In the meantime, the Russians withheld food rations from the masses leaving prisons, camps, mines, and settlements in order to aggravate, torment them and make them dependent upon the NKVD.

Prisoners and exiles in all labor camps began feverishly searching for maps of Russia to become oriented in her vast spaces. All eyes turned towards Russian Turkestan, in Middle Asia near the

Sino-Afghan border. Let's go there, we all said; whatever happens to us there cannot be worse than we have now, and should even be better. Clothing will be less of a problem in the warm climate, and the South should abound in fruit, with vitamins to prevent scurvy and night blindness. Above all, we must save the children, and they cannot last much longer in the taiga.

Apprehensive but commending ourselves to God's grace, we headed south. Such a journey meant a few months of tramping. At every railroad junction or station, and in the larger towns, we met thousands of former camp inmates and deportees—men, women, and children. They were everywhere. They scouted all the side streets of the towns, the workers' and soldiers' cafeterias, the market places, the black market, in search of a piece of bread, a bowl of hot soup, a place to get warm. A severe winter was just about to begin.

Some of the Poles were leaving the towns; others were coming in. Old acquaintances would meet in passing, greeting each other with joyous smiles and the question: where can I grab something to eat? They recognized each other by their ravenous hunger, by the ulcers on their bodies, by the lice rushing to hide themselves in the seams of their clothing. They were linked by a cigarette they would pass back and forth like a peace pipe, each taking only one little drag. They shared a bun as if it were the Christmas wafer. They shared a carrot or a turnip hidden in their trousers tied above the ankle. Their misery made them all equal. No one could guess who was hidden under the rags—officer or private, professor or school teacher, landowner or peasant, cabinet officer or village priest. They were equals, as in a cemetery, each the other's brother.

They were little more than skeletons covered with strips of dirty clothing, the bare bones showing through. Some had their feet stuck into crude shoes made from rubber tires, stitched together with wire and tied up with a cord. Others wore something like moccasins made of birch bark. Hanging from their waist on a string was a soot-covered tin can, the camp inmate's most precious property, a kettle for the food they begged: soup, porridge, soya, potatoes.

But in the faces of these creatures looking more like phantoms than human beings glowed eyes that attested to the soul within them, and to the joy that soul felt at the little freedom granted to it. Almost always, these tramps spent the night in railway stations. When passenger traffic ceased and the waiting rooms were empty, they appeared as if popping up from underground. They lay on the stone floor, on the benches, and when space was scarce, on the plinth of Stalin's statue. The penetrating cold of the stone floor made them huddle together like pups, unconcerned about the dozens of lice they might be acquiring from their neighbors.

In the middle of the night, their sleep would be interrupted by the "oobors-cheetsa," the cleaning woman, dispersing the human mass to the corners with her broom; when the broom stopped, they would relocate themselves at random. A particular difficulty of those nights was having to crawl out and over the tightly packed, twisted, piled-up mass of bodies to answer a call of nature. Whoever left his place had no chance of returning to it, because it would be instantly filled by the mass of sleeping bodies. One had to find another spot, pushing aside one body after another, never without stepping on at least one and eliciting grumbles, curses, hisses, and moans.

The road to the South was a veritable Calvary for the Polish families. From time to time, after two or three days without food, they had to break their journey in some larger city to find some. Normally, a family could at least get the "keepyatok" (boiling water) available at every railway station in Russia. It was meant for making tea, but as no one had any tea, the hungry people drank warm water, cheating their stomachs for a short time and warming themselves a bit.

Some of the transports would make planned stops for a few days at the railway stations in larger cities so that the passengers could find some kind of food—through their own "industry" and cleverness, of course. The mother and small children would wait in the train while the father or one of the older children went to the town looking for food. No one knew how long the train would wait, not even the engine driver. It thus happened more than once that the train would leave unexpectedly while the family's providers were out foraging and they would be separated forever.

The unattached exiles were better off in this respect. They could leave the train for as long as they liked. If their own train left before they were ready, they would just storm the cars of other trains. Because the guard at the door of each car would not admit anyone without a ticket, they would jump on the buffers just as the train was leaving the station, gradually gaining speed. After managing somehow to get inside, they still had to outsmart the conductresses checking tickets: they hid in corners or in the toilets, and even now and then on the roof. A passenger without a ticket, if he was handed over to the militia, faced the threat of being imprisoned again.

Freedom often seemed harder than imprisonment. A person who up till now had been a cog in the huge Communist machine had been getting at least the minimal advantages that his status as totalitarian slave entitled him to. The most important was food, which, although without fats, meat, dairy products, or fruit, still allowed the poor wretch to hold onto life. But whoever found himself outside this massive system was on his own, deprived of any assistance from the state authorities. He often felt lost. Even having money did not help if he did not have the right to buy produce at the official prices. Although every city had a black market, it operated, as in the "settlement," entirely by barter: clothing or shoes in exchange for food. Not many outsiders still had boots, shirts, or trousers to part with. But despite these unusually difficult conditions, we would not have given up this freedom for anything in the world; and it pained us to think that others still suffered imprisonment or exile.

There were multitudes of them. The most atrocious camps in Vorkuta and Kolyma refused to free their victims, very likely because the commandants had production quotas to meet and could not meet them without their slave workers. Moreover, news about the pact between the Soviets and the Polish Government-in-Exile and about the resulting amnesty reached the Poles in Russia indirectly, very often by accident. Rarely did the camp supervisors officially proclaim this extraordinary news. When the brigades, having somehow received it, demanded their release, the Russians would think up all sorts of impediments. A prisoner's records would show an allegedly foreign origin, or his name would sound German. One of the chief impediments was a passport showing Soviet citizenship, accepted by coercion after the NKVD had entered Eastern Poland.

There was no comparison between the miseries that we who had been set free were now encountering and the terrible despair of those thousands still being detained. Yet we were tramping desperately over the immense spaces of Russia, anxious to find a trace of the Polish Army. The Polish-Soviet pact had proclaimed that we were to join the military and fight the Germans, but the Russians refused to tell us where the Polish Army was being recreated, or where to find an assembly or recruiting area. Not only men but also unmarried women and mothers with children wanted to head towards those centers, seeing no other anchorage on foreign soil. At times, by a fortunate coincidence, we would get some information.

It happened, for example, near Archangelsk. A group of Polish soldiers were supervising the unloading of supplies shipped from England for the army. One day the soldiers went to the railway loading platform to watch the long line of people waiting for bread. Suddenly they heard the voice of a child crying in Polish "Orzelki! Orzelki! . . . Mamusiu, polskie orzelki!" ("Eagles! Eagles! . . . Mummy, Polish eagles!"), as she ran up to a pale, sickly-looking woman near the head of the line. The woman hesitated a moment, reluctant to give up her place in line; but her desire to learn something about her countrymen was too great. She stepped out of line and went over to the soldiers. When she found that they were indeed soldiers of the Polish Army, now being re-formed; a grimace resembling a smile appeared on her face and tears welled up in her eyes. These young men reminded her of her three grown sons who had become Soviet prisoners and been lost without a trace.

To enlist in the Polish Army and fight the Germans was the desire not only of the grown men but also of many underaged boys heading south. Just to shed the hide of a miserable stripling and become a tough, armed fighter was their most ardent dream.

For example, seventeen-year-old Stefan. No human force could drive this dream out of his head. He was alone except for his mother, who did not try to dampen the boy's ardor because she knew that even if he was accepted he would not be sent to the front right away. The two of them had been taking care of a ten-year-old orphan girl, Wanda, who was thus a sister for Stefan.

The boy was bright and determined; he would use his cleverness to reach the Army center and not let "his women" starve on the way. They had no tickets, no money, and no food except a bag of biscuits. Those biscuits had to last them a long time, so they had to get more provisions. So what? To ask was not a disgrace. Stefan took it on himself. On the outskirts of a small town, he saw some elderly women digging up potatoes. He approached and greeted them, took off his cap, and asked for a handout. A youngster with the women picked up a few potatoes, intending to give them to Stefan, but the boy's mother said, "Bros kartoshkoo; eto yevrey, nye davay yemoo!" ("Drop the potato; he is a Jew; do not give it to him!"). The boy dropped the potatoes, and the woman, straightening up, looked at Stefan. Seeing that he could barely hold back the tears, she asked him who he was and where he came from. When he told her that he was tramping around as a Polish exile, all the women sighed, sniffled with emotion, and dried their tears on their sleeves. They had also lived through horrible times, perhaps even more horrible. After the unsuccessful revolt in the Ukraine, the entire population had been deported to the taiga, whole families, including pregnant women, in the dead of a very severe winter. They had all been left in the forest; the men were given axes and saws and told to build their own quarters and manage as best they could. Until they could get their shelters built, they had passed long days and nights around a fire under the open sky, hungry and half freezing. Death quickly took the weakest, mostly children and old people.

While Stefan and the women talked, the youngster, nudged by his mother, stuffed Stefan's cap with potatoes. Stefan was beside himself with joy; he thanked the women and ran to his mother and Wanda, who were picking raspberries at the edge of the forest. They made a fire and buried the potatoes in the hot coals to bake. What a lovely smell! And how good they tasted! Poverty teaches one to be happy with very little. The potatoes, the raspberries, the forest, the sun—how wonderful this world is! If everyone were only as kind as the old women and the youngster.

A few days later a kind railway conductor let them all on the train, and they rode between two walls of endless forest. Stefan managed to make a cave for himself up on a narrow luggage rack above the wooden bench where his mother and Wanda sat. He seldom came down, there being nothing much to come down for.

After three days they reached Vologda and moved on towards the Urals via Kirov to Svyerdlovsk. Now they were on a comfortable passenger train and felt embarrassed by their poor clothing, which drew everyone's attention. Both fellow passengers and NKVD officers observed them attentively, in an unpleasant silence. If anyone spoke with anyone else, the conversation was in whispers. The faces of the Russian passengers seemed dull and indifferent; no young people were to be seen.

In Svyerdlovsk, Stefan befriended a "freed" Polish deportee, a former detective, who knew a few spots where one could get some food. During one trip in a crowded streetcar, a pickpocket lifted from the detective's breast pocket a box of tobacco, a treasure worth one or two loaves of bread. His respect for Russian pickpockets' technique grew considerably, and from then on he made sure that they did not steal the jacket off his back.

On the stretch between Svyerdlovsk and Chkalov, in Chelyabinsk, the trio decided to get off to eat and secure some provisions for the rest of the journey. After inspecting the area around the railway station, Stefan returned with a wide grin on his face. "Look, Mother, over there! I've seen with my own eyes what I heard from other Poles on the way here: there's a sausage plant! Some of the Poles have already been here for as long as two weeks, and all they want now is to get their fill."

"But Stefan, that is not a sausage plant; it's a slaughterhouse."

It was, indeed, a slaughterhouse, which seemed to be supplying the army with meat. And wherever there is a plant, it is easier to buy products, if only the least desirable. (In the warmer parts of Russia, where cotton is grown, quilted cotton jackets are easier to get than in Siberia.)

Foraging for soup and meat, Stefan was accompanied by Wanda, and they took along all the kettles they had. Stefan's reconaissance had been excellent. They brought back three pieces of sausage, a bun, and some of the greasy water used for boiling sausages. All of them got sick from their meal, unaccustomed as they were to fats. But this problem lasted only a short time, and, somewhat fortified, they soon set out again.

After only a short journey they had to get off the train, for it was going south towards Turkestan, and they wanted to go to the main recruitment centre of the Polish Army in Buzuluk, just to the west of the Urals. In one of the larger towns along the way Stefan happened to catch sight of a large Russian military cafeteria. It was dinner time, and the Red Army soldiers were sitting at the tables eating porridge out of their mess tins. (Porridge is almost a national staple in Russia, like rice in China.) Stefan's mind worked fast. He decided that, as a young man halfway to being a soldier, he was entitled to an army meal. Stepping boldly up to the young girl at the counter, he greeted her and set his soot-covered kettle in front of her. She did not move but only looked at him, sizing him up. He thought she looked angry, but as it turned out, she was merely perplexed and afraid.

"Who are you?"

"A Pole. I'm going to join the army. I'll get my uniform there."

"Are you from a labor camp?"

"No, I was on a 'free resettlement.' Now I'm free, just like you, barishnya (young lady). I'm hungry. Many days I don't have anything at all to put in my mouth."

The young girl hesitated for a long time, but at last took the risk and filled the kettle with porridge. Stefan thanked her kindly with a smile, and that obviously pleased her. As confidently as he could, Stefan moved toward the exit. It had worked. He took a banquet to his mother and Wanda. When they had eaten every last bit and Stefan, had, as usual, stuck his spoon in his legging and cleaned out his can with his finger, Wanda suddenly said, "Stefan, go again!"

"I don't know whether it would work again. They might kick me out. The first time I took the 'barishnya' by surprise, but now she's had time to think. She was clearly afraid of getting into trouble for this."

"Stefan, do try again. It doesn't cost anything to try."

"What do you know about it!"

"Then don't go," said his mother. But this sudden settlement of the problem bothered him; it sounded like an accusation of cowardice. Without a word he got up and went out.

In the cafeteria the scene was replayed, but this time the soldiers paid even less attention to him. "Barishnya, don't be angry; you see, I am not alone. I have my mother and my sister to feed. I cannot bring them in here. You know how difficult it is to get food. . . ."

The girl's sharp look softened slightly. After a moment's hesitation, she reached for the can with a quick movement, shook two large ladles of porridge into it, and without a word pushed it towards Stefan. Her gaze clung to him, inquiring, yet she managed a nice constraint. Stefan, used to such well controlled reactions from the local people, knew that this cool gaze guarded against a surge of sympathy too dangerous to display.

The eyes of Mother and Wanda, waiting near the fence, shone

with joy when they saw the full can. "What a feast!" mumbled Wanda as three spoons met in the dish. All eyes involuntarily measured the amount of porridge in the spoons to make sure that one of them, out of consideration for the others, did not take too little. Mother, however, as mothers do, gave up her last few spoonfuls. "Wanda, maybe you would go now? You are small, emaciated; you will touch the cook's heart," teased Stefan.

But after two successful attempts he was so sure of himself that he started off for the third time. Wanda was most impressed.

"This is the last time, barishnya." He spoke with a disarming expression on his face. "We will not meet again. I am going to join the army, but you have to give us something for the road. We do not need much. Just this one can of porridge."

"Let it be! Take it, and a happy journey."

She escorted the boy to the door with her eyes. Stefan, feeling her gaze, turned around and gestured a friendly goodbye.

They were among the first to arrive in Buzuluk. It was a typical small Russian town—little wooden houses, dirty, streets ankle-deep in mud. The army did not yet have regular cadres assembled; the poor wretches were arriving slowly, ragged and miserable. It was hard to believe that some of them were army officers. Looking at such volunteers, anyone from the West would have directed them all to the hospital and would not even have thought of trying to form them into a military unit.

Stefan found shelter for his mother and Wanda at the home of a pleasant Russian woman in a nearby village, where they soon found work on a collective farm; he himself returned to Buzuluk to enlist in the army.

The assembly station was a huge hall, the summer barracks of the Red Army. Autumn was approaching, and behind autumn stalked the severe continental winter. The tall roof, riddled with holes, let in sun or rain, and underneath it stretched rows and rows of multi-storied plank beds divided by passageways. Stefan struck up a friendship with a few youngsters, like him candidates for enlistment. Without their company he could hardly have endured these rough first days. All the younger recruits were footloose, with no conception of discipline. They spent much of their time providing food for themselves through their own resourcefulness; at times they could find only watermelons.

The nights became colder. Stefan's group would stretch themselves out on the topmost plank beds and cover themselves with their clothes to keep warmer. Those whose beds were near the outer edge suffered most from the cold, but they had the right to move towards the centre in a strict order of seniority at the barracks. Even so, their teeth chattered all through the night because of the nasty chill from underneath.

When he could not sleep, Stefan would look from his elevated bunk down at the corridor where a fire was burning. Around the fire, in a tight cluster, hunched the shapes of former prisoners and campworkers from Vorkuta, Kotlas, and other places of ill repute, their souls still heavy with the savagery that alone had enabled them to endure the drudgery of the camps. Stefan did not have the courage to associate with them; he would have felt a stranger among them, and he feared their brutality. They would need to live for a long time in normal conditions—in an atmosphere of mutual trust and respect for human dignity—before they could be expected to react differently.

On the other hand, their ingenuity was striking, and their humor, though grim. They talked and sang songs, first Polish then Russian. They kept the fire going with boards broken from the bunks. When their backs got cold, they would turn around. Some of them, unable to tolerate the lice any longer, took off their shirts and shook the lice into the fire. Around midnight, dead tired, they would stretch themselves around the fire to sleep.

After some time, Stefan's group was moved into a different barrack that was much less cold. Warmth emanated from the hay and straw used as litter. In addition, the volunteers were now receiving a modest daily ration of food: a herring and a piece of bread. The most insufferable aspect was the inactivity; that prompted Stefan to go to the village where he could be near his mother while waiting for the first units of the regular army to be formed. The Polish General Staff had its headquarters in Buzuluk, but it was still busy bargaining for better living conditions for the soldiers and trying to obtain such necessary supplies as nails, boards, and tools—only one of many problems.

Every day at dawn, Stefan, his mother, and Wanda went into the fields to dig potatoes and carrots. It was by now late autumn, but the harvest was not yet completed here. There were hectares of still unharvested grain, and each pair of hands meant valuable help. The female workers, all rushing to attain the "norm," moved quickly over the fields, picking only the largest potatoes and carrots and leaving the rest. The black, glistening fields, marked here and there with yellowed carrot leaves and dry potato stalks, stretched into the distance as far as the eye could see.

There was no storage space for the crops, and transportation, always inefficient in Russia, was delayed for weeks because of the war. In the meantime, the mounds of potatoes, turnips, and carrots rotted.

Generally the work was pleasant. The sun was mild; a breeze softened the air; the women laughed and chattered. When the supervisor from the collective farm was away, they found time to relax and frolic. Stefan and Wanda were using hoes for the first time in their lives, and their digging was clumsy. Potatoes stuck to the hoes' teeth. Their backs were cruelly sore. At every opportunity, they would make a fire of potato stalks and bake potatoes and carrots.

Stefan did not forget their kind Russian landlady. Every day he would throw a sackful of potatoes into the bushes and take them home at dusk. He and Wanda also made evening trips into the forest for wood. The forest in this part of Russia did not have the same charm as the northern taiga. Back home, they cut the wood and piled it behind the house, for fear that the forester, having noticed the theft, would report it to the NKVD, who would the next morning make a surprise visit looking for uncut logs.

The landlady, having been supplied for the winter with potatoes, carrots, and fuel, was very friendly to her tenants. She would invite them for pumpkin baked in the oven, which tasted something like melted caramel sugar. The youngsters always tried to get pumpkins from the collective farm fields. "Khazaika" (the landlady) was very poor and had no stock of food except what her tenants brought. She never had sugar. Once, when Stefan brought cereal, sugar, soap, and margarine from Buzuluk, she could hardly believe her eyes.

Stefan, driven by curiosity and eager to start his soldiering, went back to Buzuluk from time to time. There he saw some changes. In the Gathering Centre were many men and young women already parading proudly in their new English battledress, sent by sea around Scandinavia, though the uniforms hung loosely on their emaciated bodies. Nonetheless they altered their wearers almost beyond recognition. The food was better, though still scarce, and some of the units were already practicing the drill. The Medical Board was busy with the influx of new volunteers. In fact, Buzuluk was already full. But not far off were some units already formed: in Totskoye, the Sixth Infantry Division; in Tatischev near Kuybyshev, the Fifth Division already armed. Stories flew about the first inspection and review carried out by the Commander of the Polish Armed Forces in Russia, General W. Anders, a former prisoner in Lubyanka, still going about with a cane. The soldiers in Totskoye, still without uniforms, had marched past just as they had come from the labor camps, most of them barefooted, in nondescript tatters or in the rags of their old Polish army uniforms.

With the outward changes had come a change of spirit among the Poles in Buzuluk. Their faces shone with joy, although their recent misery still showed in their paleness and the dark spots left by avitaminosis.

The arrival of Gen. Wladyslaw E. Sikorski from England, Prime Minister of the Polish Government-in-Exile to inspect the units and to consult with the Soviet government, greatly cheered the Poles.

Stefan, having been examined by the recruiting board and labeled "A" in health, was accepted for the Unifying Course for Cadet Officers at the Army Training Centre. Now his first priority was to bring "his females" to Buzuluk. From a young chaplain recently come from England, Reverend Krol (whose beautiful uniform was such a contrast with their rags that the exiles were too embarrassed to approach him), Stefan got a fistful of medals, mother-of-pearl rosaries and crosses made in Ireland. With this trove he set out for "home."

When the Russian landlady received her share, she was delighted. She caressed the consecrated mementos and kissed them. Then she left the house and returned with a group of peasants who also wanted some. They brought loaves of bread or pots of butter. Some of the tricky fellows in the camp, having learned how much the Russians longed for such things, obtained them by devious means and peddled them in the villages.

In Buzuluk Stefan did not enjoy being with his mother and Wanda for long. Just before Christmas, for lack of space, his company was transferred to Koltoobyanka and on into the thick forest in snow waist deep. There they bivouacked in tents. Stoves were in short supply, and the temperature dropped to −50° Celsius. The Unifying Course was housed in freshly completed earthen dugouts. In the large hall were only two stoves, producing warmth only for a few soldiers close by. The fire often died out because the firewood was wet. The food was poor and rationed out in such small quantities that Stefan was always hungry.

Felling trees for fuel and loading them onto wagons, many soldiers suffered from frostbitten hands and feet. The most depressing but most essential part of the daily program was the "voshoboyka" (lice-killing session). Every soldier, under the watchful eye of the officer on duty, had to take off all his clothes, straddle his plank bed, and, shivering in the damp cold, search his clothing for lice. Some of the soldiers undertook this operation with a sense of humor, speculating about which "breeding station" their specimens had come from and calling the larger ones, with the black marks on their back, "Teutonic Knights." At a signal from the officer, everybody dressed and the hunt was over for the day.

Fortunately, the stay in Koltoobyanka was not long. About Christmastime rumors began to circulate that at the beginning of 1942 the whole army would be evacuated to warmer regions, closer to the supply bases of the British and American Armies in the Middle East, and that from them the Polish Army would receive equipment and food. Southern Kazakhstan was to be their destination, then Turkestan and Uzbekhistan.

The same route as Stefan's, though in much poorer conditions, was covered by many children from the Soviet "dyetdoms" (homes for children). Fetched straight from their schools in Poland as if to enjoy a vacation, or forcibly separated from their parents in Russia, only a very few of them got to know about the "amnesty." They held secret consultations about plans for returning to their own kin. They would select the most courageous from their ranks. These were to avoid the watchful eyes of the "educators," scout for and travel to a Polish outpost or military detachment, and there beg to have the Polish children taken away from the "dyetdoms." Even to dream of such an escape seemed insane, considering that Russian territories cover one-seventh of the globe, and the underaged delegates did not even know what approximate direction to follow.

Then there were other problems. First of all, those who escaped were pursued immediately, and if caught by the militia, they would be placed in a colony for juvenile lawbreakers. Even if they avoided capture, they needed much ingenuity just to find a safe accommodation for the night and some kind of provisions.

They would have to ferry by boat or raft, and often hide in wagons loaded with lumber or coal.

But in all those predicaments, sometimes even in danger of death, their courage was reinforced by their awareness that they were responsible for the other children. They knew well enough how feverishly those in the "dyetdom" waited; they could imagine the secret conversations after dark, and knew how fervent were their prayers for deliverance.

5

In the Cotton Fields of Soviet Louisiana

The dream of all the freed Poles was to get to the southernmost Soviet republics, those in Central Asia. These areas had been annexed by Russia in the nineteenth century in an attempt to gain access to the warm seas. Today they constitute a geographical entity as parts of the large Turkestan area. The Russian Turkestan, divided into the repubics of Turkmenia, Uzbekhistan, Tadzhikistan, and Kirghizia, is an exotic land with a tumultuous past.

Asia, as a whole, is a continent of contrasts not seen anywhere else, and in this Russian corner of it they are plentiful. Here are the high mountains of Pamir, known to the ancient Greeks as "the roof of the world," with passes higher than the highest peaks of Europe or America. From this gigantic body of mountains branch out the great mountain chains of Tian Shan, Karakorum, Kuen-lun, and the Himalayas. Pamir straddles the road from Asia Minor to China.

The granite walls of Pamir separate Turkestan from the benevolent climate of the Indian Ocean. However, thanks to the abundant snowfalls and the melting ice-tops of the mountains in the spring, this land is not a complete desert. The waters flowing down into the lowlands form many streams and rivers, two of which—the Amu-Daria and the Syr-Daria—are approximately 2400 kilometers long, flowing through almost all of the desert into the Aral Sea. Thanks to this water, and the sun's intense warmth through the six months of summer, and thanks to the loessic silt brought in by the rivers, many oases have formed here; and the towns of Fergana, Bukhara, Samarkand, Kokand, Tashkent, and Khiva are swathed in green gardens. The oases have been enlarged through a net of canals. Each drop of water is as precious as gold here. The irrigation system, technically very sophisticated, has existed from time immemorial, like that along the Nile. The winter, although short, is so severe that only one crop can be grown each year.

Turkestan has a very rich past. Through it the armies of Alexander the Great returned from the Indus River, defeated and decimated by the shortage of water. At one time the Arabs conquered its nomadic population and forced them to accept Mahomet's religion. In the thirteenth century, from the Mongolian Uplands, the horde of Genghis Khan fell upon this land with Tartar savagery and destroyed the huge Khorezm state belonging to the Persian Shah. Turkestan was the port from which all Asiatic barbaric tribes sailed through the Kirghizian steppes into Europe: the Huns, the Tartars, the Turks, and others. To its cities such as Bukhara and Samarkand came Venetian merchants, among them the father and uncle of Marco Polo, who was later invited to Peking by Kublai Khan, Genghis Khan's grandson.

To this exotic land flocked now all the Poles, as if impelled by an instinct of self-preservation from death by hunger and cold. From all directions, from Archangelsk and Vladivostok, they came, merging into a great human stream. The main stream of deportees, absorbing each day new compatriots, having reached the Ural mountains, flowed to the South. At the point where the chain of mountains ends, there opens up a large lowland called the "Orenburg Gate," "Gate of the Nations"; here the flowing mass divided. The men, regarding military service as their duty, moved west to the military garrisons being formed in Kuybishev. The women and children, the elderly, the invalid, and the sick continued south without any clearly defined destination.

Smaller groups of deportees were forming along various routes. Those from the Baikal or the Kolima areas were moving along the edge of the Mongolian Upland, directly towards Alma-Ata in Southeast Kazakhstan. Others sailed on the Volga River to Kuybishev, to contact the Polish Embassy there. This route, however, was guarded by a net of spies and the NKVD, and only a very few people managed to arrive. For these fortunate ones, the

Embassy was turned into a hostel with sleeping places on the office floors.

The mass of Poles fleeing south was like a swollen river blindly rushing ahead. The evacuation was completely unorganized. The Embassy's branch offices were just being formed, recruiting their personnel from the stream of deportees. On the road, the deportees met, here and there, delegates from the Embassy or military liaison officers whose responsibility was to direct their movements; but there was no clear information about where they were to resettle. Later on this exodus was handled somewhat more efficiently when the delegates called for the help of the so-called "men of trust," men recommended by the larger groups of deportees. But their activity did not reach everywhere because of the vastness of the areas involved and because of communication problems. Many offices were responsible for areas the size of European countries. To organize the thousands of people leaving labor camps and prisons was simply impossible. The confusion was aggravated still more by the NKVD's relocation of thousands of Soviet citizens from areas threatened by war into Asian Russia.

The Polish wanderers did not look very warlike. They were exhausted, sick outcasts, uncommonly quiet and patient but determined and resistant to hardships. The children, dotted among these masses like blue cornflowers in a wheat field, with their composed, serious faces, uncomplaining, understanding the general misery, seemed to share the patience of their mothers amid countless frustrations. Despite their extreme poverty, out of these masses emanated a certain stateliness, the dignity of a people not defeated. Permeated with faith in God's providence and a better tomorrow, they did not break down. Many who had managed to retain their meager savings refused to accept aid from the diplomatic outposts, believing that it ought to be given instead to those poorer than themselves. Relief funds were sought mostly by families of the gravely ill, those who had been robbed, and mothers with several children. In most cases, it was the group leaders who asked for relief on their behalf.

A kind word to the wretches, a friendly smile—these counted the most. They were all accustomed to each other, as if molded by their misery into one large family.

As they approached the Southern republics, the Poles discovered that their movements were being secretly controlled by the

NKVD. The trains did not stop at any stations so that people could get off. But they did not rebel, knowing that the watchfulness of the secret police would at least assure them a minimal food ration. They did suffer, however. Because they were so rarely allowed to get off the trains, they were often hungry, and could not wash themselves or their clothes for weeks. Some died of typhoid fever. At first they were tormented by the heat and lack of space, then during autumn by the penetrating chill.

According to the NKVD's plan, the whole civilian population was to be resettled in the poorest, westernmost part of Turkestan on the Aral Sea. However, despite the Soviet authorities' watchfulness, thousands of people managed to get to other republics in Western Turkestan, mostly Uzbekhistan and Kirghizia. At that time none of the Poles knew that all of Turkestan had been for years a center of the most dangerous infectious diseases in the Soviet Union, or that from time to time there were epidemics of typhoid, "enteric fever," dysentery, and malaria.

The transports meant for resettlement in the Karakalpak district, near the Aral Sea, had to stop at Farab, a railway station on the Amu-Daria River at the point where its yellow waters widen to enter the lake. There the Poles gathered by the thousands. Tug boats and barges were waiting at the river bank. Each barge was loaded with 250 people, and a string of twelve barges went downriver towards the estuary. The people were packed into a solid mass, either burned by the hot sun or plagued with cold, especially when it rained. Lice devoured them, and from the stinking bogs along the river arose swarms of tiny flies and mosquitoes. They became so thirsty that they had to save themselves by drinking the dirty river water and risking dysentery. The elderly moaned in the corners, wishing each other a speedy death. The children longed for a merciful hand bringing bread, and their mothers' eyes expressed a feeling of futility and despair. It was like being caught up in some ancient slave trade, and they seemed to be facing yet another exile.

In the course of this wandering, husbands sometimes found their wives by accident, and children found the fathers from whom they had been separated in Poland during the Soviet round-ups. Hieronim Szumowski, from the Vorkuta camp, describes the following scene:

> I was on the same barge as a group of men freed from the Vor-

> kuta camp. In the other barges were families released from some other labor camps. Since the barges sailed close to each other, it was possible to get from one to the other along a rope. We stood looking at the landscape. A few boys came near us and among them one, maybe seven or eight years old, approached one of the men and tugged at his jacket: "Daddy, is it you? Daddy, is it you?" The man did not pay attention to the boy, but when he tugged a few more times and whispered shyly again, "Daddy, is it you?" the man stared at the boy intently and finally burst into tears. He recognized his son. He took the boy into his arms; the boy embraced his father fondly and told him that his mother and sisters were "in the barge over there."

At dusk a refreshing wind let the poor souls breathe more freely and even sleep for a while. But their sleep was broken around midnight by the winds from the hills. Children began to sob quietly, their sobs accompanied by the plaintive howling of jackals in the desert. Most people had nothing to cover themselves against the chill because, in the course of their tramping, they had bartered their rags for bread. The trip lasted six days or so. After two days the desert gradually changed to cultivated fields. None of the Poles had any idea where they were going. They forgot that they had been granted "amnesty"; they just had no more strength even to think about their rights. When the barges got stuck every once in a while in shallow waters, they rejoiced, thinking they had reached the end of their journey. But they kept sailing on. When at long last they arrived at their destination, the Russians would from time to time detach one of the barges, sometimes while the human cargo were asleep. Now there was no one on shore, just vast emptiness. After many hours of patient waiting came the screech of wagons, and from the shrubs appeared tall, two-wheeled "arbas" (Asiatic carts) with a donkey or a mule in harness. One cart, two, three, then a whole caravan, and on the carts some savage-looking apparitions in tall black fur caps. These were nomads, the Karakalpaks (their name derived from their caps made of Persian lamb skins). They got off their carts and, speaking in their own language, incomprehensible to the Poles, made a flurry of gestures. Maybe they had come to help.

The deportees were allocated to local community farms: in one region around the town of Nukus, 35,000, and similar numbers in many other regions. For them the second act of slavery was just commencing, maybe even more difficult to bear than the one in Siberia. All were set to work digging irrigation canals and picking cotton. The "norm" assigned for the latter was far beyond their strength. In payment for their labor, they received some "dhzugara," a grain similar to wheat used for making crude buns. Since the earnings were too small to maintain a large family, mothers felt compelled to take their children to work as helpers. Even then it was difficult to live. There was no bread in these areas as grain was not cultivated here, the Russian government having redirected the whole economy of these areas towards the textile industry. So hungry were the Polish laborers that they scrounged for herbs such as oregano, sow-thistle, and sorrel. Sometimes the children managed to catch a dog which, to avoid watching its agony, they would suffocate in a sack. The boars so prevalent here before the October Revolution, were now almost extinct, along with the pheasant, quail, wild goats and other game, once so abundant.

When winter came a new calamity befell the exiles. Work in the cotton fields stopped, and the thousands of Poles still flocking to these areas could find neither work nor shelter. Eventually even the earliest arrivals became a burden on the poor republics, and the central Soviet authorities ordered a new evacuation of the Poles to the north, again to Kazakhstan. The first contingent was to consist of 45,000 people.

All such Soviet directives came unexpectedly and had to be carried out instantly, even in the middle of the night. So the evacuees were given only fifteen to fifty minutes to make ready for the road. At night the cashiers hurriedly doled out back pay; then the exiles were led to loading areas. Often no transportation was provided, and they had to walk the few kilometers to the train station.

One night, at railway stations in the Buchara region, the NKVD assembled some 15,000 Polish exiles, mostly mothers with children, without giving them any food for their journey. They were so exhausted by their previous experiences that they obeyed every order with dull resignation. Only their eyes showed the elemental fear of the unknown in their new exile, all the more so as they knew that the winter in Kazakhstan was severe and the living conditions crude. Thanks, however, to the energetic protests of the Polish Embassy in Kuybishev, the Soviets rescinded the re-evacuation order, and the people returned to their collective farms.

Eastern Turkestan—the Uzbeck and Kirghiz republics—was richer in farm produce than the Western part, which is mostly desert. This area was, before the October Revolution, regarded as a paradise: it fed not only the people but also enormous herds of cattle. Today it was poverty-stricken because of indolence and foolish farming methods. Both these Eastern republics were dotted with oases. On spring mornings, through the translucent fog loomed the dark mountains, the background for blossoming orchards with their bright red patches of pomegranates and for broad fields of cotton. Above the irrigation ditches grew pale green mulberry trees to soften, with an impressionist's brush, the distant ruined ramparts of medieval fortresses. Visible too, far off but unmistakable, was the grave-mound of a long-dead khan. In the foreground stood gigantic stacks of cotton wool covered with tarpaulins, their sides water-soaked, blackish and rotting, awaiting transport, sometimes for years.

The meeting ground for the natives of this land was the noisy, colorful bazaar. Above the human noise and the bleating of rams wafted the monotonous lament of the flute, now and again interrupted by the braying of a donkey. The men—strong, sturdy, with broad yellow faces, flat noses, and prominent cheekbones—would debate excitedly, dramatizing their arguments with the lively gesturing of Oriental people, their dark, cool eyes masking an acute cunning and shrewdness.

The men drank sour buffalo milk, seldom "chai" (tea), which is not as abundant as in pre-Soviet days, and chewed on roast mutton. The women, as is customary among Moslems, were dressed mostly in black and milled around the market stalls with textiles, discreetly lowering their yashmaks from time to time. Teenagers and children, chewing buns and fruits, gathered around the snake charmer. When they tired of the heat and the tumult, the adults would rest in the shade of a poplar or an acacia along the irrigation canals and listen to the bubbling of murky water and the uproar of the marketplace. They seemed to be submerged in non-existence as they sat staring at the colorful crowd that has gathered here for generations without any change in ways of living or thinking. The East is attached to its traditions, and despite the watchfulness of Soviet authorities, matters are occasionally settled in traditional ways. For example, a young girl is sometimes secretly bartered for goods by her father. Though poverty long ago eliminated polygamy, children are still sometimes married off.

This land, once known for its riches, now suffered general poverty. But the living conditions of the Polish exiles were incomparably worse. One of the victims of these conditions, Christine Maziarz, then nine years old, recalls her days of exile in this "Soviet Lousiana" as a time of constant gnawing hunger:

> I lived with my family in an Uzbek mud-hut. Right in the middle of it was an open fire with a hole in the roof just above. Misery looked out from every corner. Mother had bartered for food the last belongings brought from Poland. We ate oregano, frozen turnips, and linseed cakes (in Polish, "makuchy," cattle-feed, tasteless and indigestible). Easter Saturday came and there was nothing to eat in our home, just nothing. Not even bread. Nothing at all. Mother went about sad and mournful. My younger brother and I decided to do some begging among the natives. We peeked into a few huts but did not have the courage to enter until, after a few hours of tramping, hunger overcame our shyness. We were ready even to risk being kicked out. We entered a small yard from which the smell of baking was emanating. There stood a semicircular oven and nearby a local woman baking buns made out of "dzhugara" flour, sticking them to walls of the heated oven. For a while we stood there in the corner of the yard inhaling the smell of baking, which increased our hunger even more. The woman collected the puffed-up buns and after a few minutes took a trayful of them into the hut. We came nearer the oven, my brother and I, and carefully picked the morsels left by the woman. We were just leaving the yard with our pockets full when she appeared in the door and gave each of us one whole "lepyoshka" (bun). She was kindhearted. Maybe she understood our shyness. We ran home with great joy, having a surprise for Mum at Easter. As luck would have it, in the yard of the Uzbek that we lodged with, we noticed a cackling hen. I ran up and found an egg in the ashes. This was a Heaven-sent gift. The prospects for Easter breakfast were splendid. Our mother, overjoyed, divided our treasure into seven portions.

Poverty seldom travels alone. Her companions here were epidemics. Within a short time the hospitals were filled beyond their capacity with Polish exiles. Victims who did not find room in the hospitals were left without any care. Death was taking grownups and children alike and would have taken even more had it not been for the unexpected presence of some members of the Polish Army, evacuated from the Orenburg steppes and sent to these areas. They filled their wretched countrymen's hearts with new hope.

6

Uniformed Samaritans

The Polish Army had been evacuated to Uzbekistan and Kirghistan during the severe winter of 1941-42, the move dictated by the proximity of English supply bases in Persia and by the healthful climate. The soldiers had had a difficult time of it, living in tents on the steppes and in the Orenburg forests. Many were sick and needed a long period of convalescence.

On the way to Kazakhstan, they had traveled through some violent storms, the icy wind howling through the thin, cracked walls of the railroad cars, the soldiers shivering and huddled together. Water froze in their field flasks, and during stop-overs, they tried to steal coal to heat up the cars. Some of the more desperately hungry tried to catch dogs, without great success; but the few fortunate shared their roast dog with their closest friends. When the food supply car of the Officer Cadets School became detached from the train, its axle allegedly broken, it was stolen along with its supplies.

The army had barely managed to move into its assigned regions when an epidemic of typhoid broke out in the garrison and spread rapidly. Every morning when they awoke, the soldiers found friends who would never waken again. Thousands of infected soldiers fought death—between February and the summer of 1942, 47,411 of them.

Although the Polish Army was being destroyed by infectious diseases, the civilian exiles who had arrived in Turkestan much earlier were in an even worse situation, paying a still greater ransom to death. For this reason, when news that the military had arrived reached the collective farms and hospitals, it was received with indescribable joy, relief, and hope. Then something unexpected happened. Mothers who were ill or had sick children resorted to the desperate measure of sending their younger children to be taken care of by the Army. They did this without thinking; they were sure that a Polish soldier would not desert a child.

However, the military themselves had a critical need of provisions. For the total of 70,000-80,000 soldiers, not including the flood of volunteers at the rate of 1000-1500 daily, the Red Army allocated reduced food rations that normally would have served 26,000.

When the military engaged in more exhausting training exercises, hunger began to take its toll. The scenes of bread distribution by the orderlies in the tents are well remembered. These were possibly the most important moments in the soldiers' day. Dividing the bread assumed a ritualistic gravity, everybody attending in silence, devouring with their eyes each piece of bread, of margarine, each spoon of sugar, all weighed with pharmaceutical accuracy by the orderly on improvised scales hanging by a thin rope.

Within his soul each soldier was glad that the heavy equipment had not yet been supplied. The strenuous exercises took away his strength, inadequately maintained without a sufficient diet necessary for endurance. In bayonet practice the soldiers used light rifles whittled out of wood, and yet, with every thrust and every dodge, their legs shook from exhaustion.

A great humiliation to everyone was the horrendous loss of memory caused by avitaminosis. Forgetting the names of one's closest friends was the rule of the day. Lessons about the organization of an army, the number of soldiers in various units, the kinds and intensity of fire, the composition of the cooperating military units—all of these the soldiers found impossible to absorb. In the evening they were so immobilized by night blindness that they had difficulty recognizing their own tents. In such circumstances, military service was a hardship.

Just as thousands of volunteers arrived to join the army, huge numbers of civilians were also pouring into military regions and complicating the supply problem. With great difficulty, and after prolonged conferences with Stalin, General Anders obtained an increase of daily rations for his army of over 70,000. Actually, he was faced with the need to feed twice as many. But Stalin and the other Soviet officials maintained that the civilian population had been supplied their rations and refused to include them in the calculations.

Despite the general hunger, the military did not give up caring for the civilians, particularly the children. The Soviet authorities, however, viewed the gatherings of the Polish families near the camps with disfavor, and their irritation grew at the sight of the

Polish soldiers' generosity as they shared their meager rations with women and children. The Soviet government's reduction of the food ration to the minimum supported the assumption that they wanted to force the Polish soldiers, by exposing them to hunger, to stop helping the civilians.

Quite unexpectedly for the Polish Army, a new page of their proud history was being written—not acts of military valor, but acts of Samaritan love.

The influx of Polish families could not be stopped by the NKVD. Mothers continued to gather the remnants of their strength and head with their children towards the Army camps or send them with whatever escort they could find. Some dramatic scenes took place during their farewells, more painful than hunger or epidemics. The children did not want to part from their mothers, yet the mothers were obliged to chase them away, entreating them by everything holy to go and save themselves. "We have no more strength," they would say; "we will not survive. Go, find the Polish Army. Only there can you get help." So they blessed them and parted with them forever.

The miserable little skeletons shook with sobs in this last embrace of their mothers, aware that this parting was final, despite the consoling promise that they would see their mothers again sometime. The mothers did not believe it either as they comforted each other and sent off with their little ones all that was most precious at the time—a bun or a small bag of biscuits.

The influx of children into the army centers was large. But so strong was the desire to save the children that nurseries and orphanages began to be formed. Kindergartens, young men's work brigades, and courses for younger girls were organized spontaneously without a previously conceived plan.

Some of the children arrived on foot, others by train, half-clad, lousy, miserable, with little bundles in their hands. A majority of them had no documents, nor any referral slips. The soldiers would watch with deep emotion as the children came out of the railroad cars. Some moved under their own power; others, more like phantoms than living creatures, were held by their boney arms or half carried by nurses. The children tried to use their feet to prove that their condition was not too poor yet. Many, though, had to be carried on stretchers. In these little martyrs even sexual characteristics were obliterated. Girls with close-cropped hair because of typhoid and with rib cages collapsed, were difficult to distinguish from boys except by their clothing. The boys were dressed in the rags of their fathers' trousers, their feet in all kinds of footwear without laces, the soles with holes in them or ripped apart. The girls came wearing shabby, worn dresses or their mothers' skirts.

According to the directives, each transport of children had to be bathed instantly and deloused, have their hair close-cropped, and be quarantined. However, the directives remained on paper only, inoperable because of the lack of housing, soap, and in some areas even water.

The youngsters were located wherever possible, under a tent, in a barn, in Uzbek mud-huts. These forms of shelter were instantly turned into hospital wards as there were so many sick people that the military hospitals were accepting only the most seriously ill. The little patients lay on straw sacks in the huts, in the lobbies, in the yard in meager shade, or even on the sand. Above them were swarms of flies, spreading disease. They lay quiet, uncomplaining, their lips parched, cracked with fever and thirst. Several diseases afflicted them: typhoid, malaria, dysentery, swellings—all resulting from hunger or the monotonous diet of dzhugara and millet. Dysentery spread havoc in the exhausted bodies, and half of the cases were fatal. Under the bedsheets covering the children were the very noticeable contours of thin bones and disease-bloated stomachs. The heads were covered with scabs, the bodies badly scarred by insect bites.

Hundreds of these little victims did not live to see a better day. They came seeking help from the military only to die among their own kin. Dying, they did not complain about parting from a life that had treated them so cruelly. The seriously ill envied the ones who died quickly. Only those who had a close relative with them did not want to die but begged to be saved.

Through the time that the Polish Army remained in Russia, death gathered a rich harvest among the children, but in the initial stages this crop was terrifying. The hospital crew was unable to cope with the work load. Often the priests themselves, with no other help, dug the graves and buried the corpses. Because of the shortage of lumber for coffins, the corpses, clothed in underwear, were taken to the desert on a stretcher or blanket and thrown into a common grave. Christine Maziarz recorded in her diary:

> To the orphanage in Zamitan the skeleton-children were coming from all neighboring collective farms. I remember Sophia N. from the same farm that I came from. When she was unable to speak except in a halting whisper, she asked me for bread and begged that I take her to her mother. This request was a general call from all the children. Bread and mother. We, the healthier ones, could not give either at any price. Even the good food did not help some of them. Dysentery, typhoid, and other infectious diseases were gathering their crop in full. Every day a number of our peers parted with us forever. There were no grave diggers. We carted the emaciated little corpses to the fields on a wheelbarrow, marking the graves with small crosses made of sticks. I belonged to the group of young grave diggers; for this I received two slices of bread and a bowl of soup. I ate the soup myself and hid the bread under my kaftan for my brother Freddie. He was a year younger than I, and he always cried for our home and our mother. On a few occasions he escaped from the orphanage, but did not even know the direction to the collective farm where our mother was working.
>
> Once, on a day set for the visits to the nursery, our elder sister, Hela, came riding a donkey to bring us a few buns and "uruk" (wild apricots). Eating those delicacies, after my sister's departure, I momentarily forgot about Freddie, and when I ran out beyond the nursery gate, he was far down the road trying to follow my sister. He was running home to Mother, disregarding the fact that he was without his trousers. They had been taken from him to prevent another escape.
>
> Of all memories, the saddest for me are the funerals of my friends. I remember that field in the desert, marked by crosses, and the horrible sight of human skulls, unearthed by the wind or by the jackals. We did not have shovels to bury the corpses deeper. . . . I could never sleep well after such a funeral. The night seemed extremely long, and the howling of jackals fighting for the bodies of my dead friends chilled the blood in my veins.

In one of the hospitals was Wladek, in agony, suffering from pellagra. He was the youngest soldier in the company—seventeen years old, still only a child, the regimental favorite who had already gone through jail and labor camps for his part in underground activity. The transfusion of blood offered by one of the girls was in vain. The boy died. According to the hospital regulations, the nurse listed all his belongings, tied up in a small bundle: a Boy Scout cross, a grey shoulder-cord, and a service book. They learned that the dead boy had been a Scout, but it remained a mystery how, through all the jails, the searches, and the labor camps, he had managed to smuggle these small treasures.

The most notorious spot where the largest percentage of children died was a place named the "Valley of Death" (Karkin Batash) near Guzar. Here, nature itself conspired against life. The incredible heat would start in May, when the temperature would reach 183° Fahrenheit. The steppe would turn into a desert, obscured by clouds of clay dust. The water would dry up. The local Uzbeks would leave the valley for the summer, seeking shade and shelter in the nearby hills. The orphanage, the school for junior cadres and girl volunteers, turned into a death camp. A deadly silence descended upon it, uninterrupted by a child's song or laughter. Even the healthier children fell into a state of apathy. To shake them out of it, a new learning program was introduced. But all in vain. The only solution was to follow the example of the Uzbeks and transport the children to the healthier climate of Kitabu, an oasis abundant in large walnut trees, vineyards, and streams whose banks were covered with flowers and lush shrubs. The mountains breathed a crisp, cool air.

Like a beautiful poisonous flower, however, this area hid another danger, malaria, which afflicted many children. But the change of climate, the food sent from England, the hope of leaving Russia, and above all, the tender care gradually revived the children, though they would be marked by traces of starvation and disease for many months.

As one of the trainees of the Cadet Officers School of Artillery in Kara-Su, I had the opportunity to observe the orphans from the nearby center. Because our program and the regulations did not allow us to meet them, we saw them most often at Sunday services. There, to a rude altar built under a large tree by the chaplain, Reverend B. Zabludowski, the children would march for Mass, in twos, holding hands, poorly clad, feet sticking out of tattered boots. With close-cropped hair, their heads looking like poppy buds on thin stems, fear in their pale faces, they would stop near the altar while batteries of cadets, with their shining boots and buttons, formed before the altar in military order. Two NKVD officers always participated in the holy Mass "ex officio," with their heads uncovered but with their hands in their pockets and blank expressions on their faces. They stood up and sat down with the faithful, but stiffly, like mannequins. Behind the military would be a group of Polish civilians and among them some local Russians, who, amazed by their own courage, would hide in the crowd.

In 1942, the orphanage in Kara-Su was overjoyed by a visit of

Field Bishop Joseph Gawlina, arriving from England. All the emaciated children accepted the sacrament of confirmation and sang the song of the exiles. Composed in exile, the song asks God for mercy upon their homeland, and for the chance to go back to a free Poland. "O Lord, who art in heaven, stretch out Thy arm. . . ."

The band of little tramps, seeking salvation and an anchor under the army's care, was growing day by day, and new orphanages had to be created. Still, there were not enough of them, and the children from the most distant regions of Russia still trekked in, ragged, barefooted, hungry, but full of hope. Sometimes they would lose their composure when they arrived and, afraid there might be no room for them, would bivouac nearby for days before someone would introduce them.

Every once in a while, from the depths of European Russia or the Far East, desperate letters would arrive from children unable to leave the "dyet-doms." These were the most peculiar letters in the world, written on strips of birch bark, on the bindings of Soviet elementary textbooks, on rolls of wall-paper, on portraits of Soviet leaders. The children wrote as they knew how, knowing that no one would count their mistakes, only asking to be saved. Volunteers among the soldiers would dress in civilian clothing to make the risky journey to rescue them, unable to bear the thought of not replying to these imploring summons.

7

Bread, Medicine and God's Word

Not all of the freed Poles attempted to seek the care of the Army or the Polish Relief offices. Women, especially those responsible for small children, were afraid to make a move. It was a fearsome risk to set out with elderly parents and sick children, without money and food supplies—all the more risky when so few knew where to go and which direction to turn. Some families reckoned that they must have been outdistanced by thousands of others already and did not want to live through another painful disappointment. Many were afraid there could not be enough help for everybody because such masses had to be cared for.

The Branch Offices of the Embassy in Kuybishev sent out so-called "men of trust" to larger concentrations of Polish people in Russia, but apart from these concentrations, a multitude of lesser groups were scattered in various, distant locations, on collective farms, cut off from any means of communication.

The mission of reaching such "hidden" places was undertaken mostly by Polish chaplains. There were only fifty-four of them, thirty-nine in the Army and fifteen in the service of civilians. Their work load was heavy. Each was assigned the care of the military, hospital patients, and children in nurseries and schools; yet they managed to find time for expeditions in search of their countrymen who waited for help and words of hope.

These distant and exhausting expeditions into the Uzbek and Kirgiz land were a truly missionary work. They are referred to in the memoirs of the Reverend Wlodzimierz Cienski, Dean of the Polish Pastoral Service in Russia, who undertook several such trips to comfort his countrymen with the Word of God, with bread, and with medicaments.

The dean would be accompanied by a sub-deacon and by a nurse from the military hospital, the three of them loaded with bags, flasks, and knapsacks full of clothing to satisfy some of the likely needs. They also took a considerable amount of money to buy bread at the bazaars, as they knew the people were always short of it. The Army was very generous in supporting this effort. For example, volunteer girls from the Polish Women's Service of only one division, the Fifth, collected among themselves twenty thousand rubles for Rev. Cienski.

The errands of mercy proceeded by any means available. When it was impossible to get somewhere by train or truck, the dean and his companions would walk as many as twenty-five miles a day over a difficult mountainous terrain. The news of their arrival, in Polish military uniforms, would spread through a collective farm like wildfire. There would be no end to the questions about the Polish Army and about the possibilities of emigrating. The people would be overjoyed not to have been forgotten and to have, for the first time in exile, a chance to make confession and receive Holy Communion.

The three missionaries divided their work so that the dean heard confessions, baptized, administered the Last Rites, and said Mass; the sub-deacon prepared the children for confession; and the nurse visited the sick. There was so much work that the priests heard confessions late into the night.

Once, seeing how exhausted they were, one resolute thirteen-year-old girl offered to help prepare the children for confession, as she was the oldest among them. "Father has to hear the confessions of the older people," she said. "That is why I will prepare the rest of the children for confession, so now I will run home for the book." And she did prepare them. They sat in a ditch, listened attentively to her teachings, and submitted to the examination. Even the falling dusk did not upset them; they answered clearly and made their confession late in the evening under bright starlight. The priests, exhilarated by such godliness instilled by mothers despite exile and the lifestyle on the collective farm, forgot their fatigue.

Occasionally Russian women would steal in for confession. The priests had to be very careful not to be deceived, for there were some curious cases, and it was easy to displease the NKVD. There was no shortage of spies. Once a Russian woman came without any fear and loudly demanded that the priest baptize her grandson in a nearby house. The openness of the request sounded suspicious to the priest so he refused and declared that he was allowed to serve only Polish citizens. He would, he said, readily baptize the child if the grandmother would bring a permit from the local authorities. In reply the woman started complaining about the authorities and the Soviet ways, obviously believing that by acting this way she would be trusted. "They took everything away from us," she cried, "but we will not give them our souls." Her courage seemed too ostentatious to be trusted. Once again the priest refused. As it appeared later, he was right. Shortly after he had left, a twelve-man horse-mounted NKVD patrol came to the farm and interrogated the people about the priests' activities. Did they contact the Soviet people? Since nobody testified against the priests, and the matter of the baptism was truthfully presented, the patrol, seeing that their agent had not succeeded, left without any reprisals, though not without a reprimand to their co-worker, who was summoned from behind the gate.

Lodging for the priests was always a problem, because a few Polish families lived huddled together in small, miserable huts. However, the Poles tried hard to ensure that their longed-for guests did not have to sleep in the ditches after a full day of hard work. Once an accommodation was found in the home of an old Ukrainian woman, resettled with her two sons from the Kharkov area. Since she was not a Catholic, the priests could not understand why she welcomed them with honor and respect. When she stood at the door of her homestead and, bowing low, asked for their blessings, the dean, believing that there was some misunderstanding, explained that they were Roman Catholic, and Polish, priests. The lady explained that she respected them because they were clergymen, because they were in the Polish Army, and because neither the Polish Army nor the Polish clergy trusted the Bolsheviks. To convince them of her friendliness, she set before them a meal of Russian "pierogis," rye bread, and honey. After supper she prepared clean, comfortable bedding. As the senior clergyman, the dean was honored by being allocated the space on top of the oven padded with featherbeds.

On their journeys, the priests also had some sad moments to live through. Frequently they had to prepare for death people emaciated by prolonged exile, exhaustion, and mistreatment. The most shocking experience was witnessing deaths from exhaustion and from years of undernourishment. It also happened that people died just from the fear of hunger. Once a little boy ran up to Rev. Cienski, lamenting that his mother was dying. The priest went quickly, but by the time he had arrived, the woman was already dead. The boy started to sob loudly and in despair threw himself upon her body and cried that she had some grain and money under her. Nothing was found; someone, during the boy's brief absence, had taken everything that the unfortunate mother had put aside while depriving herself and her child. Obsessed by her fear of hunger, she would not let herself or the child touch this reserve and had starved herself to death. Shortly after, the husband died in the same way. It was not easy to rescue even the boy. At first he refused to leave the priest, but since it was impossible to take him with them, the missionaries left him in the care of a young girl who was acting as mother to a handful of her own orphaned siblings as well as to the orphans of some neighbors. Such collective families were common among the exiles. Even the poorest, the most exhausted, the weakest women often cared for someone else's children. When one of those women was asked whether she was not afraid to accept another load on her shoulders, she would say, "And what would have happened if my own children became orphans and had no one to cuddle up to?"

8

Rehabilitation

An estimated 75,000 children in various Polish centres in Russia needed instant help after the "amnesty." To create an adequate number of proper institutions would have required not only an enormous outlay of money but also an army of educators and nurses. But the possibilities were very limited.

With much effort, mostly by the Army and branches of the Embassy in Kuybishev, 139 orphanages and nurseries were established in which approximately 9,000 children found shelter. Those whose lives were most threatened were given preference.

These institutions were in no way like those in the civilized world. The children were often housed in wooden or clay huts, sometimes in tents. Everything was in short supply—bedding, linen, furniture, and kitchen utensils. Hygienic conditions were atrocious: no isolation wards for children with infectious diseases, no disinfectants to delouse clothes. For each board, nail, or broom, battles had to be fought with Soviet authorities. The primitiveness bordered on utter poverty; yet each of these relief institutions, substituting for a home, carried out its assignments to the limit of its possibilities, saving its occupants from hunger, offering some kind of roof over their heads, attempting to safeguard them against disease.

Apart from orphanages and nurseries, forty-three kindergartens were established, among them one in Bukhara, most impressively endowed and efficiently conducted.

Having no textbooks or school supplies, the teachers taught solely from memory, under the bare sky with the hard earth as blackboard. However, the teaching was a necessity, so much time had already been wasted, and only God Himself knew when these masses of children might be able to go to a normal school.

Learning progressed slowly: the children fainted, became sick, lost their memory, and above all suffered from being separated from their mothers. Teaching them was even more difficult because most of them were terrified, secretive, distrustful, unsmiling. The teachers had no way to create a psychological profile of their charges, particularly the youngest, without personal data. It was the exception if someone handing an orphan over to the nursery remembered his name or knew his age. The depositions of people who could have known something about the child did not tally. One would give one date, another a totally different one. The orphanage registered both dates, hoping that some time it could be established which was correct. As a result, some of the orphans had three dates on their passports.

In order to get to know something about the child's background, the teachers tried to reach into his memory. But what could these little orphans remember? At times some isolated pictures from the past, most often of their mother. One little girl had a recurring vision of her mother covered with a large peasant kerchief. A frail little boy remembered only his mother's hands tucking his comforter around him.

Many orphans knew their mothers only from atrocious passport photographs in which the women looked ghostly, emaciated, aged and haggard as a result of their hard experiences, work beyond endurance, hunger, and disease. But the children were not repulsed by this sight. They hid their mothers' photographs carefully in safe spots. One had a few copies of his mother's photograph and hid them in various places in order to save at least one.

The older children remembered more but did not like to speak about their experiences. The urgent aim of the orphanage teachers was to restore to the children inner peace and composure and win their trust and faith, get them used to life without fear, and help them develop confidence in themselves.

There was no counting upon speedy results, because the trauma was deep. In some children, especially older boys, the traces of a certain savagery, born in exile, were still evident. They were more distrustful than the others, lied more often, and stole when they had an opportunity. It is a simple truth that even under ideal conditions some children have undesirable tendencies. However, the teachers, who themselves had gone through prison or deportation, knew well enough what had so badly distorted the characters of some of these children, the less resistant or those more often exposed to bad influences.

Under the pressure of the Soviet system, it is possible, even though one hates evil, to get used to it as much as to one's daily bread. It is not easy to retain a distaste for lying and stealing when they serve as a protection against oppression and hunger. In fact, as the children stopped suffering oppression and hunger, in the sorrowful mix-up of their ideas they often could not assess circumstances which justified a lie or a theft. The teachers, although aware of the reasons for these deviations, were not always able to prevent them. These were complicated problems, difficult to solve.

It was painful to suffer the children's distrust of their elders, but at the same time one could not forget that in their ears still rang the seldom-kept promises of Soviet officials and supervisors.

Even now they could not shake off the fear that here also there might be no bread; therefore, they stole it for reserve, for the "dark hour," or they overate "just in case," reporting for food two or three times in the line-up. They had come to the conclusion, based on their own observation, that very few people in Russia worked honestly, that everybody tried to dodge work and when forced to it, did a slap-dash job. The children had seen the Soviet worker destroying or neglecting state property, hating with all his soul all those who (while reciting some noble-sounding slogans) were abusing him badly. Some of this disrespect for authority and for honest effort, as well as an unwillingness to contribute towards a common social benefit, permeated the Polish children noticeably.

The adults in the orphanages knew about these matters and knew also that the children's long period without religious upbringing and a proper moral atmosphere had to show negative results. Some children even displayed a disrespect for religion, because they had heard in Russia that religion is useless, that it brings no material gains while calling for senseless self-denial and self-development. Ugly swear words, blasphemies, and obscenities used constantly by Soviet labor-mates had so fixed themselves in the children's minds that, much to the consternation of their hearers, they could not resist the temptation to show them off.

Life in dirty, lice-infested surroundings had inured them to untidiness. Regrettably, the lack of facilities at the orphanages only helped them get even more used to being grubby. How could one teach children orderliness when the very basic crudeness of their living quarters—no beds, no toilet facilities, no soap, no basic necessities—counteracted the lesson?

Such difficulties, almost enough to defeat the guardians, did not, however, deprive them of their desire to work, because they were convinced that within the souls of these children, under a surface of coarseness and deviance, was a basic goodness to build on. Their work was facilitated greatly by the seeming absence of other social handicaps, including an inferiority complex, so often linked to orphanhood.

The children were not ashamed of being orphans; on the contrary, it was for some a source of rightful pride. They may have been aware, in their own way, that their parents had died in a battle fought by the whole Polish nation and that their deaths were already a tragic part of Polish history. Somehow, in spite of their own suffering, most of those homeless children evolved rather early a sense of their own value and a stamina that would help them through even more difficult times.

9

The Polish Children and the Descendants of Genghis Khan

On the collective farms in the South of Russia near the Chinese border, the Polish exiles worked among the Uzbeks and Kirghizians. They found themselves as if in a large yellow sea, not a very fearsome sea, really, but at first very strange. Here and there "the yellows" did not want to sell produce to the Polish newcomers, and their children bullied the Polish children. Soon, however, the reason for this aversion became evident: the natives suspected the Poles of being friendly toward the Bolsheviks. How could it be otherwise, they thought, if the Polish Army intended to fight against the Germans alongside the Red Army? They themselves hated the Red Army and had only contempt and open hostility for the Russians.

National pride and religious fervor were at the bottom of this hatred. The Uzbeks and the other Mongolian nations regard themselves as heirs of the magnificent if stormy period initiated by Genghis Khan in the year 1226, when he established the gigantic Mongolian Empire, known as "the empire on horseback," which stretched from Korea to the Persian Gulf and north toward the borders of Poland. They knew what to think of Russia and her present-day might. They had not forgotten that at one time all the Russian dukedoms were under Mongolian domination, and that up to the end of the eighteenth century the Russians were objects of commerce in Mongolian Turkestan. In the seventeenth century, on the slave market of Khiva, ten thousand Russians and Persians were being sold. Now the Communists were destroying all traces of their former might and trying to eradicate their religion, closing ten thousand mosques. For this, above all, the natives could not forgive them.

Their unfriendliness toward the Poles lessened as their real situation began to be understood, and their love of God. This probably did not happen everywhere, but wherever conditions permitted the two peoples to get to know each other, the awareness that they shared sources of misery eliminated pettiness and chicanery, and some Poles and Mongolians even became friends. The Uzbeks especially appreciated any show of interest in the era of their great Genghis Khan.

Not far from Khiva, until recent times a famous slave market, were thousands of Poles, working at jobs that only slaves used to do: picking cotton and digging irrigation ditches. In one locality, Nukus, 35,000 Polish deportees were employed; others were concentrated between the rivers Syr-Daria and Amu-Daria, and in the vicinity of the historic cities of Bukhara and Samarkand, at one time powerful fortresses guarding the entrance to the vast territories of the Persian shah. It was near Bukhara in 1220 that the fate of the Persian Empire was decided when Genghis Khan's armies killed almost the entire Persian population and took their children into captivity. The same thing happened later on near Samarkand. Today's descendants of Genghis Khan are happily without this cruelty, though it characterizes their rulers: the Soviets now take children into captivity to bring them up as their slaves. The inhabitants of the vast Fergana Valley are, like the Polish peasant, gentle, hardworking, and much attached to their herds and their lands.

One day, in Kara-Su, close to the Chinese border, an Uzbek brought to the Polish military camp, on an "arba," a Polish woman with a few emaciated children. It was obvious that he had become attached to the little ones, because he could not bring himself to return to his village but camped for three days in a nearby mulberry patch, patiently waiting to chat with the children when they visited him from the orphanage. His face would show no emotion; only the fine wrinkles around his eyes and a quivering of his lower jaw betrayed his joy at their visit. When the time came for him to leave, he took a few bottles of honey from the arba and very slowly deposited them at the children's feet. He took each child in his arms, picked each one up, touched head to head, quickly returned to his arba, and without once turning his head went away.

10

Release from "Paradise"

To someone who does not know the Soviets well, it would seem that all of Russia's cruel enmity against Poland should have ceased the moment she became Poland's ally against Germany, especially when, in accordance with the treaty of July 30, 1941, the Polish Army was being formed on Russian territories to increase her forces against the common enemy.

We who had come to know the Soviets at close range could not entertain any such delusions. Yet we too were astounded time after time by Soviet moves. We were particularly alarmed when a group of Polish Communists trained in Moscow first publicly expressed their opinion in matters affecting the whole nation.

A gathering of this group, "Union of Polish Patriots," took place in Saratov a few months after the signing of the treaty. Later, on July 21, 1944, the organization became the "Committee of National Liberation." With Stalin's backing, it was to impose its will upon political events in Poland and eventually force upon it a Communist government. At that time we did not fully understand the Russian game, and still nourished the hope that the Polish question would be resolved justly at the end of the war. But subsequent developments gradually laid bare the Soviet plans. We became convinced not only that Russia did not mean to give up the Eastern Territories she had seized at the beginning of the war, but that she also aimed to dominate all of Poland and turn her into a subjugated Communist state.

Even had we been aware of these machinations, we could not have foreseen that they would not be adequately resisted by the other allies. At the time we knew only that something unsavory was taking place. The strongest reaction was felt in our Army, whose members, even without this, had good reason to be wary. It became more and more obvious that the Kremlin had its own plans regarding the Polish Army. The Soviet government was, for one thing, explictly against the total mobilization of all Polish citizens capable of bearing arms. As a result, the army was considerably smaller than it could have been. Even at that, only one division (the 5th, of General Boruta-Spiechowicz) got full equipment; the remainder had to make do with a meager supply of weapons.

It was difficult to understand a situation where one party insisted on forming an army whose participation in future action could count for something, while the other would not even allow the possibility that this army might contribute at all to fighting the Germans. Such a situation could hardly be expected to encourage an atmosphere of mutual trust.

Stalin demanded that each Polish division be thrown into battle singly, as it became ready, whereas the Polish aimed for the entire army to reach full battle-readiness as soon as possible. This last Russian demand seemed most suspicious, because if the Polish government gave in to Stalin's pressure, the fate of these divisions would bc sealed. Thrown singly into the heaviest fire, they would face certain annihilation.

The tension grew to alarming proportions when news began to spread about the disappearance of 14,000 Polish prisoners of war. In September of 1939, they had been driven to Soviet prison camps, and no trace was ever found of them. Where could they have gone? There were so many of them, and not a single one survived. The thought that they had all been murdered was frightening. Completing this terrible picture were the mass deaths of the Polish population from epidemics and hunger. The only salvation seemed to be in leaving this land, which had taken so many human lives, as soon as possible.

Discussions about this possibility started in the Army and were eagerly picked up by the civilians. The whole idea seemed at the beginning like a fantastic dream of people at the end of their tether. General Klemens Rudnicki wrote:

> Under the guise of outings we were reconnoitering the passages and roads through the mountain chains separating us from Afghanistan, also the possibility of capturing trains to Ashkha-

> bad, going towards the Persian border. We studied the location of the closest Soviet garrisons, stores, ammunition depots, et cetera, where we could get weapons and supplies that we were short of.[1]

These were reckless plans, as the general himself emphasized, but understandable in people who, even at the risk of their lives, wanted "to escape from this accursed land, to escape as far as possible, even on foot, even on stretchers."

Surprisingly, a more realistic basis for the hope of getting out of Russia appeared when the Soviets agreed in January, 1942, to release 25,000 soldiers for the Polish Navy and Air Force in Great Britain. The thought that there might be a chance for further transports from then on became our only moral support, our new source of strength.

The most serious worry was how to care for 100,000 children, who were dying one by one of infectious diseases, hunger, and the stress of orphanhood. The Polish authorities tried to obtain Soviet approval for the evacuation of 50,000 of these. President Roosevelt offered help by inducing the Union of South Africa to accept 10,000 children at the expense of the American Red Cross. The Soviets, however, refused to approve this plan, citing difficulties in communication as an excuse.

When the news reached India that thousands of Polish children were dying in Asiatic Russia, the angered Polish settlement in Bombay decided to undertake instant relief action. With the ardent participation of the Achibishop of Bombay and Ceylon, the Rev. Dr. Thomas Roberts, they acquainted the English and the Indian communities with the situation and quickly launched the action. The Indian government in power at the time supported it and entrusted official responsibility for it to Sir Archibald Webb, Deputy Minister of Internal Affairs. With very cordial assistance from the Council of Indian Princes, headed by Maharaja Jan-Saheb of Nawagar, a Custodial Council was formed in New Delhi to coordinate the efforts. Many representatives of India's social and political circles, and various groups from all levels of the Indian elite, joined in the work of the Council, under the patronage of the Archibishop of Delhi.

The executors of the plan were nominated exclusively from

---

1. Stanislaw Kot, *Letters from Russia to General Sikorski*, London 1956, p. 41.

among the Polish colony, who organized the relief expedition of the Polish Red Cross from Bombay to Tashkent, capital of Uzbekistan. The expedition carried medicine, clothing, and food in six heavy trucks, bought and equipped specifically for this trip and driven by Hindus. It was not an easy undertaking. Three times on the way, they encountered difficulties from the Soviets because the luxurious trucks, as well as the quality of the gifts for the children, contrasted so sharply with the poverty they were suffering in Russia as to create undesirable propaganda for the free world.

Friends of the Polish children in India did not propose to limit themselves to this help, but planned to organize the evacuation of the children to India. Not all of these plans were realized.

In March of 1942, the difficulty of feeding the Poles in Turkestan resulted in Soviet approval for evacuating 30,000 of the military along with 10,000 members of their families. By the will of Providence, the cruel hunger that had been tormenting them unexpectedly became the instrument of their salvation.

News of the proposed evacuation precipitated a feverish stampede toward the South from all the collective farms and factories, wherever Poles were working. Even the Social Service officials began leaving their posts in order to be included in the assigned quota. Fear of losing the chance of being evacuated, possibly the only chance, overcame even the fear of new arrests, with which the Soviets were very likely to stem the great tide of people southward. This would undoubtedly cause horrendous panic and disorganization, which would increase the hunger and the diseases all the more. And even at that, there was no guarantee whatsoever that those masses would reach the evacuation points in time, especially since the Soviets, as if anticipating all that was going to happen, demanded the evacuation of the assigned quota within seven days. Fortunatley the rescue operation did not end with this one transport.

Stalin's recent tactics, changing his plans from day to day, showed his increasing distrust of the Polish Army and his clear intention to rid Russia of this patriotic force and replace it with units indoctrinated in Communism. When in June, 1942, the British suffered a heavy defeat in Africa, which threatened Egypt, Iraq, Iran, and Caucasus, Stalin, without consulting the Polish Government-in-Exile, offered Great Britain the help of Polish divisions, allegedly to defend the Caucasus from the South.

Faced with this fact, the Polish government, not yet familiar with all of Stalin's intentions toward Poland, vainly demanded a conscription to increase the Polish armed forces in Russia so that other divisions might be organized for the battle on the German-Russian front, which seemed, to the Poles, the surest and most direct road to Poland.

The mutual distrust apparent in all the Soviet activities and, above all, the total difference in their objectives, led, as was to be anticipated, to Polish-Soviet friction, resulting in the departure of 14,000 Poles from Russia during the summer of 1942. The total number of evacuees was 77,200 soldiers and 37,300 civilians, mostly military families, including 15,000 children. General Anders issued an order that the transports had to include as many children as possible, even the gravely ill, even if they had to be brought to the trains in someone's arms. Out of necessity children hopelessly ill were left behind.

The transports left from Krasnovodsk, on the Caspian Sea, for the Persian port of Pahlavi. Since the Soviet lines of communication were suffering much because of the heavy battles against the Germans, the exiles had to wait in Krasnovodsk for the arrival of a coal ship.

The sun beat down mercilessly, overpowering the weak and thirsty people on the shore. The Kara-Kum desert was fiery with heat. How precious each drop of water was here! The air, permeated with fumes from the refineries, was nauseating, and the murky, oily waters of the Caspian Sea discouraged the idea of refreshing oneself with a bath. Furthermore, there was no energy left for any activity; even the slightest movement was difficult.

At times ships carrying Soviet soldiers wounded on the Caucasian front came to the wharf, but one's senses, dulled by exhaustion, did not react. Here even death, still stalking the weaker, moved hardly anyone.

At one moment something appeared on the waves, something that looked like a pink ball. A Red Army man swam out and brought it to shore. It was the corpse of a child. The man grabbed the little cadaver by the leg, and with a swing, threw it farther away on the sand. One or two people looked, only a few voices were heard; again the dead silence fell, and the torpor. The vultures flew in from the desert and cruised above the tiny corpse.

The sight of approaching coal carriers electrified the inert masses and put them on their feet at once. But it was still too early for joy: while they were picking up their shabby bundles, they felt a growing fear at the very thought that the slightest suspicion, any kind of whim on the part of the NKVD might cause one's name to be stricken from the list.

These officials positioned themselves on the plank steps and checked the passengers coming aboard against their lists of names. It was not easy to control the excitement during this check, since the NKVD now and then brutally pushed aside a man or a woman with children if their names were not listed. The rejected one would bend over suddenly and cover his head with his hands; a woman cried spasmodically; others numbly accepted their fate. The approved people were thrown into the dark, filthy innards of coal ships, so crowded that the sick were already suffocating.

At long last came the moment of departure. The exiles carried with them, as relics, two pictures of the Virgin Mary, called the Victorious, painted by Polish prisoners of war in the former monastery in Kozielsk, now a prison, from which the Russians had, in the spring of 1940, taken the Polish officers to murder them in Katyn.

As the ships neared Pahlavi, a general panic erupted; everyone wanted to disembark as quickly as possible, to be out of the reach of Soviet authority. As if escaping a fire, the crowd pressed for the exit. In the commotion, crossing the bridge, a child slipped from its mother's arms into the water. Her cries for help went unheeded, so great was the excitement, and besides, the pressure of the crowd behind her did not slacken even for a moment. The human wave carried the mother along.

Upon landing, many people laughed, then cried, as if they had lost their senses for joy. But it was not madness; it was a passionate, uncontrollable burst of thanksgiving. To come suddenly upon normal human conditions of life was to be stirred profoundly. They forgot their fatigue and their frailty, even the full awareness that they would from now on live the life of wanderers without a home, cut off from their homeland. Only God knew when and how all this was to end.

But amid the joy, none of us could forget that we represented only a very small percentage of all the Polish people deported to Russia between 1939 and 1941, and that after the last transport of civilians and military personnel had arrived, at least one million of our countrymen, along with their children, remained dependent upon the good or ill will of the Soviet NKVD—among them many of our acquaintances, friends, and relatives. All of those thousands of terrified, wretched skeletons were one in that incredible bond of common suffering.

It was possible that later on, with the passing of time, amid the varied turns of an exile's life, one or another of us could cease caring for his fate; but just then, landing at Pahlavi, we could not. Just then, we were painfully aware of having to remain in that place; this awareness stayed with each of us, along with the grim reality of the Soviet Union and our terrible experiences there.

11

The Persian Shah's Hospitality

On the Persian beaches of the Caspian Sea, near Pahlavi, stretched a large camp, a city of countless white tents. It was here, after the miraculous exodus from Russia in the summer of 1942, that the Polish throngs found their first shelter. When tents became scarce, open shelters were hurriedly erected to accommodate everyone. The weather was warm and sunny and the routines of camp life under the sun and beside the sparkling water made the first days of freedom a joy. The children were particularly happy. Even the weakest, most exhausted began to smile again.

At field altars erected along the beaches, prayers and songs of thanksgiving were heard continually, not only at services but throughout the day. Thus, conceivably, had the children of Israel thanked Almighty God for being led out of the land of bondage.

* * *

The Pahlavi stopover was not only the first breath of freedom. By force of circumstance, it had to be also a quarantine. Here the people were inoculated and given a proper diet; dirt was scraped off of bodies; long-neglected hair was cut; lice-infested clothing was burned. In this general destruction of all objects that could spread infectious diseases, everyone tried to save precious mementos from Poland, miraculously rescued in the moves from one place to another despite the frequent searches and thefts by the Soviet overseers.

Exhaustion and the sudden change in living conditions caused diseases to break out, primarily dysentery and typhoid enteric fever. Cases of typhoid increased rapidly, and the children also fell victim to eye inflammation and the itch. Within the short period of the quarantine, according to the Bwana report entitled *Polish Pastoral Service Abroad*, approximately six hundred people died here on the sandy shore of the Caspian, at freedom's doorstep. Burials were speedy: the corpse was wrapped in a blanket, the belongings listed on a slip of paper in a sealed bottle buried alongside. It was mostly children who contracted the diseases. Fortunately, a man with the heart of an angel came to their aid, an Englishman, Colonel A. Ross. He organized a special camp for them which provided truly exceptional care, with the help of female compatriots.

The sea breeze and warm sun began to tan the haggard little bodies, and this encouraged hope for an improvement in their health. But just then the authorities started moving the refugees into central Persia, to Teheran and its environs.

The journey was made in heavy trucks through the wild Elburz Mountains. The trucks, operated by experienced Persian drivers, labored along steep, tortuous roads, slowing down for terrifying precipices and chasms. The older boys played hero, but the mothers crossed themselves often.

In Teheran, as in Pahlavi, the officers responsible for accommodations were not ready to receive such large numbers of people, nor had anyone been able to envision the state they would be in when they arrived. They were assigned quarters in the buildings of an incomplete munitions factory and in other buildings near the airport. Then a veritable tent city began to grow in Teheran's outskirts. These hurriedly organized camps were most primitive: the people slept on bare floor boards until mattresses, lamps, and other essentials as well as toys and candies for the children, were brought in by Jews, Persians, British, and Americans.

Shortly after the arrival in Teheran, more epidemics broke out, mainly typhoid fever and typhoid enteric. At once the shortage of qualified nurses was felt acutely, and two nurses even died of typhoid fever at their posts. The priests worked with almost no respite, having to give most of their time to the sick, of whom there was a multitude. Every once in a while someone had to be prepared for eternal rest—sometimes twenty or more in one day; for a long time the average was fifteen, later ten. Teheran's only coffin-supply firm was completely sold out within the first days of the epidemics. Again the corpses had to be buried wrapped only in blankets.

The Saint Lazarus Order of Monks offered their cemetery for the burial of the dead, but it filled so quickly that a new cemetery had to be assigned especially for Poles. Two thousand found rest in it. This cemetery differed from others in that it had very many crosses marked simply "NN," for the nameless dead.

On one side of this Polish cemetery stretches a row of rather small white gravestones where rest four hundred Polish children rescued from Russia but so exhausted that not even the best medical care could have saved them. They did not have the strength to fight disease. On many gravestones are inscriptions such as "Here rests Johnny," or simply "Henry, age 6, died . . . ," then "Margaret, age 4, died . . . , Rest in peace." Over two hundred of these graves bear no names. No one could tell whom these children belonged to or where they had been born.

Grief touched thousands of people. Now new ranks of orphans grew and had to be cared for. Both orphans and non-orphans had to enter normal life routines and receive schooling regardless of how long they were to stay here. Instantly orphanages and school courses were organized in all three camps. In Isphahan, the one-time capital of the Persian Shahs, a magnificent centre was created for school children, its six schools and boarding houses loaned by European and American nuns. The Shah himself made available a large swimming pool.

Whoever could, obeying his heart's dictates, rushed to help the rescued children. Bishop Joseph Gawlina, the spiritual leader of the refugees, continually bought footwear for them with his own funds, and of course candy, so important to children. The engineers of the Carpathian Division helped support the orphanage and medical treatment for the children. The Sisters Nazarethans, deported from Poland to Siberia, who had come to Persia with them, cared for them with tireless devotion. Soldiers—American, British, and Hindu—as well as Poles long settled in Persia, all tried in some measure to help nurse those droves of children back to health, to restore their faith in the existence of goodness in this world, and to help them adjust to normal human conditions. Of course, after the cataclysms they had been through, they could not adjust quickly nor did camp life and their anxiety about further tramping over the world make it easier for them.

The stay of the Poles in Persia did not seem to be planned for any length of time. Since Soviets occupied northern Persia, there was the fear that, in case of any political shifts, they were capable of grabbing the Polish refugees once more. Awareness of such a horrendous possibility, as well as the open enmity of the Soviets, had a very detrimental effect.

The Poles could not repress their fear and uncertainty. They were told not to speak about their experiences in Russia; and although it was difficult for them, they stayed silent. But their misery and their emaciation spoke for them, and evoked the commiseration of their new neighbors. The very weakness of the children was a serious accusation against the Soviet Union, so serious, in fact, that the Soviet representatives in Persia felt obliged to present the matter in their own way. In the Persian and Indian press appeared Soviet statements charging the Germans with responsibility for the children's atrocious condition. The Poles learned, to their amazement, that according to the Russians, only the Germans were to blame for their own and their children's misery. The emaciation of the children evoked so much sympathy among the Persians that soon the Soviet Union proclaimed that not only had they not caused the Polish children any harm but, on the contrary, had been their benevolent patron. They had cared for them as for war victims on Russian territory, but, unable to provide them with good living conditions because of Russia's devastation by the enemy, had facilitated their departure to countries not affected by the war.

These crude lies were easy to refute if one recalled that at the time of round-ups and deportations in Eastern Polish territories, the Germans had not been there at all; those territorires had been occupied solely by the Soviet Union under the terms of the Ribbentrop-Molotov pact. To throw the proper light on those fairy tales it should have been sufficient to ask why, in that case, the amnesty was needed. Was it in order to "free" the Poles from this solicitous care? One could cite fact after fact to bring out the truth, and the refugees would most certainly have done so despite all orders for silence had it not been that so many Poles still remained in Russia that it would have further jeopardized their already critical situation.

The fact was that they would have to leave Persia and seek other shelter in the free world. Great Britain meanwhile notified the Polish government in London that she was ready to grant the refugees hospitality in her African colonies. Others were expected to go to India and Mexico.

Re-groupings of people had already commenced, and departure lists were being prepared. Transports were organized at intervals, and the weaker refugees, children first, were being strengthened for the journey with a more nourishing diet. Clothing was also being collected.

First to depart were the military. Down the dark asphalt roads stretched columns of trucks loaded with soldiers. "Direction Bagdad!" shouted the officers. "Direction Bagdad!" repeated the boys, so certain were they that the military would not leave them behind. They did not understand that no army goes to war trailing children along with it. So, in the Persian refugee camps the departure of the Polish Army for the center of the Arabian peninsula was deeply felt by all of the Polish civilians, especially the youngsters.

Thus far the Army had been the closest, the most wholeheartedly devoted guardian of these masses of people, and above all of the children. The soldiers would be sorely missed. Never again would they cross the paths of their people, whose wandering was nowhere near its end.

PART TWO

In Africa

12

The Journey to Africa

Of all of the groups of Polish children leaving Persia via different routes to various new places of refuge, the largest went to Africa. But though Africa was able to accept the most refugees, it was the move most feared, especially by the women. The children were naturally unconcerned about where they were to go as long as there were new experiences to be had; but the mothers were panic-stricken: would resettlement somewhere near the equator in an unhealthful climate, among wild animals and half-wild people, not exhaust the last remnants of their children's strength? And would it not be altogether detrimental to the children?

They were suspicious and distrustful. The military families used all their influence to delay the departure or avoid it entirely. Their agitation was so great that the first group of five hundred listed for transport rebelled. British soldiers surrounded the camp in Teheran to make sure that nobody could leave; but under cover of night, three hundred did. Persuasive talks commenced, then lectures about Africa. The officers searched for speakers who had been there and could allay the fears. Whether these measures helped somewhat, or whether the resistance abated by itself, the transports eventually began to leave.

The first children left toward the end of 1942. Some were accompanied by their guardians; others by their mothers, grandmothers, aunts, or other elderly relatives; a few by their fathers. On the way to Africa they stopped at transit camps in Ahwaz, a town situated on the hot sand dunes near Basra on the Persian Gulf, and Karachi, India. Each transport, because of the danger of Japanese aircraft and submarines, was convoyed by British naval units. The heat on board ship was dreadful.

For some time, the main attraction on the way was the "flying fish." They moved in small shoals, gliding close to the surface of the water, emerging slightly. Their well developed belly-fins, vibrating in the water, gave them considerable initial speed, as if they were being lifted by a strong wind. Once aloft they would spread their fins to glide, sometimes briefly, other times so far on favorable winds that it seemed they would never come down but fly away into a private world of their own. The flight would end as each dived into the water as if weighted with stone. These sudden flights probably saved them from larger, predatory fish, though even in mid-air they were sometimes caught by birds.

The boys, in their lively imagination, linked those sights with tales about the wonder of mysterious life in the depths, about fish with glowing lamps in their eyes, about fish armed with clubs, forks, saws and hammers. So very pleasant was it there on that immensity of water that they were reluctant to leave the deck. The setting sun would gild the waters and trail a glitter of light, while in the east the dark waves pushed away the daylight. Simultaneously, a cooler wind would rise and the firmament would shine with stars suspended above the sea. The children would still remain on deck, enchanted. It was the right moment for them to contemplate the evening sky, and, by asking questions about what they did not understand, increase their store of knowledge and of mythical explanations.

Most of the children had not yet been to school because of their deportation and other misfortunes. Their curiosity was thus uncommonly keen: they were seeing so many new sights and living through so many new experiences. They began to learn about the wonders of the stars, about dizzying distances measured in light years, about the magnitude of heavenly bodies beside which the earth is but a small speck of dust in an infinity of whirling worlds. Small children are almost always inquisitive and reverent, demanding answers while instinctively moving toward the first cause of such mysteries—the Creator.

The glittering heavens could hold the attention of such little listeners and keep them enraptured, as their teacher moved his finger along the map of the sky and named the constellations. Caught up in this vast world of stars, without turning away, the tots would call out their questions:

"Is it true that there is a big bear and a little bear up there?"

"Who does the little bear play with?"

"Is it Jesus Christ that puts the Southern Cross up when the bears go to the woods?"

"Do the white people also see the cross, or only the black ones?"

"Does Jesus Christ love Negroes more than He loves us?"

Later on, tucked into their beds for the night, they would still whisper among themselves about the fish, the stars, and the cross. They loved that form of learning—informal talks and conversations on topics connected with the happenings of the day. Even the adolescents would put aside their books and beg: "Please, Teacher, tell us. . . ."

A few days after sailing from Karachi, the navigation officer announced that the ship was nearing the equator. All the children, down to the very littlest one, trooped out to the deck, eager to see what it looked like. They could not say how they imagined it, but they all argued that it should somehow be marked and visible.

When they crossed the equator, the sailors arranged a fancy surprise for all passengers, from little ones to grown-ups, who were crossing for the first time—the ceremony of their marriage to the sea. Old Neptune, the emperor of the seas, appeared on deck with a covey of sea-nymphs. Dressed in a fishing net, he held a trident, each of its prongs tipped by an arrowhead symbolizing thunder. With his fish-eyes he looked from his throne at the children, his thick fingers combing the beard that hung down to his waist. (The part of Neptune must have been played by the most muscular sailor, because he looked like a sea-king; the hefty seamen playing the nymphs were somewhat less believable.) Neptune's lieutenants grabbed whoever was handy for the ceremony of the "sea baptism." They would put the victim down on the table, pour salty water in his mouth, sprinkle him with some kind of powder, check his heartbeat, and then, amidst his shrieks and struggles and a thunder of cheers from the onlookers, throw him into the ship's swimming pool. When the ceremony was completed, Neptune issued each participant a certificate of marriage to the sea. Sailors free to watch the fun, clinging to the ropes, masts, ladders, and turbines, doubled up with laughter.

The ocean was quiet throughout the journey, and the weather very sunny. At times the ship neared the shores of Africa, whose contours seemed distant and inaccessible behind an opalescent veil of mist. From those shores flew voracious seagulls calling to each other as they cruised above the passengers' heads. In the sea the porpoises milled tirelessly, every once in a while jumping high above the waves, twisting themselves into parabolas, then making nosedives into the depths. When a school of them moved alongside the ship, their dark green, partly emerged, slippery bodies, traveling at around forty miles an hour, looked like live torpedoes. The sailors, always on the look-out for a chance to kid the children, told them that the porpoises, because they are grateful for food thrown to them, will never harm sailors but rather save them from drowning and carry them on their backs to the shore. For that reason sailors never kill a porpoise and, if any-one dared do it, he would hear a quiet sob, like the cry of a baby.

The children were ready to believe everything that fired their imagination. Life was bringing them a host of impressions and contrasts. Not so long ago they had been terrified by the gloomy, chilly taigas of Siberia; then there was the hot wind of the desert, though their sore eyes had been soothed by the sight of boundless stretches of the same yellow sand that ran between their toes, burning, fine and soft. Now all around them murmured those emerald-green or brilliant blue waves of the ocean. The next surprise, they were assured by the supervisors, would be even more attractive. They were going to live in the Black Land, the land of virgin forests; they were going to wear hats made of cork and eat unknown fruits full of sweet pulp.

The boys trembled with a fearful joy at every word about danger, about the wilderness. How many opportunities to display their courage! In their minds they were already romping through jungles and African grasslands. Burning with excitement about such adventures, they saw themselves as the brave characters of the Henryk Sienkiewicz novel *In the Desert and in the Jungle*: the Polish boy, Stas Tarkowski, and the English girl, Nel Rawlinson, lost in the very jungle in which they themselves were going to be living. The young people were quite ready for the charms of Africa.

The adults, however, were skeptical. They did not anticipate anything positive from Africa, more than ten thousand miles from their homeland, an unknown and dangerous region of tropical diseases, wild animals, and a killing climate. That was enough to scare anyone away from the very continent that was offering them hospitality.

When the passengers assembled to disembark, the sailors all came out on deck to say a heartfelt farewell, primarily to the children they had romped with as if with their own children. High atop the mast flew the red and white flag they had unfurled for the occasion.

13

First Impressions of the Black Land

Most of the ships called at Mombasa, in Kenya. Its harbor was called Kilindini—a name with a pleasant, funny ring to the children's ears. They could not take their eyes off the blacks, whom they were seeing for the first time in their lives, and in such great numbers. Some of these Negroes carried heavy loads on their heads, some on their backs. They were mostly tall and strong, with pitch-black skin. The older passengers informed the children that these were Negroes from the Swahili tribe, members of the large ethnic group of the Bantu. Most of all the children liked the fact that the Negroes laughed broadly and frequently, that they clapped their hands in moments of joy as children themselves do, that they shouted out at work and at play, that they slapped and joshed each other in a friendly way just as children do. And they sang and hummed all the time, merrily, but on a strangely odd note.

The little newcomers did not want to miss even the most minute detail of the colorful impressions unfolding before their eyes. They looked around with great curiosity while riding through the harbor and the city; and during the railway journey, everyone wanted to be near the window for a better look. There were so many new things to see! For the time being they absorbed it all visually. Later on they were to learn more. Admiring the beautiful coconut palms, they did not even guess how useful such trees are as producers of oils for foods, soaps, and candles, and of fibers and thatch for building construction and furniture. They were delighted by the great variety of strange flowers with their rich colors, and the magnificent, lush greenery all around.

The train left the city and entered an expanse of yellowish grasses, where everything suddenly changed. Now they were passing settlements of houses shaped like giant bee hives. In the shade of the palms and the forest, the children saw here and there a well maintained mission station; in the pastures, herds of cattle, looked after by half-naked Negroes.

"Look! They have real spears! Just like the ones in the pictures!"

"And knives! Oh how wide!"

"That is for defense against wild animals. . . ."

"That knife there is called a 'pango' in their language. I read just recently. . . ."

And the black children along the way dropped their games and rushed closer to see a train full of white children. Panting, they stopped suddenly, amazed at seeing so many white faces at the windows. Subjecting themselves to mutual inspection, the little Negroes, curly hair close-cropped, stomachs bare and distended, smiled their bashful smiles. Then the waving of hands began—black hands and white hands.

The appearance of wild animals, enjoying full freedom here among the grasses of the great Kenya National Park and Game Preserves, particularly the large variety of gazelle and antelope, caused quite a commotion in the compartments. There were not enough windows to look out of. The roar of the train, the hiss of steam, and the clouds of smoke made the animals raise their heads. But they did not run away, and one could see the gazelles—their long necks, their moist, vibrating nostrils, their large black eyes, and the horns adorning their heads: some straight, short, conical, spread like a V; others like a long fork with parallel prongs, some bent slightly backward, others bent aggressively forward. The horns of the antelope were even more impressive, notched and twisted as they were into tight or loose spirals. The animals were grazing in herds on both sides of the railway track; in the distance one could see giraffes and a lonely ostrich. Sometimes, it is said, a rhinoceros attacks a locomotive, for which it pays, of course, with its life. To scare off such suicidal animals, the train is brightly lit at night.

As the train neared Nairobi, the capital of what was then British East Africa, the ground rose to five thousand feet above sea level. On this elevation there was wind and crisp air; the sun lost its power to burn, and the vegetation grew more lush, emanating the same freshness as in some milder climates of Europe. When the train came to a halt, a giant elephant tusk suspended in front of the railway station drew exclamations of awe from the little travelers. This stop-over in Nairobi provided time for a tasty meal especially prepared for them and a lively send-off by Nairobi's Negro orchestra, impressive in their tall headgear, silver epaulettes, and gold buttons, with gleaming black skin, playing their strangely stirring national anthem.

Only the children going to Uganda traveled through Nairobi; others, going to Tanganyika for instance, went from Mombasa toward Mt. Kilimanjaro; still others sailed on, south of the equator, to Rhodesia and the Union of South Africa. In Africa distances are measured in thousands of miles. During these long journeys the Black Continent revealed its wonderful exoticism and its astounding diversity.

Our children were greatly taken by the jungle and other moment-by-moment surprises. Their eyes widened at the sight of tropical orchards planted in neat geometric order. New to them were the mangos and papayas and the clusters of coconuts and bananas.

"How much fruit there is!" they would exclaim. "How tasty it must be! How it shines in the sun!"

Although unaware of it, the children were most often attracted by the jarring force of Africa's contrasts: "Just look at that Negro! Leaning on his spear and looking at an aeroplane!" "Those Negro women with tall jars on their heads and children on their backs! What are they doing here, near those beautiful new white houses?" Such contrasts were countless: there, the white man's lawns and gardens, tennis courts and golf courses; here, the Negroes' round, thatched-roofed, smoke-filled huts among thistles, cacti, and hawthorn. There, the great coffee and sugar cane plantations of the wealthy, magnificently maintained; here, the miserable little fields of the poor. Even the skin of the Negroes was not uniformly black. The children spotted many fairer-skinned Negroes in whose veins flowed Semitic blood. Noted one little fellow, "This one looks as if he's made of milk chocolate."

The most striking contrasts were climatic. When the children first caught sight of Mt. Kilimanjaro in all its majesty, covered with perennial snow, there was no end to their amazement at so much cold at the equator. The climate often changed unexpectedly within the same zone. One would be traveling through scorched, dry areas at one moment, then move through steamy ones the next, for the steppes radiated heat and the jungles oozed humidity from foliage and mosses. In the lowlands the sun scorched one mercilessly, and in the hills the almost Alpine air misted one's breath.

"How many wonders in this Africa!" observed the children.

"We will not have time to see it all because the war will soon be over, and we shall be going home." But, in fact, there was no home to go to, and the jungle's hospitality was to stretch, against all expectations, over seven long years.

14

Where the Jungle Reigned till Not So Long Ago

The newcomers were housed in camps scattered hundreds of miles from each other over the whole of British East Africa, in both Rhodesias, and in the Union of South Africa, an area much larger than Europe. Most of the camps were far from any town, frequently in the deep bush, some in very picturesque areas: Camp Masindi, hidden deep in the jungles of Uganda; Camp Koja spread on the banks of Lake Victoria, largest in Africa; Tengeru near Kilimanjaro; Camps Kidugala and Ifunda in the mountains and the lush vegetation of the kingdom of the lions. Kidugala, just on the border of the Nyassaland, because of its scenic landscape, was called the "Polish Rabka," a well known spa in Poland; Camp Abercorn, on the charming southern bank of Lake Tanganyika, won for itself the name "African Switzerland." But not all of the beautifully situated camps enjoyed good climate, and many of them had serious problems with malaria.

The reason for this dispersal of the camps from the equator to the Cape of Good Hope remains still a secret of the British government. The most suitable country would undoubtedly have been Kenya because of its mountain climate, akin to that of Europe. The Poles were not settled there possibly because it already held internment camps for several thousand Italian prisoners of war.

In the terminology of the British colonial administration, Polish centres were called "settlements" or "refugee camps," though neither term was accurate. They would have been more appropriately called simply "camps" since the Poles, having been deported against their will, were not refugees. We all used the British terms, however.

The twenty-two African Polish settlements had a total of 19,000 inhabitants, including some 3,500 men of advanced age, incapable of military service; over 6,000 women; approximately 8,000 school-age children, among them about 1,500 adolescent girls. In other words, children and young people made up about half the camps' population.

The camps varied in size, and could accommodate from 350 to 4,000 persons. Among the largest were Tengeru and Kidugala in Tanganyika; Koja and Masindi in Uganda; Lusaka in Southern Rhodesia—each housing a group of orphans. Two strictly scholastic centres were located in Kenya and the Union of South Africa.

Unlike those in India, the African settlements had a rather small percentage of educated people. Most of the families brought to Africa were those of small landholders from Eastern Poland. Vacancies in the professional groups needed for work in the schools and in the camp administration were filled by personnel from the so-called "Cypriot group," composed of around a thousand persons not connected with the rest of the people through experiences in Russia. These were the people who, immediately after the defeat in September, 1939, had left Poland, gone to Rumania, and from there, at the invitation of King George VI, continued on to Cyprus and eventually landed in Southern Rhodesia. Later on the percentage of professional "intelligentsia" was increased by a number of elderly officers withdrawn from military service.

Representatives of the Polish Government in London, of Social Welfare, of Religious Matters, and of Education were located in Nairobi.[1] Here also were the Polish Red Cross, together with representatives of Catholic Relief Service-National Catholic Welfare Conference and of the Spiritual Guardian of Polish Refugees, Bishop Gawlina. Two publications from Nairobi were very popu-

---

1. In 1945, when the Western powers withdrew recognition of the legal Polish Government in London and established diplomatic relations with the Communist regime that had been thrust upon Poland, care of the refugees in Africa and in other countries was transferred first to UNRRA (United Nations Relief and Rehabilitation Administration), later on to IRO (International Refugees Organization). The change had little practical influence upon conditions prevailing in the camps but wherever the care of these organizations was inadequate, the NCWC-CRS (National Catholic Welfare Conference, Catholic Relief Service), the charitable organization of the American Episcopate, came to the rescue and rendered uncommonly valuable service.

lar among the Poles, the weekly *Glos Polski (The Voice of Poland)* and the bi-weekly *Nasz Przyjaciel (Our Friend).*

In charge of the camps were retired British Army officers, with general management and administration in the hands of the Poles. Medical care was not adequate everywhere. In Camp Abercorn, for instance, there was no doctor for a full year. The duties of the camp physician were carried out initially by an optician; later on, by a retired naturalist who earned for himself the nickname "Fly-catcher" because he spent his free time netting butterflies.

For the twenty-two settlements there were only eighteen priests, an inadequate number in view of the fact that the schools, with their enrollment of eight thousand children, also urgently needed catechists.

Food supplies, on the other hand, were satisfactory everywhere. Only some settlements experienced a shortage of vegetables. The inhabitants ate in communal dining halls or brought their meals from the communal kitchen to their own quarters. In some camps families were given produce so that they could do their own cooking privately. Seldom did the camp provide electricity for each hut. Settlers were supplied with kerosene for lamps, but electricity was provided only for administrative offices and commanding officers' quarters, rather rarely for the church, priests' quarters, or the residences of camp officials.

The camps were originally conceived as primarily convalescence centres, where people could restore their health and strength after their grueling experiences. No one was forced to work. If, however, anyone wanted to, he found a job within the camp: on a farm, in the hospital, in stores or workshops, in educational programs, schools, administration, in the kitchen, or in security service. Leaving the camp to earn money was forbidden on principle. Some of the Poles believed that the local authorities feared they might want to install themselves in the British colonies for good. It was loudly discussed in the camps that the Polish consul, Wierusz-Kowalski, was told to leave his post the moment it was revealed he was trying to acquire official funds to buy land on which to settle Polish farmers. The Polish Government-in-Exile did not, however, favor the dispersal of Poles abroad, nor their search for work on their own, as it intended to direct them to Poland after the war. (Who could have foreseen the post-war situation?)

The first days of camp life in Africa were probably the most emotion-filled. Let us see what some young people, encouraged by their teachers to keep diaries, recorded about their globetrotting.

Krysia Maziarz, already mentioned in Part I, wrote about the Tengeru camp:

> For me Tengeru had its own specific, unique character. On a very large area, forested by magnificent specimens of African flora, on crystal-clear little Lake Duluti of volcanic origin and criss-crossed by numerous paths, Tengeru was a large, sprawling village. But it did not become a village all at once.
>
> I remember Tengeru from its first days of existence. I was ten years old then. The half-naked Negroes, with the chocolate brown skin, members of the Masai tribe, cut down the trees with giant axes. They also burned out the elephant grass for long days and nights. The fire was the only element which could successfully fight the jungle for living space for the people, and at the same time, get rid of the venomous reptiles. That is why at night we were almost always encircled by garlands of fires.
>
> The sight of the Masai capering at the fire, their wild cries, and their dull groans, were terrifying to us, evoking visions of cannibals dancing around a human sacrificial offering meant to be devoured. It seemed to us that any moment the whole wild gang would come to our little huts, pounce upon us, and eat us up.
>
> Traces of wilderness were to be seen everywhere. The trees, left standing among our huts to provide shade, had been stripped of their bark by wild animals whose hiding place this had been before our arrival. At night the jungle and the savanna resounded with mystical, strange music, interwoven at times with the noise of night birds, the roar of lions, and the crying howl of the hyenas. Monkeys at the edge of the jungle would make raucous noises as if arguing violently, and under cover of night would raid the corn fields. Sometimes we heard some big game moving through the jungle, breaking the dry branches underfoot. The plague of malaria-carrying mosquitoes was the one most feared. Lesser somewhat, but not much, was the plague of steppe fleas, the so-called jigras, parasites that lodged themselves in the softer parts of the human body, most often under the toenails. They would encyst themselves there, lay their eggs, and cause acute inflammation. The Negroes were of priceless comfort whenever this happened. With the greatest composure and with the skill of a surgeon, they could extricate the whole sackful of eggs with a needle.
>
> As time passed by, the camp assumed a familiar look. All around the whitewashed clay huts against the green carpet of grass were the merrily contrasting flower beds with roses and

> hollyhocks predominant. Often at the entrance to a hut sunflowers greeted one, bowing top heavy.
>
> During the favored evening strolls through the camp, the glowing moon silvered the grass roof of every hut and caused every trimmed hedge running along those curving paths to project ink-black shadows at one's feet. These strolls filled us with yearning and transported us to worn paths under the thatched roofs of Poland, and to fields sown with golden grain smelling of clover and buckwheat. Sometimes it seemed that the moon, through its magic power, had transformed this equatorial land into the Polish countryside. Each hut lit up with lamps would wink at us in a friendly way. In front of the huts, in the semi-darkness, the women would settle for their chats, just as if they were sitting on earthen benches running along the front of their peasant cottages back home. The night would softly bring us toned-down echoes of conversation, the distant sentimental songs of the scouts, and, from the direction of the orphanage at the center of the camp, the evening song prayer "Wszystkie nasze dzienne sprawy" ("All our daily affairs"). . . .

To extend Krysia's description, which reveals her love for the Black Land, we should point out that the Tengeru camp was just at the equator but in the southern hemisphere, some fifty miles from Kilimanjaro and near the foot of another mountain, Meru, 14,960 feet high. Above the crags of the Meru there was always a garland of clouds; chased and scattered by the wind, they seemed to be loosely attached to the peak, like a white flag. The slopes, covered by virgin jungle, were full of wild animals. Seven miles from the camp was the township of Arusha, with a railway station and a bus depot.

The camp itself was located 4,500 feet above sea level, its entrance guarded by an "askari" or policeman. The camp looked like a large park, for the most beautiful trees had been preserved to retain moisture and enhance the landscape. Hedges, flower beds, colonies of cacti and agave, as well as grass covered the ground so that only here and there, looking like a mushroom in a forest, the white wall of a round hut peeped through, its window a black patch and its roof covered with banana or palm leaves. Judging by the number of termite mounds and by occasional columns of wandering ants, although the animals had given ground, millions of insect armies still held that area.

In the center of the camp was the church. There were also recreation halls, schools, the theatre, the cooperative shop and the "Civic Centre." The theatre, built against the solid wall of the forest, offered films, live performances, and concerts, and accommodated gatherings of camp inhabitants. Beside the church on an area covered by grass, an evergreen hedge had been cultivated, evenly trimmed and shaped so as to spell POLAND 1942, the year the first refugees arrived at the camp.

Further on were the administration buildings, the stores, and the impressive residence of the British officer commanding the camp. On a hill just above coffee, papaya, and corn plantations, was the small brick hospital, conspicuous because of its whiteness and its large windows. On the northwesterly side was a prosperous farm operated by refugees. Close by, in tranquil seclusion, was the cemetery accommodating those who died as the result of disease, nostalgia for their homeland, or old age.

Toward the dark immensity of Mt. Meru was an entirely different view. The terrain, descending in terraces toward the valley, seemed to be running away, leaving behind the mountain streams and gorges, causing the vegetation gradually to lose its lush greenness, the trees to become rarer, dwarfed, graced with less foliage. It was the typical African savanna, changing its colors with each gust of wind, assuming ever new hues with each shadow of a cloud, and above all this, the visibly shimmering waves of hot air.

A great adornment of the Tengeru camp was beautiful Lake Duluti, its deep, clear water reflecting the densely forested hills surrounding it. Along the banks of this one-time crater, covering an area of twenty-five acres, grew white and yellow water lilies. Flocks of brightly colored birds nestled in nearby thickets.

Because of its location and considerable altitude, the Tengeru camp enjoyed a pleasant climate. At sunset, a bracing wind blew from the glaciers of Kilimanjaro, and it was hard to believe that malaria still had a hold on these camps.

* * *

To move from the camp in Tanganyika to those in Uganda is to go to an ever-green land whose name was unknown to the world only a hundred years ago, a veritable paradise and Africa's most beautiful jewel. The two life-giving elements, water and sun, are here in abundance, and food of all sorts abounds. Its pastures are lush; its groves bear a large variety of fruit. All around are impenetrable forests. Where the Nile loses its direction and spreads into a sea of muskegs and lakes, in an area one and a half times as large as Switzerland, grow the papyri eighteen feet tall. Hippopotami and crocodiles splash in whirlpools. Rhinos, elephants, and herds of other animals cross the expanses of tall grass. European birds spend their winters here to mingle with species that live here year round: storks, cranes, ducks, swallows, lapwings, longbills, hoopoes, pelicans, and landrails—millions of birds wading the marshes or flying over the muskeg dotted with floating islets of spongy water plants.

For six thousand years Uganda's papyrus forests guarded this paradise against Egyptians, Greeks, Romans, and other intruders. Whole generations of Uganda's Bantu inhabitants led peaceful lives without the need to fight foreign aggressors. Two harvests each year doubled their heavenly bliss.

It is mistaken to assume that before the white people arrived in Africa it had no culture, that its inhabitants were a disunited, disorganized mass. On the contrary, the Negroes in Africa have had, and still have, their states, their history, their politics, their social structure, their mores, and their native art.

Uganda boasts an unbroken dynasty of thirty-four generations of kings (kabaka). About 120 years ago one of them, wise and respected Mtesa, received, with honors, an Englishman, J. H. Speke, the putative discoverer of the springs of the Nile. The wise Mtesa was foreseeing the fate of his land when he reminded Speke: "The large rivers swallow the small rivers; since I saw you, I steadily think about it."

There are indications that the influence of the pharaohs of Egypt may have reached here. Ugandan kings, like the pharaohs, still play the harp, and their warriors, heroes distinguished in battle, blow into antelope horns during their ceremonies. On Ugandan pasturelands grazes a type of bull seen nowhere else except in Egyptian flat relief sculptures, with their tall, straight backs and their large horns shaped like the lyre.

A Ugandan legend preserves a rather unusual description of the beginnings of the world, and the first man's fall into sin. According to this legend, the first king of the earthly paradise was a good man who had been given immortality. He was called by the Creator on several occasions to the top of the mount near Kampala, the present commercial capital of Uganda. The Creator gave him advice and guidance about governing his people, acquiring wisdom, and enlarging his store of possessions. During one of those meetings, the Creator taught the man how to cultivate banana plantations, the most productive in the whole world, and on the side how to brew beer from bananas. The man liked the brew so much that he drank more than he should and shuffled home drunk. When he woke up sober the next day, he remembered that he had left the bananas on the mountain and went back to get them. But at the spot where he was used to meeting the Creator, he saw waiting for him the Angel of Death. The Creator's fearsome envoy killed the king, his wives, and his children. The Ugandans say that because of the king's stupidity, the Angel of Death is still ruling the world.

To this exotic Uganda came three thousand of our children, including about four hundred orphans. Janka Kusa remembered vividly her first day and night in Camp Masindi, on Lake Albert near the border of the Belgian Congo (now Zaire).

When they arrived in Uganda, she and the other children had been sent to a transit camp that was not quite completely ready for them. They were to live in hastily built primitive huts whose roofs rested on poles and whose walls were made of thick layers of elephant grass. Inside were tiered plank beds on a grassy earthen floor; outside were ferns of various kinds, twisting lianas, and a multitude of ivy nets. They sensed, before even seeing them, the dark walls of the jungle around the camp, and they began at once to appreciate the mystery of Africa.

At the moment this whole world was, for these arrivals from the North, a deep mystery, attractive but also taunting. The first night was fearsome, Janka reported. The earth was swathed in deep darkness. From the jungle came noises of wild birds and groans of buffalo. Each rustle they took to be a snake crawling near or some large animal stealthily approaching. Once a powerful drum beat resounded from far off, accompanied by wild shrieks. With dawn the fears receded, and in a short time, the children got used to the strange language of the jungle and the noisy games of the Africans.

Conditions in the transit camp were rather hard on the children; therefore, after a few days they were moved to the town of Masindi. Here the neat brick houses of the mission served as their quarters. Between these little houses grew "real grass," as Janka called it, instead of the unfamiliar six-foot-high grass of the first camp, and nearby were orange and lemon orchards. In the mission church, a great surprise which brought tears to everyone's eyes, she recalled, was the appearance of a Polish missionary, Father Piekarczyk of the congregation of the White Fathers.

After a few weeks the children were moved again, this time to the permanent and better equipped Camp Polonia, named by the refugees themselves. The huts were made of clay, the floors inlaid with red brick, the roofs woven of grass. Here also, Janka noted, were "flowers in the flower beds and water taps with running water." Within a short time, thanks to the efforts of Father Francis Winczowski, the priest in charge, the refugees built a brick church and offered it to God as a token of gratitude for their release from Russia.

In order to comprehend the beauty of Africa, and such exotic sights as her huge, natural animal gardens which every year attract hundreds of tourists and hunters from around the world, one has to travel over her vast distances. The young Polish exiles have the right to be proud of the knowledge they acquired of the Black Land on several safaris. Since these journeys were too tiring and even dangerous for the youngest children, they expressed much disappointment in their letters later on at not being allowed to go. They even doubted that there were wild animals in Africa since none ever came into the camp. A little boy from Kidugala wrote: "We dreamt about Africa, imagining her as fearsome, wild, and full of various wild animals. Now that we are in Africa and see her with our own eyes, we see that it is not so. We are as if in a desert: all around us are the mountains with trees rarely growing on them and with some bushes."

A young cubscout let his imagination compensate for the sights he missed, only sensing that beyond the camp was the rich life of animals, birds, and insects: "The beautiful stars are seen in the sky, belonging to various constellations. The moon sails among the stars and shines merrily for the benefit of the animals and the snakes. . . ."

Africa, as seen through the eyes of the very youngest inhabitant, full of fantasy and courage, does not seem to be as fearsome as grown-ups described her. Six-year-old Bazyli Zaranko, from the elementary school in Ifunda, Tanganyika, writes: "Here in our camp you go where you want to, and nobody except maybe the manager of the settlement can scare you."

In addition to the mixed settlements in which grown-ups lived with the young people, there were two educational centres exclusively for the young, Rongai in Kenya and Oudtshoorn in the Union of South Africa.

The Rongai centre was organized in January, 1945, for orphans collected from the various African camps. Situated 117 miles northwest of Nairobi and about fifteen miles from the equator on a plateau 7,000 feet above sea level, it had ideal health conditions, as well as educational facilities. Its accommodations were also very good: eleven boarding houses built of brick on the site of an abandoned airport, with roomy dining halls and dormitories. More little houses were built as classrooms.

There were four hundred children in Rongai, half boys and half girls, with a pronounced majority of smaller children and orphans. In the centre were a kindergarten, an elementary school, and a secondary school, with the humanities as the main curriculum. The eighty-seven teachers, administrators, and their assistants included twenty nuns, Sisters of the Holy Family of Nazareth, and one Felician sister. The nuns, who had accompanied the children since the Russian days, undertook to teach them and operate the boarding houses.

Rongai was truly a kingdom for children. Their memories of Rongai remain their most pleasant ones. And no wonder! The air was dry, the nights cool, at times even cold (an eight-year-old girl, Maciusia, complained in a letter to her mother: "I sleep under eight blankets. You have no idea, Mum, how tiring it is carrying such a weight all night"). There was no shortage of varied pleasures such as swims in the pool, games in the playgrounds, excursions into the mountains, and the nuns' splendid food, especially their magnificent desserts such as pineapple and whipped cream.

The land was free of malaria, and the little hospital was empty most of the time. The classrooms were adorned with pictures of animals and with animal horns, and the whole centre was maintained in exemplary order. Flowers grew everywhere. A popular saying was "In December or in May, flowers are lovely in Rongai."

But, alas, to the children's great disappointment, the Rongai centre lasted only two years. British authorities ordered the centre to be liquidated, without stating a reason. This was an unpleasant surprise, one of the many in the lives of the little wanderers, who had to add the word "liquidation" to their vocabulary.

They were sent to orphanages in Kondoa, Ifunda, and Tengeru in Tanganyika.

More than two thousand miles south of Rongai, almost at the tip of the Black Land where the two oceans meet, was another educational centre, the so-called "Home of the Polish Children," on the outskirts of the town of Oudtshoorn in Cape Province, which together with Natal, Oran, and Transvaal formed the Union of South Africa.

This was the refuge of 501 children saved from Russia by the invitation of the South African government. They had been transported from Persia to Africa on the steamboat "Dunera," which after one month's sailing docked at Port Elizabeth on the 9th of April, 1943. The group included boys called *junaks* and girls *mlodsze ochotniczki*, reserve army volunteers. They had originally been destined for Palestine, but the near total physical exhaustion of the children suggested that we not take the risk of transporting them across the Arabian desert.

The Union of South Africa assigned the children to former military barracks near Oudtshoorn, one-story brick buildings with sheet-metal roofs. In the ceilingless barracks they found the beds made with blankets, even night-tables. Compared with the misery in Russia, it all seemed luxurious. Still, all military grounds are depressing, with a certain air of emptiness. But soon lawns appeared, and flower beds, walks lined with shrubs, and a vegetable garden; luxuriant castor oil plants sheltered the living quarters from the scorching sun. The camp, under the management of the priest, Canon Francis Kubienski, changed beyond recognition.

While camp life was being organized in Africa, transports were still arriving from Persia bringing youngsters who had been detained in hospitals. As each new transport neared Africa, lists of the arrivals were published in each camp so that relatives could claim members of their families. Zdzislaw Kulesza, one of the first to arrive at the centre, described how he felt as the lists were read: "We assembled in the dining hall. With great excitement we listened to the priest who was reading the list of the found brothers and sisters to whom fate was kind. The names were pronounced slowly, one after another. Although we usually made so much noise that not even the explosion of a bomb could have been heard, at this time there was such silence that one could have heard the humming of the tiniest insect. Each one of us hoped to hear his own family name now. However, good fortune smiled on only a very few. Their faces radiated happiness, but those disappointed in their hopes quietly sobbed in the corners. After the reading we had our dinner, sprinkled with tears of sorrow or of joy. However, there was more of sorrow and bitterness."

Sometimes children considered lost or dead were found accidentally, as were the Studzinskis. Zosia and Jozia, aged eight and nine, were playing in the orphanage yard in Tengeru when suddenly they were asked by their friends going by, "Zosia! Jozia! Did you ever have a little brother?" "Yes, but why do you ask?" "We ask because the last transport from Karachi in India brought a little boy to the boys' section and his family name is the same as yours." "Maybe he is our little brother. We don't know. Show him to us." "Was your brother big?" asked their classmates. "By now, he should be about the same size we are. He and Zosia are twins."

The sisters went to the boys' quarters with their curious friends. Suddenly the girls stopped, fearing that they might be laughed at if the boy was not their brother. The boy brought in was looking around in fear and distrust, his ears burning. He shifted from one foot to the other, twisted his fingers and looked at the toes of his dirty shoes. Zosia sized the boy up, and in the tone of an investigator asked, "Is your name Studzinski?" "Yes," said the boy quietly in a half-shy, half-exasperated voice, "so they say."

A further investigation established the boy's identity, and from then on Stas was taken care of by his sisters. He was overjoyed at not being all alone in this world, and the girls were proud of having a brother.

The young people of the Oudtshoorn settlement wanted to get to know the country that had offered them its hospitality. The very location of the camp was delightful. On one side stretched the river Grollclaar, a tributary of the Olifantsriver, in which the children could bathe. On the plateaus sloping towards the river on both sides was the town of Outdtshoorn, some one thousand feet above sea level. Half of the inhabitants were white, the other half black. The town was the center of the agricultural area of the Cape Land, the most thickly populated of all the provinces of South Africa. The two river valleys comprised 70,000 hectares of very fertile soil, perfectly irrigated, which produced abundant crops of tobacco, clover, corn, and vegetables. In the orchards grew fruits of almost the whole world, shipped, fresh or dried, in large quantities to other countries. Beside the orchards stretched vineyards and gardens whose magnolias and mimosa first attracted the eye. Above all, the town of Oudtshoorn had become famous as the centre for ostrich breeding, an immensely profitable venture which the townspeople had been engaged in for eighty years. Because ostriches are also still found there in large numbers in the wilderness, the Cape Land is considered the home of this gigantic bird.

The large dell in which the Polish educational centre was situated was encircled by a chain of mountains reaching to over 6,000 feet. There our youngsters visited the famous stalactite caves of Cango, with their elfin castles of stalactites and stalagmites. On the walls near the entrance were drawings of hunting and war scenes, very likely made by the original inhabitants of the land, the Bushmen, who were succeeded by the Hotentots, Kaffirs from the Bantu tribe, and finally the Dutch Boers and the British.

In the same chain of mountains the children visited another very charming spot called Rust-en-Vrede, the area of waterfalls that every year attracts thousands of tourists. The road to these natural wonders leads through mountains covered with dwarfed trees, through dells and ravines filled with tufts of agave and cacti above whose blossoms fly beautiful tiny hummingbirds.

Contact between our Polish children and South African young people was restricted to a few sporadic meetings at scout gatherings, theatrical productions, or exhibitions of handicrafts. Because many of the Dutch farmers had become miserly, a visit to any of their estates was a rarity. Contact with blacks working at domestic chores in the camp was more likely. Exploited by white men, given to alcoholism, most of them lived on the verge of utter poverty. The refugee children out of sympathy gave them whatever clothing they themselves did not need and thereby won their admiration and attachment.

The longer the children remained in the centre, the quieter their life became. At times it was hard to believe that a cruel war was raging in this world, that, having commenced in Poland, it was still turning cities into ruins, every day increasing the number of orphans to suffer yet more misery.

15

Let's Learn!

The large concentration of school-age children in the African Polish camps required a proportionately large team of professional teachers and educators, male and female. But they were not available: younger male teachers were at the front, and there were few qualified females.

In these circumstances people without qualifications had to be accepted. Some had a higher education but no teaching experience; and, although they were full of good will, their newness to the task hindered the work of education to a large extent. The children had already suffered a delay in learning; and their normal process of development had been so interrupted that they ran loose, especially the older ones, and resisted all the norms and rigors of school discipline. They had somehow to be given surrogate parents, but that was not easy, and our teachers worked very hard.

One of the younger, more energetic teachers in Africa wrote, after a few years of the exhausting pace of her classroom:

> I simply fall asleep while standing on my feet, and quite often in the course of a day I do not know whether I am coming or going. I lose my equilibrium, not only spiritual but physical as well. The world whirls before my eyes. For the last few years my work has gone on incessantly, from early morning till eleven at night.

Probably not all the teachers worked that hard in the African climate. Some did not have enough stamina; others may have learned how to save themselves; still others may have managed by easier means. Much depended on local conditions. But one thing is certain: if the Polish schools in Africa did a satisfactory job (and in the opinion of many they did, despite all obstacles, difficulties, and organizational shortages), they did so thanks to the people who were so totally devoted to the children and so self-denying as to be heedless of the inordinate drain of their time, strength, and energy.

In all, fifty-seven schools were organized: twenty-one elementary, seven secondary, with a general education program, thirteen trade schools, and several specializing in arts programs. In Tengeru, where two thousand children of school age were being taken care of, were three elementary schools, a secondary school with a general education program, and special schools for teaching fashion, commercial arts, agriculture, mechanics, and music. Methods courses were offered periodically for medical orderlies and for teachers. For girls of post-school ages there were courses in sewing, embroidery, basket-weaving, and domestic science. Graduating students could at times fill the gaps in the teaching ranks.

Teaching was done in Polish, with English as a second language. At the end of the war, when it became apparent that Poland was not going to be a free country and Poles were planning to relocate in various parts of the world, Spanish and French were added.

Elementary schools were the most numerous because the younger children were in the majority. Those who had completed their elementary education were switched to a secondary school. Some of the older boys did not relish the idea of going to secondary schools, particularly those offering only a general education, and preferred the briefer training in a trade so that they could quickly earn good wages and become independent. But there were few trade schools, and even they were deficient in many ways. Whether they liked it or not, then, the older boys had to follow a program of general education. Since most of them had been born in villages, the percentage of such students in these schools was very high, a rarity in the years before the war.

The Polish school system in Africa was headed by a delegate from the Ministry of Religious Affairs and Public Education, of the Polish Government-in-Exile in London, whose office was in Nairobi. The accommodation of the schools was looked after by the local colonial authorities. Many school buildings left much to be desired. Of course, one could not expect solid structures in temporary camps located in the bush, but the huts so hastily assembled in native style were less adequate than they should have been even in the circumstances. In Tengeru, Tanganyika, for instance, teaching was conducted in large barracks which looked more like stables than schools: mud huts covered with leaves and grass. Under the roof along the walls was a space three to four feet wide for ventilation. Conditions were not much better in Uganda, where the barracks did not offer sufficient shelter from rain and classes had to be stopped occasionally during a tropical storm. Since teaching was also frequently interrupted because of malaria, it was difficult to provide a proper course of learning.

Nor did the casual construction of the buildings adequately separate the students from the ever-fascinating surroundings outside, and they had trouble concentrating during classes. It has often been said that the schools in Africa are open to God's world. However ideal this sounds, the fact is that God's world in Africa was so irresistibly enticing that it was difficult to fend off the temptation to run away from school into the bush or the jungle, up a tree, or down the path to the lake.

The teaching program was sorely hampered also by the shortage of textbooks for students as well as teachers, though this shortage gradually became less serious. School authorities eventually managed to provide some reference books, modest libraries, and a few good teaching aids.

God's African world, though a constant distraction, did itself become an invaluable teaching aid. Thanks to the natural science exhibits and frequent sight-seeing excursions, the youngsters began to seek out the best specimens of plants and insects for their "own school." At Masindi, Uganda, they created a complete botanical garden. Some schools had collections of rare butterflies, others impressive herbariums. One natural science teacher, a lady, developed in her hut a veritable museum of African curios. Each school wanted to have something to boast about, and they all engaged in a lively, happy competition. The teachers maintained this strong motivation by their own example, enriching their natural science courses with expeditions to less accessible spots such as Mt. Kilimanjaro. The students began to make progress in their education, and the future seemed much brighter.

In the meantime, however, deep, complex disturbances in the children, often irreversible because of their displacement, had to be treated. With many children, the cordial family atmosphere of each establishment helped. But with others, such deep traumas were almost impossible to eradicate. Some patients were treated by the visiting supervisor of psychological hygiene, the psychiatrist and psychologist Doctor W. Szyrynski, who was acting representative of the Ministry of Religious Affairs and Public Education in Nairobi. He had in his care from June, 1945, to February, 1946, almost all the camps in Africa, including children, educational staff, and parents.

For the teachers lectures and seminars were arranged in general psychology, educational psychology, psychological hygiene, and psychological testing. Available to the staff were up-to-date materials on teaching methods and the science of education provided by the monthly publication *Sprawy Pedagogiczne (Problems of Education)*, printed in the Middle East. Psychological counselling was introduced to help educators guide problem children. Parents learned more about the psychological sciences and could better understand their youngsters who, because of the extraordinary conditions of their lives and their own increasing sophistication, were inclined to become domineering.

On many students, whose fancy was caught by the scientific organization of work, educational guidance had a beneficial influence. They began to notice a more systematic approach to each lesson, better planning, and more enthusiasm. Also by promoting and extending the scouting program, Dr. Szyrynski engendered in many boys fresh hopes for real accomplishment.

To tackle head-on the problem of delayed schooling, the more gifted students, thereafter known as "jumpers," were given the chance to skip a grade. Aspiring youngsters gathered often in the teachers' huts to work late into the night preparing themselves for such advancement. Healthy students with solid potential were placed in an experimental accelerated program, only somewhat abbreviated, where they completed a year's work in six months. This experiment, devised by Dr. Szyrynski, produced good results. Senior scouts also worked as aides to the younger teachers.

All of these students who, under such difficult conditions, showed so much perseverance, enthusiasm, and self-sacrifice, received well-deserved recognition from their elders and began to be respected and imitated by their peers.

16

Predominant Traits

The nightmare of banishment from their homes, deportation to the Soviet wilderness, and all the other injustices beyond their comprehension was reflected in the children's behavioral patterns throughout their stay in Africa.

The teachers observed with compassion that they often returned to this gloomy, stormy past while reminiscing, as if they could not get away from it. From the very beginning their nostalgia for home, for mother, father, sister, or brother, dead or detained in Russia, haunted them all. True, the force of new impressions and the calming influence of the camps' security and peace managed to screen out the old sorrows from time to time. Most children took keenly to learning, sports, games, entertainment and mischief; they laughed charmingly, merrily, as only children can. Yet deep in their souls they were still aware of the harm they had suffered.

Sometimes it manifested itself unexpectedly. Most often the children revealed it unconsciously in their school essays, even those on topics far removed from their past. In an essay entitled "How I See Myself in the Immediate Future," they would describe at length the wrong done to them by the Bolsheviks and treat their vision of the future in a few vague sentences, indicating that everything was in the hands of God or that the future was very uncertain.

Some of them were aware of the changes in themselves, in their mode of life, and in their character, thanks to improved conditions and educational guidance. Gradually eradicated were such negative traits as explosiveness, lack of self-control, insubordination, and vindictiveness; they began to show more composure and tenderness. But for the Soviets they had always the same comtemptuous epithet: "barbarians."

They were different from children their own age living under normal conditions. After what they had gone through, they were desperately afraid of war and developed the habit of praying for peace. They were always guarded, not ready to trust. However, the educators did not lose hope, for they believed that time would heal these children. Significantly, the children in general wanted to make up for their losses in learning and upbringing and, most importantly, had idealistic attitudes toward life and a high degree of morality, in spite of all their unpleasant experiences. The adversity they still remembered helped many of them attain a spiritual immunity to evils yet to come. They learned to fight adversity and developed a deep compassion for the handicapped and suffering. Some of them dreamed about achieving positions which would enable them to comfort those who suffer physically and morally. They spoke often about their desire to be useful to their country. Although they were possibly only repeating the words of their elders, not being able to imagine their own usefulness, they discussed it among themselves seriously, acknowledging meanwhile that they should bend all their efforts to learning. They knew that in war-devastated Poland it would not be as easy to learn as it was now in Africa.

Twelve-year-old boys were expressing views of life on a level of experience seldom achieved at that age. They arrived readily at universal truths: that life is not play; that from the point of view of eternity, it is very short and insignificant; that it has many more trials, troubles, and sorrows than moments of happiness and peace. One little girl observed in a school assignment that although the worries of grown-ups are greater than those of children, to children their own worries are no less important and no less painful.

Generally speaking, however, the children were not given to undue worry. They accepted easily whatever spoke of the triumph of good over evil. They listened eagerly to the tales of their elders touching on this subject, because they had already had enough of evil. They themselves, of course, were not always well-behaved or amenable to correction, but many were well-disciplined, sensitive, and full of humor and courage. The women teachers exercised a great influence on the formation of such a character; though some were not certified teachers, they all were able to create a loving, tender, motherly relationship with most of their pupils. If, years later, these young people could not forget Africa but remained nostalgic for her in far-away countries, they longed above all for that atmosphere of "family" where grown-ups encouraged laughter, humor, and freedom.

Because the children's observations were full of charming,

naive humor, the teachers and even the publication *Nasz Przyjaciel (Our Friend)* were forever quoting them. For example:

> The feast of Christ the King is approaching. It is evening. A tropical storm is raging outside. The mother, a teacher, sits correcting school assignments while her ten-year-old daughter meditates and prepares herself for confession. Suddenly the girl asks, "What kind of sins do grown-ups commit?" The mother, a bit dumbfounded, says that she does not understand the question. The girl responds with a conundrum: "Grown-ups do not have dads and moms. They do not have to obey them, so they do not sin by disobedience. When they lie, they say they are 'only kidding'; when they say nasty things about other people, they call it 'a conversation'; and when they use foul language, or swear, they are 'nervous.' "

One of the teachers of Grade Five found in a set of papers the following account of the ceremonial visit of Bishop Byrne to Tengeru: "While the bishop was administering the sacrament of confirmation the choir sang beautifully and the orchestra was acknowledging." Another child wrote: "When the bishop came to Tengeru, our parish priest, while greeting him, gave him a sermon, then the bishop in turn gave our priest the sermon, then the bishop gave the sermon to everybody in English, and our priest translated it into Polish." For the finale of one celebration during this visit, the orphanage presented a play called "Saint John's Night." One girl reported: "Our parish priest encouraged the people, during his sermon, to come and see the evening performance, and the bishop, although very tired, came also, and he liked it very much." A little altar boy wrote touchingly: "In the afternoon we invited the bishop for tea in the recreation hall. There were lots of people; however, I was not invited as being too small. Had to be satisfied with imagining the taste of the goodies."

17

Restrictions and Inadequacies in Trade Training

In South Africa, efforts to found enough trade schools and maintain them properly were thwarted by two problems: the lack of qualified instructors with up-to-date knowledge and the inability to procure technical equipment. The choice instructors were at the battle front, and in Africa there was no hope of getting equipment even if there had been funds for it.

These problems did make many of our most competent boys bitter, disenchanted, as they tried to reconcile themselves to the situation and justify it. They overexerted themselves, operating whatever primitive, defective, obsolete equipment they could find, even if only to make such simple objects as sine bars, knives, old-fashioned clothes irons, keys, and rulers. They knew they were capable of more sophisticated work. It is not surprising that boys with such mechanical aptitude felt doubly awkward in the general education program. Already delayed in their schooling by the war and deportation, here they were serving time in grades far below their age level, with no interest whatever in the subject matter. To aggravate the situation, some teachers failed to understand their frustration. As a result some of the boys developed a pronounced dislike for theoretical science, and some even subscribed to the nonsensical and dangerous notion that they were being denied admission to trade school only because their presence in the general program assured their teachers of employment. They became arrogant, and felt that they were doing their teachers a favor.

School authorities were in a quandary. To dismiss these difficult students seemed the simplest solution, but what to do with them? To expel them would be to give in to hooliganism in an isolated camp; to send them to distant towns at such an early age, without family ties or guidance, would be perilous for them. With properly organized trade schools, all these problems would have been avoided; and the selection of young people, especially boys, at the start of school, would have brought excellent results because these youngsters regularly demonstrated a capacity for absorbing knowledge. The Polish people are talented, quick, inventive; Polish tradesmen and qualified laborers have always been serious competitors in the world's labor market. They can work intently; they know their jobs, and they quickly grasp the subtleties of whatever they are doing.

An incident which occurred in Tengeru demonstrates how gifted our boys were, and how seldom their energies and talents were used properly. One normal school day, a boy was brought by a friend of his to the camp's hospital with a bullet wound in his chest, the bullet lodged near his heart. The friend reported at first that the two of them had ridden their bicycles into the jungle a few miles from the camp just for an excursion. Suddenly, he said, they heard a shot as if from the road, and his friend was hit. Later on, under cross-examination, he changed his story, admitting that they had staged a duel with guns, as in American cowboy films they had seen. In their enforced isolation our young people had learned of the civilized world primarily through films and often modeled themselves on what they saw there: a life mostly stormy, adventuresome, filled with glory and easy living.

Later in the investigation it was revealed that the boys' firearms were home-made; several boys had been making handguns, knives, and primitive rifles (what more suitable during a war?), using primitive tools stolen from the industrial school, sometimes even fashioned stealthily at the school itself, with look-outs to keep the instructor from suspecting anything. The British experts were full of admiration for their excellent craftsmanship. The revolvers did not misfire; their barrels were well made and their ivory handles were decorated with scenes of animal life, such as a lion stalking its prey, every muscle finely carved, or with Polish eagles. The very thought that these young boys could have started manufacturing weapons on a large scale and marketing them at a low price was enough to make one shudder.

Because of the handgun affair, the commanding officer of the camp closed the school for a month and reopened it only after he was certain that the school would be supervised by an experienced educator who could maintain a stricter discipline.

It was obvious that our young people wanted to learn more. Some of them sneaked out of the camps and worked for Italian tradesmen, without pay, to get acquainted with engines and learn how to operate precision military machines and lathes. Some of them even learned Italian. After one or two years of general education, the boys left school. Some "touched" the technical school for six months or a year and, when this was not enough, went to work in trade shops in Arusha, Dar-es-Salaam, Nairobi, Kampala, and other towns. Within a short time they became skilled tradesmen.

The problem of technical training was best solved in the School Centre in Oudtshoorn, Union of South Africa, thanks to the government itself, which made it possible for Polish youngsters to attend English trade schools with modern equipment and well qualified instructors after completing a preliminary course at the Centre's technical school. They went to one of twelve schools, those mostly in Capetown, Johannesburg, Port Elizabeth, and Pietermaritzburg, where one group, the "mechanics" from Tengeru, even found good jobs. Some of the girls were able to study at the School of Commerce in Johannesburg.

Meanwhile, though some boys continued to express frustration, the majority accepted the conditions as they existed, and completed their education without protest in whatever schools they were assigned to. Yet a surplus of secondary-school graduates did not augur well for their lives in the future. This became particularly obvious when, at the end of the war, Poland's freedom was not restored and the period of "sitting in the jungle" threatened to stretch into years and years. Universities were distant and unattainable, and the enforced idleness of the graduates undermined not only their own morale but that of the younger ones still in school. "What do we get from learning?" they asked. "What do we have to learn for? After we finish school, we will be in the same condition, eating the bread given to us and wallowing in sloth." Such apathy and defeatism crept in here and there. Fortunately for the atmosphere in the camp, however, these malcontents were not numerous. And a year after the war ended came prospects of emigration to various other countries for a long, possibly even permanent, stay.

These problems with the camps' schooling should not, God forbid, lead to the conclusion that the whole educational system had failed. This would be unfair to the genuine accomplishments of both teachers and students. The students spent five or six hours a day at school, including Saturdays. They did homework assignments, attended special meetings, and managed to take care of regular chores. Disregarding their bleak prospects for the future, they worked hard and remained ambitious. Their teachers often observed admiringly that the work load of these children was far greater than that of the average white colonial settler, whose work days in this climate usually were limited to two hours in the morning and two in the afternoon. If one considers the hot, humid climate, the tropical diseases, the after-effects of diseases suffered in Russia, and the lack of vitamins which caused a deterioration of memory or even mental deficiency in some children, then it has to be admitted that the system worked remarkably well. Most children made excellent progress against these heavy odds and completed their schooling with laudable results.

Many of them, after leaving Africa proved their mental maturity in many occupations in workshops, in offices, in the teaching profession, and in commerce. Many received university educations in other countries, often with distinction. But their greatest attainment, which enhanced their adult lives wherever they happened to land, was the good character they managed to shape despite so many adversities.

18

The Influence of the Environment

Time was passing. In this tropical climate the youngsters developed rapidly. Suddenly most of the boys who had arrived as frail, emaciated ten-to-twelve-year-olds were strapping, baritone-voiced young men. And as the number of teenagers increased, so did our problems.

It is an established fact of life that the problems of adolescents disturb the peace of the older generation. However, in well organized, stable societies with lifestyles firmly established, most of the problems of the youth are resolved as they surface by the social environment which shapes young adults and helps create standards for them.

But what standards could evolve from the unstable environment of refugee camps? Formed by the circumstances of war, fortuitous and impermanent, they could only perpetuate instability. Of necessity these were unbalanced environments, without the normal texture of interrelationships, without the range of cohesiveness of professions, occupations, and businesses found in structured societies. In these camps were only an administrative staff, an educational program, medical auxiliary services, domestic crafts, and a few trades. The young people had no attractive examples of cultured professional men or well adjusted tradesmen, no functional social framework, therefore no clearly designated social obligations. Any adolescent concept of society based on this temporary camp model was bound to be distorted.

The situation was made worse by the fact that every home was fatherless. Women were in the majority; if there were any men at all, most of them were sick or very old. Generally speaking, the noble village housewives, although at times too lenient with their children in order to "compensate" for what they had suffered in Russia, still taught them the concept of God and implanted in them good ethical principles; but frequently, by the time the children had finished secondary school, their mothers had no further influence on them.

There was still another problem. Refugees were not allowed to look for work outside the camp; since food and keep were ensured, no one was to worry about his livelihood. As a result, though many women had more than enough to do caring for their own children, the majority were idle. The teenagers saw what prolonged inactivity could do to the mentality of mature women who had been used to hard work on their own homesteads in Poland: the listlessness of those with no materials for creative work, the apparent indolence of those with nothing to do.

This state of affairs was bound to demoralize them, if they could not understand that the causes were to be found in the anomalies of camp life. They made harsh judgments, which evoked unpleasant clashes with their mothers, whose authority was already deeply undermined. A father's authority might have remained firm, but in such abnormal conditions, mothers could do little with their adolescents.

The orphanages were in the same predicament. The women educators were sometimes unable to manage adolescent boys, and male teachers with a firm moral authority were just not available.

In boys' sports programs the lack of supervision by men was sorely felt. The playgrounds were busy and noisy, but physical education was conducted indolently and chaotically, without regard to its basic physical and moral objectives.

When one considers the abysmal neglect of our children's upbringing during the long years when most men—fathers, leaders, guardians, educators—were at the front, their fighting and dying seems to have been in vain. As Dr. Szyrynski, the Inspector, was leaving the Army in the Middle East to go to Africa, some of the older soldiers came to him with letters to their wives in their hands. They were very worried and asked him to speak to their wives. Their requests were almost identical: "What is the sense in writing to us about their clothes, the corn, the monkeys, the Masai or the huts? We know they are better off now than before. Let them tell us how the children do at school, how they grow, and how they behave. If they cannot bring the children up by themselves, let them ask wise people for help. Surely there are such people. They will help. Woe to anyone who depraves our children. We don't know what we would do. . . . So let our wives think about this, and let them write about it!"

How much greater the fathers' worry would have been had they known how badly their sons in African camps needed them. If they had known, for instance, what dangers beset those sons from a group of criminals who had landed in the camp after being dismissed from the Army—psychopaths, hot-heads, moral degenerates. Possibly the military authorities decided to send this asocial element to the jungle in the hope that their isolation from the world would render them harmless. To compound the evil, a few of them were entrusted with camp functions, as educators in the boarding house, or as security guards. Because they were clever enough to hide their past, wore uniforms, and boasted about their heroic deeds at the front, they were at first considered models of manhood and only after precious time had passed were recognized in the camps for what they really were. But by that time they had led several boys toward drunkenness, thievery, and vulgarity. One boy from Abercorn described in a letter the kind of problem that sometimes developed:

> One evening I was escorting my friends home, together with Frank. Behind us moved some other boys, all the while shining their flashlights on us from all sides. On the way back Frank and I were alone. Suddenly somebody fired a shot in our direction.

> The bullet hit a tree a few feet away. Frank was carrying a revolver and wanted to fire it in the direction of the shot, but I restrained him. All around we heard mysterious whistles and shouts, and then there was a hail of rocks. This continued every evening, but we did not bother about it.
>
> One day, however, as we were coming home from the cinema, we were stopped by a gang of camp boys with the policeman at the head, a man discharged from the army. We were trying to go around them when one of the goons addressed Frank, "I've heard you want to fight me." This was our greatest enemy. Frank replied that he did not want to start any trouble on the road, and we went on toward the camp. We had moved barely a few steps when the troublemaker hit Frank on the head from behind. Frank turned around and hit him back. Then the whole gang converged on us to beat us up. Frank instantly pulled out his revolver and threatened to shoot if the attacker moved another step.
>
> The gang drew back and Frank put his revolver back in his pocket. After a while we headed toward the camp. Just then the policeman sneaked up behind us and jumped Frank, throwing him to the ground. The other guys came to their leader's aid.

Frank emerged from this encounter with an injured jaw and his revolver stolen by the gang. The policeman abused both boys in foul Russian language. The whole episode was like a fragment from an American gangster film. And this was the sort of adult male who often served as a model to teen-aged boys in the camps.

It was not only such Polish outcasts that endangered our somewhat mixed-up boys. Fraternizing recklessly as they did with native youngsters, allegedly to learn the local dialects, they were taught native swear words as a joke. And this relatively harmless association led to more serious involvement in "contacts" and commercial deals in the marketplace.

Fortunately, not all young people are equally susceptible to undesirable influences and bad examples. Many boys in the camp managed to resist both and not only emerged untainted themselves but also extricated some of their weaker friends.

In spite of this dark side of camp life, the percentage of perverted or debauched youth was relatively small. One can conclude, then, that the total effect of education in the camps was, despite all the fears, positive, a tribute to conscientious teachers, devoted mothers, scouting programs and religious organizations, and the great majority of worthy youngsters who responded to these efforts themselves and helped save their weaker friends.

19

The Orphanage

Orphans and half-orphans were regrettably numerous in the Polish camps of Africa. The largest centre was located near Arusha, in Tanganyika, in the middle of the sprawling settlement of Tengeru. Besides being assured of their education in the elementary and secondary schools of this settlement, the orphans were free to use its recreation halls, libraries, and other cultural and educational facilities. Frequent contacts with the camp community enlarged their frame of life and diversified, in more or less desirable ways, their orphanhood.

The Polish camp, a sort of rear guard in its homeliness, fenced the orphanage off from the strange, half-wild environment. Its sociability brought joy to the children because they understood it: camp people spoke the same language they did; everyone prayed the same way in church as at home. Their strong common bond was their identical past, the same hard experiences. Some of the women in the camp appeared to the orphans very much like their mothers, lost in Russia. Thus the whole camp, in its kindliness and cordiality, with its advantages and its faults, was close to the children's hearts. Conversely, the orphanage was the darling of the whole camp society, as its members proved irrefutably at a moment most critical for the orphans.

The orphanage was divided by sex, the two sections separated by the workshops of the mechanical school and the barracks for grown-ups. It consisted of more barracks whose walls were of mud bricks "fired" by the sun for a month to an extraordinary hardness. The roof of palm leaves and elephant grass, its wide eaves protecting the interior from sun and rain, rested on poles rising from the walls. The space between the walls and the roof provided ventilation, but also gave access to insects and reptiles. The windows too were open, but fitted with shutters to guard against dust and wind. The floor was of hard earth.

The beds were like a scout's plank bed. On a wooden frame with plaitwork made of grass was a mattress also stuffed with grass, much more cool and comfortable than spring mattresses or rubber ones; there was no other furniture. Behind the partitions were rooms for guardians. Each barrack was crowded with around twenty beds, and the least disorder was noticeable. The guardians maintained impeccable cleanliness and order here because any laxity would threaten the barracks with an infestation of vermin. Because the passages between the beds were narrow, all the children's riches were locked in frail metal suitcases, pushed under the beds or placed near them to become makeshift night tables, with useful knick-knacks and often a figurine or picture of the Virgin Mary. Above the beds hung mosquito nets, rolled up in daytime, loose at night. The children had to hang their clothes on wooden pegs, always a certain distance from the wall because of termites.

The older boys and girls lived in little round huts that lodged four persons. These were cozy and comfortable, warm during the rainy season, cool during the torrid summer thanks to the insulation of thick layers of banana palm leaves and the roundness of the walls that could diffract the sun's rays.

Within the confines of the establishment were the kitchens, and near by, greedily waiting, the marabous, the ugliest relatives of the stork and the garbage collectors of Africa. Our repugnance to these birds was caused mainly by the large craw protruding obscenely from their bare necks, but also by their bald heads. Were it not for their powerful beaks, they could be mistaken for vultures. Whenever the cooks appeared at the door to throw out garbage, the whole flock would surge madly forward, some fighting for scraps of refuse while still in flight, others scuffling on the ground. With their metallic dark-green plumage, they became a gleaming mass of squawks and squabbles.

About a city block from the kitchen were the laundry facilities, baths, dining halls, and storage buildings. In the evenings the orphans gathered in the two recreation halls where there were a piano, table tennis, a record player with a good supply of records, games of chess and checkers, a library, and a corner for reading. The youngest children had their own corner too—the kingdom of dolls, clowns, teddy bears, toy soldiers, balls of all sizes, and rubber wheels.

Behind the orphanage buildings was a large playground with a volleyball court, another for basketball, the soccer pitch for the rounders, and a croquet court; for the tiny ones, scooters, swings on poles, slides, and pendulum swings. Every year the management of the orphanage staged carnivals in the playground with various attractions for the children of the whole camp, sometimes including gymnastic displays.

However modest, the quarters and furnishings were dear to the children's hearts, for most of them spent their childhood here, some their whole adolescence. In their reminiscences they recall this as the "bucolic-angelic period" of their lives.

The soul of the whole children's kingdom was Mrs. Eugenia Grosicki, a knowledgeable person, self-controlled, resolute, and loving. One of her greatest accomplishments was the creation of a family atmosphere, and if the harm a child had experienced had left an indelible stigma on his soul, she sought at least to eradicate his discouragement and false shame. She often explained to her charges that they came from good, God-fearing families, honestly working for their daily bread. If today they happened to be orphans, it was through the wickedness of corrupt humans. Their parents were innocent victims who had become heroes and who, while living as poverty-stricken exiles in Russia, had done their utmost to save their children from perdition.

The orphans got a good upbringing here. The girls, more amenable to refinement than the boys, benefitted from it most. The educators, generally good, carefully selected, were totally devoted to the children. It was enough to walk through the orphanage to see the results of their supervision. After classes, the girls would often sit in the shade of the large trees at a long table to do their homework. They would stand to greet their teachers, and as a token of respect bow their heads in welcome; they would speak in quiet, soft voices and strive to control their gestures. Their faces, mostly pale from malaria (even the African sun will not tan the faces of its victims), revealed a captivating tenderness. They smiled readily, but their smiles were always shadowed by something very doleful, something that could only come from their awareness that they were orphans. They followed the conventional forms of propriety very naturally, without pretense; and they won the hearts of all the rest.

The boys were less industrious, less disciplined, and less careful about their outward appearance. Physically they were developing splendidly, what with exercise, plenty of sun, good air, and baths. They threw themselves into volleyball and soccer, defeating the Hindu and the Greek teams. They were so acrobatic they could run on their hands and climb trees like monkeys. In using the catapults their aim was deadly. Regretfully, though, they frequently disdained learning and regarded it as hazardous to their health. Good manners were too restricting to be observed. A man who has frequent contact with nature and faces a largely primitive environment is inclined to simplify his life, restricting his needs to those most essential. These boys were making physical strength, cleverness, and courage their chief ideals.

Such barbarity encouraged by those lax conditions in Africa became gradually more evident. Male teachers were in short supply, and since those who did teach often had no idea of what that process is all about, they were sometimes cruel. The women, naturally more tender than men, had little authority over the adolescent boys. Actually there were no adequate sanctions to enforce discipline; they were not afraid of anything, for they knew they would get shelter, clothes and food, no matter how they behaved. Depriving them temporarily of entertainment or restricting their freedom brought no change in their behavior. They particularly liked to escape to the jungle at classtime. Even the girls did that at times. They would swing on the lianas and track birds and animals for hours. They would explain their absence as due to an attack of malaria, and in Africa, that excuse could always appear to be true.

Hiding places in Africa were abundant: besides the jungle, the Negro marketplace, Negro villages, and vegetation on the lakeshore. Once some boys hid for a few days in a nest they had made in the crown of a huge tree. They would come down only to be counted and to eat, to be seen momentarily by the supervisors, then would spend the school hours in the nest, telling stories, playing cards, and eating fruit. The hideout was discovered quite by accident when one day the nest disintegrated under the boys' weight and they fell, one after another, like ripe pears through the crackling branches. One broke a leg, another an arm.

The unruly boys did not, however, organize themselves into tough, street-wise gangs, as in civilized countries. Nor were they serious offenders; they did not destroy property or attack people, and they stole only orphanage property. Though mischievous, they were kindhearted. Their juvenile extravagances originated primarily in the anomalous conditions of their childhood, which warped their character in a merciless and very early battle for survival. In Russia every deportee, children as well as adults, thought chiefly about clinging to life, and whatever made that possible was justified. Near starvation, people were forced to steal, and stealing necessitated lying. Worked beyond their strength, they were forced to cheat. The system created the offenses, and all of the victims despised the system and hated those who had devised it. These shocking conditions were bound to influence the children in ways fatal to the development of a good character.

Distrust of authority, instilled in the children in Russia, still inhibited their souls and plagued their teachers and administrators in Africa. This psychic trauma manifested itself most often in fear, especially among children who had lost their parents in Russia early and been left to their own resources as very small children. They trusted no one and looked at everyone out of the corners of their eyes, stubbornly silent in the presence of their elders. This was the behavior of deeply hurt children and was the attitude of most "difficult" boys who got into serious trouble and of course, made problems for their supervisors. It was particularly difficult to teach them not to steal.

They would steal mostly communal items such as bed sheets, blankets, clothing, underwear and footwear. Then, as they had in Russia, they bartered their haul for fruit. Whatever they could not get rid of elsewhere, they would sometimes barter at Negro marketplaces, where stolen articles brought practically nothing because fruit was so cheap. The boys, and even the girls, did not regard this as a sin and even openly boasted about it. Their thievery was all the more amazing because plenty of fruit was always available to them at the camp. Their habit of stealing, long engrained in them in Russia, had become a compulsion.

Not only did some of the orphans feel a compulsion to steal, they were also gifted con men. Many orphans corresponded with soldiers, personally unknown to them, who had taken an interest in them and sought to offer brotherly care while serving at distant front lines. Though this correspondence reflected a sincere mutual attachment, some of the children began to abuse the kindliness of their distant friends, and played on their sympathy by presenting living conditions in the orphanage in extravagantly dark colors. The Polish soldier, remembering the Gehenna of exile in Russia, was eager to alleviate all sorts of misery, particularly of orphans. He therefore doubled and trebled his donations. This distasteful con game, perpetrated in Africa and India by orphans who were getting used to "making money on the side," was assiduously hidden from their supervisors.

Those who maintain that man's perdition is caused by his first bad habit are absolutely right. The first defect is registered in his soul; like a little ember it causes the first fire, and then a lengthening chain of fires. First bad habits were to be noted among the boys who were smoking, drinking and doing cruel things. Smoking was forbidden as a danger to them, and drinking the intoxicating banana beer, home-brewed by the blacks, though infrequently indulged, was equally dangerous. Another bad habit developed by some youngsters was card-playing. It began as a means of killing time but later on, with money at stake, it became a compulsion. In being cruel the boys thought to acquire "cold-bloodedness." This degeneracy they expressed by strangling cats, torturing them, or holding them by the tail and slamming their heads against a tree. Each indulgence in any of these practices led to a further stifling of conscience.

It was unlikely that one boy, all by himself, would indulge in such behavior, but a large number were entering this first phase of adolescence, among them several already aggressively destructive. Their evil tendencies infected those who feared to be thought sensitive or cowardly. Group living encourages such infection, and the bad example of a friend often becomes a double dare. The boys' guardians, nevertheless, still nurtured the hope that each one, trifler or bully, could be helped to discover other diversions than these destructive ones.

20

Work and Entertainment—The Theatre in the Jungle

The energy and agility of the young people in this difficult climate was often astounding, and not only in those who spared themselves at learning. It was observed that poring over books and sweating over studies still allowed for a considerable "swing" beyond the school. The need to be physically active was satisfied through scouting, playground fun, excursions, recreation-hall games, competitions and other such activities. The urge to be creative was often fulfilled through cultural organizations—literary circles and drama clubs. And much energy, initiative, and goodwill went into the newspapers soon being published.

In Oudtshoorn appeared a weekly publication, *Krzyz Poludnia (The Southern Cross)*. The Boy Scouts edited their own paper; and other youth publications were imported from the Middle East, the most popular being *Junak* and *Skaut*. Some literary creations were adapted for stage presentation. Religious plays, nativity plays, and patriotic programs were staged on religious feast days and national holidays. Both grown-ups and children helped prepare and deliver lectures, recited poetry, played the violin and the piano, or delighted their audiences with choral and solo singing. Frequently such celebrations were linked with gymnastic displays and with guest teams competing in volleyball, basketball and soccer.

The agricultural secondary school in Tengeru staged annually the old Slavic festival of the harvest (Thanksgiving), and the young people participating in it appeared in Polish national and regional costumes which they made themselves, performing lively Polish dances such as the "kujawiak," "oberek," and "trojak," and the graceful, majestic "mazur" and "polonez."

In the evening the people would gather in recreation halls for games or so-called "teas," for pictures or talks, recorded music, a chat, a song, or a game. Such occasions as "Santa Claus" Day, post-Christmas and post-Easter gatherings, the school principal's name day, and end-of-school-term celebrations gave the young people an opportunity to strengthen their friendships, and encouraged them toward communal undertakings.

The organization of school celebrations, parties, and excursions remained their own responsibility. At the end of each school term the trade schools would arrange exhibitions of articles produced by the students; some of these exhibitions were on a large scale and were held in neighboring towns. Exhibits of knitted garments, women's wear, folk embroidery, metalware, and leather goods attracted crowds of interested admirers eager to buy these handicrafts. Since they were responsible for advertising the exhibitions, the youngsters prepared posters, leaflets, invitations and stall decorations besides ensuring an adequate supply of Polish food at the refreshment stands. The entertainment department always demanded hard work. The orchestra had to be got ready, the accompaniment, the singing, and the dancing. Some of these amateur performers were so talented that they gave great promise of becoming successful professionals some day.

Thanks to the efforts of Mrs. Grosicki, supervisor of the orphanage, a theatrical ensemble of eighty young actors was organized in Tengeru. This troupe managed to win the recognition not only of their own people, but also of people living beyond the camp. Although the performances were originally scheduled for the camp alone, some were given by invitation in Dar-es-Salaam, the capital of Tanganyika, and even in Nairobi, the capital of Kenya. The Nairobi daily paper, *The East African Standard*, reviewed each presentation there, with high praise for the performers. The superintendent of the orphanage, who also directed and produced these plays, and was the author of several of them, always bore in mind that the theatre should be educational. One of his main objectives was to keep reminding the children of their own country as it was before the war, and in the days before that. Intelligently selected plays, reminiscent of times now so distant yet ever close to the heart, reached deeply into the people's souls and brightened many hours of the drab monotony of camp life.

The theatre was open to the sky in the thickly forested valley. The stage, situated among bushes and tall trces, was only a platform with a ceiling of green leaves and lianas. Its backdrop was a thick wall of green vegetation. Nobody feared the rain because there was no rain during the period called the "dry season." The audience area gradually inclined away from the stage up the gentle slope of the valley. The best theatres in the world would have been envious of such facilities.

This beautiful setting was bound to affect people as they took their places, so stimulating was it to the imagination. That is why, when the curtain was raised and, to the sound of lovely faint music, enchanting things began to happen on the stage, many a mother sighed with delight. When some tableau brought forth familiar images from Polish history, folklore, or legend, the sighs deepened, and here and there, a mother would wipe tears from her eyes and whisper to her neighbor, "That is how it was with us there, exactly the same!"

The Nairobi papers referred to these productions as "shows of such a range of color as the Royal Theatre stage has not seen in a long time." One can imagine how overjoyed the young actors were when they read such press reports, especially thirteen-year-old Janka Papuga, acknowledged the most talented performer in the ensemble. The praise was, of course, shared by the Italian orchestra accompanying the shows with Mister Sabatino as conductor. Profits from these presentations were assigned partly to charities such as the "Food for Britain Fund," British War Invalids, or Polish Refugees in Germany.

Imaginatively and artistically the children of the settlements showed their country to the Africans. As *The East African Standard* recorded it, they gave them "a peep inside Poland." It can be said without any exaggeration that the theatre of the orphanages wrote one of the most colorful pages in the history of the centre.

21

In the Heart of the Natural Zoo

The experiences of our orphans were of such singular variety as to constantly stimulate their curiosity and enhance their education.

Uprooted, moved, shifted so many times, forced to make new contacts and adjust to new surroundings, the children eventually realized that their own arrival in Tengeru caused the migration of large numbers of wild animal families. When Negroes armed with axes and saws declared war on the jungle, felling trees and uprooting bushes to make room for the Tengeru settlement, most of the large animals sought shelter in the murky, humid recesses of the forest at the foot of Mount Meru nearby.

To see the large game from close range one had to make a safari deep into the steppe or the jungle. From the letters of their peers, the children at Tengeru knew that lions appeared in the neighborhood of the Kidugala camp; that in the Koja camp on Lake Victoria the Polish children could see baboons, hyenas, crocodiles, and even at times hippopotami.

It was not easy to make the children understand that some animals, like lions and leopards, do not ordinarily come out to feed before night. Eventually they reconciled themselves to this oddity of animal behavior. They were warned, however, that one could encounter a lion suddenly, eye-to-eye near the farm fence, near the hen house or the stable. In the vicinity of the Koja settlement, a leopard was stealing poultry, killing cats, and even attacking cattle, until it fell into an ingenious trap set up by the settlement dwellers. A few miles away, on the highland of Mount Meru, a large herd of elephants stampeded from time to time through the farm of Mme. Trappe. The surrounding plantations were very often ravaged by monkeys. The baboons proved to be particularly destructive and wicked, prowling in herds of fifty or more, ruining crops. At the time the Polish children were near Lusaca, Rhodesia, a marauding old lion, decrepit and partially blind, killed a Polish missionary, Brother Francis Bulak, on the grounds of the Jesuit mission. Brother Francis had gone out with a flashlight and a loaded rifle to chase the prowler away from the cattle. In the morning the lion was tracked down and killed.

Wild animals as a rule run away from man and can sometimes be scared off by a clap of the hands, a shrill whistle, or a gunshot. But they will attack a man when hungry or afraid, when protecting their babies, or when slowed down by age. In South Africa natives used a rather peculiar, now forbidden, method of getting rid of baboons. Caught alive, the baboon was shaved, painted blue, and then set free. His odd appearance scared his confreres away from the area.

When the large animals moved into the depths of the jungle away from the neighborhood of the camp, the chidren of the Tengeru settlement found a measure of consolation in the beautiful birds that remained there. How delighted they were when, in hiding, they would watch the flights of the toucans, the comedians of the bird world, their plumage rich in contrasting colors and their beaks disproportionately large. They were fascinated too by the sun birds. Like hummingbirds, they are about the size of one's thumb; their wings in motion make the humming sound of the bees as they linger suspended above the flowers to collect nectar or tiny insects. Here and there the children would see a bird of paradise, its tail a few times longer than its whole body, its plumage an impressive range of purple, black, white, and hot orange.

These magnificently feathered birds were associated in the children's imagination with the characters in a fairy tale in which the prince or princess turns into one of these beautiful creatures through the magical powers of a sorcerer. Yet it did not escape their attention that none of these exquisite creatures was capable of producing the musical songs they expected to hear. Some made sounds like the grinding of a saw or the gibbering of an agitated deaf-mute; some seemed to be imitating the whistling of a happy hooligan or even the syncopated snapping of fingers; others sounded like the rattle of a toy or the ruffle of a drum. It was left to the small, grey, humble little bird to fill our hearts with its enchanting song.

Just as the birds did not fly away when the human invasion commenced, neither were the snakes ready to move. They merely crawled into the thick grass. But since some were dangerous, they had to be smoked out of their hiding places.

Once a few boys were browsing near the edge of Lake Duluti with their dog Kubus. He was jumping in the grass, smelling at holes in the ground, barking madly at the frogs in the bushes, and every once in a while reporting to his young masters, then running off again. One time, however, he did not come back, and the boys became apprehensive. When their calls and whistles brought no response, they dispersed to search for him. Much to their horror they found him in the coils of a python, about to be crushed. This was unbearable to the boys. One of them got out his pocket knife, ran toward the monster, grabbed it "under the chin," and in a wild fury began to strike the head. He himself did not know how he managed the courage; he just felt desperate. The python's glittering body suddenly went limp in the hands of the boys and they freed the half-crushed Kubus. The dog recovered quickly but remained very subdued as the boys returned to the camp in triumph, carrying the dead python on their shoulders.

As for the Tengeru settlement, it had no serious trouble with reptiles; nor did any of the other settlements. In the Masindi camp, however, occurred a frightening incident described by a little girl, Wanda, in a letter to the editors of *Nasz Przyjaciel (Our Friend)*.

> There was an incident in our camp which could have ended tragically. There are some derelict huts in our camp. Beside one of them grow some beautiful flowers. One lady wanted to pick the flowers when suddenly she saw a head like that of a fish. She thought it was a dog stretched in the grass. Walking on she saw a body stretching far out. She recognized the python and began to move back. Lots of people came. Mister Edwin arrived with his shot gun and shot the snake, which was 27 feet long.

The rescued lady was extraordinarily lucky because encountering a python at close quarters mesmerizes humans so completely that they stop stock still, and it takes only one quick recoiling movement for the reptile to lock its victim in its deadly grip.

Occasionally there were tales about cobras blinding people by spitting in their eyes, but when the ever-ready remedy was applied instantly, the blindness would soon pass. Frequently these snakes were found hanging down from the rafters of the huts, above the beds. It was mandatory to check at night to make sure none were hiding under the bed or in a corner. At times a snake was found rolled into a ball at the gate of someone's garden. These were not pythons, nor always poisonous, but the risk was there always.

None of us was as afraid of the snakes as the Negroes were. Once I saw a few Negro camp cleaners spot a few poisonous snakes hanging down like long green pea pods from the branch of a tree. The Negroes shouted in terror: "Nioka! Nioka!" ("Snake! Snake!"), their eyes wide with fear. Only for these and for the simba (lion) do they feel such dread.

A deep appreciation for the unconquered forces of nature must ever remain with these new Polish children of the jungle. They would watch in fascination the smoking out of the snakes from the grass in the settlement area. Of all the reptiles only the lizards were allowed to remain—multicolored, always unperturbed, arranging furious races on the walls of the huts. Once, sitting on a veranda, some of the boys and I noticed the branches of a bush moving ever so gently. then we saw something monstrously ugly crawling at a snail's pace along the stem. The creature was stretching its little legs with their three-toed feet seeking a hold and helping itself along with a lengthy prehensile tail. It looked like a miniature antediluvian saurian. The head was topped by a triangular, pointed cap. The skin was grainy and spotted with colored dots. The most peculiar feature was the eyes, rolling like searchlights seeking out enemy aircraft. Capable of moving independently, one eye could look up while the other looked down; or while one looked forward, the other could look backward. Those eyes filled us with an almost superstitious fear. They seemed to be all-seeing. All the while that ugly fellow held his eyes on me I thought of the legendary basilisk whose piercing look was fatal.

Appearances deceive in the animal world. This fearsome and abhorrent creature was the innocent, quiet chameleon, looking for insects to eat. Its tongue, a formidable tool as long as its body, can coil itself in the mouth like a piece of chewing gum, but let a fly appear and the tongue flashes like a rock from a slingshot. It never misses.

I tried to pry the chameleon from the branch and place it on the earth, just to test its ability to change colors. It objected with a dull hiss and pinched me. We won, though, and gently carried out our experiment. Against whatever background we placed it, its skin, outfitted with shrinking and expanding grains of coloring, changed its hues to match.

The children made many such wonderful observations, sharing with me their experiences and discoveries. They could sit motionless for hours, like patient scientists, watching every movement, every detail. I would not be surprised to learn that a good number of these Polish children in Africa chose to become biologists, zoologists, or naturalists. They discovered that the smallest of all the creatures they met were often the most aggressive and dangerous. The tse-tse fly was not to be found near the Tengeru settlement, but there were malaria-carrying mosquitoes and many other nasty pests ready to attack. We were surrounded by a giant army of insects in thousands of varieties, sometimes unique specimens. They kept reminding everybody of their existence, so annoying were they. Not only Krysia Maziarz's earth fleas but other pests as well would get under the skin and multiply there. It was enough to push the tall grasses aside with a bare arm to have hordes of parasites lodged instantly under the skin. The doctors had to extricate them at once to prevent infection. It was forbidden to put on unironed underwear if it had been hung out on a bush to dry, because the tiny, agile intruders were capable of getting into it. Most problem cases occurred in the Koja camp.

But, annoying as they were, these insects were only loose vanguards for elite armies, well trained and well organized, which inflicted the heavy damage. Once on a dull night in the hut of my neighbors, quite a commotion broke out. Awakened and curious, I looked out the window. Mrs. Maria Puzinowska and her daughters, in their nightgowns, were furiously shaking something off themselves and tramping on it in a frenzy. After a while the father came out of the communal kitchen carrying a shoveful of burning charcoal and scattered it around the hut. It was easy to guess that my neighbors were being attacked by wandering red ants. These ants advance in Tartar fashion. Nothing except fire and water can stand in their way. They must have climbed the wall of the hut and entered under the elevated roof. No hut of this sort can obstruct them. As usual, this was an army of hundreds of thousands that could have gone through the hut and beyond had it not been for the people who moved; to the ants that was the signal to attack.

The soldier ant, outfitted with strong pincers, bites its victims so deeply that when it tries to separate itself, it leaves the pincers embedded in the flesh. Negro mothers carry their babies on their backs for fear that the marching ants will devour them in their cradles. Housewives keeping chickens must release them from the henhouse before the ants attack and guard them somehow; otherwise the black hordes leave only the bones behind them.

In the morning I spotted the next army of ants heading toward my hut. Wishing to secure a quiet night for myself, I threw out a few papayas, each the size of a soccer ball, for their meal. With enough to eat till the following day they forgot everything else. The next morning, all the flesh of the papayas was eaten up, but the thousands of ants sticking to the thin film of the skins were still drinking the juice. It was not too difficult to upset their marching plans. On a shovel I transferred the papayas together with the ants to the garbage, where the banquet continued.

It would seem that these red hordes are only a frightful nuisance to humans, but even they serve a good purpose. They are looked upon as Africa's most useful insects because of their function as "grave diggers." They neatly devour the carcasses of dead animals not eaten by hyenas or jackals, leaving clean white bones and thereby preventing the spread of epidemics. They also eat other insects and thus help maintain the ecological balance, though the camp inhabitants could hardly be expected to regard them sympathetically.

But the most destructive creatures, therefore the most hated by the Polish settlers, were termites, twice as big as the marching ants, with fat, soft, whitish bodies and brownish-red heads shaped like helmets. Ordinarily they live underground, beneath the mounds they erect. These termite castles are of different shapes and sizes, some reaching as high as eighteen feet. These dwellings maintain an even temperature by an ingenious system of ventilation. The termites leave their underground home only at night; sometimes, to reach their prey undiscovered, they build tunnels. In one night they can chew up anything: socks, shoes, wooden picture frames, books, or sisal door mats. Only rock, concrete, iron, and glass they cannot tackle. They often lived in the walls of our mud huts. As the floors were also made of hardened mud, the termites would often erect a mound right in the middle of a hut in one night. All settlers, grown-ups and children alike, had to declare war on them. When one hit the earth with a pickax where termites were working below, there would be a dull, hollow sound. The children entertained themselves locating these spots and alarming the grown-ups.

One summer the termites selected for their kingdom the grounds of a vegetable garden adjacent to our presbytery. After a while the earth in the garden became hard as a rock, first in a small area, then rapidly in the whole garden plot; all vegetables and trees withered, a sure sign that the termites had established their kingdom there. One of the ways the British settlers used to get rid of the termites out in the open was to pour honey in front of the termite colony and attract to it not only the termites but also the marching ants. This joint feasting soon changes into a mass slaughter of the blind, fat termites.

The more radical way to dispose of them is to destroy the queen, for when she is gone the life of the whole society becomes disorganized, the rules of discipline break down, the termite workers, soldiers, gardeners and nurses—all their community—lose their reason for existence and perish. Many reflections could be spun out of this, but the man in Africa does not think about it. He has to protect his own rights. Can one surrender to termites?

We tried the second method in the presbytery garden. We hired a Negro with a pick. He started the job early in the morning, digging up the underground kingdom, bit by bit. It was not an easy task, because the structures of the little architects become a petrified mass of earth. The underground corridors are spread far and deep. The trick is to hit the spot where the queen resides. The Negro dug all day long, having the company of the children for most of the time. He sweated, rested, and took up his task anew, trying to find the royal chamber. All around the dug-up pit the termites milled mindlessly, and patiently the onlookers watched.

Just before sunset the Negro raised the trophy triumphantly above his head to show it to the boys and girls. He sat down, exhausted, and deposited on a leaf a little sack pulsating with life. After a brief rest he wrapped the trophy in a leaf, went to the administrative office, and showed his treasure to all the officials in turn. Upon receiving praise and a few shillings, he raised the termite queen high, rolled his eyes happily, and ate the sack raw, with gusto, as if it were the greatest delicacy. "Mzuri, Bwana, mzuri! . . ." ("Lovely, sir, lovely! . . .") he murmured, patting his stomach with one hand, clutching his earnings with the other.

22

Adventures of the Scouts

Believing that the scouting movement in Africa provided an excellent means of education, we wanted as many Polish school chldren as possible to become boy scouts and girl scouts. The scouting way of communing with nature, we hoped might restore the spiritual balance and inner harmony which many of the children had lost. We were not disappointed in this hope, though the program attracted fewer boys than girls. Except for certain restrictions imposed by the rigors of colonial life, the Polish scouting activities offered splendid opportunities for exotic adventures as well as the regular gatherings, camp fires, celebrations, marches, parades, gymnastic displays and maneuvres.

One of the "marches past," in the camp of Lusaka in North Rhodesia (now Zambia), was reviewed by the daughter of Lord Robert S. Baden-Powell, founder of the World Scouting Movement. In Oudtshoorn, the Polish boy scouts recorded February 24, 1947, in their diaries as a most memorable day, when the town was honored by a visit of the British Royal Family, King George VI and his queen and the two princesses, Elizabeth and Margaret. During the reception ceremonies, King George stopped before the Polish banner and spoke with our boys about their life at the educational centre. Queen Elizabeth, in the meantime (attracted by their colorful folk costumes), delighted the girls with her compliments.

The summer camps and excursions to the jungle, the steppe, neighboring missions, craters, and lakes, were very popular with the children. They often figure in the recorded descriptions of camp life, such as this excerpt from a letter by Janina Bartkowiak, at a girl-scout camp some 150 miles from her settlement at Tengeru:

> I enclose a snapshot from the camp in Kikore. It was made on the front step of the Rest House in which we lived. The giant skulls seen in the entrance hall belonged to rhinos. Two years ago an Englishman from the Kikore area killed six of them; the seventh one killed him. That is why only six skulls are displayed. On the wall of the veranda is an epilogue to this adventure, an oil painting showing the Englishman's battle with the rhinoceroses, a felled tree, and underneath the tree, his grave.

A home sporting six rhino skulls had obviously made a great impression upon the girls. But much more important to them was their own discovery that communing with nature was a matter of deeply appreciating the wonder of it, of allowing its mysteries to press in upon them as they looked, listened, touched, measured, and responded. Each hour of the camping-out experience offered its fresh sensations and its lessons in natural lore.

Little Joseph Migut was able to catch in his journal a variety of feelings during an unsuccessful camp fire in Tengeru:

> It is said that people never argue when they look at the stars together. I would add or when they look together at sparks coming from a camp fire.
>
> In the evening, with weather ideal, our troop assembled on the clearing in order to start the camp fire. Just as the dry twigs shot up with the crackling fire, there came a horrible downpour of rain. The troop scattered in a wink, seeking shelter. My detachment hid in a hollow tree trunk. The space inside was about ten feet high, but the tree seemed to be healthy, judging by its huge crown of leaves. The downpour caused such a mood within us, fifteen of us hidden in the hollow tree, that we were soon shouting the way the Negroes do, while the rest of the troop, standing under another tree, were being drenched. Our joy did not last long. Our troop leader, fearing for the health of the boys being soaked under the tree, ordered all of us to run to a farm not far away. There we dried our clothes. When the rain stopped for a while as we were returning to the settlement, suddenly we were enshrouded by an impenetrable darkness, dampness, and cold.

Silvester Krzaniak of the boy scout camp in Uganda described a New Year's Eve in this way:

> We all slept like logs but then, all of a sudden, the signal of the alarm trumpet put us on our feet. Just as I was finishing dressing, Marian and Ted dropped in. They put down before me a beard, a moustache, and a cane and told me that I was to take the part of the "Old Year" during the campfire at midnight. I was not happy about that. I had to improvise all by myself. I barely had

> time to think what to do or what to say when everybody was heading towards the campfire site. As I was lagging behind a bit, so as not to be spotted by anyone in my costume, not very far from the fire site a tardy girl scout caught up with me; but seeing this horrible figure standing in the path, she just started yelling. Other boys and girls ran to her rescue. I managed to hide. As was discovered later on, the frightened girl was the "New Year." The poor "New Year" was scared by the "Old Year." Anyway it all ended up with the "New Year" chasing the "Old Year" away.

The mothers in the settlement, just like mothers the world over, were always full of worry about those summer camps and bivouacs. They would possibly have been less anxious had it not been for the whisperings of concerned neighbors and the rumors they spread. The same Silvester Krzaniak recorded this in his memoirs:

> Life in our boy scout camp generally passed quietly, but occasionally we would be upset by talk in the settlement about our mode of living. There were rumors that we had to go two miles to get water, that we were starving and so on. Our mothers became angry, at times even desperate. They sent food parcels to the camp: bread, cakes, and eggs. Once the postal truck even broke down under the weight of those parcels. The whole settlement must have been amazed when on one occasion we sent back the whole transport of food parcels.

One summer the girl scouts pitched their tents on a plateau near Mount Meru, nearly fifty kilometers (thirty miles) from the Tengeru settlement. The location was excellent, the ground rising in gentle folds toward the mountain. From this side the peaks of Meru were bare, forming a chasm difficult to reach. A Negro legend says that Meru, an old volcano, will erupt again at some time, and that this will mark the beginning of a new era for the tribes living nearby. Looking at the bivouac from above one saw the stretch of dark green splotches, the jungle, and the bright green splotches, the mountain sides, and glittering in the distance, the mirror-smooth surface of the lakes.

The girl scouts' tents were pitched less than one kilometer from the farm buildings belonging to Mme. Trappe, a settler of German descent. At night, herds of elephants trekked through her farm, plundering and destroying her vegetable garden, and rhinos also visited her. We learned that two very ferocious Alsatian hounds, left outside for guarding the farmstead, had fallen victim to some nocturnal predator, for both had disappeared without a trace.

Because of the danger, the girls maintained double guard duty on the bivouac and, of course, the fire was kept going all night long. Each little noise in the darkness was scary, but the girl scouts returned here almost every year, as courageous as Amazons, proud that now, on a stretch of the natural African zoo with all its dangers, they could practice the Scout principle: A girl scout loves nature and strives to get to know it.

Once I went to their camp for a weekend visit. At my disposal was a little one-person tent on the outskirts of the camp. When night set in, I sneaked into it but could not fall asleep for a long time as I listened to the crackle of the fire, the whisperings of the girl guards on duty, the silent jungle holding its breath, its animals hiding from the claws of the night hunter, the leopard.

Cold morning chased me out of the tent with one more hour to go till reveille. I began to assemble the field altar while one of the guards picked wild flowers to decorate the altar. The world was silent and peacful, the peak of Mt. Meru shrouded in milky mist. Above the grasses as the mist blew away, emerged the outlines of Elephant Mountain, so named by the Polish children because it resembles the hind quarters of an elephant.

Reveille was sounded and the camp filled with life, with song—"Kiedy ranne wstaja zorze . . ." ("When the morning lights rise . . .")—with prayer said in unison, with the flag hoisted to the top of the mast, with Holy Mass and a lesson. Toward the end of the service a drizzle began, and masses of clouds lowered upon the camp a thick curtain of fog. Soon the missal's pages became wet, the grass and bushes were adorned with pearls of dew, and we were penetrated with chill.

After breakfast we paid a visit to the fearless Mme. Trappe. At close range, she was a short, frail, thin woman with a sallow complexion and sharp, intelligent black eyes. A fine net of wrinkles under her eyes betrayed her advanced age, but she was rigged out in a short-sleeved shirt and a pair of shorts. Her lips, always ready to smile, stiffened somehwat when from the house came a young man, tall, broad-shouldered, stiff, and as silent as Mt. Meru. Mme. Trappe introduced him as her son. A short while later a tanned rather coarse-looking woman wearing riding britches pushed through the group of girl scouts. This was Mme. Trappe's daughter. When introduced to us, she looked around as if suspiciously, dryly said "good morning," and left. A while later she appeared at the front of the house on a fiery horse. Her horsemanship was admirable, and she jumped the horse over natural obstacles with great ease, her light hair bouncing rhythmically on her back.

When she disappeared into the thicket, our hostess invited us to sit down and went to the kitchen to make tea. We noticed then that the furniture was old and the house poor, except for its hunting trophies. At the entrance to the veranda stood the hollowed-out leg of an elephant used as a wastepaper basket. On the walls were a few pairs of buffalo horn, set on massive heads, which were covered with a thick layer of dust, as were the animal hides scattered on the floor. In the place of honor over the fireplace was a collection of shotguns and rifles. On the mantlepiece, on the lowboy, and on the cupboard were dust-covered photographs, one of them of the recently introduced daughter with a tame panther at her feet.

As we were looking at this photograph, Mme. Trappe came in with a tea tray. Explaining that the panther was gone, she put the tray on the table and lowered herself heavily into an armchair as if overcome by a flood of unhappy memories. One of the girls poured the tea while, at our urging, she told us the family's story. She and her husband, she said, had lived lives of solitude, finding the greatest pleasure in their communion with nature. Their son and daughter were born in the jungle, knowing nothing of their parents' homeland. Domestic and wild animals were their true friends; they felt their fears and understood their love for freedom. The work of the farm and the discovery of nature's secrets filled their lives. In contrast to the many enterprising tourist hunters who came here, their young siblings preferred to see a pair of warm, living eyes under a beautiful pair of horns. The encounter was always a surprise for the animal. For a brief moment man and animal would size each other up, the man tenderly, enticingly, the animal curious but distrustful. Often when the man's innate fear seemed stronger than his own curiosity, the animal would turn around and tear away from the man, stopping only for one last look.

Young Trappe would shoot an animal only when it was a danger to himself or to someone else. He once killed a hippopotamus which had upset a boat full of Negroes, mutilating one of them. The brave Negro had held his spilled bowels against his body with his hat and dashed for help toward the farm. The yellow tusks of this hoppopotamus are now hanging in the parlor.

At long last the lady touched upon the topic most painful to her. With great tenderness she spoke about once having had a stable of beautiful race horses. The war came. When the British placed all Germans in internment camps, her family was not spared. They had had to sell the horses for almost nothing. The young panther, set free but not wanting to leave, tucked his tail under and moved slowly toward the jungle, stopping often to look back, not believing that he was really being exiled. Chased away again, he bared his teeth threateningly and puckered his nose.

This narrative, bitter though it was, brought some relief to Mme. Trappe. Her sadness passed, and the girls asked her to tell stories about other wild animals, as many as possible. She was more than willing to. She had only contempt for the lion, she said, regarding him as a coward and an idler, never as the king of animals. She respected the elephant as the most intelligent creature, though the African elephant and buffalo are among the most dangerous of all quadrupeds. Even wounded, the elephant can chase a hunter with the speed of a horse. Saving oneself from an elephant's vengeance is possible only by climbing a tree large enough that the elephant cannot uproot it by ramming it with his forehead.

In the afternoon the girls visited the farm and surrounding areas. At the edge of the jungle, near Mme. Trappe's vegetable garden, were the colobus monkeys, the rare species with bushy tails, black hair, and white bellies. Since at one time the pelts of these monkeys were in such great demand on the world's markets they became nearly extinct, the remainder are now under strict protection. In the orchard the girls saw passiflora vines wound around the tree trunks and the fountain-centered pond at the entrance to the garden.

In the meantime guests had come to the camp for a swearing-in ceremony, an awarding of badges, and the "camp fire." The kids were playing ball when suddenly somebody reported the appearance of an elephant. The camp was empty in no time flat, and the tall side of the ravine filled with people. The elephant, unaware of so many curious eyes, cavorted in the thicket, pulling its proboscis over the branches of a tree to stuff the leaves into its mouth. Having plucked the greenery off in one spot, crackling over branches and snorting, it moved its heavy body to another spot, and again the powerful trunk, like the tentacle of an octopus, twisted and turned among the branches. After finishing his meal the animal stepped down to a stream, sucked water into its trunk and noisily showered its body.

After drill practice and lectures the next day, the girls had another opportunity to watch elephants, this time a herd of over twenty, grazing in a ravine into which, from high above, fell a small mountain stream. The girls wanted to be as close to the elephants as possible, but a Negro, sent out by Mme. Trappe, warned that they should not move forward any more. Nobody understood Swahili, but the Negro's nervous gestures indicated clearly that there was some danger close by. Moving to a more suitable observation point, they noticed that the volcanic shell under their feet was rumbling as if the ground were hollow and in some spots the grass was hidden by a thick layer of ash.

At the lunch break some of the older scouts and I followed Mr. Trappe, with a few Negroes, to the lakeshore to watch the hippopotami. The excursion was almost a fiasco. Because of the heavy clouds overhead, the animals were not coming out of the water despite the insistent urgings of the Negroes, who were disappointed and dissatisfied with their leader. Somewhat piqued, he asked us if we would be afraid to go deeper into the bush; it would be dangerous, but we would see many hippopotami. Though a few girls gave up and returned to the camp, the rest of us were eager to set out. At the head of our procession were two Negroes, armed with pangas and javelins, to scare away the wild animals that might be concealed along our path. The Negroes threw rocks into the bush to frighten away creatures in hiding. Behind them was Mr. Trappe with a Mauser rifle at the ready. We, unarmed, followed a few steps behind them. The sun stood at the zenith, pouring down its heat and blinding light. The terrain was undulating. The deeper we went into the kingdom of animals, the most anxious became the Negroes, so lightly armed. From time to time they would turn their heads, checking that Mr. Trappe had his rifle ready. After a longish march we climbed up one of the hills dominating this area and saw in the distance the shining waters of its small lakes. From here our guide could point out various species of animals. There, far in the distance, a buffalo was making its way with a heavy step, its head held low. Mr. Trappe reckoned that the buffalo might be wounded, because its appearance at this time of the day was unusual.

Seeming to perceive the danger coming from man, the buffalo comes out to pastureland and watering areas only after sunset or before dawn. This is the most cunning animal, and the most difficult to hunt. Lions are its most dangerous enemy, always attacking in a pack. A fight between the lion and the buffalo is said to be one of the most dramatic of spectacles. Although the buffalo loses on the battleground, it often inflicts heavy injuries, sometimes fatal ones, on the lions.

At one moment a pack of wild dogs with brown, bristling coats appeared in the clearing, so ferocious that even the mighty lion fears them. On the lakeshore the rhinoceroses moved around or rolled in the mud. They must have caught the sound of human steps because the cows were moving with a mincing step. Nature compensates for their poor sense of sight and smell with a keen sense of hearing. Their hearing did not fail them now because suddenly they turned around and plunged heavily into the lake, bubbling the water with their huge, lumbering bodies.

It was around three in the afternoon and the air was humming with the song of crickets when Mr. Trappe said we must return. The natives relaxed, dropping back to keep in line with us, paying little attention to the bush.

Suddenly, about sixty feet away, we heard a snort, and from the thicket rose up a huge black body that rushed at full speed towards our leader. He had no time to take aim, but shot in a reflex action. The animal fell some fifteen feet in front of him. We all ran up, curious, though greatly shaken by the experience. In front of us lay the rhinoceros, one large horn on its snout, the other faintly showing under the hide, from its temple a trickle of blood. With its legs tucked under, it looked like a stranded blimp. We looked at the marksman admiringly. He stood there shaking all over, holding the rifle close to his chest, his jaw muscles tightened like ropes. As he regained his composure, we all slowly realized that had it not been for that deadly shot, the excursion could have ended in tragedy. With a sudden gesture he started us moving again toward the camp. When we looked back at the dead animal, the vultures were already hovering over its crinkly form. These birds serve their animal companions not only in death but also in life—picking from their itching hides the fierce flies and other insects, to give the animals relief and themselves food, and warning their hosts of imminent danger—yet another example of the even exchange of services in nature.

Mister Trappe, after cooling down a bit, explained to us that to escape from a rhinoceros is not such a difficult feat. It is enough to jump aside, and the animals will rush past like fury, stopping farther on to wonder why it did not encounter the enemy on the way. The rhino, because it has very poor eyesight and little sense of smell, often suffers from the delusion of danger and charges in vain, sometimes injuring itself as its 3,000-4,000-pound body crashes into a tree. The adventure ended with Mr. Trappe ordering the Negroes to remove the horn from the dead animal's snout. Though not so valuable as ivory, the horn can always be sold.

In spite of all of our precautions, our scouting venture in Africa suffered a tragedy whose echo reverberated through the troops in all the settlements. In September of 1947, a youngster named Jerzy Miedzyrzecki died during a competition at a Jamboree. Staszek Czernek, a friend of his, describes Jerzy's death:

> The Jamboree was held on Lake Victoria. Twenty of us came from Tengeru camp, only nineteen returned. It happened thus. As is normal at jamborees, several competitions were included in the program. Jerzy was competing for the first time, I for the third. The object of the exercise was to follow the terrain until we reached a certain spot marked with a flag, there to receive further instructions and follow them.
>
> Our group of ten from Tengeru, having outdistanced all other groups, reached the flag first, but close after us came the Negro scouts. Together we read the instructions, and following this the Negroes started running on, Jerzy and I after them, leaving our own tired colleagues behind. We ran like crazy. The jungle was terrifying. Fallen trees impeded our run along the narrow path, similar to an animal trail. Soon we got ahead of the Negro boys, and as we ran on, their voices became fainter. The path led us to the lakeshore. The final objective was not very far off. Jerzy spotted a boat nearby and jumped into it, while I was looking for the topographical signs or a letter of instructions. In the meantime the Negroes arrived. Instantly I jumped into the boat. We pushed off and sailed on, while the Negroes, having no other choice, ran along the shore, tearing through the bushes. Silence fell. There was only the jungle and the two of us on the lake. We were not too far from the shore when suddenly the boat capsized. I fell into the water but managed to push myself from the boat and it righted itself. Now Jerzy, having managed to remain in the boat, bailed out the water with his hat. I detached my haversack, hooked my feet against the boat, and tried to guide it towards the shore; but the boat, made out of a tree trunk, began to sink rapidly. Jerzy also took off his haversack, and we tried to swim ashore in our clothes. I asked Jerzy, "Can you make it?" He said, "No, Staszek!" However he swam on, and I helped him and

encouraged him. We reached the weeds through which I was breaking a path for him. He made those, but the next ones were some fifteen meters farther on. Here Jerzy seemed to lose his courage despite my urgings. I heard him cry, "God! Forgive!" He was drowning. I brought him to the surface. He looked dead; his head and his hands hung down limp, and yet he had been under water no more than five seconds. Desperately I pulled him toward the shore. My arms became weak, and I felt myself going under. With the last ounce of my will I grabbed Jerzy once again, made a few jerky movements, and at that moment touched bottom. I rushed toward the shore, tripping over the water plants, and on the shore tried to resuscitate him, though I myself was losing strength. At that point the rest of our group arrived and began to help. The fight for Jerzy's life lasted two hours. But all in vain.

According to the medical statement Jerzy died in the water of a heart attack. So ended our troop's ambition to be the first ones to breast the tape ahead of all the other nationalities.

23

Profiles

The priests assigned to the Polish camps in Africa played an important role in the lives of the refugees. Two very meritorious chaplains of the Tengeru settlement had much to do with the building of character in our young people.

Not tall, but rather corpulent, Father Jan Sliwowski was returning at a slow pace from the church to his supper at the presbytery. He had left in the churchyard long rows of boys and girls still waiting for confession. Sunset was at hand, but the heat was still bothersome, and beads of sweat shone on the reverend's face and his bald pate. His eyes sought the restful greenery of the presbytery garden where colonies of oleander displayed their pink and red flowers.

Only minutes later, when Father Jan walked back to continue his duties, the yard was almost entirely enveloped in darkness. Dusk in the equatorial zone arrives suddenly, like a giant black bird shadowing the earth. The stars were appearing; flowers perfumed the air. Father Jan stepped back to look with tenderness at the church whose roof with its raised eaves was a large black patch on the darkening horizon. Through the bamboo grating which, together with the low cemetery fence, formed one wall of the church, he saw the faint outlines of youngsters queued up near the confessionals, patiently awaiting their turn. The church was dim, lit with only the flickering flame of the eternal lamp.

This never-extinguished flame was something like the beating heart of this tireless custodian of the temple. How much love and labor he had invested in it! For a long time he had been the only one to care for the whole parish and all its schools. The work had often seemed beyond his endurance. Before each first Friday of the month he was there in the confessional five days a week, from one o'clock in the afternoon till midnight, sometimes longer, and in the morning just before Holy Mass. Before the high holidays more than three thousand penitents confessed, and on Easter Day or Christmas, Father Jan distributed the Holy Host to an average of twelve thousand.

It had not been anything like that when he first came to Tengeru to be the spiritual steward of the camp. He was often in a very pensive mood then, unhappy with his flock. At the time of oppression, he remembered, they had vowed, promised, beseeched, and pleaded for mercy. Yet, once led out of their oppression, they showed, like the ancient Jewish people under Moses, very little gratitude. In Africa they loafed, grew lazy, and became indifferent to God and His graces. The confessional stood empty. Only a few women came once a month for confession, though the shepherd waited hours for his flock. This spiritual torpor among his people kept him awake at night. He devoted all his energies, multiplied through prayer by the grace of God, to winning souls. He rushed into thatched-roofed homes, recreation halls, schools, to prevail upon some, harangue others, shame still others, and counsel everyone according to his or her temperament, degree of awareness, and confirmation in the faith. The flame of his spirit warmed some, burned others; enlightened some and blinded others. For Father Jan generated either love or hatred. Most of the parishioners truly loved him as a father, but there were also those who called him a tyrant. To the ones who hated him he called out, "Do to me whatever you want; you can kill me even, but do come to the retreat!" Before the Feast of Christ the King, when he saw that only a very few people thought about cleansing themselves of their sins, he threatened that if at least two thousand people did not come to confession, he would not arrange the celebrations, nor the forty-hour service; he would rather, he said, arrange it for the pagans, just anywhere, under a tree perhaps. He vowed to leave his parishioners to themselves and go away. His ardour consumed him.

One of his former pupils, Miss Jozia Ulanicki, recalled what happened: "The people came, some for fear that the shepherd might carry out his threat and leave the parish, others out of shame. The church was crowded with people sitting and standing. There was no room to kneel down. Within three years Father Jan had almost the whole population of the settlement coming to confession and Holy Communion on the First Friday of the month. He was distributing Holy Communion from six to eight a.m., nonstop."

That the inhabitants of the Tengeru camp were devout, faithful Christians was the fruit of the heroic efforts of this servant of God. The statistics alone are stunning. The Living Rosary Society had 2,400 members, the sodalities 1,500; the crusades numbered almost 1,000 children in their ranks, and the altar boys' circle had 70 boys. Father Jan taught in the several schools for forty hours a week. Because the refugees did not have documents, he issued birth certificate affidavits en masse. He completed building the church commenced by Father Dziduszko, the first pioneer of the parish. He built the presbytery, planted the large, beautiful garden around the church, and started the Catholic recreation hall. And he still found time to organize numerous excursions for the youngsters to animal reserves, mission stations, lakes and craters. Imprinted on the souls of all of his people was his unwritten law, the habit of monthly confession to stay in the grace of God. No wonder Father Jan's name is recorded forever in the hearts of his flock.

"It seems to me that I shall never forget him," wrote Jozia. "He had the soul of a child, so tender and sincere. I never will forget the day of his departure from the settlement. The people's eyes were swollen with crying. When during his last Mass they intoned the hymn 'Pod Twa Obrone, Ojcze na niebie' ('For Thy protection, Oh Heavenly Father'), instead of the song, there resounded sobs and moans. During the Lenten Psalms in the evening, although the church was full and everyone was genuinely worshiping, the church seemed empty because one very dear man was not there."

After Father Jan left, his work was taken on by Father Piotr (Peter) Roginski. He was one of those Poles who, besides an ardent faith, have a firm attachment to the fatherland. At the time of the Polish-Bolshevik war, Father Piotr had interrupted his theological studies to don a military uniform. He hailed from the colorful Vilno area famous for the miraculous picture of the Madonna of Ostrabrama venerated for centuries in Poland and Lithuania. Therefore, shortly after he arrived at Tengeru, he placed on the main altar of the church a faithful reproduction of the picture.

Whenever I recall his African days, I see him bending over a microscope checking a sample of his blood for malaria parasites. He was tall and looked rather robust; in his white linen cassock, he resembled a peasant of the Kosciuszko era when Polish peasants under Kosciuszko united with royalty to fight Russian soldiers with scythes. One noticed first his soft, silver hair; then his face, ennobled with suffering; his warm, benevolent smile; and his eyes shining with wisdom and strength of will.

His health had been seriously damaged in Russian labor camps and was now further impaired by the tropical climate of Africa. He had left the refugee camp in Morogoro, over 100 miles west of Dar-es-Salaam, the capital of Tanzania, when it was liquidated because of malaria, and had had to battle monthly attacks: shivering, aching bones, violent headaches, and feverish ravings. Though these miseries were somewhat alleviated by doses of atabrine, quinine, and paludrine, the remedies were all more bitter than wormwood and very likely to cause loud humming in the ears and weaken the heart.

Spiritually Father Piotr was just as he had been in Poland. He liked solitude, and God only knows how many ideas were born in his head during his meditations; sometimes they appeared unworkable, eccentric, even inane, but all were born of his ardent love for God and his fellow humans.

Father Piotr knew no compromise. He told the local British people frankly what he thought of the Yalta agreement, and a few other bitter remarks sometime later were the cause of his having to leave Africa. His sometimes harsh methods of presenting the truth or condemning evil even disposed some of his more sophisticated parishioners against him.

He would take advantage of even the most important celebration to disseminate his anti-repatriation propaganda. Once, when homesickness and their inactivity in the camp caused a few residents to decide to return to Poland, Father Piotr realized that his counselling against it was not enough. During the observance of a religious and patriotic holiday, soon afterward, he presented one of his unusual programs, a one-act play. The stage represented a cattle truck filled with exiles consigned to Siberia. The familiar drama was recreated there: children crying for bread and water, mothers wringing their hands in despair, one fainting from the pains of imminent labor, all huddling together as in severe cold, Russian soldiers answering the children's cries with roars of laughter, throwing them a salty fish and a handful of rice. To the pity and terror evoked by this drama, the presence of the awful pail and the suggestion of filth and foul air added the dimension of revulsion. At the end of the show, the author and director appeared on stage in dirty rags, a gloomy relic he had saved from his prison days in Russia.

One day a request came from two fathers in Poland asking that their two sons, living in Tengeru, return. The boys, now over sixteen years old and still harboring vivid memories of all the hurts inflicted on them by the Communists, refused. When the matter reached the British authorities and the International Refugee Organization, the boys were ordered to go home to their fathers or be deported. When the order came, the two boys disappeared and were presumed to be hiding in the jungle. As days went by and the run-aways failed to return, the authorities feared that they had perished. The mystery was solved by accident: One evening as I was returning from the recreation hall to the presbytery, I noticed Father Piotr hurrying to his room and closing the door. I remained on the veranda, fascinated by the cockchafers swarming around the ceiling bulb. From time to time one of them would hit me and fall to the earth as if dead. I picked one up and put it in my open palm. Soon its temporary paralysis, a natural means of self-defense, passed and the cockchafer began to move its tiny legs, trying to take off. Just then, though the night was calm, the oleander bushes began to move. There were the run-aways, waiting for Father Piotr to give them blankets and bread for their hideout. A few days after, the British authorities cancelled the deportation order and the two boys returned to camp hale and hearty.

Father Piotr loved young people. His life's precept, incessant activity, he applied to his care of them, making sure they were always busy and had no time for evil thoughts. He arranged lectures on a variety of subjects, and was in seventh heaven when from England came a used slide projector. He taught dogmatics, ethics, and the history of the Church in the secondary schools, always giving these subjects a humanities orientation.

And woe to anyone who dared hurt a child. He once discovered an elderly sexual deviate in the act of planning harm to three underage girls, brought him to the presbytery, and in the presence of the would-be victims threw the old man to the ground and administered such a beating that his groans and cries of outrage attracted a group of curiosity seekers. When three other adolescent girls dropped school and started going out with Hindus from Arusha, Father Piotr threatened to call their names from the pulpit if they did not stop. They were seen later, all three of them, kneeling in front of Father Piotr's bench at every evening service.

The hot climate, the inactivity, the abnormal social conditions, and the closeness of the huts constantly threatened to undermine the moral resolve of certain young people, but their teachers and their priests were always there to strengthen them. On some evenings, Father Piotr took more direct action and, armed with a powerful flashlight, stalked the "lovers' lanes," especially in the theatre area near the jungle, to chase the young lovers home. Such ways of inducing people to walk the straight and narrow path labeled him an oddball, though they reflected only his uncommon ardor in the service of God and his neighbor. Father Piotr, in whatever work he undertook, even the quietest, was a maniac, a fanatic, taking heaven by storm for himself and his flock.

His merits in the field of education and religion were acknowledged when he was promoted to the position of canon and decorated with the order of "Polonia Restituta." I was captivated by his goodness and humility. When I first arrived in Tengeru and stopped in front of the presbytery, he gave me his heart at once. After I had washed and had a meal, he took me by the arm as though I were his younger brother, and walked with me around Lake Duluti. Such a little time was enough for both of us to understand and to love each other. His humility stirred me deeply whenever he knelt at my knee for confession. As a priest he knew that the only important thing is to seek God and to honor and love Him most of all in His children.

24

Mr. Korzen and the Children of the Camp

In the neighborhood of the church at Tengeru stood an old hut, its sides bulging like a barrel. Mr. Ignacy Korzen, its occupant, was used to shifting his possessions to the center of the room whenever he heard that unmistakable sound of powerful insect jaws at work. Items made of glass or metal were safe, but clothing, boots, and matting could disappear overnight. The nasty termites had almost completely hollowed out the walls of his hut.

But Mr. Korzen was seldom there anyway, since he spent most of his time in and around the house of God, where he was sexton and jack of all trades. He soled boots, made leather suitcases, kept church and rectory equipment in good repair. He also knew cabinet making and could mend a cart wheel or build a boat; but because such skills were wasted here in equatorial Africa, he learned others. One day, spotting a swarm of wild bees falling upon an oleander bush, he transferred them tenderly with his bare hands to a box and built a hive for the young queen and her court. From the beeswax he started making candles for the altar, but, being of inferior material, they snorted and crackled so during the services that they frightened even the priest and these products of Mr. Korzen's apiary had to be abandoned.

Not so with his horticultural efforts. Thanks to his industry and knowledge, everything in the church garden grew splendidly. He did have a problem with his beautiful red and white roses: they kept disappearing. Whenever a member of the teaching staff celebrated a name day (and with over ten schools in the camp that was fairly often), the best of the blooms vanished. Rarely did Mr. Korzen apprehend a thief, and though he guessed that such a gift from a pupil would relax the teacher and ease the school day, he could hardly bear the losses. God help anyone who would steal flowers meant for the church! He wanted to be after the thief with a stick. When he did catch some young secondary-school ladies in the garden, he gave them worse than a beating:

the tongue-lashing of a servant of God in high dudgeon. To keep peace thereafter the priest had to give special permission for any name-day flowers to be appropriated.

Though he loved animals and had taken in a stray black angora cat and her many offspring, the sexton developed an intolerance for dogs. So prolific were canines bred in the African climate that the law allowed only one dog per hut. The dog-catcher, a deaf mute, would pursue the illegal dogs for days on end, armed with a shotgun but with no cooperation from anyone. Until the round-up was over, little boys would take turns hiding with their pets in the jungle. The number of dogs remained undiminished.

But they were not, according to Mr. Korzen, to be tolerated in or near consecrated ground. Even when they behaved themselves, quietly following their young masters into the church, he would explode with anger and unceremoniously shoo them out, often upsetting the service or interrupting the sermon.

Farming had been Mr. Korzen's calling in Poland, where he had owned some fertile land near Nowogrodek. But the war had separated him from his farm, his wife, and his children. When in 1920 shortly after World War I, he had fought against the Bolsheviks, they had imprisoned and tortured him to get the names of the other soldiers in his detachment. Stood up against the wall of a barn to be shot, he awaited death calmly; but the investigator, certain his spirit could be broken, cancelled the death sentence in favor of further torment. As a memento of those days, one of his hands was atrophied and stiff.

Mr. Korzen was in the prime of his life when he came to Tengeru, though his terrible experiences had aged him before his time. His broad practical knowledge made him renowned throughout the camp, and his tales of personal adventure earned him great popularity with the young altar boys. His every yarn about hunting and fishing in his homeland was luminous with the beauty of lakes and forests immortalized by Adam Mickiewicz, Poland's great poet.

Some of his spirited African narratives were of questionable veracity, but they managed always to mesmerize his audience. His tongue smacking with pleasure or his eyes misting with pain, he would throw himself into his story-telling: One day, he said, he went out a fair distance from the camp to buy eggs. Making his way through cornfields and coffee and banana plantations, he reached one of the Negro settlements, a few small huts hidden in a thicket. Before one of the huts sat an old woman. For an outrageously inflated price she sold him a dozen eggs. But they were small, not bigger than pigeon eggs. The Nowogrodek peasant knew what an egg should look like, and he was not going to be swindled by an old black woman! About to back out of the transaction and leave, he was suddenly surrounded by Masai warriors, knives in their belts, javelin blades and greased bodies shining in the sun. They stood motionless, leaning forward slightly. Their angry eyes flew from buyer to woman, from woman to buyer. Their stance spoke for them: "Either buy those eggs or else. . . ."

Mr. Korzen was not entirely sure of himself. Speaking slowly in his broken Swahili, he reiterated in a loud voice, "You want too much for your eggs! They are very small!" The old crone begged; the warriors threatened: "She is old. She cannot work. She has lost her teeth." The situation was tense. What was he to do? Run away? They would catch him, take all his money, and. . . . Suddenly an idea came to him. He himself was not so young and deserved to be pitied too. To prove it, he took out of his mouth a plate of the whitest artificial teeth. With a wide gesture he showed them to all. The Masai gasped and ran away. What in the world were those warriors afraid of? "They must have taken me for a sorcerer," he decided; but before they could recover and return, he dived into the bush and rushed back to camp.

One memorable African experience took place before he came to the camp as sexton. He had been working, he said, for a British farmer, a keen hunter who supplied wild animals to zoos; so he had several opportunities to participate in the hunting. He well remembered going at night in an armoured car to a pre-selected spot to hunt lions. As bait, the carcass of an antelope was thrown out. As soon as the hunters heard the gobbling, the groans, and the crunching of bones, they directed searchlight beams on the lion family at dinner. The lions, blinded, froze, and in that moment the Negroes popped from their hiding place, grabbed the cubs by the scruff of the neck, and scurried them into the car. The lioness sprang to the chase, clawing at the car door to rescue her brood, but the armoured vehicle was a stronghold. Inside was the soulful whimpering of the cubs, the bated breathing of their abductors, and the silent quaking of Mr. Korzen, while outside, after each frenzied attempt, the lioness filled the air with a desperate roar.

Now the greatest pleasure of the sexton's life was to sit in the recreation hall after a day of exhausting work. There several other men gathered "for politics" and played chess or checkers while waiting for the "Voice of America." Germany had surrendered, the war was over, and the Western World was overjoyed. Not the Poles. For them only one enemy of mankind had been defeated; the other one, Communist Russia, still flourished, glorified as the West's faithful ally.

At the signal for the program, the chess and checker games were suspended, and eager listeners surrounded the radio to catch news of the world. Each day they followed the slow process of decay within the Allied block. Homebred politicians, they could assess each happening and draw conclusions better than many a statesman. They had experienced Russia and well understood Russian promises and solemn assurances about restoring the nation's freedom. They were capable of facing the truth: Russia's friendship with the West was nothing but a massive deception.

More revealing than any radio news, however, were the letters Mr. Korzen received from his wife and children in Eastern Poland, now illegally incorporated into Russia. Penned by one of the younger girls, they reported accurately if laconically their misery, the requisitioning of their cattle for the community farm, the heavy taxes to be paid in produce, the forced enlistment of farmers in the collectives. Tears welled up in his eyes. When the child asked, "When are you coming back?" he recognized the diplomacy inserted to assure the censor's permission for continued correspondence. When the mother requested material help, he knew that she was really urging him not to return. As an "enemy of the working class" he could look forward only to liquidation. Wilting with nostalgia, Mr. Korzen would then start his parcel-sending campaign. He would buy underwear, soap, sugar, leather for footwear, material for dresses, buttons, and thread. He would solder cans and fill them with lard. Then when his collection was complete he would seat himself one evening in the center of his hut and spread around him all the precious gifts. He would lovingly take up each one, calculating the pleasure it should bring, and arrange them all in careful order in a carton, each gift a gift of love from a loving father, linking a chain of hearts from continent to continent.

He would sometimes envision what would happen if he returned home. How would he enter? How would he act? What would their first words be? Would they know him? Better not tell them. He has aged a lot. They might not recognize him. He will approach them as a stranger, see how they live, how they manage. He will ask about the father, whether the older children remember, whether they long for him. . . . He will enjoy seeing tears of sadness in their eyes. Then he will tell them—surprise!—and transform their sadness to joy, and dry their tears. His wife should recognize him. True, he has changed, but then so must she have too. The years do their work; we are not the same as we were. But the soul is young, and love is fresh forever. . . . So he would dream as he packed his boxes.

25

The Camp in Kondoa

The large bus was carrying me into the depths of Tanganyika, to the Polish refugee camp in Kondoa, where I was to conduct a week-long retreat. It was the start of my first year in Africa, November 1947, the beginning of summer when the hot dry air forces every living thing to seek shade; this air, pulsing through the windows, and the monotonous hum of the engine were making me sleepy. I looked out over the sprawling flatland of the steppe, hopelessly bare, sun-scorched, and ugly. Many areas in Africa have no charm at all.

As the only white person, I had been given the privileged seat beside the driver, a taciturn Hindu. Behind us, wearing a muslin sari, was a Hindu woman with her husband; and in the rear behind a partition were the Negroes, cooped up like chickens in a hen house. The bus stopped every so often to pick up a new passenger, who caused considerable commotion in the back compartment while getting settled. The squawking of hens being carried to market was deafening; tied down with string, they made one huge, noisy, struggling mass of feathers, fighting with the people for space.

Gradually the human noise subsided. Conversations became quieter, occasionally broken by an outburst of merriment. With his equanimity and readiness to laugh and frolic, the African Negro seems seldom troubled by such crowded conditions.

I had left Tengeru in the early morning and had rattled along on the bus for half a day on uneven sandy roads. We were travelling through the lowlands, the breeding ground of the tse-tse fly, where enormous virgin forests had been cut down to discourage it. Only here and there were a few solitary trees, giant baobabs. Cattle not afflicted by sleeping sickness were usually driven to more distant, healthier parts of the country.

On entering and leaving this infested area we were held up at disinfecting stations. The bus drove into a long shed, the "askari" (military officer) quickly locked the door, and other black attendants walked around the bus spraying clouds of liquid DDT, its acrid smell irritating the nostrils.

Further along the road the driver pointed out a Negro bee-hive hut and explained that one time a young married couple living there had been attacked by a decrepit lion, unable to hunt antelopes. When the lion managed to jump through the window, the terrified couple ran, but the lion caught up with them and felled the young woman with one stroke of his paw. The husband ran away in terror.

This reminded me of the story told by a missionary about the "lion men," natives dressed in lion skins who, encouraged by sorcerers, attacked the inhabitants of a village not far from our route. They would mutilate the bodies of their victims, mostly women and children, with lions' claws to simulate a lion's attack and divert suspicion from themselves. Finally one of several women attacked while going to the stream for water managed to escape; she told her fellow villagers, who had for years lived in terror, of the truly remarkable lions who could stand on their hind legs. This clue convinced the police that they were dealing with a gang of criminals, and soon all the "lion men" were apprehended, convicted, and executed in Dodoma in central Tanzania.

Close to Kondoa the soil became more sandy and brick-red, criss-crossed by wide seasonal rivers now dry but torrential during the rainy season after a downpour. Their banks were covered by some miserable bushes whose thick leaves store enough moisture to carry them through the dry season.

Toward evening I could admire the flames of a steppe fire fed by the wind, and the dark silhouettes of blacks looking like spirits as they set more and more grass on fire, to cover the farthest fields. Wild breezes rocked this sea of flames, twisted them into angry coils, combed them out, and scattered great galaxies of

Bishop Joseph Gawlina of England visits Polish orphanage in Karkin Batasz (Death Valley), Siberia, 1942. (Courtesy: J. Hoffman)

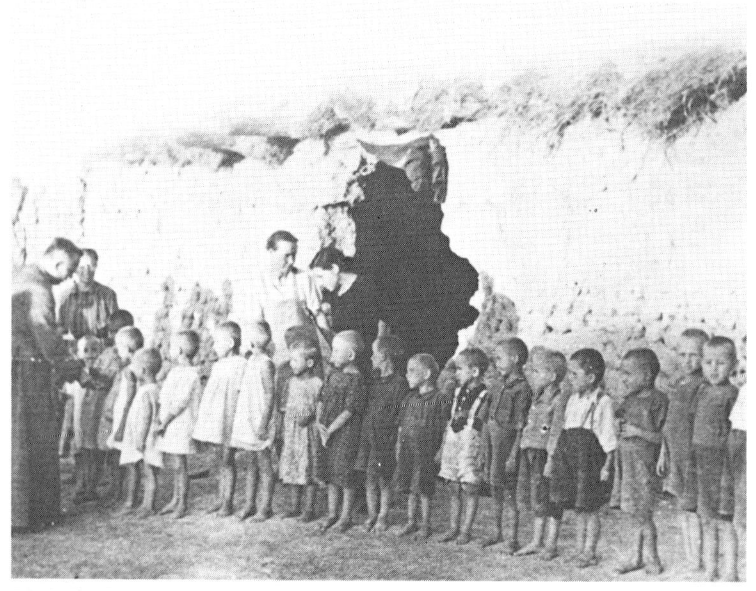

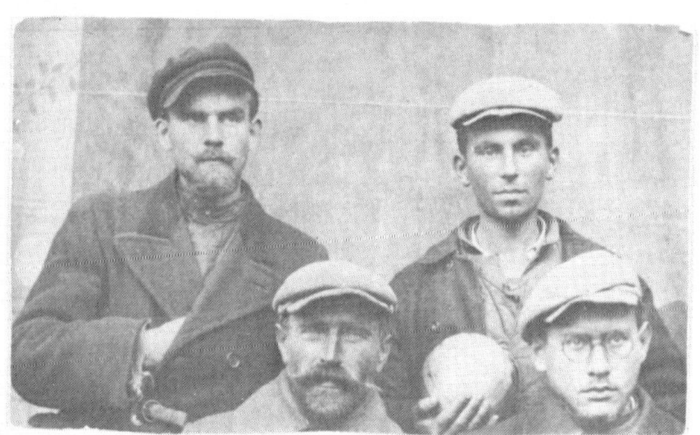

Liberated from labor camp, Soviet Russia, Nov. 1941 Fr. Lucjan at right-front. (Author's collection)

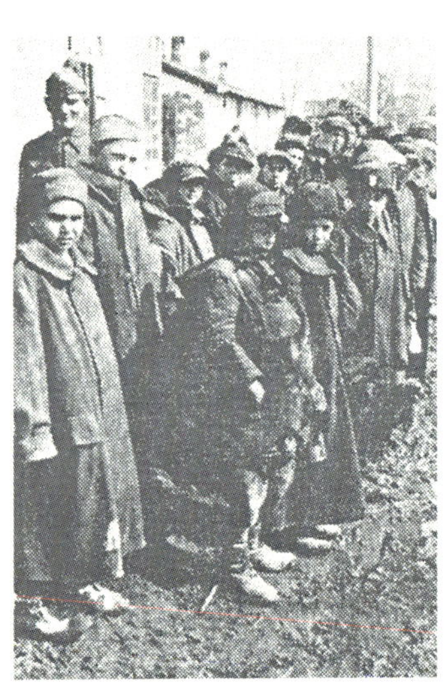

Under the Polish Army protection. 1942. (Veritas collection)

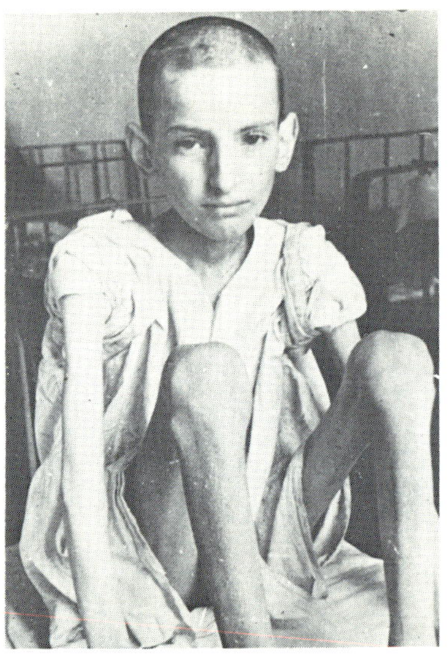

Recuperation after Russia in Teheran Hospital, Iran, 1942. (Author's collection)

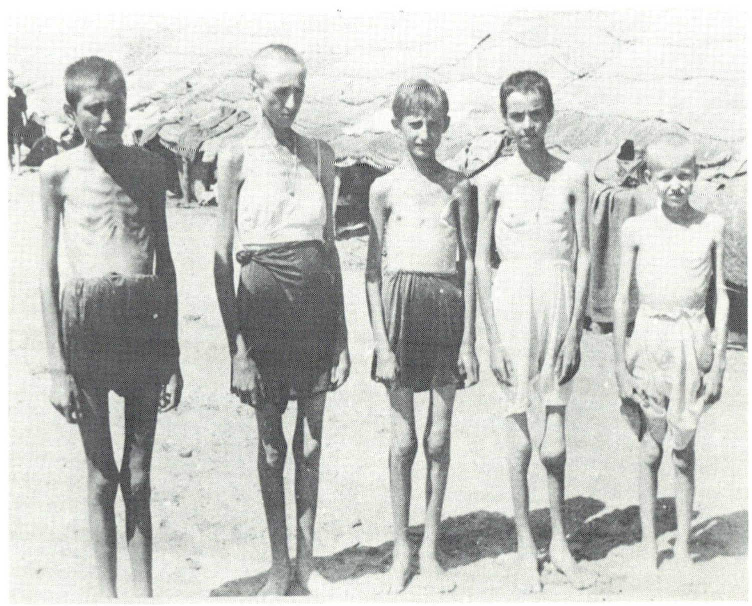

Polish children on the shores of the Caspian Sea, Iran, 1942. After escape from Russia. (Author's collection)

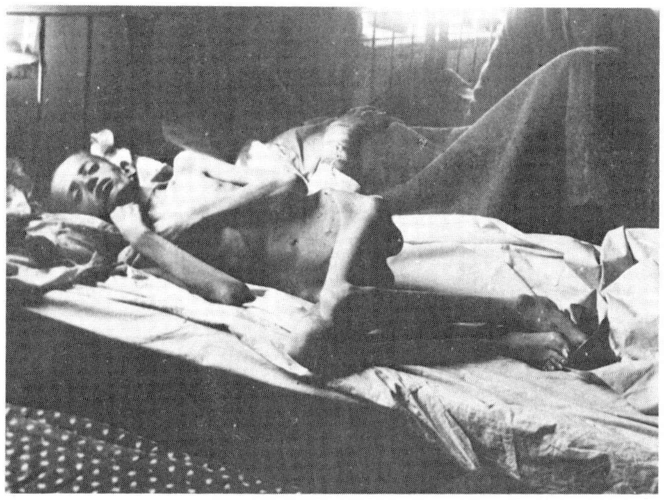

Recuperating from Russian Escape. Teheran Hospital, Iran, 1942. (Author's collection)

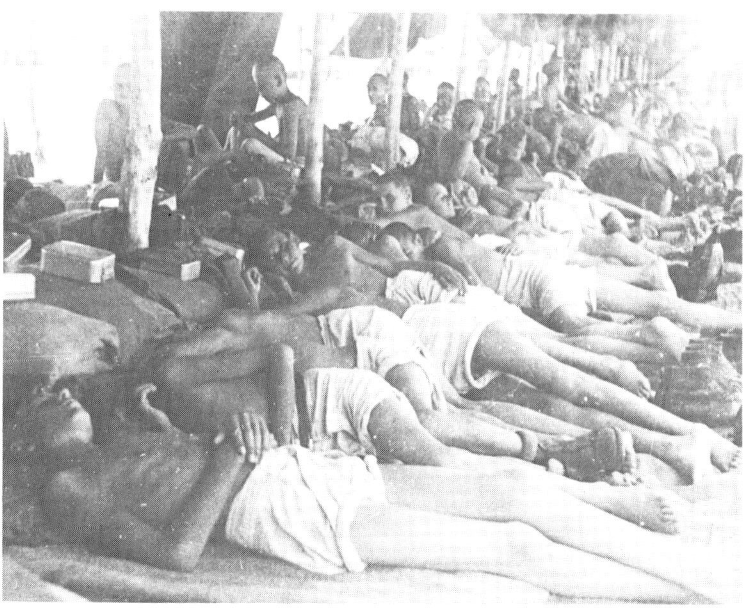

Polish youngsters rest upon arrival from Russia. Pahlavi Transit Camp, Iran, 1942. (Author's collection)

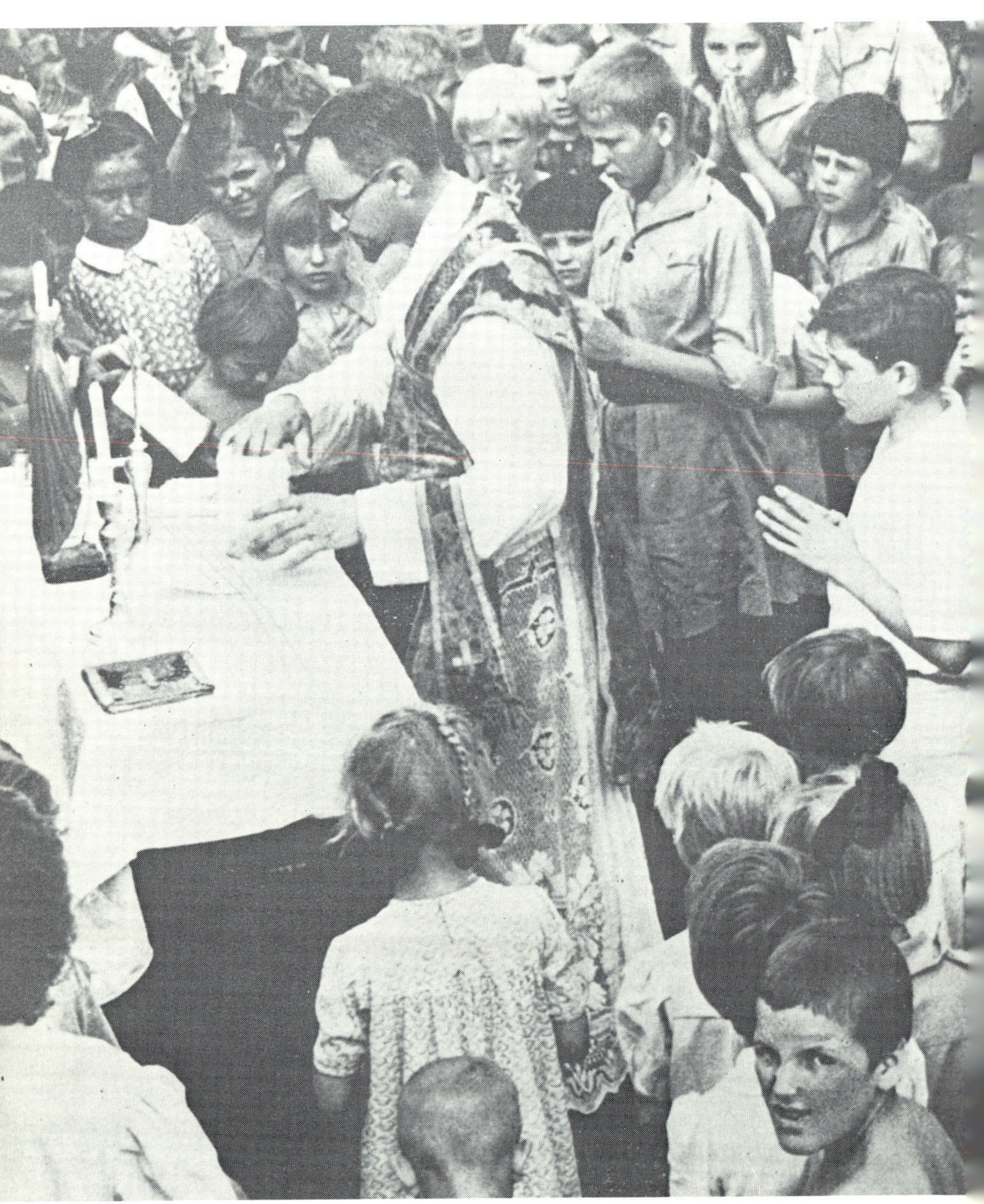

Shipboard Mass on the way to New Zealand. Indian Ocean, 1942. (Author's collection)

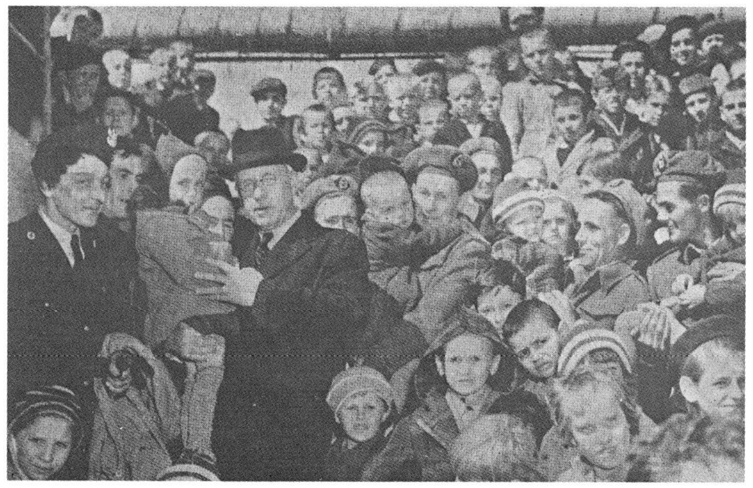

Government Representatives of New Zealand welcome Polish orphans on their arrival from Soviet Russia, 1942. (Author's collection)

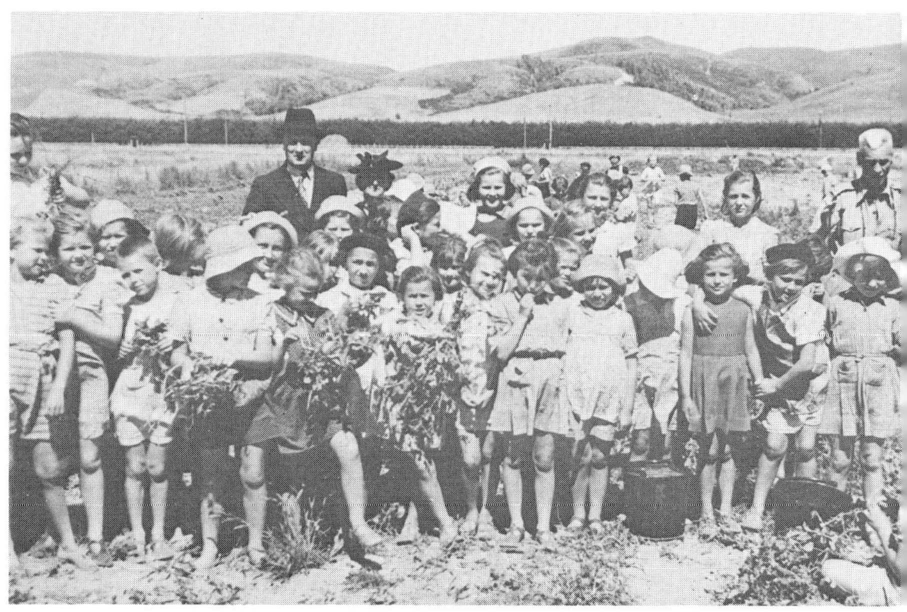

Polish orphans on New Zealand soil. Just arrived from Soviet Russia, 1942. (Author's collection)

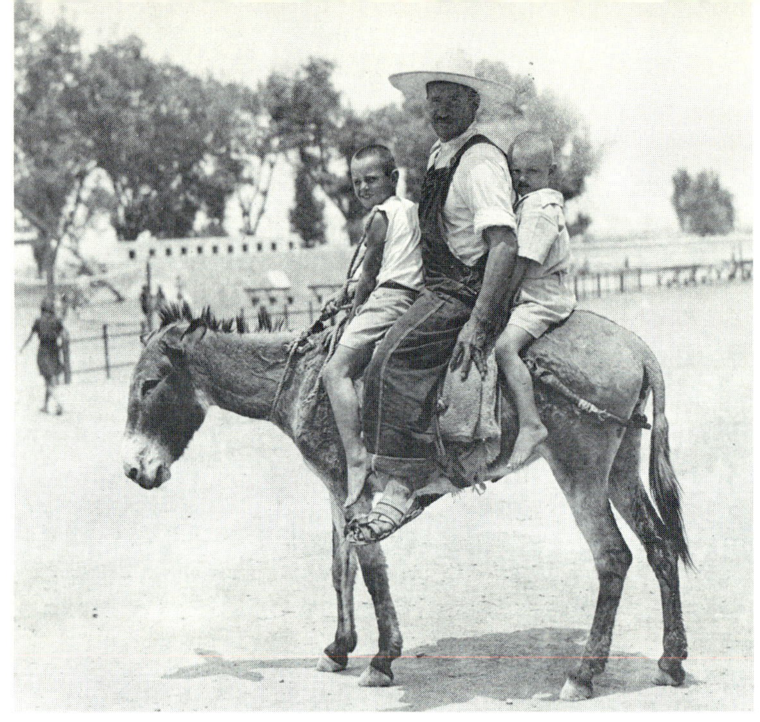

Polish youngsters with Mexican farmer. Santa Rosa, 1942. (Courtesy: Felician Sisters)

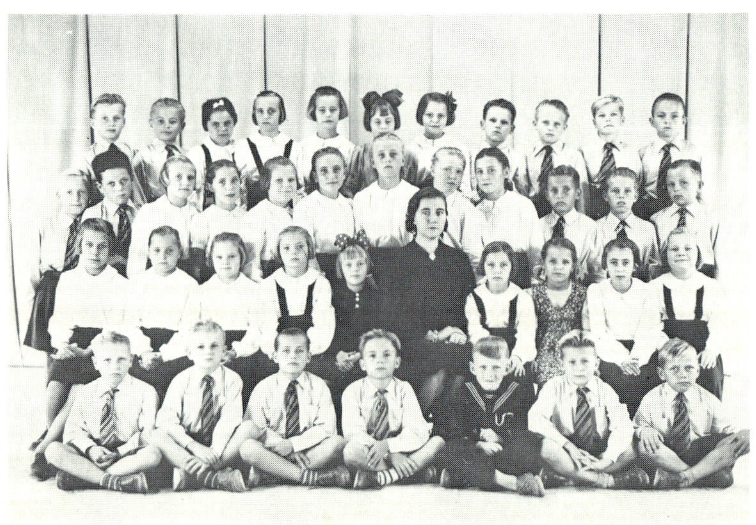

Santa Rosa, Mexico, 1945. Fifth graders with their teacher. (Courtesy: Teresa Kmiec-Wryk)

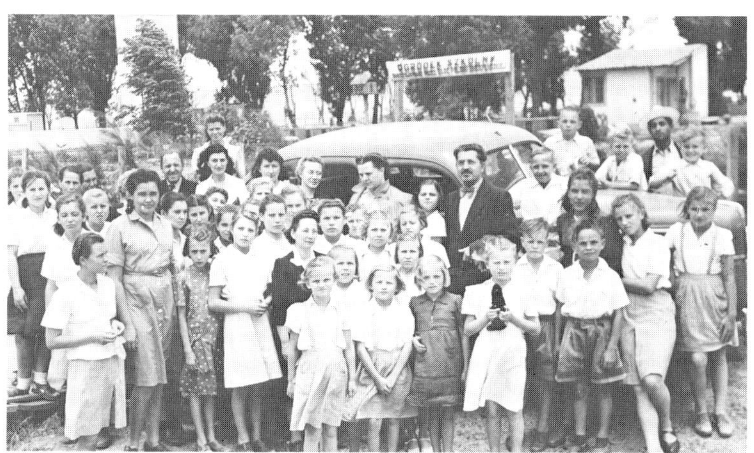

Santa Rosa, Mexico, 1945. Orphans bid farewell to their tutor, Sr. D'arc, a Felician nun, returning to Chicago. (Courtesy: Teresa Kmiec-Wryk)

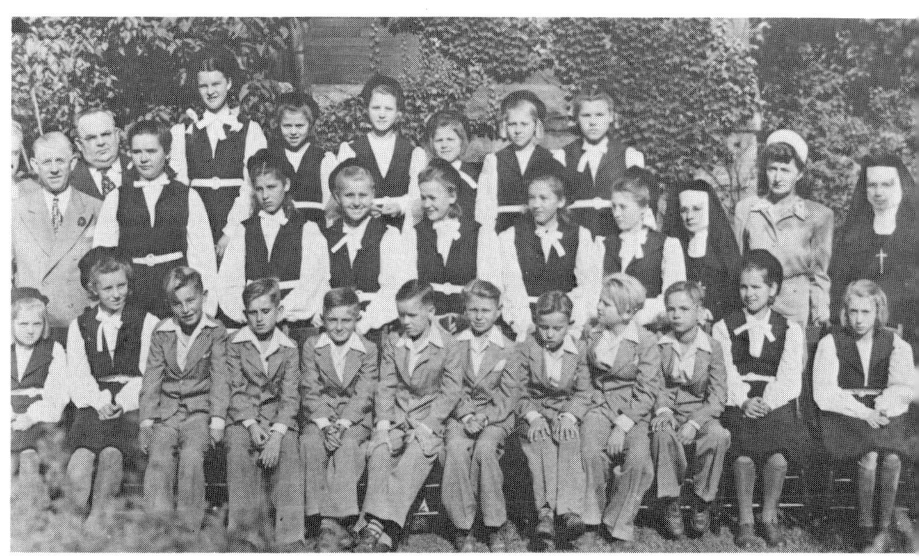

Orphans brought to Buffalo, N.Y., U.S.A. by the Felician nuns after liquidation of Santa Rosa Children's Camp in Mexico, 1945. (Courtesy: Mrs. Harriet (Bugiera) Duffie)

Inscription of evergreen hedges, 1942. Marks year of arrival of orphans in Africa, Tengeru Camp and Mount Meru. (Photo: M. Dobosz)

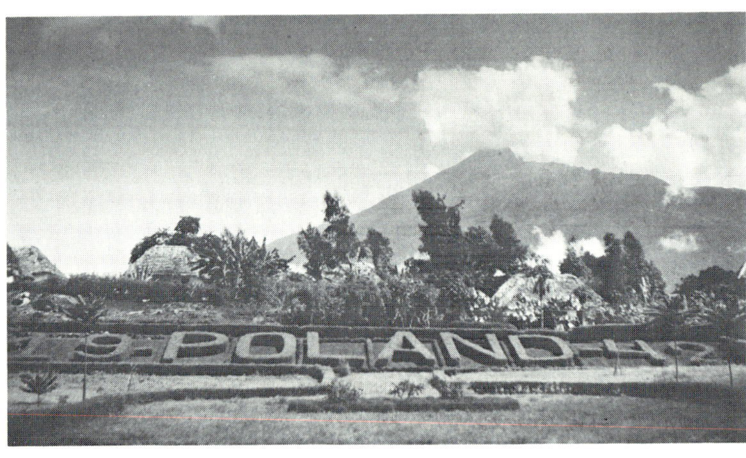

Sixth graders of Tengeru Camp, 1943. Second year after escape from Russia. School buildings in background. (Courtesy: J. Fulmyk-Lorenc)

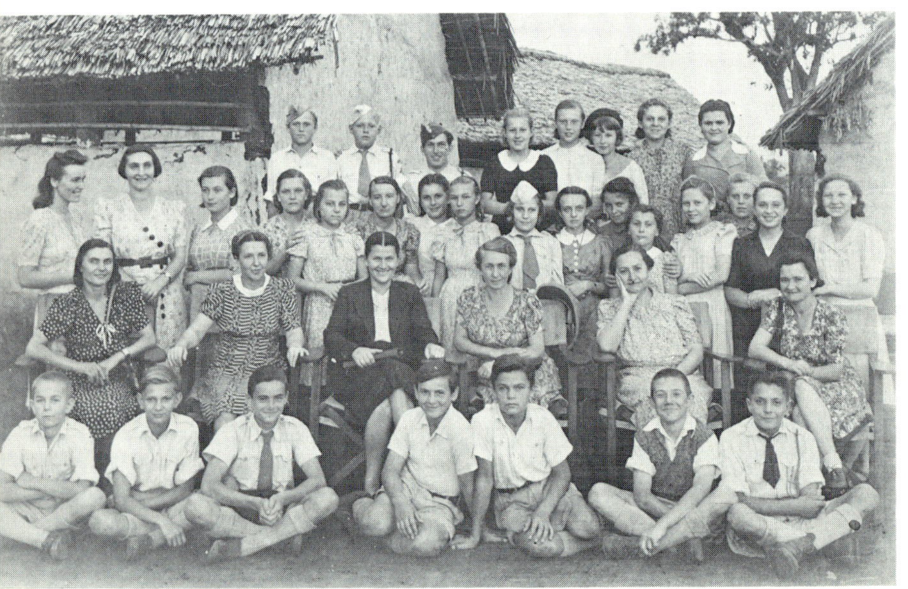

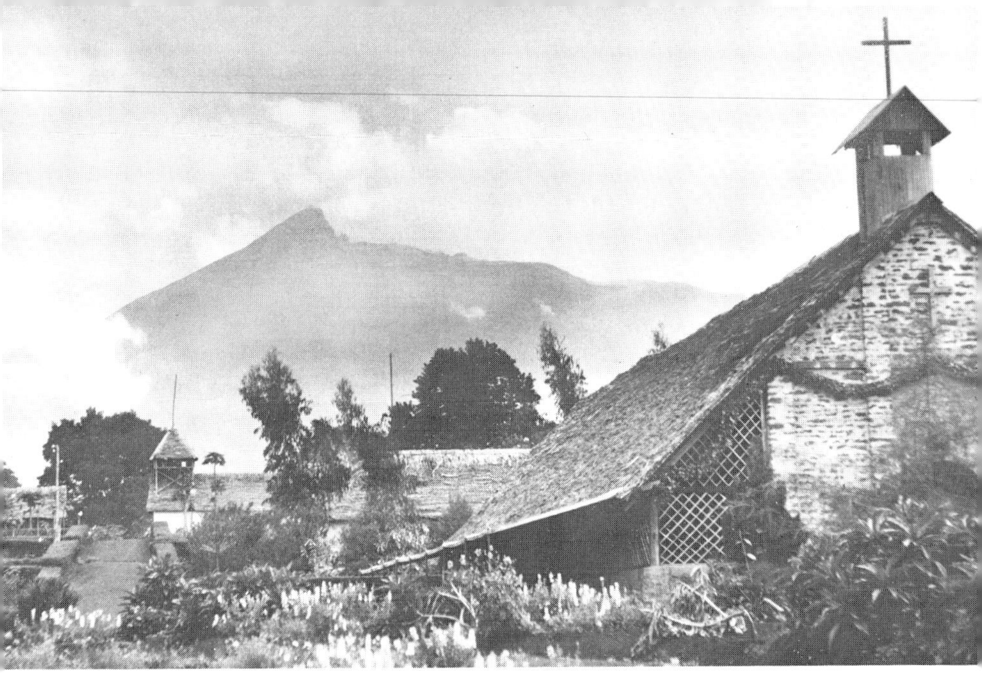

Tengeru Camp church and Meru Mountain, 1949. (Photo: Mr. M. Dobosz)

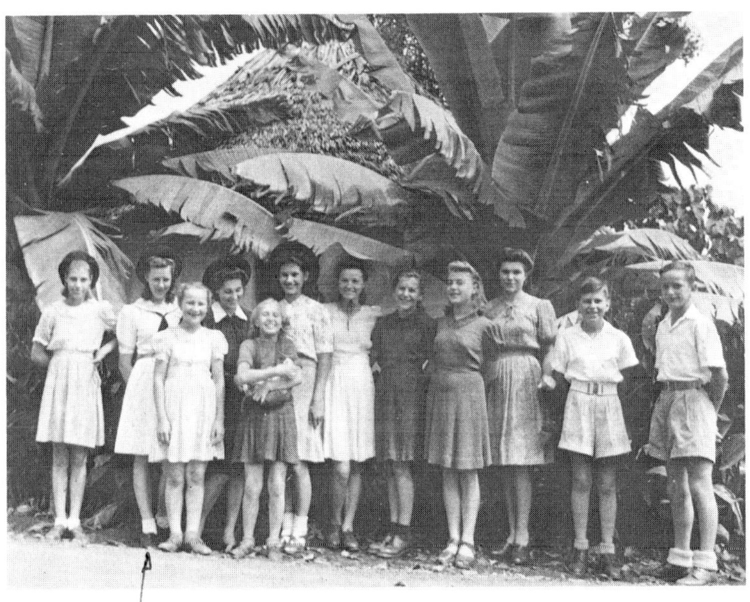

Sunday morning, Tengeru Camp, 1946. (Courtesy: J. Miszuta-Petit)

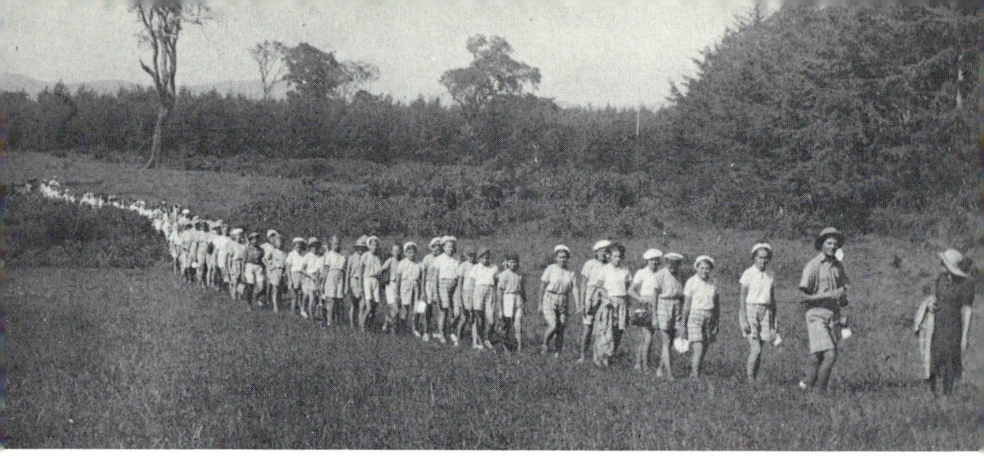

Safari to the bush. Tengeru Camp, 1946. (Courtesy: J. Miszuta-Petit)

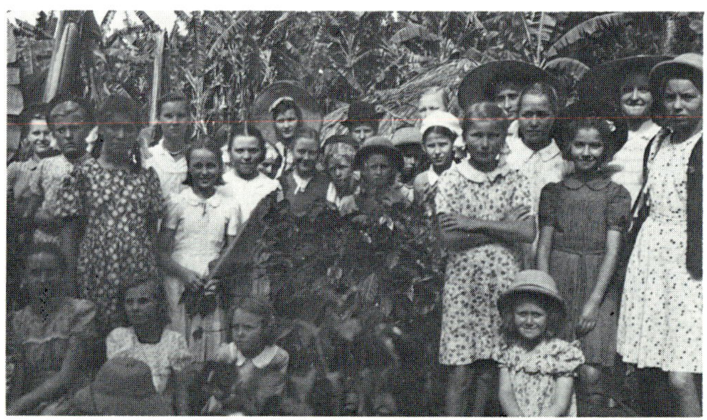

On the banana plantation near Tengeru Camp, 1948. (Photo: Fr. Lucjan)

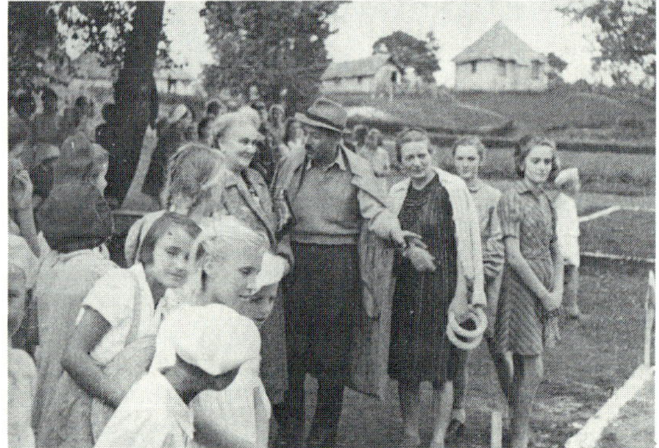

Mrs. Grosicka and orphans. Tengeru Camp, 1946. (Courtesy: J. Miszuta-Petit)

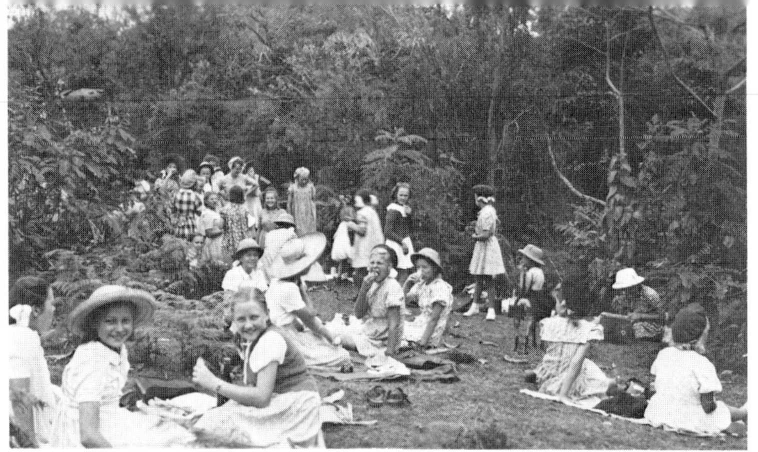

Picnic near Tengeru Camp at the foot of Mt. Meru Tanzania. (Photo: Fr. Lucjan)

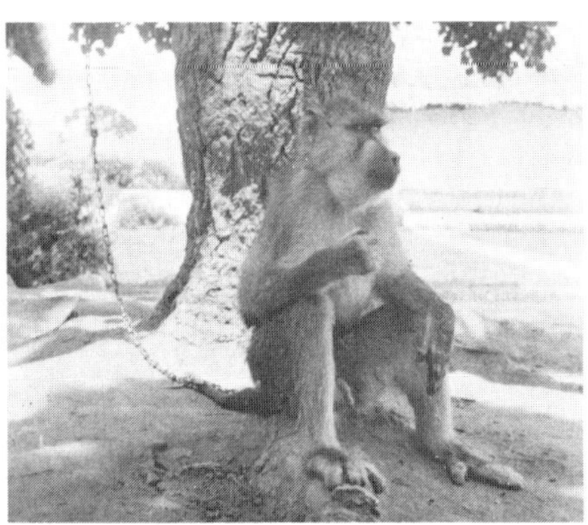

Tengeru Camp, children's mascot. (Author's collection)

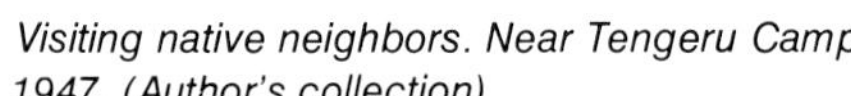

Visiting native neighbors. Near Tengeru Camp, 1947. (Author's collection)

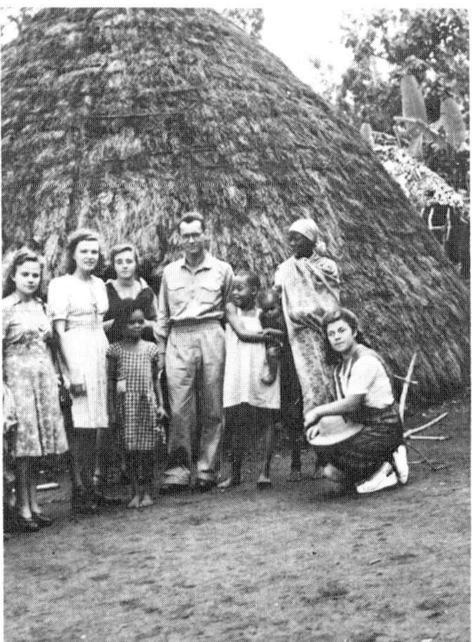

Fr. Lucjan's hut. Tengeru Camp, 1948. (Author's collection)

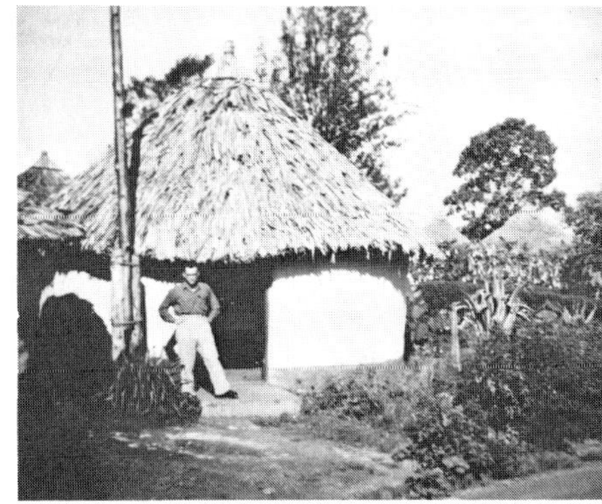

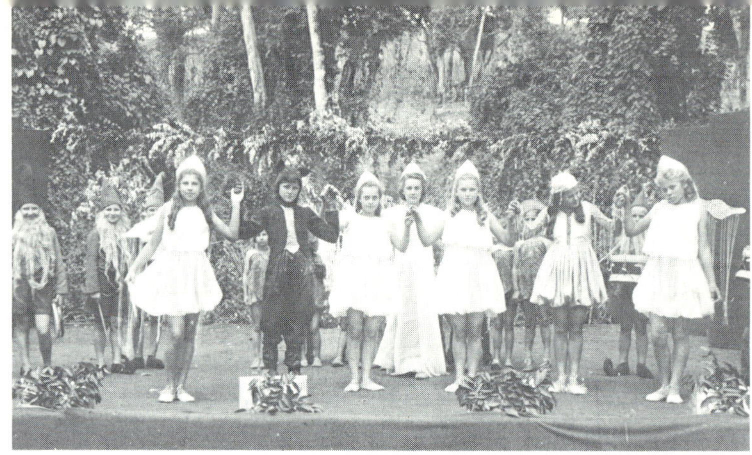

Theatre in the jungle. Tengeru Camp, 1947. (Courtesy: E. Grosicka)

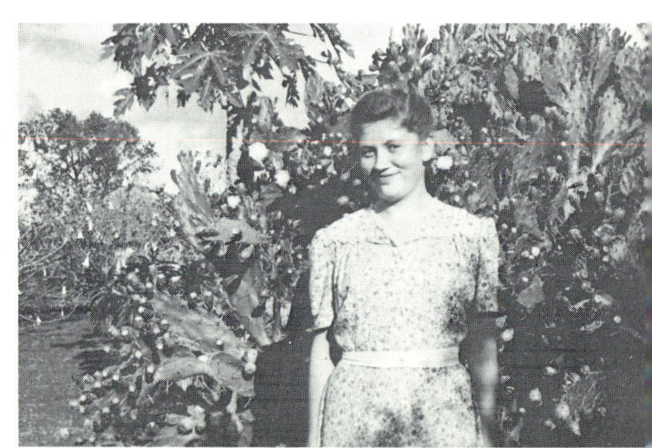

Lucja Dryganiuk among the cacti, Tengeru Camp, 1948. (Photo: Fr. Lucjan)

Theatre in the jungle. Tengeru Camp, 1947. (Courtesy: J. Miszuta-Petit)

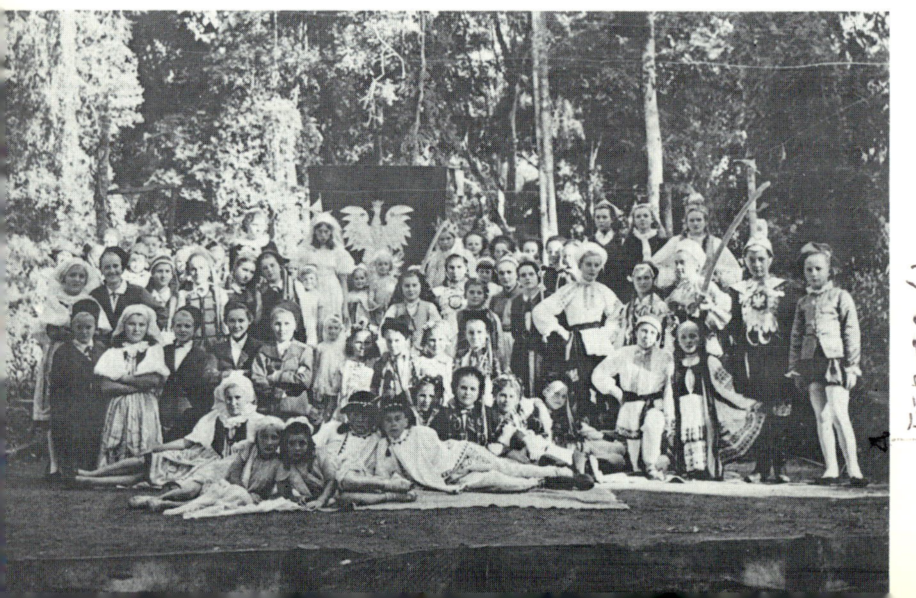

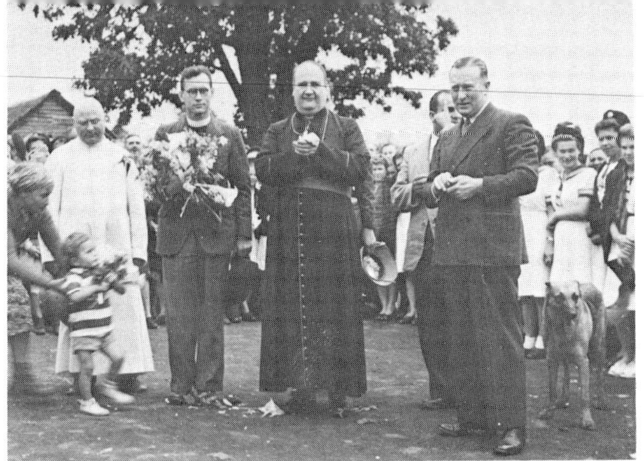

Apostolic Delegate, Archbishop David Mathew. Tengeru Camp, 1947. (Author's collection)

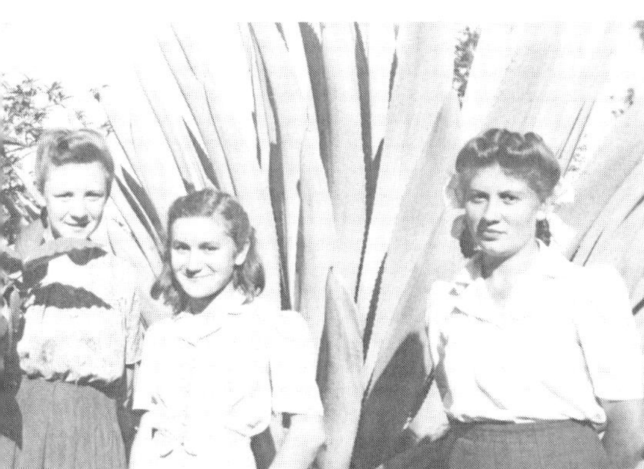

From left: Danuta Puzinowska, Janina Fin, Lucja Dryganiuk. Tengeru Camp, 1949. (Photo: Fr. Lucjan)

Our Lady's Sodality, 1947. Church provides background. Tengeru Camp, Tanganyika. (Photo: M. Dobosz)

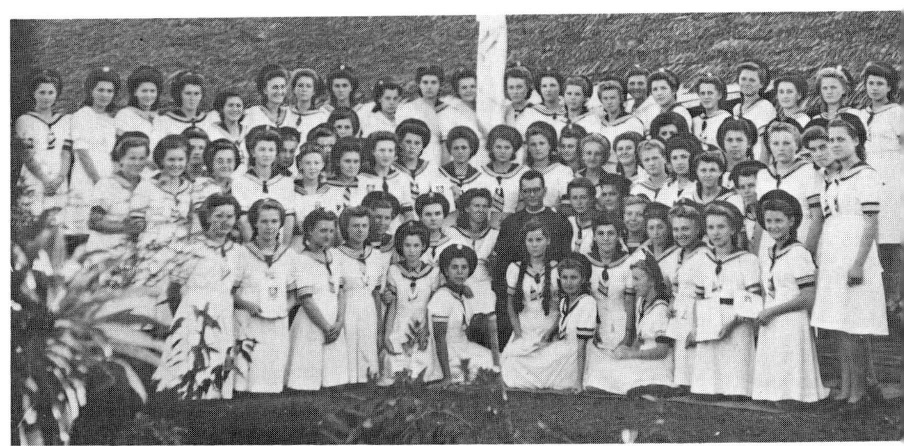

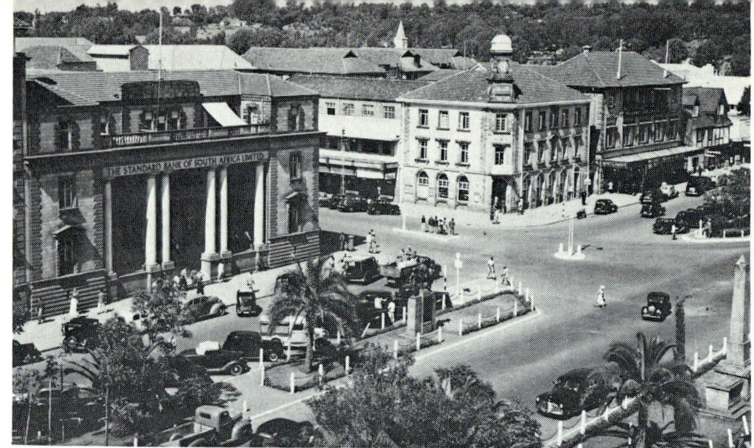

Nairobi, Kenya, where young people found work.

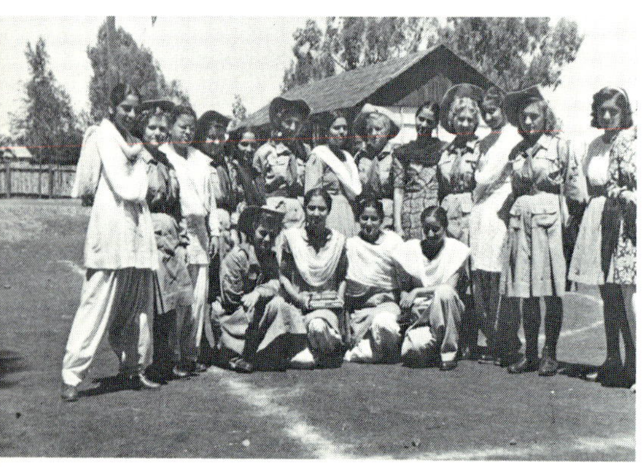

Polish girl scouts from Tengeru visiting Hindu girl scouts in Nairobi, 1949. (Author's collection)

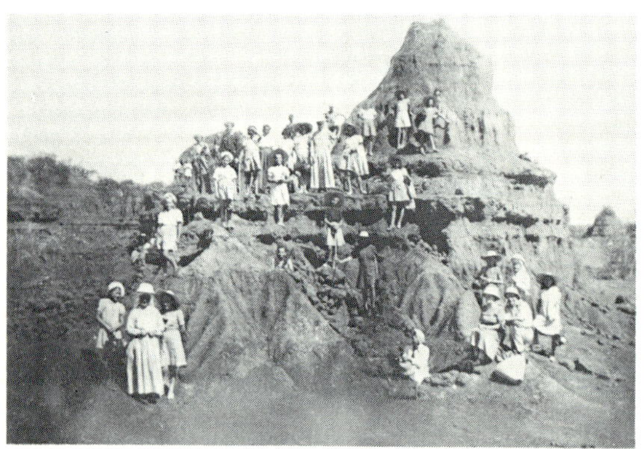

Children from Rongai Camp on a termite mound in Kenya. 1946. (Photo: H. Szumowski)

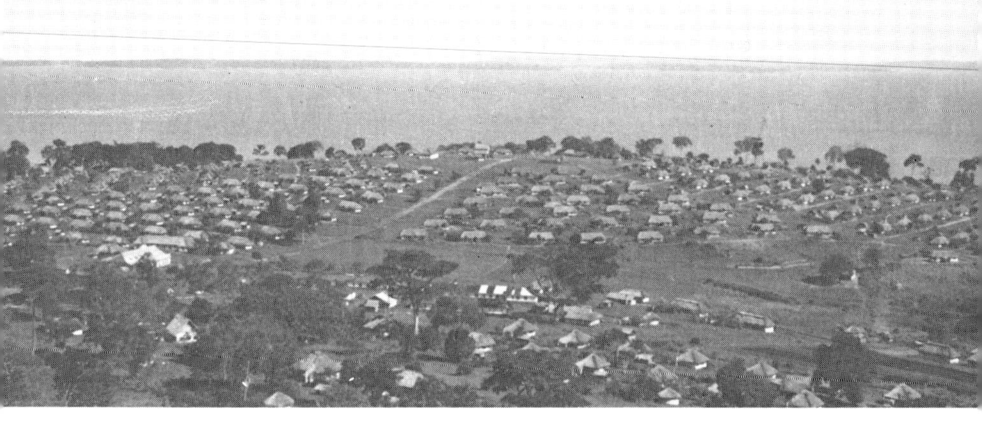

Koja, Refugee Camp, Uganda. Lake Victoria, 1949. (Photo: Fr. Lucjan)

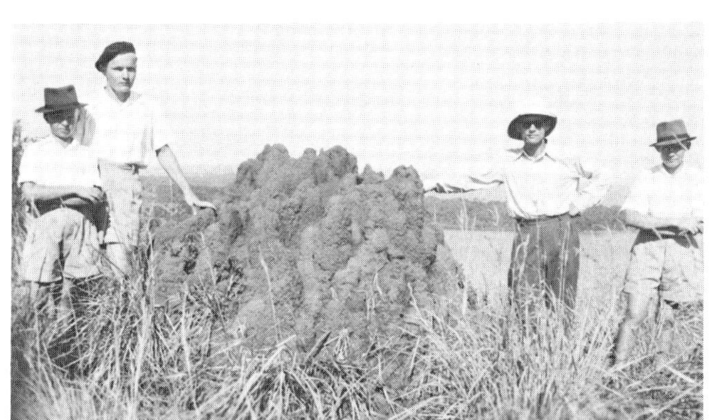

Termite house. Koja Camp, Uganda, 1949. (Author's collection)

Grave of Jurek Miedzyrzecki. Koja Camp in Uganda, 1947. (Photo: Fr. Lucjan)

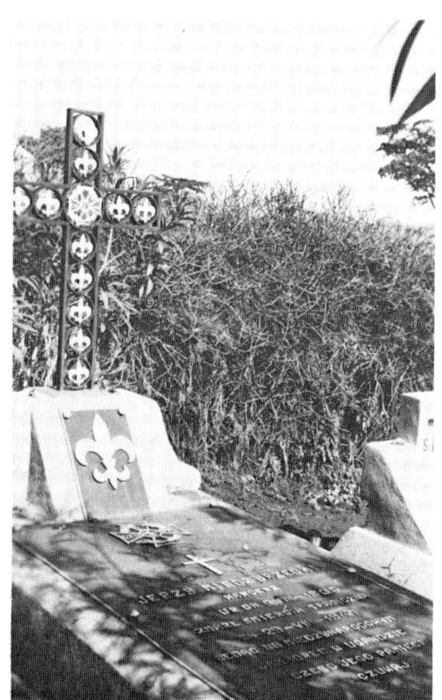

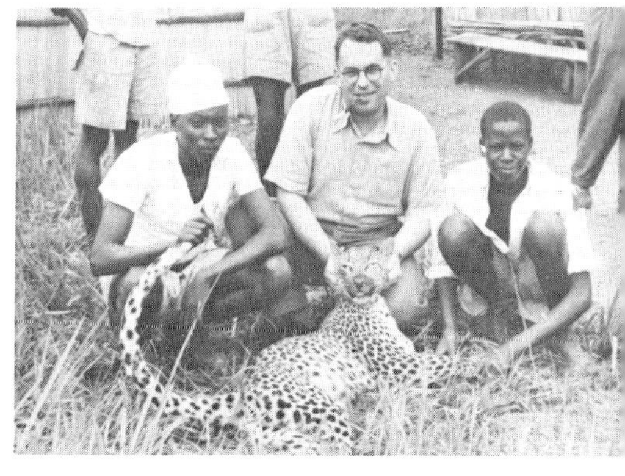

Fr. Ryszard Gruza with felled leopard. Uganda, 1951. (Author's collection)

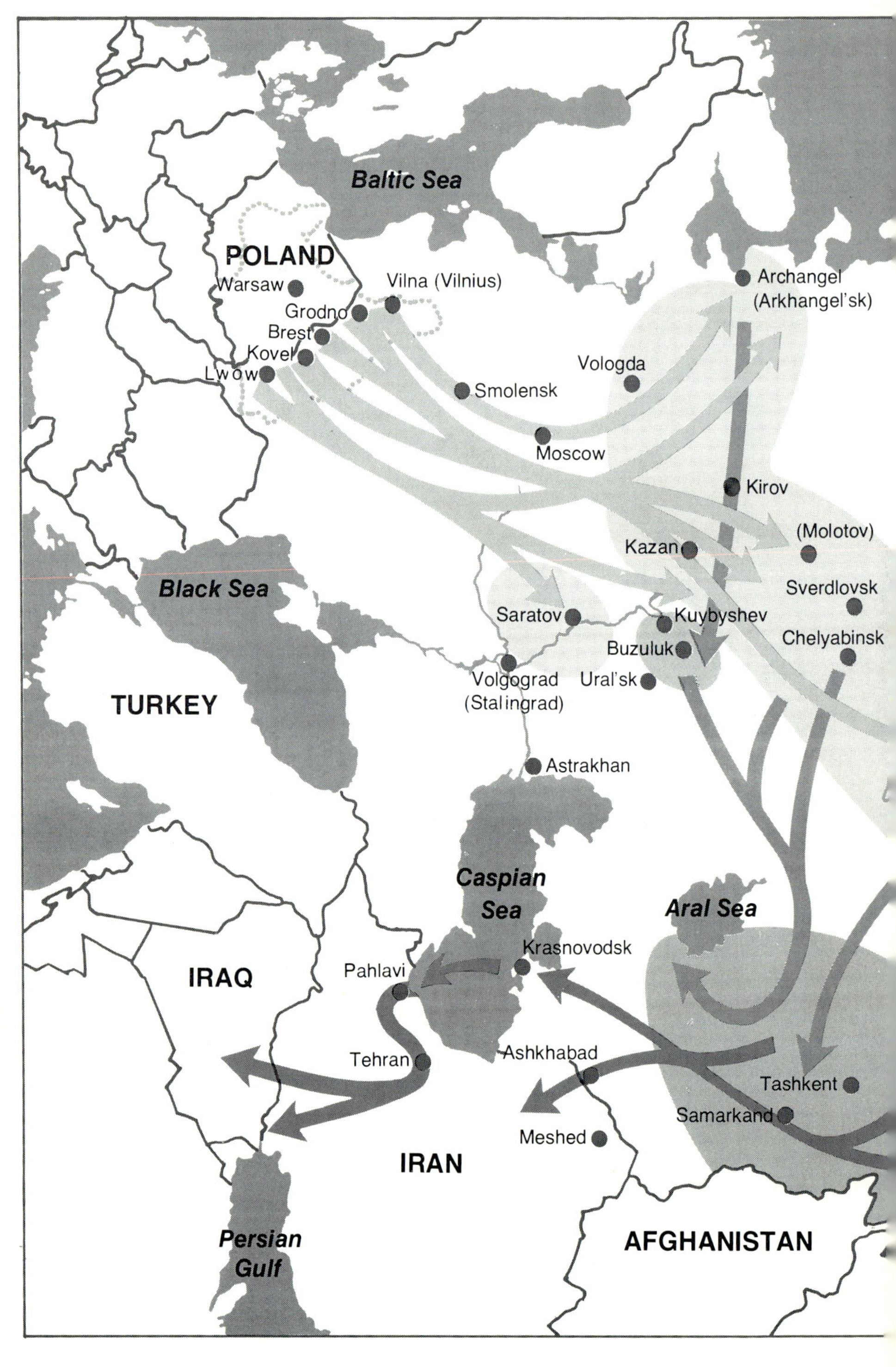

Baltic Sea
POLAND
Warsaw
Vilna (Vilnius)
Grodno
Brest
Kovel
Lwow
Archangel
(Arkhangel'sk)
Vologda
Smolensk
Moscow
Kirov
(Molotov)
Kazan
Sverdlovsk
Black Sea
Saratov
Kuybyshev
Buzuluk
Chelyabinsk
Volgograd
(Stalingrad)
Ural'sk
TURKEY
Astrakhan
Caspian
Sea
Aral Sea
Krasnovodsk
Pahlavi
IRAQ
Tehran
Ashkhabad
Tashkent
Samarkand
Meshed
IRAN
AFGHANISTAN
Persian
Gulf

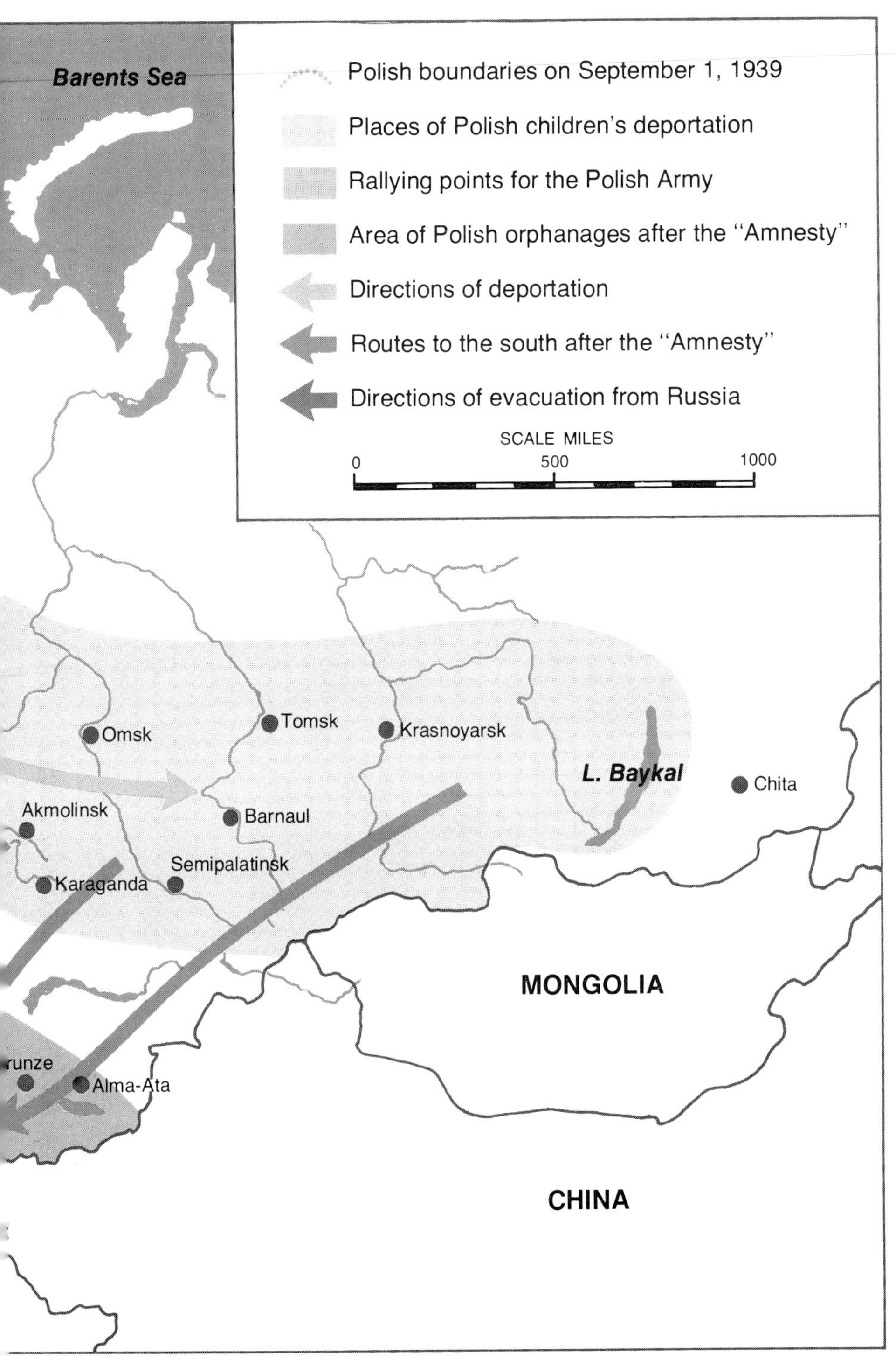

Places of Polish Children's deportation

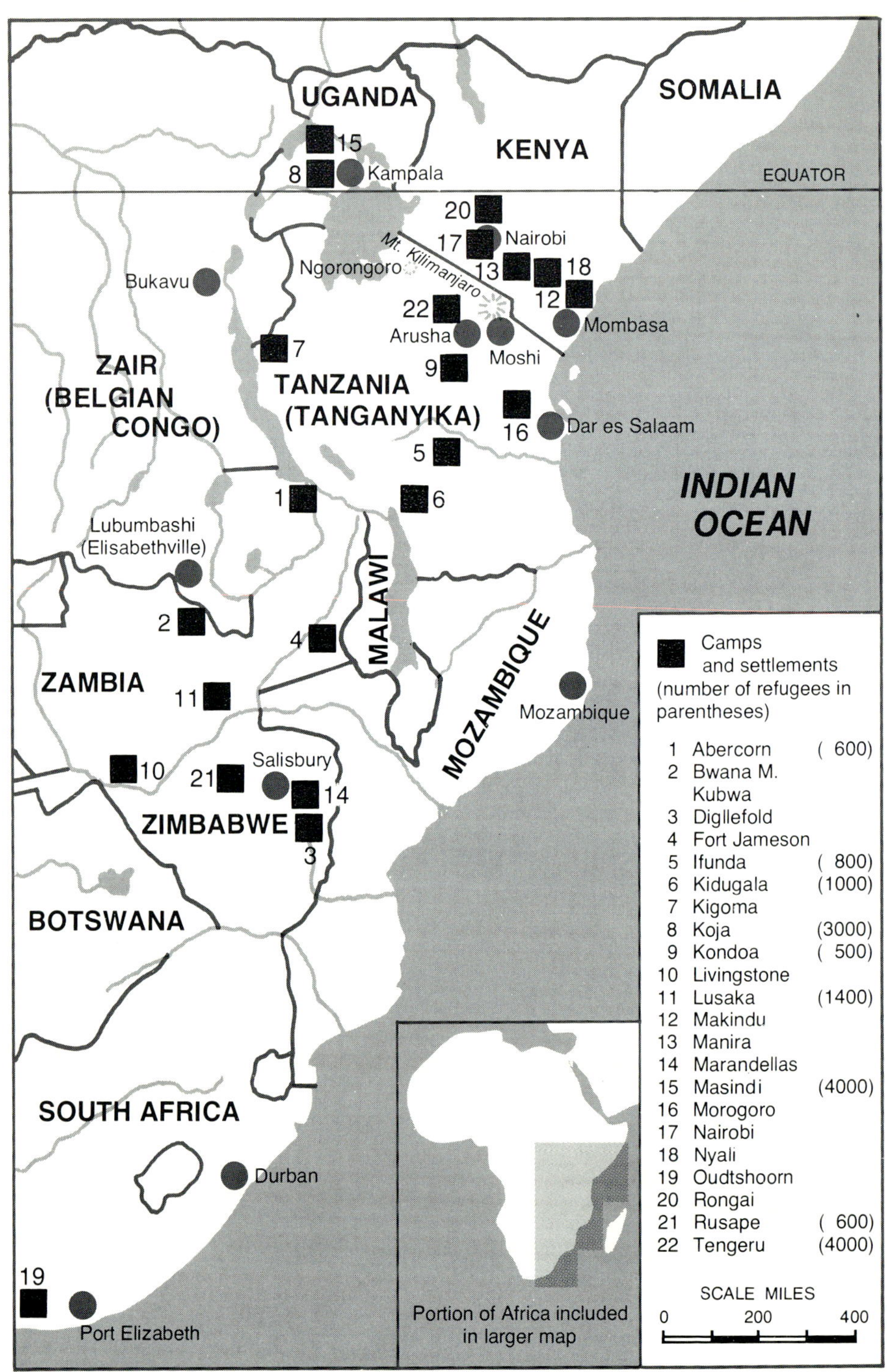

Polish Refugee Camps in Africa 1942-1950

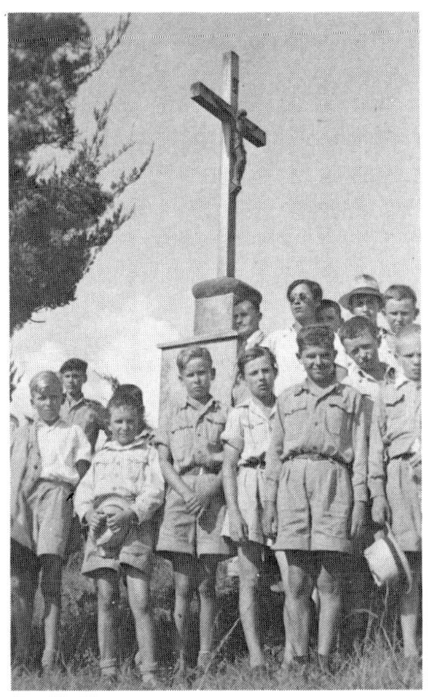

Kilema Catholic Mission. Mt. Kilimanjaro, 1949. (Photo: Fr. Lucjan)

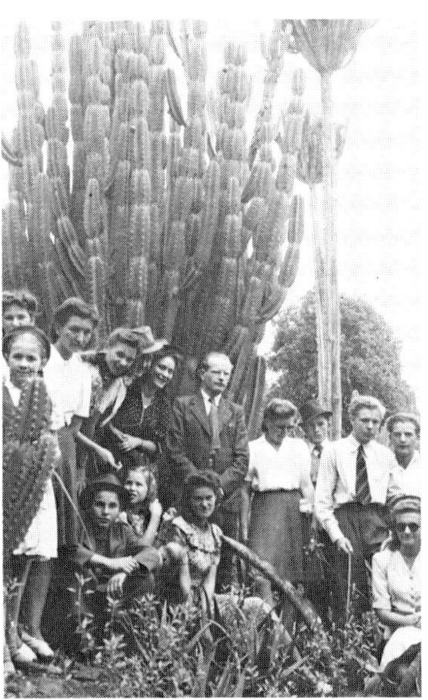

On Safari with Fr. Zeno Wierzbinski, 1948. (Photo: Fr. Lucjan)

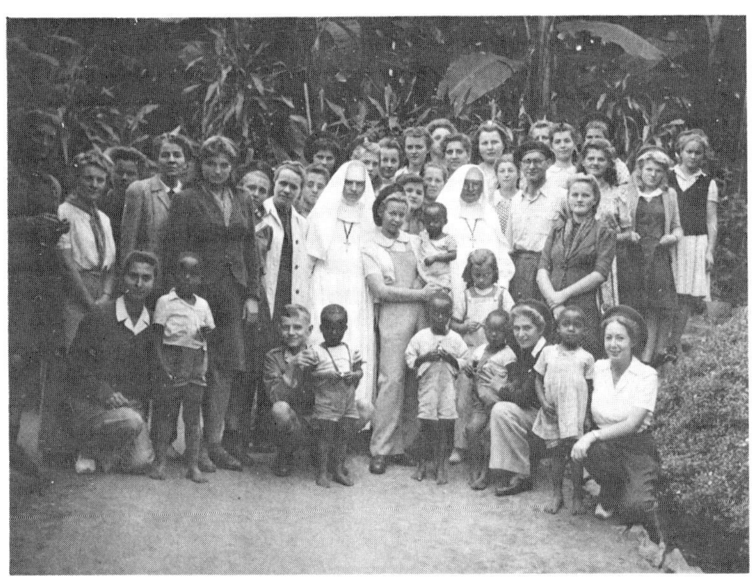

With Mother Matilda, 1948. Kilema Catholic Mission on the slopes of Mt. Kilimanjaro. (Author's collection)

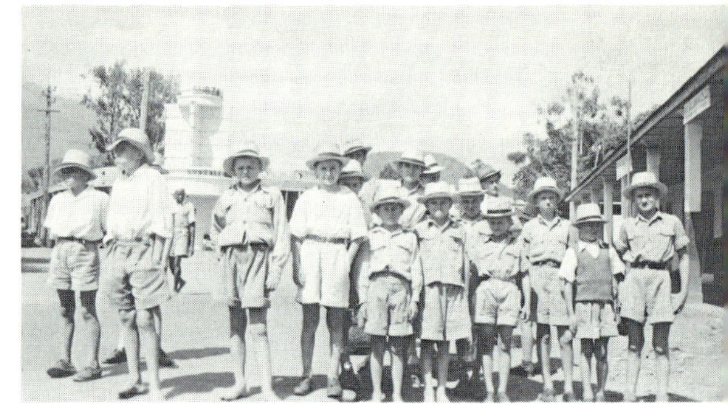

On an excursion. Arusha, Tanganyika, 1949. (Photo: Fr. Lucjan

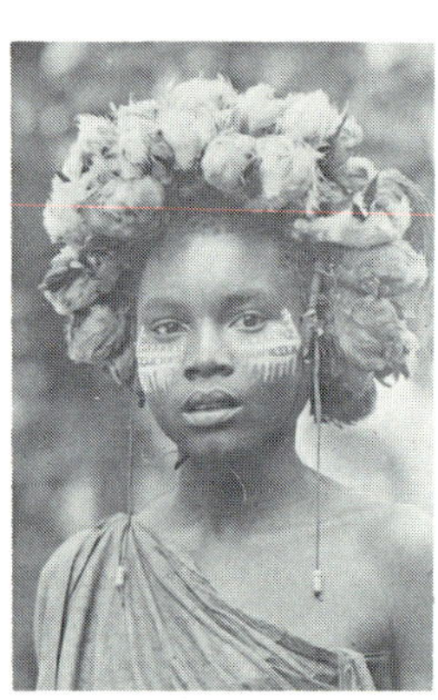

Native Boy in headgear of colorful birds, Arusha, Tanganyika. (Photo: Fr. Dziduszko)

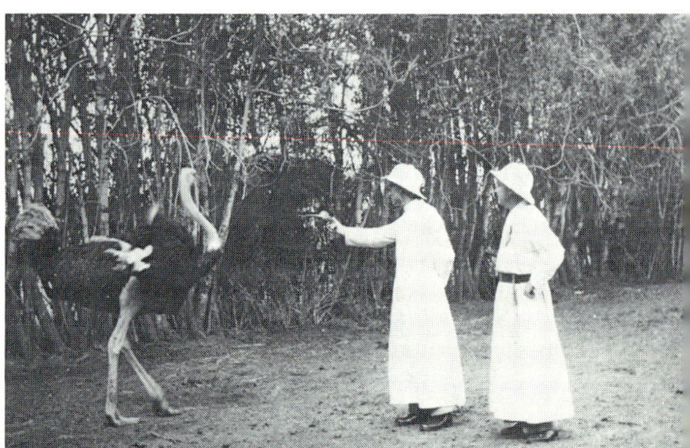

Kondoa Camp, 1948. Fr. Lucjan, Fr. Barbanelli, and domesticated ostrich. (Author's collection)

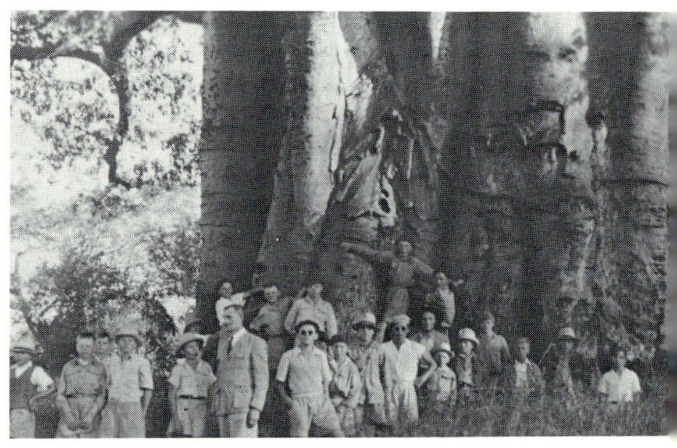

Under a baobab tree at foot of Mt. Kilimanjaro, 1949. (Photo: Fr. Lucjan)

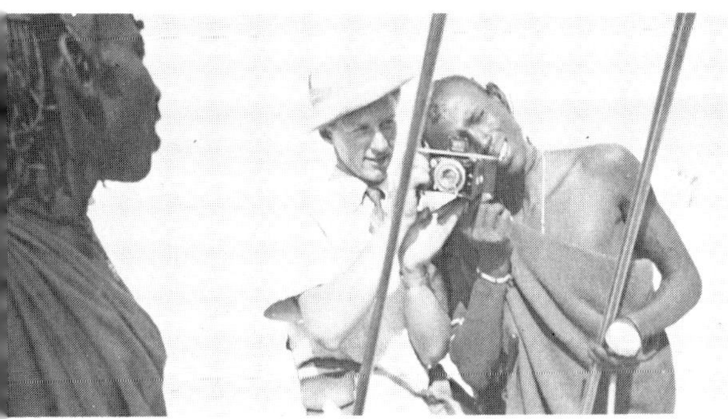

Our guides to Ngoro-Ngoro Crater, 1948.
(Photo: Fr. Lucjan)

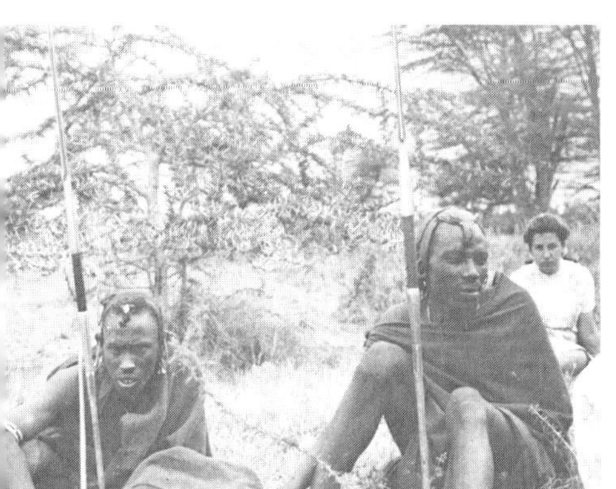

Our guides to Ngoro-Ngoro Crater, 1948.
(Photo: Fr. Lucjan)

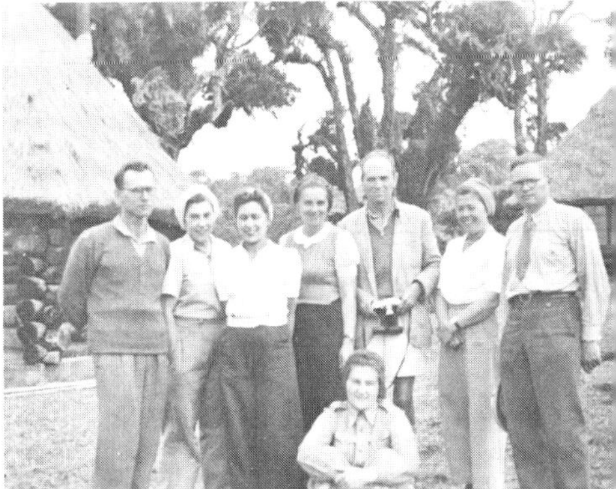

Teachers at tourist camp, Ngoro-Ngoro Crater.
Fr. Lucjan at left, 1948. (Author's collection)

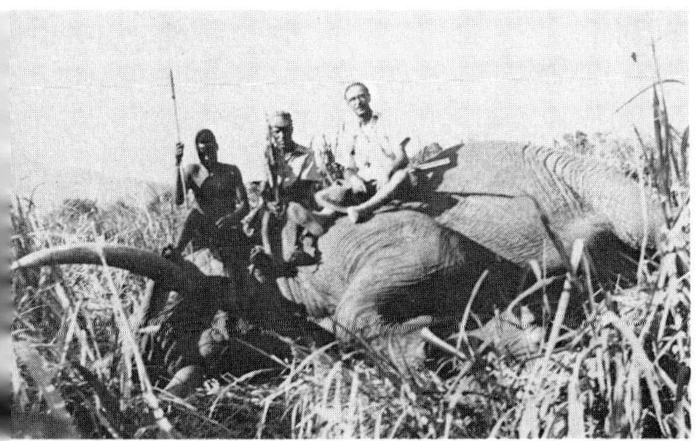

Our Dentist, Dr. Flach with just-killed
elephant, 1951. (Author's collection)

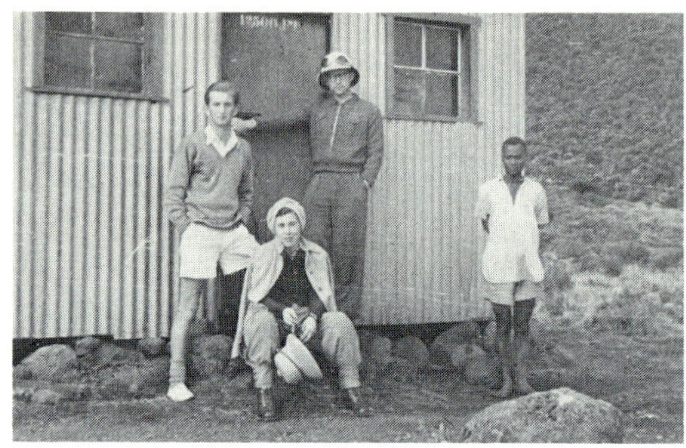

Climbing Mt. Kilimanjaro. Peters Hut at 12500 ft. T. A. Naylor, Miss Maria Sidor, Fr. Lucjan. 1949. (Photo: Prof. J. Hoffman)

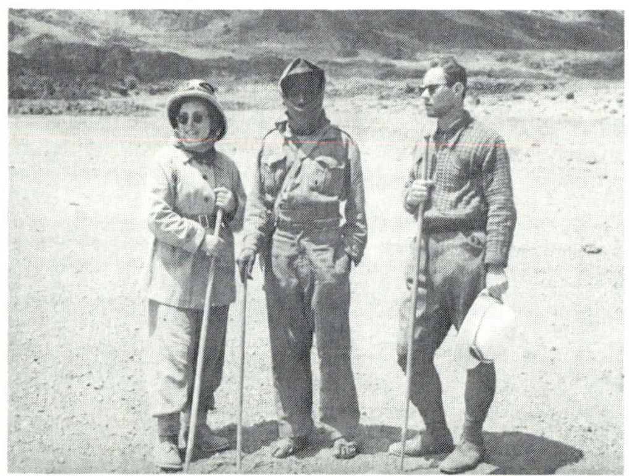

A desert high in the Kilimanjaro Range. Miss Maria Sidor, guide Johann, Fr. Lucjan. 1949. (Photo: Prof. J. Hoffman)

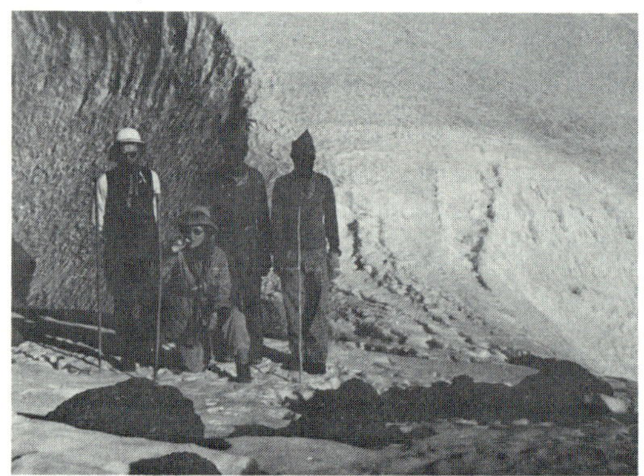

Glacier at top of Mt. Kilimanjaro. Fr. Lucjan and Mrs. Sidor and guides. Jan. 26, 1949. (Photo: Prof. J. Hoffman)

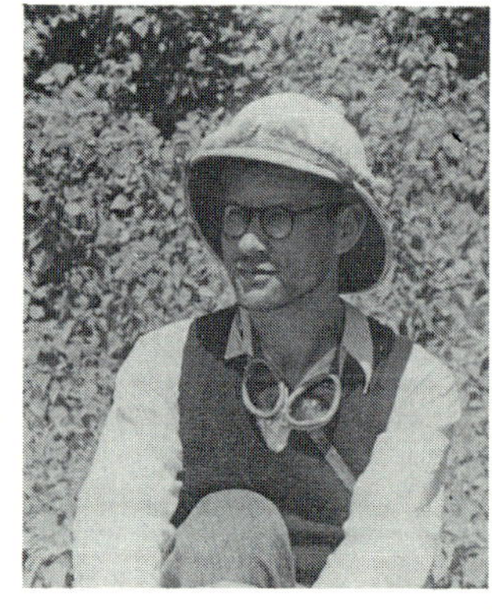

Fr. Lucjan after his return from Mt. Kilimanjaro. 1949. (Photo: Prof. J. Hoffman)

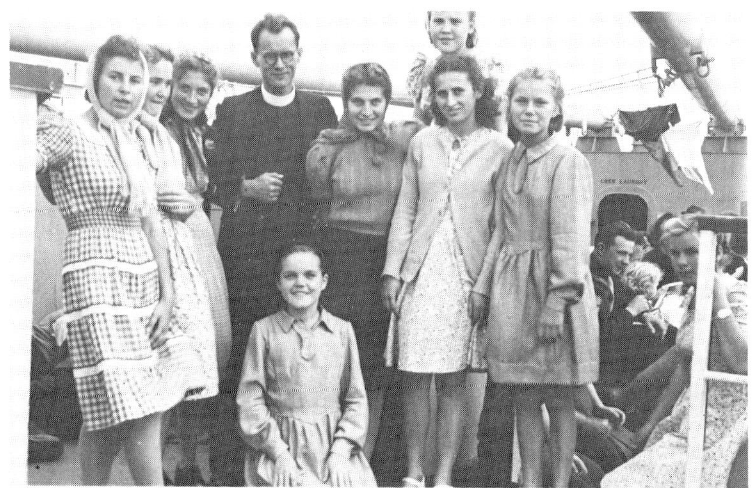

On the Deck of the SS Gerusalemme leaving Port Mombasa, Kenya, 1949. (Author's collection)

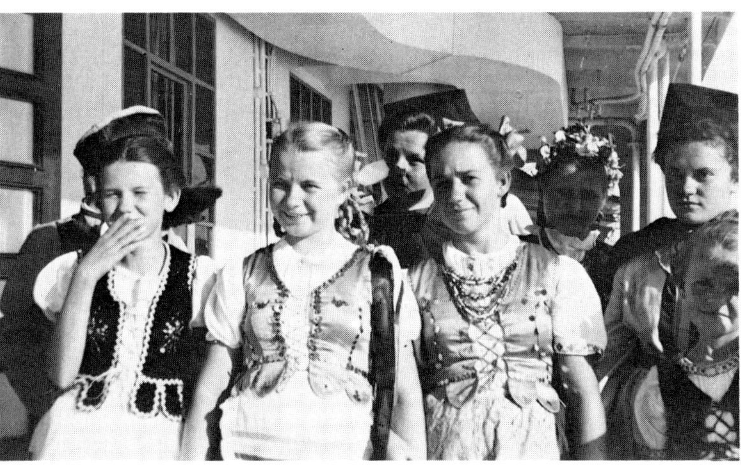

Performers in Polish regional costumes. SS Gerusalemme, Indian Ocean, 1949. From left: Krystyna Tymicka, Bronislawa Kusa, Irena Przychodzen, Zofia Matusiewicz, Kazimiera Chedoga, and Janina Papuga. (Photo: Fr. Lucjan)

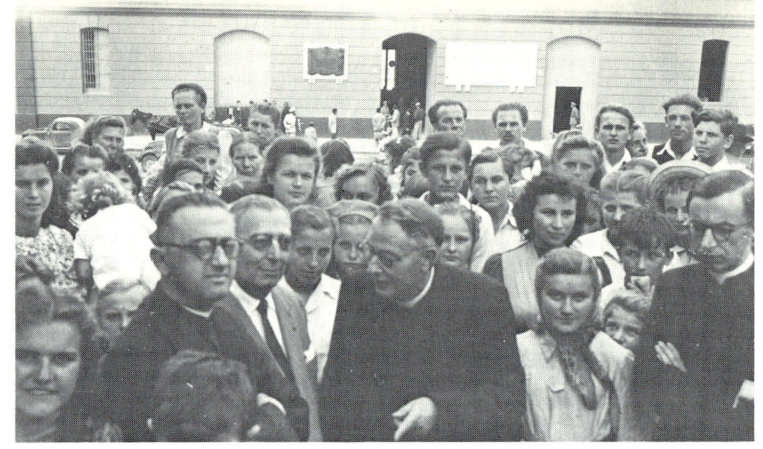

Church officials greet orphans. Port Bari, Italy, 1949. (Photo: Fr. Lucjan)

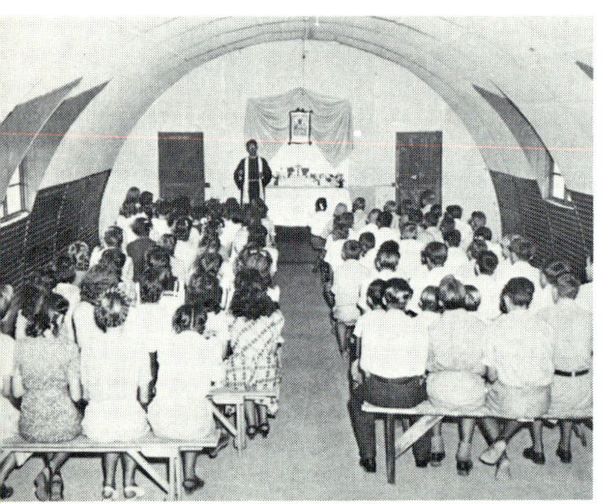

Fr. Lucjan preaching. Salerno, Italy, 1949. (Author's collection)

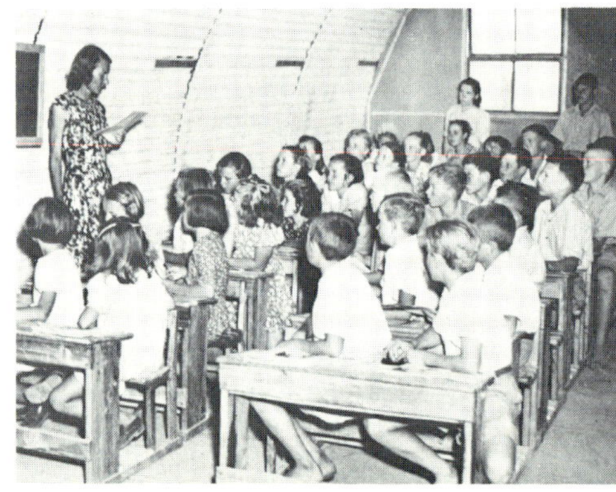

English lesson. Salerno refugee camp, 1949. (Author's collection)

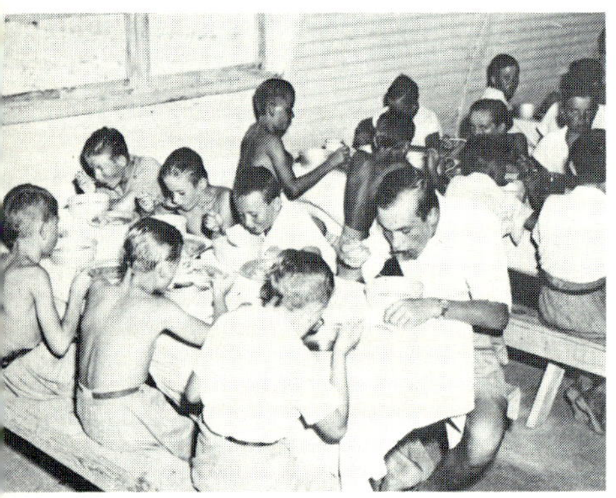

Lunch time. Salerno, 1949. (Author's collection)

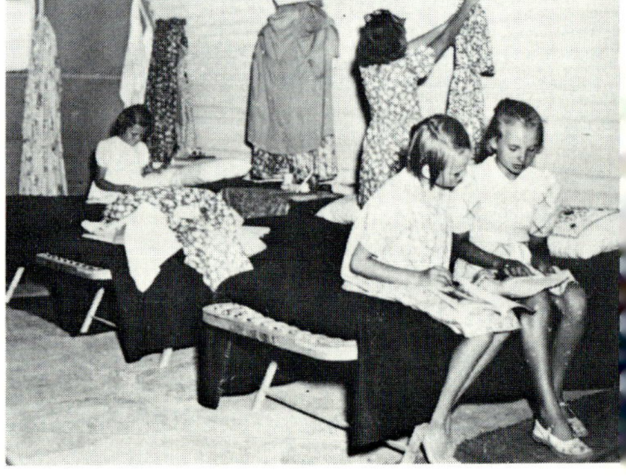

A quiet hour in the refugee camp. Salerno, Italy, 1949. (Author's collection)

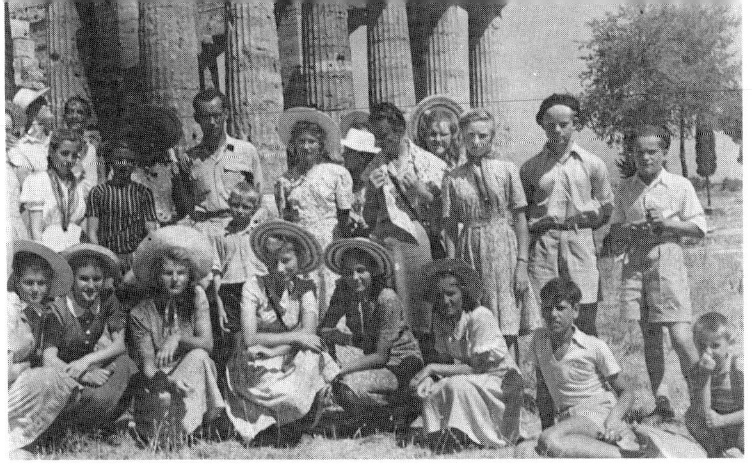

On excursion, 1949. Greek temple, Paestum, Italy. (Photo: Fr. Lucjan)

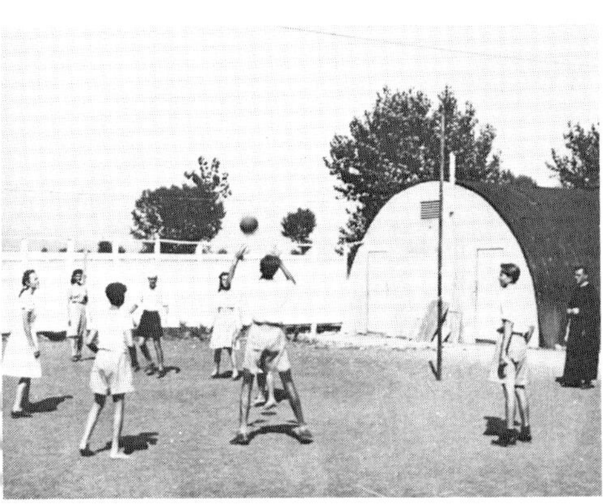

Volleyball in Salerno, Italy, 1949.
(Author's collection)

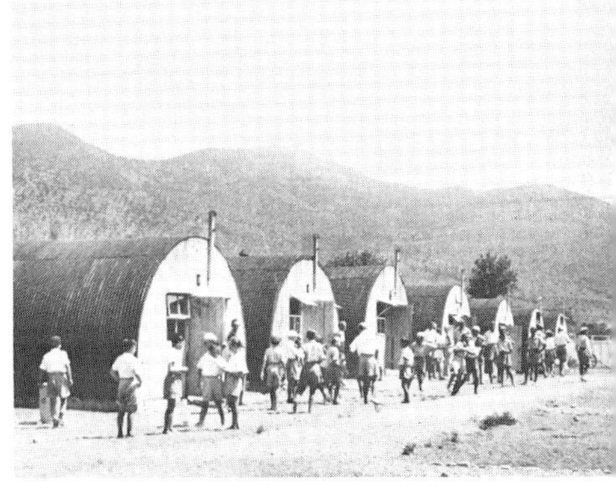

Living quarters for the children. 1949.
Formerly U.S. military barracks. Salerno, Italy,

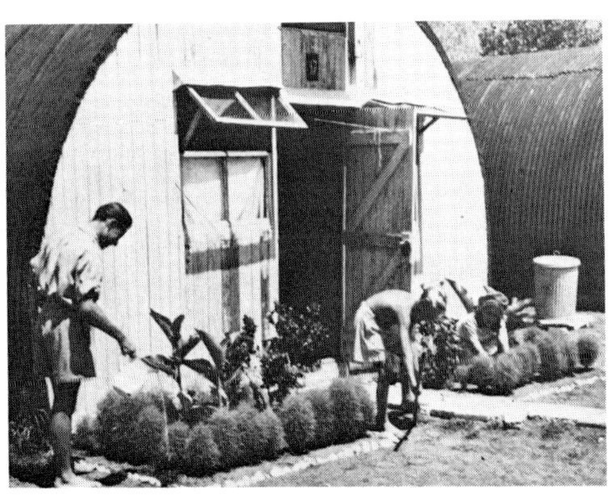

House becomes home in Salerno.
(Author's collection)

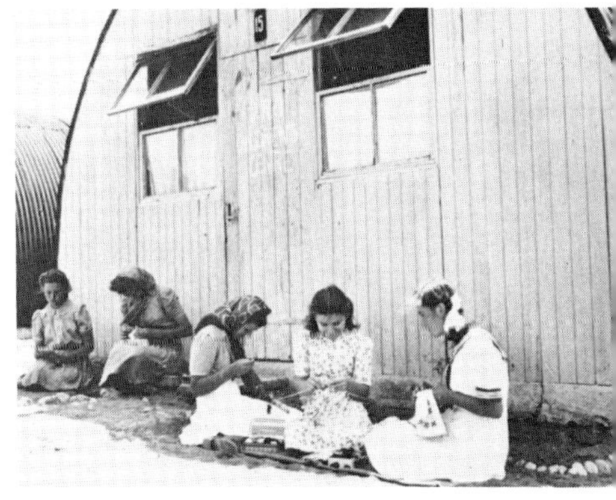

At leisure in Salerno, Italy, 1949.
(Author's collection)

Stop-over in Innsbruk, Austria, during escape from Italy to Germany, 1949.

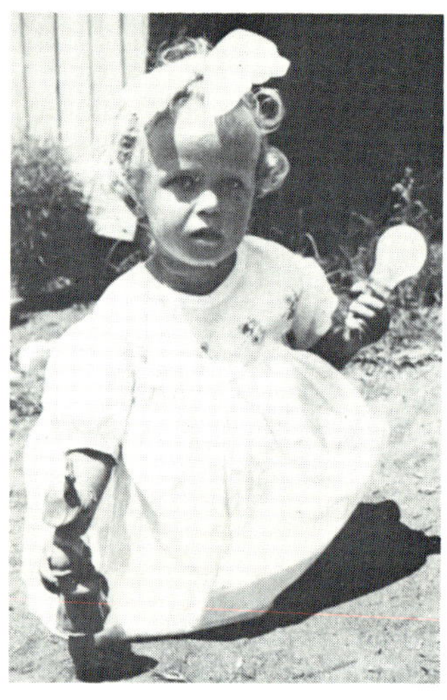

Youngest orphan "Nena". Salerno, 1949. (Author's collection)

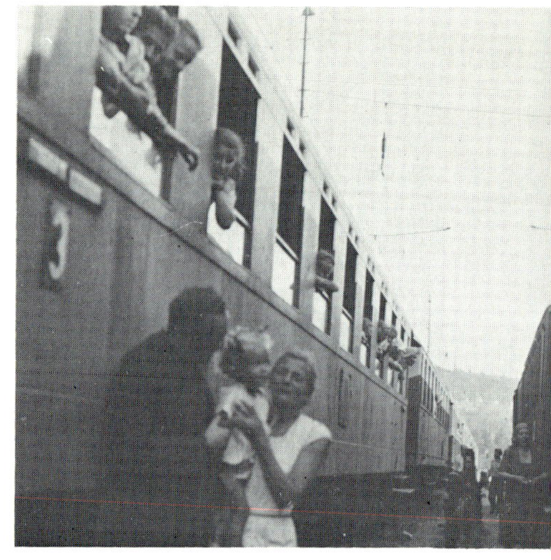

Msgr. Meysztowicz, Mrs. Grosicka on platform. (Photo: Fr. Lucjan)

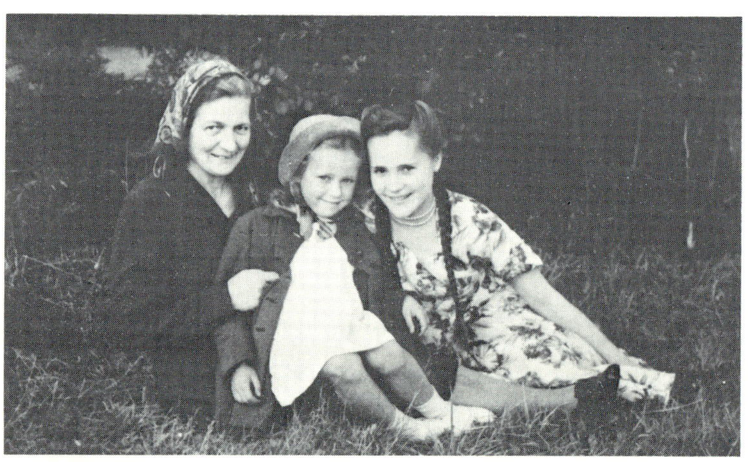

Mrs. Eugenia Grosicka with her adopted children Teresa (Nena) and Janina Papuga. Leicester, England, 1952. (Author's collection)

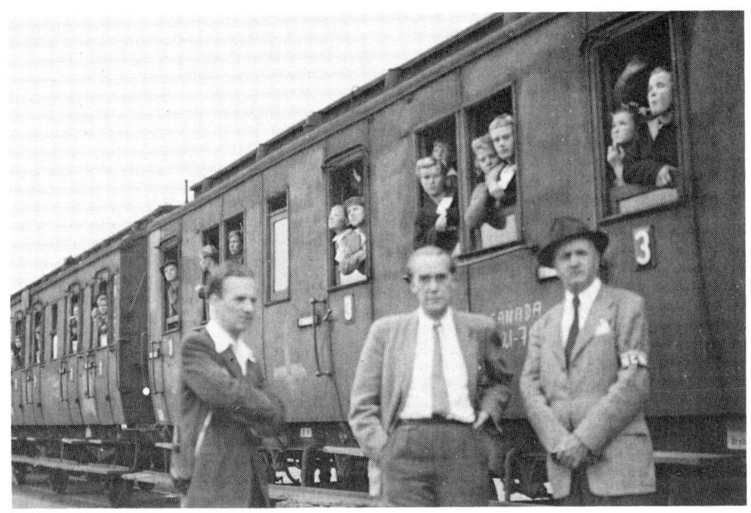

A forced stop-over at the Brenner Pass. Children had no visas to West Germany. Escape from Salerno to Bremen, Aug. 1949. (Photo: Fr. Lucjan)

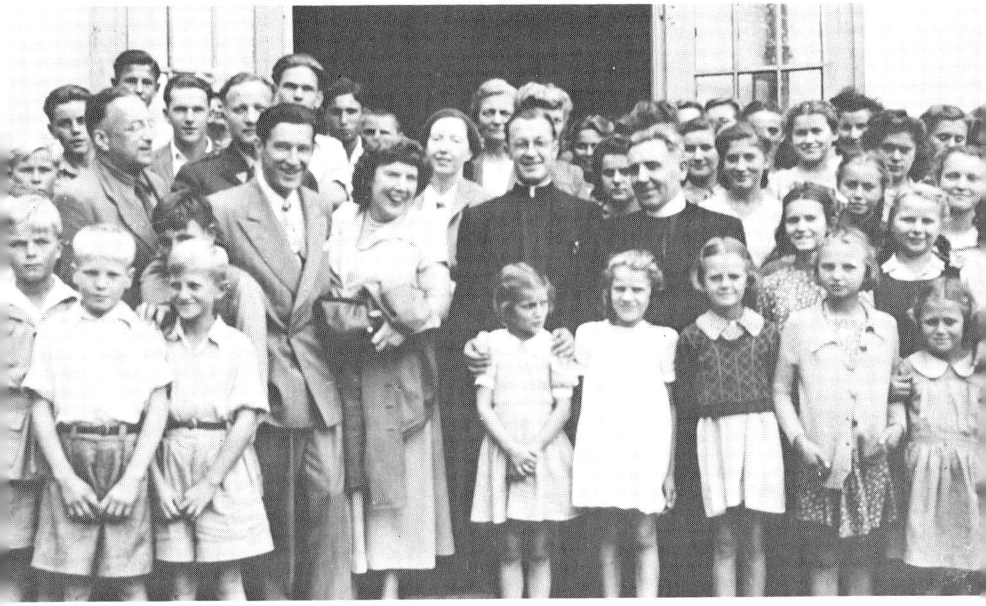

Orphans arrive in Bremen, Germany, 1949, with Msgr. Walerian Meysztowicz and Miss Dorothy Sullivan. (Photo: Fr. Lucjan)

W. Gardzilewicz and M. Kacpura. Rawdon Boarding School, Quebec, 1951. (Photo: Fr. M. Dostaler)

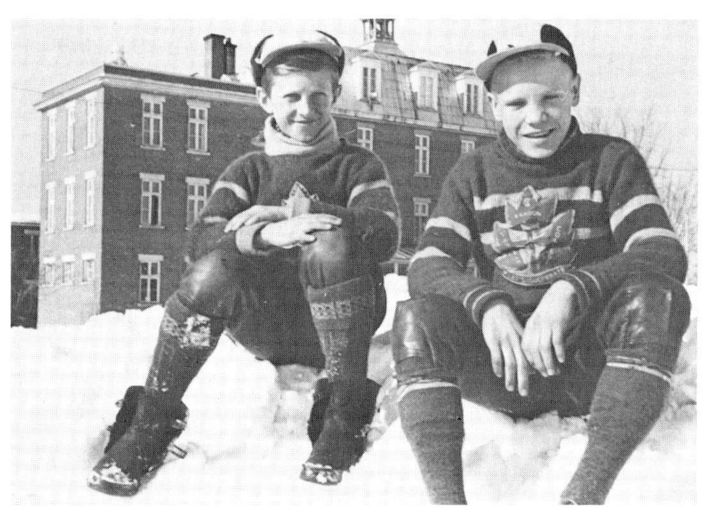

Paul-Emile Cardinal Leger, Archbishop of Montreal, Quebec hosts group of Polish orphans and their guardians, 1951. Fr. Jean Caron (far left) and Fr. Lucjan (nearest boys, right). (Author's collection)

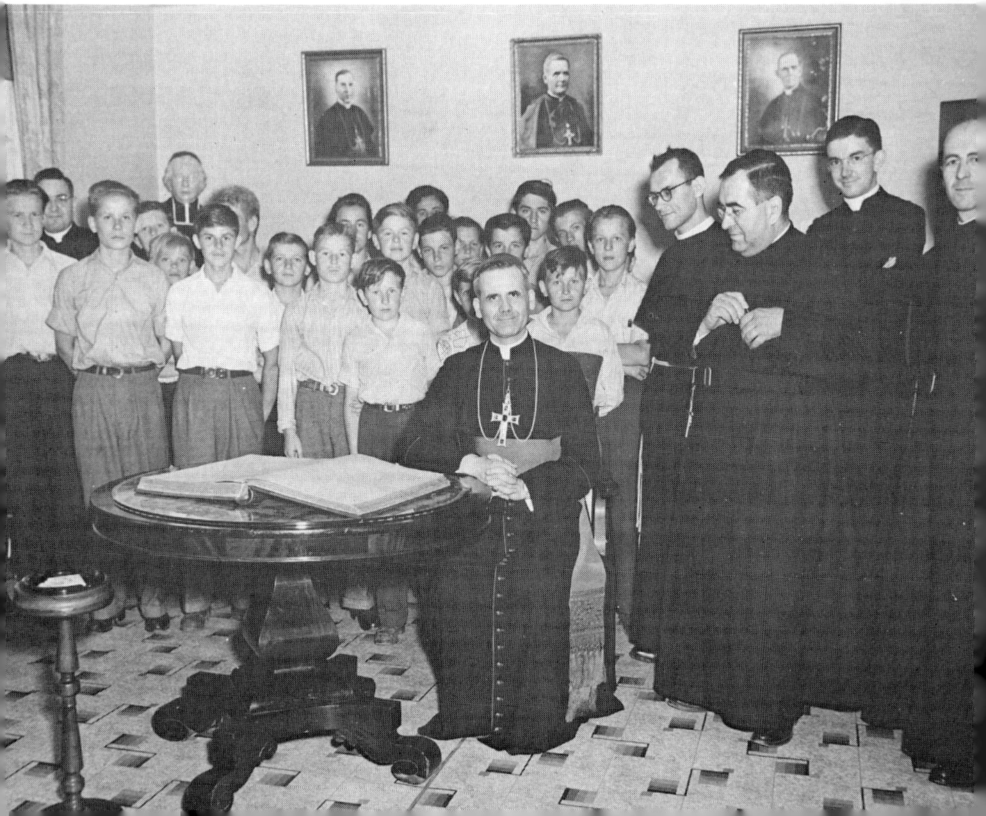

Maisonneuve Trade School, Montreal, 1951. Fr. Lucjan with Michal Bortkiewicz. (Photo: Fr. M. Dostaler)

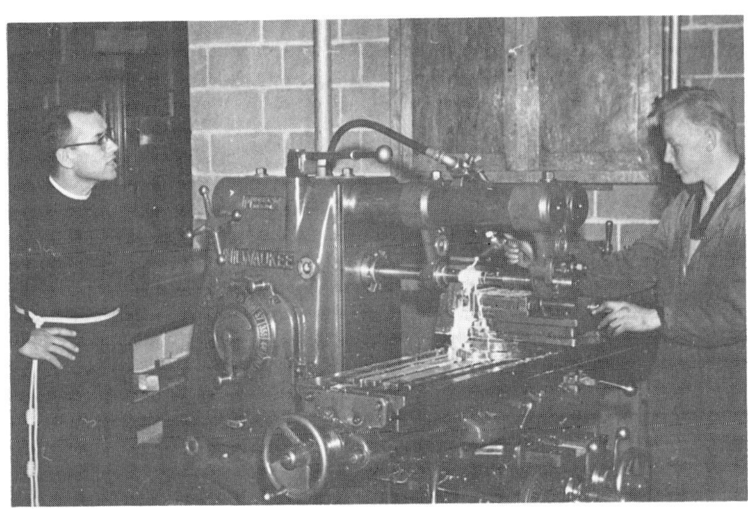

Maisonneuve Trade School, Montreal, 1951. From left—In background, M. Otto, J. Jurgielewicz, W. Szczepaniak, H. Pawlowski, B. Moch, and their instructor with Fr. Lucjan (Photo: Fr. M. Dostaler)

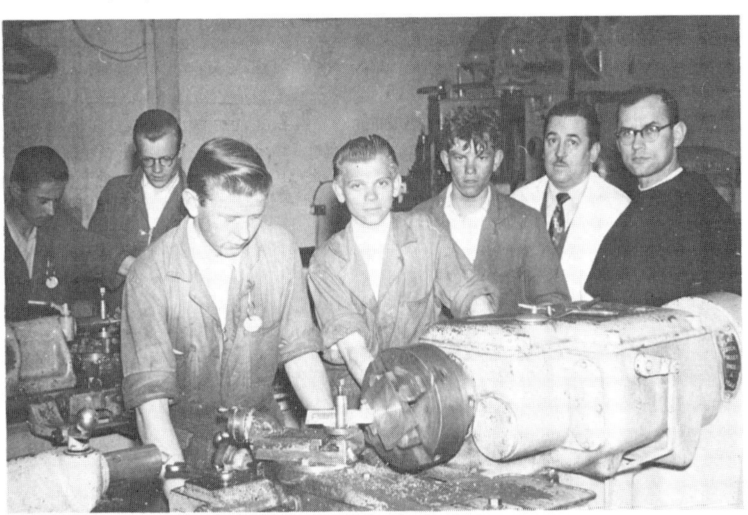

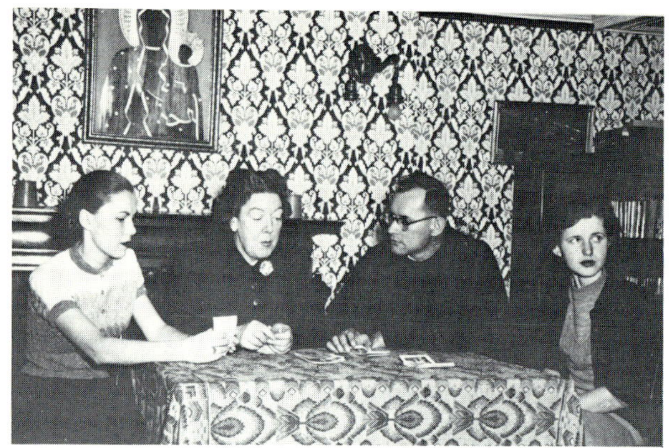

Miss Dorothy Sullivan, Fr. Lucjan, Danuta Gradkowska and Jadwiga Strzelecka, Sisters of the Resurrection Youth Centre, Montreal, Canada, 1954. (Photo: Fr. M. Dostaler)

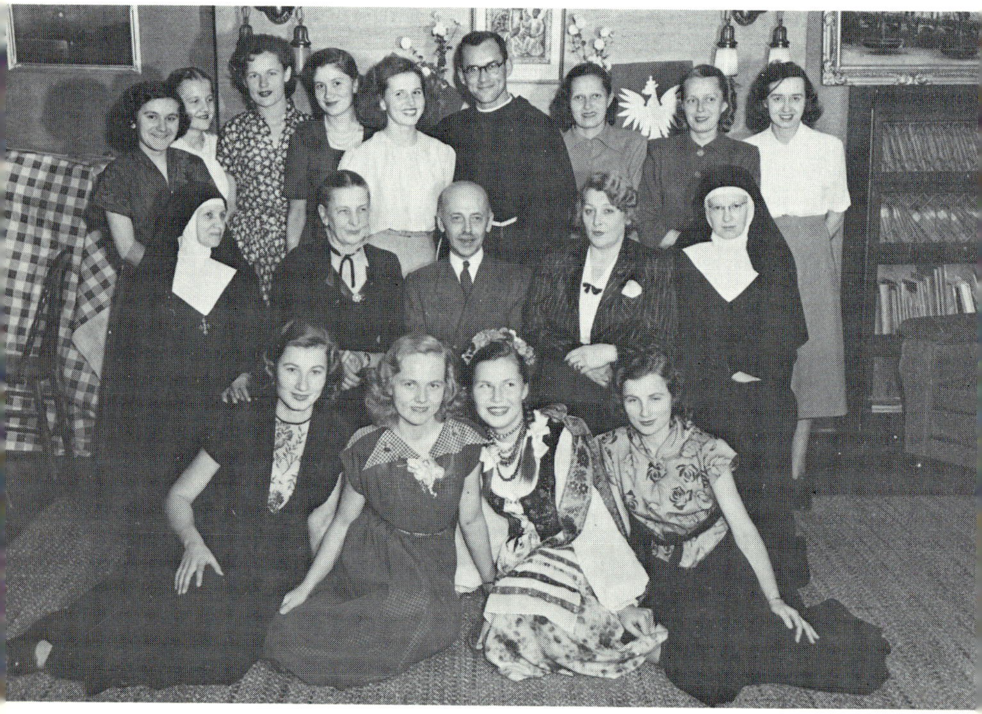

Polish underground commander, General Bor-Komorowski, visits Convent of Sisters of the Resurrection, Montreal, Canada, 1953. (Author's collection)

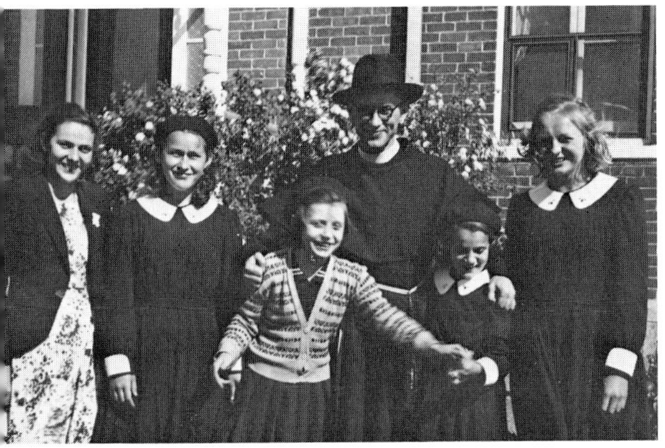

From left—Helena Kropa, Maria Waniuk, Wanda Cyran, Fr. Lucjan, Magdalena Mazur, Eugenia Giren. St. Paul de Joliette Boarding School, Que. (Photo: Fr. M. Dostaler)

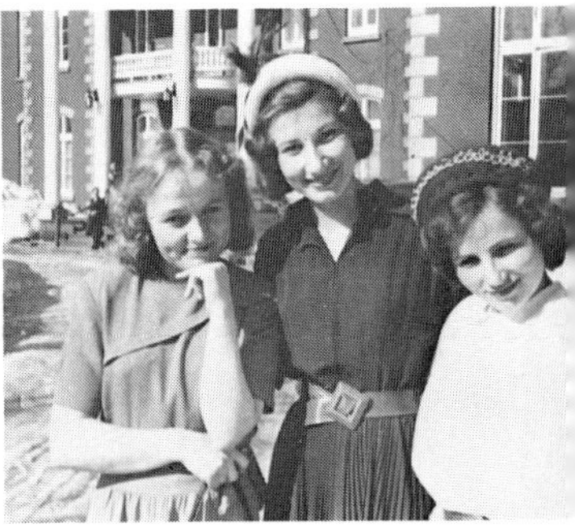

Student Nurses, Montreal, Que. 1954. Zofia Bojnowska, Paulina Syjut, Kazimiera Mazur (Photo: Fr. M. Dostaler)

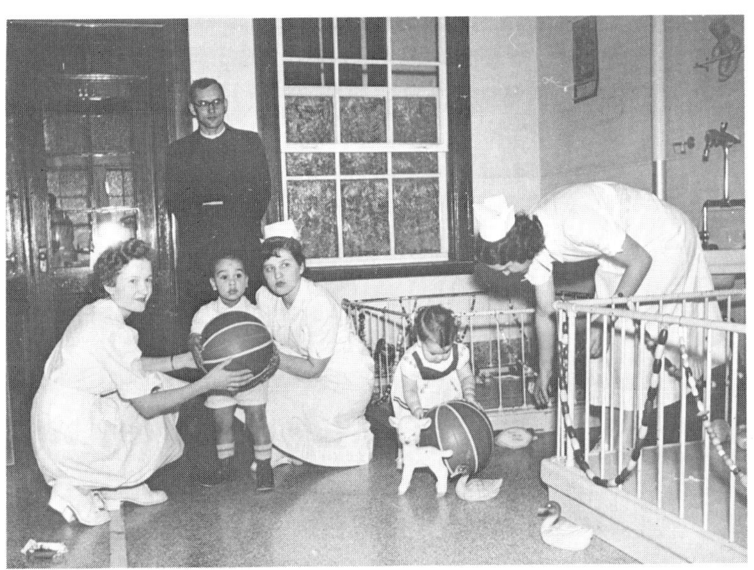

Student nurses at nursing school, Montreal. Bogumila Michniak, Zofia Matusiewicz, and Jozefa Studzinska with Fr. Lucjan, 1954. (Photo: Fr. M. Dostaler)

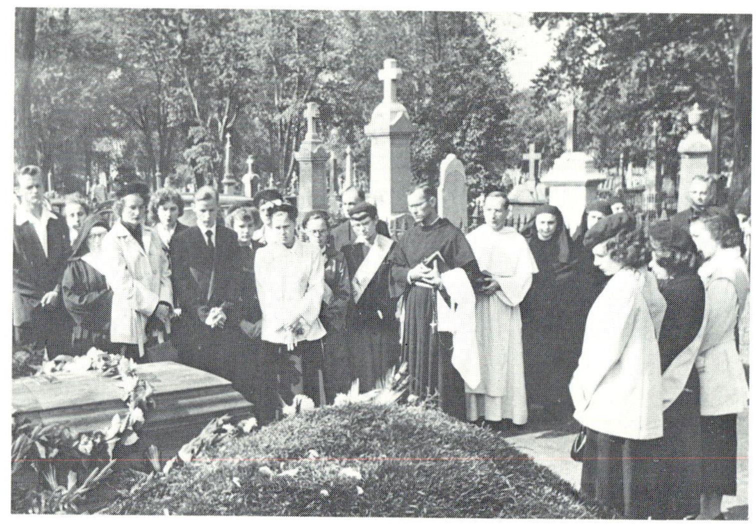

At the grave of Stefania Kraus, Cote de Neiges Cemetery, Montreal, Que., 1953. (Photo: Fr. M. Dostaler)

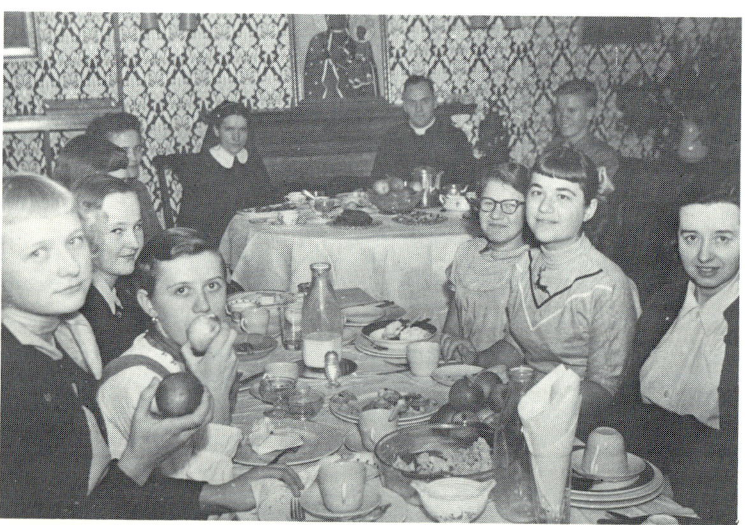

Farewell to novice Sr. Stanislawa Kacpura (at Table with Fr. Dostaler), leaving for Rome, Italy, 1954. (Photo: Fr. Lucjan)

sparks into the sky. The muttering, crackling sound resembled a hissing in the grass. And, in fact, the natives were firing the steppe to protect their huts from various reptiles—and taking a vengeful pleasure in roasting these enemies.

That night, I finally arrived at Kondoa, one of our smallest camps, with only four hundred inhabitants. Their rectangular homes were drowned in darkness, and only the pale light of kerosene lamps filtered through the shutters.

In the morning I began a tour of the camp. It was located close to the Italian Catholic mission of the Order of Passionist Fathers, where the Apostolic Nuncio, a distinguished Irishman, resided. Since no Polish priest was available, pastoral duties among the Poles were carried out by a Passionist missionary, Father Benedetto Barbaranelli. After five years of work he had learned to write and speak Polish perfectly, with only a slight accent, and was now carrying out all his pastoral duties in Polish. He even knew Sienkiewicz's Trilogy and other classics of our literature.

There were in the orphanage twenty-four uncommonly quiet, well mannered children, who would, within a year, after the camp was liquidated, be sent to the Tengeru orphanage. It was from them that Father Benedetto had learned to speak Polish. The retreat lessons were most beneficial to my listeners as well as to me, thanks to the atmosphere of single-minded concentration dominating the camp that week. Almost all the residents participated.

In moments of relaxation Father Benedetto would roll up his white cassock and take me for rides on the back seat of his motorcycle, tearing along rough paths and jumping the bumps with all the aplomb of a seasoned commando. I spent most of my free time, however, getting better acquainted with the people. After five years of monotonous camp life in Africa, and especially since the Communists had occupied Poland, the adults had lost all joy in life and become apathetic, their faces stern. The children, on the other hand, seemed excited about their exotic lives. They told of a pet ostrich they had had that used to saunter among the huts, looking curiously through the windows and filching small objects like pieces of soap, boxes of buttons, and photographs. The thief usually gave himself away, they explained, for the very bumps in his neck showed the shape of whatever he had stolen. They admitted to having kept a young hyena on a chain until it bared its fangs and they realized its distress. In the mission playground they still kept two ostriches that ate hot potatoes from their hands.

One of the Italian missionaries, Brother John, was a special friend of the orphans. He had served as homestead supervisor for several years, and when he left, he gave the children snapshots he had taken with the camera they had considered such a novelty. For his mother he was taking back to Italy the skin of a leopard killed inadvertently by a truck that had blinded the animal with its headlights.

The mission work of the nuns was evident everywhere, but I especially remember their tender care of a Polish woman I visited in the little camp hospital, who was dying of the dreadful disease black malaria. Nor can I forget their special love for a little three-year-old black boy. Deserted by his mother and left to die in the jungle, he had been found as a crying infant by a bicycling missionary. When I saw the child, he was absorbed in examining a music box, a miniature of the Basilica of the Most Holy Virgin Mary in Lourdes, which Sister Krystyna, a former Russian deportee, had just given to him. It was playing the sweet Polish song "Po gorach, dolinach. . . ." ("Over the hills, and over the dales. . . .").

On Saturday evening Negroes from far away began to congregate for Sunday's Holy Mass. With their frisky children, they arrived, weak, hungry, and thirsty after walking barefoot the whole day in the scorching heat. From early morning on, they began to fill the church. They sat on narrow, low kneeling benches, with no back support. They were a true example of the living faith that only simple, childlike hearts are capable of. Throughout the Mass, they sang as the early Christian communities did. All of them, old and young, sang the Gregorian chants that they rehearsed each Sunday. When their black preacher began teaching them the gospel lesson, they fixed their eyes on him and listened intently. Singing, listening, praying, and receiving Holy Communion together, they were united as living members of the one Mystical Body of Jesus Christ.

The Holy Mass, the singing rehearsal, the catechism lessons, and vespers filled the entire day. The Negro, following God's command, celebrates the Lord's Day with all his soul, and from this conscientious fulfillment of his obligations in the presence of God draws peace of mind and joy of heart.

In the afternoon, the Polish people gathered in the Catholic

Action recreation hall to say farewell to me and thank me for the retreat, the children seated in front, the grown-ups behind them, their faces emanating kindliness. Miss Wanda Wyrzykowski, one of the orphans, sang a beautiful song. In this melody, in the speeches and poems of the children, and in the gratitude and pure cordiality of all the faces I saw the same spirit as in their black brethren. These people had skin as white as birch bark, those had skin as black as ebony; but all their souls were filled with the same love of God and with His Grace.

26

On the Ngoro-Ngoro Crater

The end of July 1948 had come. The sky would soon be free of the clouds that had obscured it since the onset of the rainy season late in March. African spring was around the corner. Dawns were misty, but the days were already weaving the sun's gold threads into their texture. Local roads ceased to be hazardous and seasonal rivers dried up: this was the ideal time for sightseeing—not too cold, not too hot. This time the youngsters, now in their sixth year in Tengeru, had chosen to trek to Ngoro-Ngoro, a large crater about 120 miles southeast of Tengeru.

We set out early one morning in three open trucks rented from a Hindu transport firm in Arusha. Each member took a day's supply of food, because we planned to spend a night at the shelter. The girls and lady teachers wore slacks and blouses, with kerchiefs on their heads; the boys had decked themselves out in African style, with shorts, short-sleeved shirts, and cork helmets or green wide-brimmed hats. The early morning chill forced everyone to wear a sweater as we awakened the camp with our joyous singing.

After passing through Arusha, we were on a desolate steppe stretching to infinity, its barrenness broken only by the flat umbrella crown of an occasional acacia tree. Almost a whole day of not exactly pleasant travel lay ahead of us. By eight o'clock the sun was sailing high in the sky, and off came the sweaters. By ten we were being scorched. The trucks trailed clouds of yellow dust.

There were small breaks in the monotony. Now and then we passed a group of giraffes close to the road, their reddish-beige coats with their striking white design standing out sharply against the sun-scorched steppe. This bizarrely shaped animal so baffled ancient zoologists that they called it the camel-panther; and a more recent naturalist conceded that it has the hair of a panther, but added that it has the torso of a horse, the neck and thighs of a camel, the ears of a buffalo, and the legs of an antelope. It made a sensation during the reign of Napoleon when the first one was brought to Paris, accompanied by four Negroes to tend it and three cow nurses to feed it. Before long, its silhouette was appearing in designs for fabrics and china, and its ungainly appearance was figuring in satires.

At the moment, the giraffes with their large brown eyes observing us from the African grass looked very surprised. Their ever-moving ears, sticking out behind hairy little horns, would catch the roar of the engines, and their whole stance would reflect a child-like naiveté, a gentle tenderness, and a lively intelligence. Then suddenly one of them would give a signal and they would dash away, necks straight, spines sloping toward the rear, as if their hind legs were shorter than their forelegs. They would stop after a few powerful leaps, then out of curiosity turn their heads back toward us while some of them started browsing acacia leaves from among the thorns with their long tongues. We were enchanted.

Farther on we spotted ostriches. At times their legs sank into the grass and they floated on a sea of greenery; then where the grass thinned out we could see their long, powerful bare legs. Their tails, sparsely covered with dirty feathers, did not at all resemble the magnificent snow-white plumes adorning knights' helmets and royal hats.

In the bushes along the road darted guinea-hens, bustards, and quail.

By afternoon we had reached only a small, dull village, but beyond it we could see the massive forest-covered mountains that hid the Ngoro-Ngoro crater. Our children greeted the stop-over with the enthusiasm of an Arab for an oasis and fell upon the mangoes, papayas, bananas and soft drinks being peddled by the usual Hindu hucksters. As they unwrapped their lunches, their joy in life revived. We now began climbing into the mountains and the air became a bit cooler as we looked back down on the empty, flat, apparently lifeless steppe.

We reached the crater about two hours before sunset and ran to its rim to look down into the giant basin, twelve miles across, its steep slopes reaching down to a flat bottom seven thousand feet above sea level. Here, far below us, were two lakes, one with fresh water, the other heavy with nitrates. Because the basin is shaped something like the African continent it is called Africa in miniature. Just as a thick mist began falling upon the dell, we left for the shelter, where we were most impressed to find, in a meadow among the trees, six cottages with roofs of silvery white grass, much like those at Zakopane, the mecca of mountaineering sportsmen in Poland. The shelter, operated by the government of Tanganyika with a permanent Negro staff, consisted of a large mess hall, a kitchen building, and the cottages, each with a fireplace.

While the Negroes were bringing logs for the fireplaces, some of the girls busied themselves preparing our supper as others made the beds. The rest of us scattered to look over our surroundings. In the forest nearby grew colonies of young bamboo and on the meadows, heather, orange-red gladiolus, thistle, daisies, and clover, not found anywhere else in Africa. Some of the boys ran up with sensational news: they had seen a panther on a tree limb, and with one stab of his lance the Negro guide had killed it.

At dusk, by the light of candles, kerosene lamps, and the fireplace, we ate our meal; then everyone gathered around the fireplace for singing. After the evening prayer and meditation came the boy scouts' farewell to the day:

> Comes the night, the sun is gone,
> Off the peaks, off the fields, off the seas!
> Go to sleep, not alone:
> God is close!

Night had come.

The wind assaulted every cottage, whistled in every chimney, tore through the cracks of the timbering, and tugged at every door. Even with the fire still burning on the fireplace, we felt the cold, and the day's impressions kept us awake. Whenever we heard a distant moan, we imagined a lion stalking in the dark. For the plains of Serengetti and Ngoro-Ngoro itself are known for their concentrations of big game. Lions could be seen here in prides of ten or twenty. Someone had told us about a newly married English couple who had just arrived at this shelter for a vacation when the husband had to leave suddenly for urgent affairs in town. He returned the next day to find his young wife completely gray from terror as a lion had tried to break into their cottage during the night.

After our breakfast the next morning we descended into the crater and encountered almost at once a Masai woman, her head shaved and shining with grease. She wore all of her womanly riches: on her neck and legs and arms masses of brass rings, necklaces and multicolored beads; the whole lot must have weighed several pounds. Even for money she would not allow herself to be photographed, and she watched the camera with a superstitious fear.

The sun flooded the bottom of the crater showing more clearly the details we had seen only dimly the day before—the nitrate lake; the stream winding through the bush; the forests, which from the shelters had seemed just like the bush. Between the forest and the nitrate lake grazed thousands of zebras and wildebeests, animals similar to the domestic cow, black with steel-gray stripes, with beards and slightly lower hindquarters. Just to the side a bit was a herd of antelopes and gazelles, all watchful as if ready to run away. Seeing so many animals scared us, and we looked at our Masai guides for signs that we were in any danger. They were composed. The wildebeests, which were barring our passage to the lake, started a frenetic dance, their hoofs thudding in a wild gallop. We watched anxiously the lowered heads, the flowing manes, and the raised tails. Our boys, with their meager Kiswahili vocabulary, could not find out from the guides whether or not we were in danger. The animals continued their frolic, sometimes turning around suddenly like a cavalry unit and stampeding in the opposite direction, then again stopping to kick and shake their heads. Some of the girls became hysterical and demanded that we return to the shelter right away, but the guides maintained their Olympian composure. We had heard it said that the Masai belong to the bravest tribe, but we had also heard that African natives are frequently brave because they are not aware of a danger. They should, however, know these animals, we thought, and they did have in their hands long twin-edged lances. We thought it best to remain calm and motionless.

Suddenly the antelope ran away, followed by the obese zebras, and last of all the wildebeests. Our passage was finally free. But they did not run far and, apparently sensing that they were at a safe distance, resumed their peaceful grazing. Only the zebras closest to us raised their heads, their donkey ears twitching as they nervously watched us proceeding toward the lake. At the lakeshore we were suddenly overcome by fear that the animals might gather again behind us and cut off our return. Soon, however, we recognized that we were in no danger at all. We later learned that wildebeests are the clowns of the animal world and often show off. I tried to get near them to take photographs, but in vain; they stampeded again and ran away, the earth thudding under their thousands of hoofs, the forest sending back an echo like the sound of a distant storm.

As we returned past a Negro village we noticed that the cattle grazing in the neighborhood had their hide cut up in many places. The Masai eat red meat as a rule and drink milk and warm blood from the oxen, believing that it gives them strength and manliness. It is for this reason that they breed so many cattle, steal cattle, and even wage wars over cattle. Along the way we admired the flowers peeping through the grass and the natives' bee-hives—thick hollowed-out tree trunks, closed at both ends, hanging from trees. The Negro women evidently do not know how to smoke out the bees to collect honey, for theirs is invariably full of wax and dead insects.

While we were stopped for a rest, one of the lady teachers wanted to buy a lance from a Masai, and it seemed that the transaction would be completed successfully. She had already given him a few bank notes. But just then a friend of his got into the act and, suspecting trickery on the part of the white woman, urged his friend to return the bank notes and demand perforated coins instead. Because the teacher did not have enough coins, the deal fell through.

As we resumed our walk back to the shelter, a few girls had an attack of malaria caused by the long, strenuous march in the scorching heat and by the great fear they had felt at the sight of the wild animals. Some of them had fainted while we were still at the bottom of the crater, but the other girls had revived them with water from the stream while a few boys went on ahead to bring back cold tea and lemons. One of the sick girls had to be carried, the others led; and the steep, craggy slopes covered with bushes and rocks made our return into a kind of calvary.

Later, in the afternoon, as we were getting ready to leave for home, an axle of one of the trucks broke. The organizers of the excursion were greatly disturbed because it meant that part of the group would have to remain here for another two days. Since there was no telephone, two trucks would have to return to the camp and one of the drivers would have to notify the transport company in Arusha and return with the new axle. That the axle broke just at the gate of the shelter rather than somewhere in the steppe at night was our only consolation. The youngsters who had to stay were, of course, overjoyed. Even the girls lying inside the padded truck, whose numb fingers and stiffening toes had to be rubbed by their companions, wanted to remain.

After the two trucks had left, the fortunate youngsters remaining behind discussed the possibility of hunting for some game since there was no food. But my briefcase was full of things to eat, because, having been invited for "guest treats" at each mealtime by different groups of boys and girls, I had not touched my rations. So we were all saved from starvation.

The next two days we spent in games, entertainment, and short excursions in the neighborhood of the shelter. After we returned home, we learned that the sick girls were in the hospital. And it was obvious that their companions had been giving very colorful accounts of their excursion, because none of the mothers of the girls in our delayed group had slept until we returned.

27

At the Mission Station in Kilema

One of the spots most frequently visited by organized excursions was the Catholic Mission in Kilema in the foothills of Mt. Kilimanjaro run by the Fathers of the Holy Spirit and staffed by the Sisters of the Precious Blood. Here was much to admire and emulate: excellent management, high standards in the schools, practical instruction for Negro girls, and everywhere, orderliness. The Mother Superior, Sister Matilda, our compatriot, enjoyed exceptional respect from her group of German sisters, and everyone acknowledged that this humble sister from Poznan was, with the Lord's help, accomplishing a task comparable to Dr. Schweitzer's.

It is only about sixty miles from Tengeru to Kilema. The road traverses grass-covered plains that stretch in endless monotony, but in the distance is Mt. Kilimanjaro, floating in rarified air, coming closer and closer. In January, 1949, three of us teachers and a group of young people made an excursion from Tengeru to Kilema, with the intention, later on, of climbing the highest peak of Kilimanjaro "on behalf of the camp."

In the area of sand dunes we passed wide-trunked baobab trees and farther on, traveled through the area of plantations, more thickly populated with women and children tidily dressed. Here the Negroes we met smiled at us and threw us a merry "Jambo" (Good morning). We must be nearing the mission.

The roar of our truck engines climbing serpentine roads attracted the black youngsters, even children from deep in the forest. As we neared the mission buildings, a large group chased after us. We stopped in the shade of some very old trees in a square before the large stone church and were at once surrounded by a crowd of Negro children admiring, wide-eyed, the women's hairdos, colorful dresses, and footwear.

In a few minutes Sister Matilda ran toward us, elderly but sprightly, with a radiant face and cheeks rosy as a young village girl's. Tenderly she hugged the children in our group, once in a while wiping away a tear. She was overjoyed at the visits of the Polish children, and they felt completely at home with her. With her they could be themselves. Yeah! our Sister Matilda has a very good head, and that's a fact! But Sister Matilda also had a very good heart.

In these little wanderers she saw her distant homeland. Besides, she knew most of the children; for in 1942, with the first news that Polish children were coming to Tengeru, she had gone there to receive her countrymen, and later to help and advise them.

After a meal in the refectory, Sister Matilda led us to a large "tembu," or elephant tree, where in a grotto enshrouded in ivy and flowers stood a statue of the Immaculate Virgin Mother. For the mission this shrine was the source of graces, frequently visited.

In the shade of this tembu, with jungle murmurs all around, the cornerstone of the mission had been laid and the first Holy Mass said on the Feast of the Assumption of the Blessed Virgin

Mary; and into her care the whole mission work had been entrusted.

The children listened with great interest to the history of the mission's founder, Father Augustine Commeninger, who had had to drink the "brotherhood toast" of animal's blood with Fumba, chief of the Chagga tribe, who gave the ground for the mission. At that time Sister Matilda had been only sixteen years old back in Poznan, a girl named Jadwiga preparing for mission work. Now, advanced in years, she reminisced. She had served her novitiate in South Africa and received her religious name, Matilda. We tried to imagine her as the sixteen-year-old Jadwiga arriving in Durban in 1895, being lowered from her ship in a basket and carried by boat to the shore lush with spring flowers.

And after that?

After that, she said, she began growing into African ways and getting acquainted with the Negroes, learning to deal with the frailties of their primitive nature and seeing them as God's children.

And what then?

They learned to trust her, she said, and accept her advice and help for they knew they could learn much from her.

Sister Matilda's good health and solid build suggested uncommon youthful physical strength. This was confirmed in a story that one of the sisters told us later. Soon after first coming to Africa, Sister Matilda noticed that the hens, geese and ducks were disappearing from the farm. Suspicion fell upon the Negroes. One day, however, as she stepped into the barn, she saw a huge snake coiled in the corner, the bulges in its body betraying it as the poultry thief. She had not been in Africa long enough to know that she was facing the fearsome boa constrictor, and she was not going to let the felon go unpunished. She grabbed a hay rake and thrust it into the reptile's body. Slowed down by its digestive processes, the boa tried to escape; but Sister Matilda, leaning all her weight on the rake, pinned him to the wall, called a Negro girl, and finished him off with an iron bar. But that was not the end of her battle against poultry thieves. Sister Matilda eventually killed another three boas. Their bodies were all, one by one, stretched out under a tree and their bellies opened. In the first were six ducks, in another an antelope complete with horns. Because these conquests, though heroic, could have cost Sister Matilda her life, she received a reprimand from her superior—and the admiration of those who kept her prowess alive by retelling the story.

Her young guests listened raptly as Sister Matilda recalled the troubles she had had trying to teach the Negroes how to improve their plantations, gardens and huts. But her efforts had not been in vain.

After telling her story she led us to the church and through a wide tree-lined walk to the cemetery, where the pioneers of the mission were buried along with Father August. The children knelt and said prayers. Then they headed joyfully for the farm buildings near the tall banana grove. Since they were mostly from villages, the children enjoyed seeing the horses, the cows, the hens, and the aggressive rooster. To some of them the farm-yard sights and sounds and smells brought misty memories of their own family homesteads.

Visiting the school, we were allowed to enter the classroom during lessons. In their own language, Ki-zulu, little Negro pupils greeted the visitors in unison and sat down with an exemplary discipline, never taking their eyes from their teacher as she began to ask questions of one after another. Every once in a while one of the students would glance at the white children, but they were all so excited by the lesson that every question was greeted by a forest of raised hands.

These children were learning practically the same things that children the world over learn in primary schools. Sister Matilda observed that though some of them often exhibited above-average intelligence, their development was retarded by their parents' ignorance, fostered by their primitive living conditions. During recess, the music and singing teacher assembled her small pupils on the playground to sing for their guests. The finale was given by the brass band made up of little musicians obviously proud of their music-making. They would occasionally sneak a glance at us to see how impressed we were. Later, at the orphans' shelter, where among the ebony-black curly heads the pale locks of a little mulatto stood out, the children looked neat and healthy and were not afraid of us.

Sister Matilda's favorite enterprise was the school for the older girls, where besides cooking, washing, ironing, sewing, weaving, and basketry, they were taught nursing and child-rearing. Sister Matilda spared no praises for the Negro girls, their piety, ardor and obedience; and while she was at it, she explained to us that a healthy morality, natural in Negroes, is a fertile ground for sowing Christian precepts.

Chief Fumba, though friendly toward the first missionaries, had died still a pagan. At the time of his death, according to members of his tribe, a fiery ball had flown from his hut, made an arc in the sky, then rolled down the mountain into the grasses and disappeared from sight. His son, Kirita, had proved a relentless enemy of the mission. The British authorities discovered that he had even made an alliance with the bellicose Masai tribe to murder the missionaries. According to the plan, Father August's head was to be put on a long pole to adorn the entrance to the chief's hut, but the white nuns were to be spared, for Kirita appreciated their work and their skills so much that he intended to marry them all. The British banished him to Aden for seven years.

Meanwhile the mission had been dealt a severe blow. Just after the first World War, the British authorities ordered the women missionaries to leave Tanganyika, and they had to go to their outposts in South Africa. Only black nuns were left in Kilema and for the first time took over all branches of the mission's work. When the white sisters, including Sister Matilda, came back five years later, they discovered, much to their amazement, that the black sisters not only had stayed firm in their calling but had performed their duties well, even though they had neither the organizational acumen nor the experience of the white sisters. Parts of the enterprise had suffered—the buildings especially—but others had flourished, and Sister Matilda was overcome with emotion to learn that they had even built a reserve supply of potatoes.

With the triumphant return of the white sisters to Kilema, the mission experienced an abundance of God's graces. Kirita's successor, Joseph Maliti, an ardent, exemplary Christian, consecrated his country and his people to the Most Sacred Heart of Jesus. The men formed a Saint Joseph fraternity, the women a Saint Anne's Society; and the young people entered the ranks of Marian Sodalities. In Kilema-Chini a theological seminary was established for natives; in Singa-Chini, a teachers' college; and in Huruma a novitiate for black girls. A shelter for poor girls and widows was also organized in Kilema.

In the meantime Kirita had returned from his banishment and resumed the leadership of the tribe. If he found some profound changes, spiritual and cultural, in his people, Kirita was not the same man either. In a touching scene he made friends with the missionary he had wanted to murder; and though he was refused baptism for some years because of doubts about the sincerity of his intentions, he was received into the faith on his deathbed. In gratitude for such a great grace of God, the missionaries erected a large memorial cross on Mount Gangu. We climbed up to this shrine.

The view from the top of Mt. Gangu gave a good prospect of the whole impressive complex. The mission buildings with their corrugated tin roofs shone brightly in the sun. In the dell of green fields stood a large statue of the Virgin Mary, "The Guardian," dating back to the days when Kilema had been plagued by locusts from beyond the Red Sea and had been left without a leaf. In the blue distance across the Moshi valley directly opposite Kilimanjaro, the Pare Mountains rose above Lake Jipe reflecting pink clouds. To the east and to the west of the memorial cross stretched a chain of mountains, covered with vegetation, all part of Kilimanjaro.

It was just the same as it had been in 1904, when the missionaries first came to Kilema with Sister Matilda. They had arrived in a caravan making its way slowly against this magnificent panorama. A few hundred steps in front marched a young missionary to scare away wild animals. Behind him walked the bishop, priests, and sisters, including twenty-five-year-old Sister Matilda. Then came the blacks leading the pack animals, with a donkey cart loaded with chests, bringing up the rear. Of course the natives were armed, and the sisters' protective red habits, black scapulars, and white veils looked like a moving oasis of bright flowers against the sun-scorched steppe.

The caravan had been traveling for a week. According to their journal, they started each day's march at three in the morning by the light of the moon, much brighter here than in the North. Since the sun rises at five-thirty, already is very high by six, and by nine is unbearably hot, the caravan would stop for a rest till three in the afternoon. Then it was time for the missionaries to do their spiritual exercises, meditate, and recite their breviary. After a meal, they set out again until sunset, around six. When dusk came, the caravan would be already encamped. Some of the Negroes would rig up a zeriba, a prickly fence to protect them from wild animals; others would build a large fire and cook maize for supper and breakfast. Then the dark of night would enwrap them all, with only the wide tongue of fire twisting through the darkness like the eternal lamp in a sanctuary. Priests and natives stood guard, while the others slept, wrapped in blankets.

After a week's trek the caravan arrived in Kilema, where the natives greeted them with joy and the children shouted, "Wamama wamekooya! (The little mothers have arrived!)."

In 1957, Sister Matilda celebrated the golden jubilee of her missionary work, and her grateful black charges staged in her honor a play based on the novel *Fabiola*. She had outlived the founder of the mission and many other co-workers dear to her; and she had lived to see the conversion of the bloodthirsty adversary, Kirita, who by accepting baptism became the symbol of the renaissance of the Black Land in the spirit of Christ. Understanding this symbolism, Kirita's son buried him on Mt. Gangu at the foot of the cross where Christ stretches His arms over the land of Kilimanjaro.

On our way back to the camp, crossing the steppe, we paused. The distant mountains were darkening; the icecaps of Kilimanjaro were shrouding themselves in blue and purple. The sun would soon go down. Above the Kilema mission stood the cross, the symbol of a different, eternal light that disperses the darkness in human souls.

28

Assaulting Mt. Kilimanjaro

Every morning about seven the sun lights up the peaks of Kilimanjaro, enthroned above low-lying clouds and as if covered with rose petals. The tallest peak reflects back the sun until the clouds rise from below to obscure it. Toward evening the curtain of clouds drops down, and the ice-capped dome reappears, glittering at times like sugared pastry. Then as the sun sinks lower and lower its colors change through a kaleidoscope of pink, white, celadon, blue, and finally blue-black.

For the Masai pagans this sparkling dome of snow and ice was for centuries, like the golden cone atop the pharaoh's obelisk, the Ngaye Nga, or home of their god. The words Kilima ya Njaro mean "Shining Mountain"; it is also called the Crown of African

Mountains, the Lion in the Dales, and other names. Local legends, spun before a human foot had touched the peak of Kilimanjaro, say that on it is a magic white medicine. But it also seemed strange to the natives that "berda," the chill, came from this radiating dome, and they held it in superstitious awe.

Since 1848, when it was first discovered by missionaries, Mt. Kilimanjaro has been a great attraction for tourists as well as Africans; and many have attempted to climb it, among them several Poles. Before we took up its challenge, it had been conquered in 1910 by Dr. Antoni Jakubski, a professor and the first Polish climber to reach the peak. During their stay in Africa, several Polish refugees had made the attempt. Among those who succeeded were two boy scouts—sixteen-year-old Stanislaw Czernek and Miroslaw Krazynski—and two adults—Dr. Wiktor Szyrynski and Father Jan Sajewicz. Now our group of four were, in February, 1949, to test ourselves on Kilimanjaro: Jan Hoffman, a historian and geologist specializing in Volhynia regional culture; Maria Sidor, a high-school teacher and naturalist; a British military pilot; and I, also a boy scout.

The massive Kilimanjaro mountain chain is evidence of a major cataclysm that occurred when, under the pressure of internal volcanic vibrations, the crust of the earth cracked from the Taurus mountains in Asia Minor all the way to Beira in South Africa. In the tectonic ditch that resulted, rivers started to flow and lakes and seas formed—the Sea of Galilee, the Jordan River, the Dead Sea and the Red Sea—and on the African continent the great lakes Victoria, Tanganyika, Alberta and Nyassa. In Africa this elongated chasm is called The Great Rift Valley.

The cracking of the earth's crust also pushed up mountains on both sides of the rift, and three groups of volcanic mountains were formed: Rungwe, Kilimanjaro, and Ruwenzori. Kilimanjaro is the fifth highest mountain on earth, after Mt. Everest in the Himalayas, Mt. McKinley in Alaska, and the two highest peaks in the Andes. It rises in gentle slopes from the great Moshi Valley to two peaks, Kibo (19,565 feet) and Mawenzi (17,000 feet), separated by a saddle ten miles long at an Alpine altitude of 14,000 feet.

Kilimanjaro represents all the climates of the world, with the flora of each. At four to six thousand feet grow coffee, corn, bananas and yams. From six to ten thousand feet stretch virgin forests which lose moisture as they ascend and become dwarfed in the high region of silver green moss and low vegetation. In this climatic zone live practically all species of African fauna—elephants, leopards, buffalos, lions, and others—and the forests are filled with multi-colored birds of many species, some not yet fully classified by ornithologists. Above the forests stretch the coombs, covered with tufts of heather, orchids, blood-red pompoms of hoemanthus, gentians, corn flowers, and most spectacularly everlastings, giant blue lobelias standing like obelisks, and tall, grotesque groundsels, looking like giant artichokes whose roots, forking out, end in bunches of leaves and flowers.

Above thirteen thousand feet, life becomes gradually extinct until there is no trace of animals or even insects. The occasional flowers are pollinated by the wind. Dr. Reusch, one of the first conquerors of Mt. Kilimanjaro, a scientist, allegedly found a leopard buried in the ice on the Kibo peak, and a bit farther on a deer, evidence of a chase; but that is rare at such an altitude. Finally, just where the plant and animal worlds end, nature moves into another mode with giant rocks of brown basalt scattered over the slopes and covered by lava, monuments of the cataclysm. Here and there stand perpendicular sheets of rock several feet high, as if polished by a giant. Mosses of a pleasant rusty green and grey cling to the rocks. Higher still, even the mosses cannot subsist, and the landscape seems to be the aftermath of a gigantic fire that left behind only blackened rocks and volcanic ash, with layers of gravel deposited by the glacial flow on the slopes of Kibo.

The three of us started from a hotel at the foot of the mountain; we were joined at the last moment by a young British pilot, who later gave us aerial photos of the Kibo crater. We had eleven Negroes from the Chagga tribe with us: nine "pagazi" or carriers; Daudi, a cook; and Johann, a guide well known to tourists. The Negroes set out at a trot, their heads loaded with huge bundles and cases, their bare soles flashing red as they disappeared from our sight. We would see them again only at the longer stop-overs or in a mountain shelter. We stepped into a narrow path that formed a dark, humid tunnel through the jungle. Each day we did about ten miles, ending at a shelter for the night. These shelters were mute historians of our predecessors on Kilimanjaro, with their graffiti-inscribed walls and bedboards: words of advice and aphorisms recorded for posterity. They advised us to go no farther; they declared "Never, never again!" Our boy scouts left notice of their presence by engraving their fleur de lys with the initials O.N.C. (Ojczyzna "Fatherland," Nauka "Learning," Cnota "Virtue") near their emblem, a Polish boy scout in silhouette guarding the four great Polish rivers, Varta, Vistula, San, and Bug.

As we stepped out onto the sunny carpet of grass and flowers for our first stop-over, a storm broke below us over the jungle, chasing the layered clouds and shredding them with lightning. At times a beam of sunlight penetrated the clouds to show us the Kilema mission buildings far below. We were even now high enough to feel the change of temperature. On the second day we climbed through cold mists racing over the slopes, chased by a fearsome whistling wind. At night we huddled around the shelter's fireplace, listening to the howling wind tearing at the sheet-metal roof. We all woke up the next morning with colds and headaches and washed in a mountain stream with icicles forming on the rocks and ice lace encrusting its edge.

At last we reached the saddle, at the same altitude as the Alps. On our right were the crags of the Mawenzi peak shooting skyward, looking like the dainty turrets of a gothic cathedral. Between these tattered crags, in the rocky ravines, was snow and a deadly silence. There was no sign of any life at all. By noon the sun was burning so deadly hot, despite the high altitude, that it was dangerous to take off our cork helmets for a bit of relief.

Having traversed the saddle, we stopped toward evening at the last rest spot, "Kibo Hut," where the last section of the road begins to the peak of Kibo, 3,950 feet higher. On the side that we were about to climb, the ice-caps do not begin until 18,700 feet because of the warm monsoon winds. (On the opposite side the ice-cap starts down at 12,500 feet, and the climb is therefore far more difficult.)

In the shelter that evening we experienced most of the unpleasant problems to be expected at such altitudes where air pressure is only half that at sea level: nausea, lack of appetite, mental exhaustion, insomnia, and swelling around the joints. The Englishman, used to such altitudes, felt good, ate hungrily, and soon went to bed; but in the middle of the night he was seized by severe cramps and fever, so could not make the last stage of our climb. We started at half-past two in the morning. Johann had wakened us while the others slept in, for they were to wait for us at the shelter. We had to reach the peak before sunrise so as not to risk climbing the steep ash-covered slopes with the temperature reaching a possible 73° Celsius (163° F.).

We had to hurry to keep within the round yellow glow of Johann's lantern. The severe cold, with a temperature down to −14° Celsius (4° F.), caught us unprepared even with our warm clothing, and the climb was so difficult that after an hour we all thought we were going to die. Our legs kept sinking in thick layers of volcanic ash up to the calves, and the stuff was so slippery on this steep gradient that we would, with great effort, climb seven to ten steps only to slide back three or four. It took us almost two hours to accomplish no more than three hundred steps. We had to make a Herculean effort, forgetting everything, even companions, and concentrating all our will power on the imperative "Keep going! Move ahead!" The blood pounded in our veins, our hearts beat frantically like a bird caught in a net. Each movement was irritating, and each breathless word from a companion. Silently, bitterly, I reproached myself: "You fool, why did you get into this?" Other climbers before us had suffered cramps, hemorrhages, and mental disturbance, and had had to be carried down a few thousand feet before they returned to normalcy. I remembered a disturbing legend about an Abyssinian king, Manelik I, who had to climb Kibo as penance for his sins. He died just as he reached the rim of the crater.

Finally, at 7:30, our agony ended as we reached the peak amid pyramids of ice. Johann congratulated us and drew a large circle with his hand to show us the magnificent reward of our labors. We did not know what to admire first. The sun, momentarily hidden behind the Mawenzi mountain chain, was throwing a massive shadow down on the saddle. In a moment it rose above the frozen turrets of the peak and seemed to be coming toward us, large and brilliant. Some ten thousand feet below spread a sea of white clouds with islands of ice-caps, stalactites, stalagmites, and trillions of snowflakes glittering like diamonds. Even Switzerland cannot boast such a view: past Kibo's sister mountain, Kilimanjaro, all the way to ice-covered Kenya some two hundred miles away. Faintly, to the east, we could make out a misty streak which was the Indian Ocean.

At our feet was the oval crater of Kilimanjaro, about a mile and a quarter in diameter and reaching in spots a depth of one thousand feet. The crater is rimmed with cones, eternally ice-covered, called Stella Point, Leopard's Point, Gillman's Point, and—tallest of them all—Kaiser Wilhelm Spitze.

At Gillman's Point we inscribed our names in the commemorative book hidden in the rock; we read the inscriptions of former expeditions: film crews, scientists, and other climbers like us. The Polish boy scouts had written the words of a song:

> We plod ahead, climbing always higher,
> To reach the peak of Kibo;
> There shines our scouting badge!

Maria Sidor left a rosary in a can as a memento. At the Kaiser Wilhelm Spitze, we were told, is a Bible, and one missionary is supposed to have said Holy Mass on that peak.

When we returned to the shelter the Negroes crowned us with garlands of immortelles (strawflowers) as a token of our triumph, and there was great joy in Kilema. A group of youngsters from the tailoring school met us there to take us back to the camp. As we travelled through the steppe, the night air alive with cricket songs, the girls sang the scouting song about that strange nostalgia for sky-reaching peaks felt by those who have once reached the top:

> He who once has reached the peak,
> Whose brow has touched the cloud,
> The loftiest he will always seek,
> The pure, the just, the proud . . .

And for us it was true. Despite the weariness in our bones, we were already making plans for the next climb.

29

A Safari in Kenya and Uganda

In March, 1949, near the end of the African summer, I found myself on a bus traveling the 180 miles from Tengeru to Nairobi, where I was to conduct a retreat for the Polish settlers there, mostly young adults.

Just outside the Tengeru camp, we had been briefly delayed by police who were rounding up all the Negroes in the area to investigate the murder of a Hindu who, while carrying mail on a motorcycle, had been killed by a javelin thrown from a thicket into his head.

A little farther on, a hyena jumped in front of the bus and ran ahead of us for a good mile until its despair directed it sideways into the bush. After circling the base of Mt. Meru, we reached the rolling steppe plateau. The hills around were white with what seemed to be wild flowers but on closer view were thousands of storks congregated for their annual flight north. While some conducted a noisy rally, others flew in to join them.

Possibly many of them were bound for Poland, because storks that spend the European winter in East Africa fly along the Nile, then skirt the borders of Palestine and Lebanon, and finally cross over Asia Minor to relocate in Central Europe. (Those that winter in West Africa take a westerly route over Lake Chad, Morocco, and Spain.)

Now and then we passed Negro villages like oases, with occasionally a hotel for white tourists where African fauna, such as little parrots, were for sale. Close to the road were Hindu jumble shops with tailors seated in front of them making underwear and other garments for their black clients. Plodding through the village were Kikuyu women carrying bundles of merchandise or firewood on their backs, their bodies bent forward as the weight of their burden rested on a belt stretched around their foreheads. The women of the other tribes, in the habit of carrying their loads on their heads, hold themselves erect and move gracefully as if dancing a ballet. A half-naked Masai, leaning on a lance, stood on one leg, the other resting against his thigh as is customary with many Negroes. At one time the Masai were fierce enemies of the Kikuyus, stealing their cattle and fighting bloody wars to retain them. Now, protected by law, the Kikuyus live in peace.

Near the village we would see tiny boys guarding herds of grazing goats and sheep; one of the boys sat on his heels, chewing a piece of sugar cane and observing the traffic. These tiny shepherds would not be free to have some fun until evening, after the herds were driven into the corral.

On the road to one village we passed an old Negro driving donkeys laden with British-made cans filled with water. His ears, weighted down by brass ornaments, reached his shoulders; and the tattoo on his chest, the sign of his tribal allegiance, resembled a richly engraved breastplate. All over his body was an intricate pattern of incisions and eruptions shaped like beads. Such ritual mutilations are seen only rarely now.

As we neared Nairobi the road began to rise, the air was crisper, and the vegetation grew more luxuriant. Nairobi, then the capital city of East Africa, was as attractive as any modern city in an old-world country in the magnificence of its buildings, the width of its streets, and its cleanliness and orderliness. Although it was a mixture of many architectural styles, it was beautiful and lively—a far cry from the small camp of railroad men installing the line from the coast of Uganda in 1896. Here in Nairobi met, without integrating, four races: Negro, Hindu, Arab and British, differing in dress, language, religion, and mores.

Natives from the Kamba tribe, coming from the bush, were either half-naked or in their characteristic "throws" made of skins or in blankets worn directly on their bare bodies. The Negro women wore loose garments like togas in fantastic designs and vivid colors. The local Negroes went barefoot and wore shorts and shirts with the tails hanging out. The black soldiers of the King's Royal African Rifles looked like dolls in their slick black-and-blue uniforms with shining brass buttons. Dark-complexioned, black-eyed Hindu women with pomade on their hair and the tiny red dot on their forehead moved through the crowds with silent grace in their exquisite muslin saris. From time to time a Negro Moslem woman was seen, with precious stones mounted in her nostrils. Occasionally amid this exotic throng appeared a ginger-haired young Britisher in shorts and sport shirt.

Along with Roman Catholic and Anglican churches were mosques with muezzins in minarets summoning the faithful to prayer: "Allah is great; Mohammed is his prophet; come for prayers!" The cinemas showed the newest American, British, and Italian films; in restaurants one could order any type of cuisine in the world. Store windows displayed as elegant clothes and jewelry as could be found in any European or American city; and books were sold from all over the world. From a native of the Kamba tribe tourists could buy regional artifacts, primarily carvings of tribal warriors, which resembled ancient Egyptian figurines. One of the city's suburbs, Mutainga, residence of the more affluent whites, was actually a large park, its villas hidden among lush, carefully maintained gardens.

The Polish group in Nairobi was small, primarily young people. Girls who had learned English and also some kind of trade had first come from area camps to work for the British Auxiliary Territorial Service (ATS). When the military units were dissolved, they had found jobs in various Nairobi firms. A similar group of boys were working in the machine shops.

Coinciding with my stay in Nairobi were the unforgettable celebrations in honor of Our Lady of Fatima, especially an evening procession with lighted candles, torches, and lanterns, manifesting a living faith that united all people irrespective of tribal or national differences. In the Irish church, the faithful recited the rosary throughout the night. All sang as thousands, among them many lame or crippled, processed in front of the statue of the Mother of God, kissing its feet prayerfully. A pilgrimage of Polish youth planned for these celebrations had to be cancelled when they were denied permission to leave the camp.

In the company of Monsignor Wladyslaw Slapa, I went on to Lake Victoria in Uganda to visit the Polish camp in Koja, where we were to conduct a retreat for the children and young people. We traveled the approximately 500 miles by car, through a landscape much more interesting than the Tanganyika steppe. The road wound through plantations, forests, and grasslands. Despite the almost European climate, the white people protected their heads from the deadly ultra-violet rays with cork helmets or wide-brimmed green felt hats.

Leaving Nairobi, the road climbed steadily along the easterly wall, the so-called Escarpment, to 7500 feet above sea level. Between the Easterly and Westerly Escarpments runs The Great Rift Valley, which since time immemorial must have been filled with water to judge by lakes dotting its bottom. Making the dizzying descent along the inner slope of the Rift, we passed one of its many volcanic craters, the Longonot, long since extinct, and then Lake Naivasha, ringed by dark mountains and shining in the sun. Not much farther on was another lake, small, shallow, and mucky, whose surface seemed to be covered with fiery red rose petals. Suddenly they began to rise like leaves scooped up by the wind, creating a pink cloud against the sky: red flamingos, their wings darkly splotched, beaks protruding, legs stretched back. An unforgettable sight, this flight of the flamingos above the scorched Rift bottom stretching a hundred miles.

Beyond the nice little town of Nakuru, the asphalt road climbed again to the opposite escarpment, higher than the other by fifteen hundred feet. At its edge we crossed the equator in a temperature of over 120° F. From this crest the road descended precipitously toward Lake Victoria, 3,720 feet above sea level. Here in the Kericho area we drove through tea plantations, rows and rows of beautifully maintained bushes with leaves so thick and green they looked like rich velvet.

We stopped for the night in a small lakeshore town called Kisumu, where after dark the hippopotami roam the streets. The night was hot and humid, and from the back rooms of the hotel came the noisy singing of British farmers spending the weekend in town. We tossed on our beds like netted fish and found it impossible to sleep.

The highway circling the northern shore of Lake Victoria was the color of ocher, hard and smooth as asphalt. Ginger-colored termite mounds rose from the ground like rocky, misshapen steeples, some as high as tall trees, some attached to trees—much larger than any we had ever seen in Tanganyika. As we drove beside marshlands of papyri and water-lilies and splashed through overflowed areas, we guessed that we were nearing the Nile. On little islands in the distance we could see cocoanut palms and euphorbia, their fans swaying in the wind, their trunks like giant candelabra.

Now and then the road dived into thick jungle where each tree seemed to be fighting for sunlight. On their trunks and limbs hung garlands of liana, poison ivy, and other more firmly spun creepers. Wherever the sun was unable to penetrate, the underbrush was lusterless and sparse, but wherever it could even glimmer through small leaves and flowers, it transformed their lacy patterns into stained-glass designs. At the edge of the forest, where the sun seldom comes, grew a thick wall of vegetation impenetrable except to animals. We met only a family of baboons who watched us warily.

Just beyond the little town of Jinja, the road crossed a bridge over the foaming cascades of the Nile. They no longer run free, for a dam has since been built to power generators so huge that they produce electricity for all of East Africa. The enormous reservoir of fresh water that is Lake Victoria, second largest in the world after Lake Superior, has also become a blessing to Egypt; its even flow of water can now irrigate large areas of the desert.

Placed among rocks at the site is an historic marker honoring the first white man to see Lake Victoria, John Henning Speke: "Speke found this source of the Nile in 1862." The inscription suggests that somewhere the Nile must have another source, and some learned men so argued in a dispute that began almost at once. Because of this argument, Speke, who must have anticipated favors from Her Majesty's government for having named his discovery after her, had to be satisfied with permission to use on his coat of arms a crocodile and a hippopotamus, animals allegedly present at the birth of the Nile. Because of its great length, the Nile, honored by ancient people as "Father of Rivers," is often called an artery, carrying life from the very heart of Africa, Lake Victoria.

The last stretch of road to the Polish camp in Koja curved through a forest of great trees whose wide-reaching crowns met overhead to form a tunnel. To emerge from that natural archway and see the camp from the slope of the hill, nestled as if in the palm of a hand, was to see at once how well planned it was. It did have only a few trees; all its white-washed huts were bathed in sunlight. But they were arranged in neat rows along either side of wide streets. On an elevation at the center of the camp was the chapel-altar protected only by a roof and a removable screen. Its framework resembled that of the Ostra Brama in Vilno, famous street shrine of the Blessed Virgin Mary, whose picture, painted by the artist Froudist, is venerated daily by townspeople and pilgrims. In front of the chapel stretched a wide, grassy area where groups of people congregated for services, ever exposed to the tropical sun or the downpours of the rainy season. On a tree-covered slope opposite the camp were the administration buildings, nicknamed "The High Life." In the dell between the hills were hospital huts, often occupied by young patients afflicted with malaria or bilharziasis caused by a parasite. Behind the hospital, in a fenced-off area of flowers and shade trees, was a cemetery. One uniquely ornamented grave attracted particular attention, that of seventeen-year-old Jerzy Miedzyrzecki, the young man whose death at the Boy Scout Jamboree in Uganda I have recorded in Chapter XXII. The entire surface of the gravestone and cross was decorated in stainless steel with the Boy Scout insignia, the fleur-de-lys.

When we had time, we made short excursions with the young people into neighboring areas, accompanied by the local parish priest, a jovial Franciscan, Father Joseph Gruza. Most often we headed for Lake Victoria, whose wide horizon made it look like a sea. Emil Ludwig calls it "the giant mirror of the African sun." Although its shores were dotted with palm, acacia, mimosa and oleander, and its wide blue waters and its little isles beckoned bathers and boaters, an evil fate hung over it. It was contaminated with bacteria called bilharzias (after Theodore M. Bilharz, 1825-1862, a German parasitologist), which enter the blood through the pores and cause serious disorders, among them loss of weight and pernicious anemia. Every marsh and every quiet bay also teemed with malaria-carrying mosquitoes, and access to some of the islands was forbidden because of tse-tse flies. On others, cared for by missionaries, lived those walking corpses, the lepers.

Because of its contamination and its multitudes of crocodiles, bathing in the lake was forbidden. This was a restriction difficult to obey, for the children loved water and water sports. Some of the older boys could not be frightened by the threat of punishment or by bilharziasis or by crocodiles until fifteen-year-old Marian Sliwa paid for his recklessness with his life. He and two other boys went one day to the lake with the idea of swimming across a large bay. Women hanging their laundry among the trees reminded the boys of the danger, but they ignored the warning and jumped in. When they were some considerable distance from shore, they were horrified to see a crocodile heading toward them, its eyes bulging, its nose cutting the smooth surface of the lake. People on shore watched with dread as the boys separated, trying frantically to escape the monster; but Marian, the nearer, could not swim fast enough, and the crocodile reached him with a few powerful strokes of its tail. It opened its jaw wide, grabbed the boy at the waist, tossed him up, and in a moment disappeared with him under the water. A motorboat raced from the camp to retrieve the remnants, but nothing could be found. The crocodile, in fact, almost caused another tragedy; apparently struck by the grappling hook, it almost capsized the boat with a powerful blow from its tail.

* * *

Until recent times, Uganda had little to do with the white civilization. Though under British protection, the Negro did not feel he was living under an occupation. The British government, from its headquarters in the city of Entebbe, was, at the time of our visit in 1949, preparing the natives for self-government. Now, though still a member of the Commonwealth, Uganda is considered a partly free country with the freedoms of assembly, speech, and press; the government has banned internal travel, also national news agencies and foreign newspapers since the reporting of Idi Amin's policies. According to U.N. statistics it is one of the least developed, lowest-income countries of the world and one of the most seriously affected by adverse economic conditions. Its many tribes have been historically conditioned to enmity and rivalry. But Uganda is blessed with the potential of rich agricultural production besides its principal income crops of cotton and coffee. With the construction of the gigantic electric power station, Owens Falls Dam at the headwaters of the White Nile; with governmental enforcement of firmer law and order; and with the promise of closer and friendlier relations with her natural allies, Tanzania, Zambia, and Mozambique, its chaotic economy should stabilize.

Increasing nationalism and anti-colonialism make it easy to accuse the colonial powers of exploitation. Of course, the slave trading, banditry, and robbery of the seventeenth and eighteenth centuries covered the white race with ineradicable shame. But the greatest enemies of the black people were the Arabs and the tribal chiefs themselves, who rounded up the prospects, killed off those unfit for sale, and tied the rest to one long chain for the lengthy march to the coast and the ships of white slave-traders. No one but God can count the tears and the sorrows of these innocent human beings, of the young men and women taken from their mothers, of the weaker victims left along the road to be eaten alive by ants, vultures, hyenas, and jackals.

Some good has come from the seventy-five-year occupation by the British. A few white people, outraged by the slave trade and inspired by the Christian spirit, fought against these wrongs. Some even died in this fight at the point of an Arab sword or the poisoned arrow of a native. But thanks to their determination, the natives became more educated and now are able to occupy positions in all branches of cultural and economic life. In their humanitarian task, the colonial authorities were greatly assisted by the missionaries. The British, especially those who were born in Africa, and the missionaries who had worked there for years, knew and understood the natives. Generally speaking, their relationship with them was something like that of an elder sibling with a younger who regards it as his duty to watch over the younger until he grows up. Uganda now has one of the most Christianized populations in all Africa.

The capital of Uganda is Kampala. On one of our excursions we visited our countrymen in the hospital there. As we rode past construction sites, fields, plantations, and pastures, we saw Negroes at work, smiling, good-natured, happy. One would sing as he sat on a roof tying elephant grass to the rafters; another, breaking the hard soil with a pick, would work to the rhythm of a song, sometimes a church hymn. Though his tasks were often hard, the Ugandan, always open to distraction and ready to play, did not put much of himself into any job.

Like ancient Rome, Kampala is spread over seven hills, some occupied by the king's palace; Makerere College, the first African university and probably still an affiliate of London University; the Catholic church; the Anglican cathedral; and the mosque. Our sick countrymen were very glad to see us. The young ones were generally in good spirits, though the older ones viewed the future with misgivings. When the camp was finally closed down, who would think of them? Who would care for them? Which country would receive them?

Our last days in the Koja settlement coincided with the onset of the rainy season, preceded by an influx of tiny flies shaped like mosquitoes. They were everywhere: in the course of a conversation, they would fall into one's mouth, get into one's nostrils, sit on the food, fill every slight crack, attack lighted windows in dense masses, and enwrap every electric lamp in a grey cloud. They always appeared when there was a full moon, and during their invasion every type of work was difficult, especially any requiring an electric light. After a few days they suddenly disappeared without a trace.

Then came the thunder, and all across the horizon the dark sky opened, pouring down streams of water while, low overhead, the dense clouds burst like old barrels. All living creatures sought shelter; all nature, as if humbled, bowed down. And from the earth simultaneously rose mists so thick they obscured the world. Above the lake area, the thunder roared like a barrage of cannons and the lightning reveled, silhouetting trees and huts in brief, blinding flashes and spotlighting the terrified faces of the youngsters who dared to watch it. Its forked tongues joined at times into wide ribbons; their giant sparks seemed about to set the world on fire, as the thunder continued its salvos. Then in this humid glow, more needles of lightning would appear to stitch the horizon together again.

We came to regard such tropical storms as most appropriate for the fierce, unharnessed natural beauty of Africa.

30

The Communists Claim the Orphans

The year of victory for the Allies over the hordes of Hitler was 1945, but for the thousands of Poles in Africa it had no significance whatever. They could no longer return to their homeland, occupied now by the Communists, who had caused such harm as could never be undone or forgotten. Though the African camps continued their existence for some years after the war, by 1947 the pressure of the International Refugee Organization to liquidate them had increased considerably.

Since the Polish Armies, when military activities in Italy and Western Europe ceased, had been moved to Great Britain for demobilization, the possibility of reuniting the scattered families there was being considered. The women and children who had husbands, fathers or brothers in the army were therefore among the first to leave Africa. The others began trying to get permits to go to other countries, especially Australia and Argentina. Emigration to the United States, restricted to a quota, was possible for very few. The small number who returned to Poland were those half-orphans who had been urged to do so in letters from fathers or mothers there.

The greatest worry of the refugee community in Africa at that time was the fate of the remaining orphans. Early in 1947, the children from the liquidated camps in Africa and India joined the Tengeru orphanage, their fate taken care of by a Guardianship Committee formed in 1945, when the Allied governments withdrew their recognition of the Polish Government-in-Exile. The nominal President of the Committee was the Bishop of Dar-es-Salaam, Edgar Maranta, though the actual responsibility rested with the elected vice presidents, Poles from Tengeru. The Highest Court of Tanganyika empowered the Committee to care for the orphans and decide what would be done with them.

In the summer of 1947, their case took a very unfavorable turn. The organization assisting refugees, the UNRRA, intent on cooperating with the Communists, wanted to accede to their demand that the children be sent to Poland. The resulting wave of anxiety only caused the demand to become firmer and more insistent. The desperate defense against this forced repatriation of the children was reflected in numerous dispatches, notices, and records of meetings of the Guardianship Committee of that period. The summer of 1949 brought the matter to a climax: the children must leave the Black Land. That was exactly what the Communist regime in Warsaw wanted. Upon leaving Africa the children would be outside the jurisdiction of the Guardianship Committee and deprived of the moral support of the refugee community.

After 1947, when the UNRRA handed over the care of the refugees to the IRO, the liquidation of the refugee camps was accelerated. To the IRO the repatriation of the orphans seemed to be the simplest task of all, and they therefore dealt with the Tengeru orphanage first. They proposed to the Guardianship Committee that the children be transferred to those parts of Europe where immigration commissions of various countries were still operating. The children willing to go back to Poland would be able to leave for Poland from there.

Under normal conditions the IRO proposal would have been accepted without opposition. The Poles in Africa, however, had serious reservations, because in post-war Europe the widely spread Red regime of Warsaw could easily assimilate a group of orphans. Reports from Europe brought news of the compulsory repatriation of thousands of adults and children behind the Iron Curtain, and the consequent tragedies. The anxiety about the fate of the children in Africa was justified and increased by reports from New Zealand, where the Warsaw regime was categorically demanding the repatriation of all Polish children there.

In Tengeru we had no proof that the IRO proposal was in any way connected with Polish Communist diplomatic maneuvers; nonetheless we questioned the intentions of the organization. Much later, after the storm had blown over and the children were already in Canada, we learned that these suspicions had been well founded. In his speech during the 111th Session of the United Nations Committee, Mr. J. D. Kingsley, Director of the IRO, reported that the Communists in Poland had demanded permission from central IRO authorities in Geneva to meet with Polish children living in Africa. Twice the IRO had proposed that the repatriation committee come to Tanganyika, but the Warsaw regime had rejected the proposals. The people in the Tengeru settlement, together with the Guardianship Committee, had been right in fearing that to send the children to Europe without visas was tantamount to having them shipped to Poland.

The sudden liquidation of the Educational Centre in Rongai in 1947, without any stated reasons, was itself very puzzling. Just as the children were boarding the train, it was rumored that the whole transport was to go to Mombasa, en route to Europe. This would have been the first attempt to separate the children from the organized refugee community. The Guardianship Committee intervened instantly, and the children were translocated to the orphanages in Tanganyika and Uganda.

Facing the increasing unrest, the Committee took steps to obtain asylum for the children somewhere in the free world. Because of the numerous, well organized concentrations of Poles there, the most suitable country would, they thought, be Great Britain. If Great Britain could not admit the whole group, then it would be a case of finding fictitious relatives and guardians among Polish war veterans. The Committee commenced discussions first with the Polish Combatants Association, then with the Women's Voluntary Services. In the meantime they were also in touch with organizations in Argentina, the United States, and Ireland. But all in vain. Some of the appeals were not even acknowledged. In the meantime the matter was becoming desperately urgent.

In October of 1948, there was some hope that the older orphans could be sent to Great Britain, because the Labor Recruiting Board of the British Ministry had been enticing Poles to work there. But not many orphans had reached the minimum age.

Nervous tension grew from week to week in Tengeru, as the IRO and the British authorities exerted constant pressure on the Guardianship Committee to have the children sent to Europe. Then in November, 1948, the representative of the IRO in Tengeru, F. Lorriman, proposed that the children be sent to Italy, promising that they would be enrolled in schools there and cared for by a Catholic organization in a Polish environment. Pressed for details, he was able to give neither the name of the camp nor the organization, and the Committee disproved his assurance that the cost of the children's education in Italy would be less than in Africa. Italy had been devastated by the war. Transportation costs to Australia, Argentina, or Canada were cheaper. From Mr. Lorriman's vague statements, it seemed that were the orphanage transferred to Italy, it would remain under IRO supervision, and none of us had confidence in that organization. In view of these uncertainties the Committee postponed reviewing the proposal until they could get more precise information.

The stance of the Committee was clear, and the postponement to the children's advantage. The Committee maintained firmly that even in transit through Europe they must be provided with visas to ensure that they could get safely to the country where they were to settle. Without at least a guarantee of asylum for all the children in a free country, they would not be safe in Europe, especially since it would take much time to obtain visas and this delay would be to the advantage of the Polish Communists. The Committee also strove to ensure that, if the children were sent to Italy, another organization, duly authorized by legal authority, would take over their guardianship. The unknown organization suggested by the IRO did not constitute a sufficient guarantee.

The position of the Guardianship Committee was fully endorsed by the ambassador to the Vatican of the Polish Government-in-Exile, Dr. K. Papee. In his opinion, transporting the children to Italy under existing conditions "is by all means inadvisable." He also noted that "the Polish Embassy at the Holy See . . . delivered, on the 31st of March, 1947, a memorandum recommending the fate of the children to the Holy Father's attention, also pointing out the danger of possible repatriation. The higher powers of the Vatican showed a great and sincere interest in this matter and, as I learned, undertook the necessary steps to include the Polish group in the contingent of orphans from Europe, the one that was to be received and taken care of by the Canadian Episcopate, and to be resettled in Canada."

But the pressure exerted by the IRO to send the orphanage to Italy as quickly as possible resulted in the demand that the guardians prepare the children for the trip at once. The time allotted was so short that it was all but impossible to liquidate the affairs of the orphanage and get around 150 children ready to leave. The Committee therefore appealed to the Governor of Tanganyika for a postponement, still hoping that the Vatican might succeed in its negotiations with the Episcopate of Canada, or that Great Britain might be induced to receive the children.

Meanwhile the unrest in the camp was increasing steadily,

and affecting the children. The nightmare of the past was reawakened in them, with its attendant suspicion, distrust, and fear. Despite all our efforts, these prematurely mature children shared in all the emotional tensions of the camp. They well knew that once again their fate was at stake, and they wanted to know everything that was going on. They sent out their own spies to lurk around buildings where the Guardianship Committee was meeting and around huts where the adults were chatting.

On the 4th of April, 1949, a rumor went around that the IRO was threatening to withhold all financial aid for the orphans unless they left for Italy by the deadline, the 28th of April. The news electrified, and infuriated, the whole camp, both children and adults. But at that moment came news from the Vatican: Canada had agreed to take the Polish orphans from Africa under the guardianship of the Canadian Episcopate. The episcopal officials also sought permission of the federal government to conduct medical examinations and visa-related formalities in Tanganyika. "Under those conditions," wrote Ambassador Papee, "the transfer of the children to Italy is now, more than ever, pointless; therefore, steps have been taken to prevail upon the IRO to abandon the project."

But there was no reaction from the IRO headquarters in Geneva, only dead silence. The days were hurrying on, and the closer the deadline approached, the greater the bitterness in the camp. Its residents missed no opportunity to show their animosity toward the IRO delegate in Tengeru. The children seemed to be the most affected: fear showed in their pale faces, and their eyes seemed to be asking, What is going to happen to us? They gathered here and there in corners, debating the reports of their spies. In the classroom they were absent in spirit, their eyes unfocused, their homework unfinished, their interest deadened.

Their minds were disturbed even more by the drastic step of the Director of the Refugees in Tanganyika, A. L. Pennington, until then a friend of the Poles, who in the middle of April notified the British Commanding Officer at the Tengeru camp that the dealine was irrevocable. Simultaneously he overturned the decision of the Highest Tribunal that had affirmed the Guardianship Committee as the legal guardian of the children who had arrived from the Rongai centre, from Kenya, and from India. Over them, he stated, the Committee had no authority whatever, and should any child resist leaving, he would be subject to deportation as a destructive and anarchic element.

To fill their cup of misfortune, the Polish Citizens Committee in Nairobi, represented by the Delegate of the Ministry of Religious Affairs and of Public Education, Seweryn Szczepanski, and the Reverend Monsignor Wladyslaw Slapa, supported the IRO plan. This unfortunate stance not only astounded and angered the residents at Tengeru but also strengthened the hand of the IRO delegate, Lorriman. All of this depressing news made the orphans resolve to escape into thc bush if they were forced to leave. They could hardly be persuaded to abandon such a dangerous idea.

The Guardianship Committee still resisted the IRO's decision to send the children to Italy without visas. Three days before the deadline, Mr. Lorriman, surprised by the resistance and by the mood in the camp, decided to confer with the Committee and speak with the orphans personally. He did not talk with the children, however, because the whole camp was already irritated and because camp representatives demanded that he call a general gathering of all the residents, to explain why he was putting so much pressure on the Guardianship Committee. Mr. Lorriman answered drily that he had nothing to clarify, since he had been ordered to relocate the children, and that the attitude of the people in the camp did not concern him at all. A serious confrontation was avoided by the British Commanding Officer, who gave permission for the gathering, promising that he would come himself and prevail upon Mr. Lorriman to participate.

On the 27th of April, the eve of the official deadline, the gathering was held in the camp theatre at the edge of the jungle, with all the Polish refugees present and Father Zenon Wierzbinski presiding. The whole community voted for a resolution supporting the position of the Guardianship Committee and resolving not to allow the IRO to take the children away without visas, or at least the assurance that they would be granted visas immediately upon arriving in Europe. The older members of the community stood solidly behind the orphans; they decided to adopt them if the IRO should carry out their threat. The last words of the resolution were, "We regard it as our most sacred duty to protect the orphans of our soldiers or those who died in Russia; and, therefore, we cannot give the children into ill treatment in the camps without other care than that provided by the officials of the International Refugee Organization, in whom, after many painful experiences, we have much too little confidence."

Such community support had a very soothing effect on the

fevered, fearful minds of the children. A discordant note, difficult to bear, was the Polish radio broadcast from Nairobi that very day. Almost every refugee listened to the program because of the emotional tension over the fate of the children. They were dismayed to hear S. Szczepanski urge them not to resist the orders from the IRO but to send the children to the port of Mombasa the next morning.

The next morning at 6:30, in a drizzling rain, the trucks rolled into the camp to take the children and their luggage to the railway station. The orphanage was very peaceful. The huts, with beds carefully made, stood empty. In this hour so crucial for them, the children went to Holy Mass. Then the Guardianship Committee ordered the normal program for the day. The truck and railway transports were canceled. At that point the chief of the IRO for the whole of Africa, H. A. Curtis, announced that the IRO would make good its threat and withhold credit for the maintenance of the orphans until they had left Tanganyika for good.

Thanks to the kindness of the British authorities, however, the orphans continued to be fed and provided for from the maintenance stores. The Guardianship Committee, in a memorandum to the IRO, accused it of resorting to blackmail and reiterated their motives for resisting its order; they asserted correctly that, in so doing, they were expressing the will of the whole camp community. These were anxious days for the members of the Committee. It was a fact that they had the whole camp community behind them, but it was also true that they were acting without legal authority; their actions were not, in fact, even supported by the Polish Government in London, an attitude they could not understand. Was it possible that their appeals and letters of alarm had not reached the proper hands? On the 27th of April, after the memorable gathering of the camp, Father Zenon Wierzbinski had sent a letter, on behalf of the Committee, to the President of the Council of Ministers, asking for an opinion on the propriety of the Committee's position. The letter remained unanswered. Nor did the Committee receive any support from the Refugee Guardians Office in Africa, which acted on the authority of the London government.

In so grave a situation, the Committee, not wanting to prolong the tension, reluctantly decided to send the children to Italy. But though they finally had to surrender, their stubborn resistance had three positive effects: the authorities handling refugee affairs were made acutely aware that the children were not mere merchandise to be dumped at random; the Committee won a precious few days to set up in Italy a new guardianship empowered to receive and care for the children; and there was now time to outfit each child properly for the journey.

The final official date for their departure from Tengeru was the 2nd of June, 1949. The camp turned into a veritable beehive. The orphanage crew feverishly arranged for transportation. All the programs in the Secondary School and the Tailoring Shops were suspended so that teachers and pupils could make suits for the boys (two each) and dresses for the girls (three each). The Mechanical School repaired metal suitcases and soldered cans for lard and butter; the Carpentry Shop made chests for extra food rations (12 lbs. per child)—the "iron ration" in case of shortages in the European camps. The camp's supply stores issued new blankets, bed sheets, sweaters, boots, and other necessities. Our hearts burst with pleasure to see the authorities so generously ensuring that the children would suffer no deprivation in Europe.

The children were overjoyed that Canada was going to take them in and, like children the world over, excited at the prospect of traveling to new lands over new seas. Canada's very distance made it alluring, mysterious. Excited conversations were heard everywhere. Crowds of children visited the huts of friends and families. They hastily took photographs in front of the "beehive" huts and the church; among the flowers; in groups with favorite dogs and cats. They were saying farewell to everything they most cherished: the corners they had played in, the stream in the jungle, the lianas; the schools they had worked so hard in for such long years; the cemetery where a relative was buried. To help keep up their spirits, they saved the persons dearest to them to see at the very last moment. But the closer the moment of parting, the sadder their faces, and those they were to leave behind. Some of the orphans ran to the jungle for a good cry. The day before they were to leave, they went to say goodbye to their church and to commit themselves into the care of Our Lady of Ostra Brama at the main altar. Many received Holy Communion. This parting was as sad as every new parting would ever be for these children.

At long last the trucks moved, with their 150 children, toward the railway station, where the train was waiting. The IRO had, at the last minute, decided to include a group of more mature orphans who were now capable of deciding their own fate; some who were morally unbalanced were to become problems for the adults accompanying the group. The head of the transport was the experienced manager of the orphanage, Mrs. Eugenia Grosicki, who years ago in Russia had taken some of these children from the arms of their dying mothers. Seeing that she was going to Italy, the children stopped being afraid that they would be sent back to Communist Poland. They knew how tenderhearted she was, and how uncommonly courageous. To help her, a few other persons, including myself as chaplain, went along also. Many other friends of the children accompanied them as far as the port in Mombasa. At the railway station, among those saying farewell, stood Father Zenon Wierzbinski, a member of the Guardianship Committee who had kept the fate of these orphaned children so close to his heart. Soon the train was carrying the beloved youngsters away into the wide steppe.

They went off singing a merry song, but the people who had so gallantly fought for their welfare were heavy-hearted and filled with apprehension. Each of them silently commended the children to God and His Most Holy Mother for safekeeping.

31

Parting with Africa

In Mombasa the children lived in a staging camp in a suburb named Nyali until they embarked—almost a week. The camp sat under umbrellas of cocoanut palms not far from the ocean. Some of the children remained in camp, playing on the seashore, collecting colored shells, and swimming; but the more curious wanted to spend their last days in Africa seeing the port and the town, so I agreed to take them sightseeing. Downtown we bought souvenirs and picture postcards, photographs of Negro types and of wild animals, and carvings of ebony and ivory. Mombasa was a new experience for the children, since they did not remember passing through it seven years before.

This city, called the gateway to East Africa, has an intriguing history. Although for the average European African history begins only at the moment the white man arrived, the history of the East African Coast goes back to the days of the pharaohs and the Phoenicians. It is assumed that this region is a part of the mysterious land called Pont, referred to in Egyptian chronicles dating back four thousand years before Christ. In the fifteenth century B.C. a woman pharaoh named Hatzsepsut sent a fleet of five ships to this land to import precious stones and sandalwood. It is quite conceivable that Mombasa was the port at which the Egyptian fleet called. This event is commemorated in a low-relief etching on the wall of the temple dedicated to the queen-goddess in Thebes. It shows an admiral of the fleet, dressed in white, stepping down onto the land with gifts, mostly weapons and cheap trinkets. To meet him comes the King of Pont, tall Pe-re-hu, with his obese wife. The huts on the shore resemble the domed dwellings of the present-day Negroes. According to the carving, the port was situated in a deep bay, almost identical to the one forming the old Mombasa harbor.

Along the eastern shore of Africa ran the ancient gold route; the place names, right down to the Union of South Africa, suggest a Phoenician origin. It is conceivable that the Phoenician expeditions to the exotic land of Ofir (present-day Zimbabwe) trekked along this route to wherever their colonies were, exploiting gold-bearing lodes. It is known from the Bible and from Abyssinian chronicles that it was from the land of Ofir that the Queen of Sheba sent gold to King Solomon for the construction of the temple in Jerusalem. The ancient mines and ruins can still be seen today in Zimbabwe.

Touring the old port, we had the impression that history had stopped dead in its tracks. Unlike the new one, where the most luxurious modern ships call, the old harbor was crowded with light, agile dhows, the Arabian sailboats unchanged for thousands of years. Their noisy Arab sailors seemed to be the same fanatics, the same obtrusive traders as in ancient days, always ready for an argument and a fight, and still using the same navigational terms their ancestors learned from the ancient Persians.

On this shore, so history has it, were once located the fabulously rich warehouses of the Bagdad sultan Harun-al Rashid, whose ships carried off to the North, in exchange for Persian merchandise, gold, ivory, sandalwood, ebony, monkeys, and slaves. One of his men was the legendary Sinbad the Sailor, whose fantastic adventures are woven into the fable of *The Thou-*

sand and One Nights. Along these shores also operated such well known pirates as the Turk Ali Bey and Captain Kidd.

In 1498, Vasco da Gama called at Mombasa on his first journey to India, though the bellicose natives did not allow him to dock and he had to go a bit farther, to Malindi. About that same time, other Portuguese had been colonizing the East Coast of Africa, building fortresses and fighting Arabs, vying for supremacy in the slave market. Mombasa happened to be the staging area for black slaves, sold in the markets of Zanzibar. One of the Portuguese fortresses here is Fort Jesus. We walked on its grim, red-grey embankments that once guarded the port, the little windows in its neat turrets looking like eyes gazing down at the dark blue waters of the ocean. Just below the fort, in the monsoon season, fierce waves break against the coral reefs. Today it is the most peaceful spot in the harbor, indeed in the whole town; and its silence invites one to contemplate the grand days of its prime when pirates, traders, and colonists fought for its walls.

Going across the bridge to Nyali, I mentioned to the youngsters that not far from here died the brave Negro Matthew Chemgwimbe Wellington, who took part in one of the expeditions seeking Dr. David Livingston, lost in the heart of the Black Land. Matthew, once sold as a slave, had returned to Africa after untold adventures and had the honor of carrying the sick Livingstone from nearby Lake Tanganyika. The explorer died, but the faithful Negroes brought his body to the Coast and deposited it before the British consul in Zanzibar. Chemgwimbe remembered his bwana (good master) until he died, recalling him with tears in his eyes.

On the 4th of June we boarded an Italian steamship *Gerusalemme*: 150 children—seventy-nine boys and seventy-one girls—their supervisor, Mrs. Grosicki, three other women, the crew, and I, chaplain and deputy manager. By coincidence we also had the company of F. Lorriman, the IRO official, on his way to Canada for a vacation.

Many of our friends were gathered on the wharf, and ever so many friends of the children—English, Polish, Hindu, and Greek—all saying their fond farewells. Soon the outline of the town and the harbor slipped from sight. Fort Jesus, against its background of green vegetation, was the last to disappear. Then the Black Land was sunk into the ocean. We were alone.

PART THREE

Through Europe

32

Aboard the SS. Gerusalemme

The sea was calm, and the voyage was pleasant. The ship's command undertook to make the two-week journey enjoyable by constantly organizing activities for the orphans. They competed with great gusto in eating spaghetti with tomato sauce without using their hands, eating apples suspended on a string, carrying water in a spoon from one basin to another a fair distance away, and undergoing many other tests of coordination and dexterity. The cleverness and agility they had developed in their frolics on the steppe and in the jungle came in handy now, and enabled them to win top spots among the children aboard. Mrs. Grosicki organized ethnic dance programs in the first-class salon, to the accompaniment of the ship's orchestra. The spectators who filled the salon always applauded generously and gave the dancers candy; one time they even took up a collection and presented 400 shillings to Mrs. Grosicki for the children's benefit.

Every day there were concerts, and the children swam in a pool made out of sail-cloth and watched the porpoises and flying fish. Often one could hear our girls singing from some corner of the ship. The sailors were delighted by our children and couldn't do enough for them. One sailor, a born comedian, pretended that he wanted to learn Polish and entertained them with his comical pronunciation of words that are difficult for foreigners.

Our young people, then, had a period of freedom from worry. But for us, their guardians, each day brought a new concern. Almost from the day we left Tengeru, we had been upset by the behavior of a few adolescent boys and girls attached to our transport. Undisciplined, arrogant, and rude, they began to have a bad influence on the younger ones. They suspected us of possessing a large sum of money, allegedly meant to be shared, and demanded to be given "what is our due." They maintained that they did not need any favor or any care, and urged the others to disobey those who were "stealing" from them. When one of the young girls stood up for us, an older girl slapped her. Then, there was the immodest behavior of a few older girls toward the men and older boys: we worried about their own reputation as well as about the bad influence they could have on the younger girls.

These wayward charges also developed less dangerous, though equally vexing, habits. They began drinking table wine at lunch and dinner; we finally had to ask the ship's stewards to dilute it. A few of the boys began smoking cigarettes on the sly, and wearing large hats, often dusty and sweaty. Though necessary and thus entirely appropriate in Africa, this headgear was an affront to the properly dressed passengers and made the boys look like gangsters. I ordered them to put away their hats; those who disobeyed had them thrown overboard.

Sailing around the large African promontory, we called at Aden, anchoring some distance from the port. From behind the curtain of stuffy air quivering with heat emerged the dark silhouettes of bare mountains. After Aden we made a nightmarish passage through the Red Sea, a basin enclosed by the Sahara sands on the west and the Arabian desert on the east. Life on the ship subsided; people moved drowsily along the deck or lounged on deck chairs, sweating profusely; few came down to the dining room.

Beyond the chain of desert mountains to the west lay hidden from our view the "Gift of the Nile," Egypt, the most ancient kingdom of the Western world. We sailed into the Suez Canal at night, and by three o'clock the next afternoon we were passing a small town, El-Qantara. Knowing that it would interest the children, I told them that along this route more than nineteen hundred years ago the Family of the Holy Refugees, Saint Joseph with the Saintly Mother and Jesus, the Child, had traveled to Egypt. El-Qantara has, since time immemorial, been a stopping place for caravans on the East-West route. With my mention of the Holy Family's flight, things became livelier in our orphan family; children tired from the heat livened up, and we grown-ups told ourselves within our souls that nothing happens without God's will and we therefore submit to it in faith and trust.

El Qantara, a poor town the color of sand marked by a tall, slender minaret, was well known to the soldiers of the Second Polish Army Corps under General Anders. During the war, near that town and not very far from the Canal was the Polish Military Hospital No. 8, in which I had been one of the chaplains before leaving for East Africa. The camp's water tower, still standing there, was a very good orientation point. The children were fascinated by everything pertaining to the Polish soldier, and showered me with questions. "Please, Father, are the Polish soldiers still there?" asked Zosia. Her eyes became misty when I said, "They are, Zosia, but they are not alive. They are resting in the military cemetery, there beyond those tall trees, sleeping the sleep of the brave. Among the graves, on a pedestal, stands a dark cross with a raised sword affixed to it. This monument symbolizes the truth that such a grace as freedom has to be fought for, and that the road to victory is always the road of the cross, of pain, and of sorrow."

In a maze of images, I saw again the distorted faces, heard the broken whispers of the young soldiers dear to me whose eyes I had had to close. I thought with pity of the one who had joked about reporting to the company of corpses.

"Poor soldiers," murmured Bronia.

"Please, Father, those vultures cruising over there in the distance, they are not going to tear up the corpses of our soldiers, are they?" said Hela.

"No, the soldiers were buried in coffins deep in the earth, not as in Russia, where our dead, wrapped only in a bedsheet, were buried under a thin layer of sod. All military cemeteries are being carefully maintained. People of many countries offer money for this purpose, and the keeper plants flowers on behalf of those who remember their soldiers."

"But this is a horrible desert," said Janek. "As far as the eye can see there is nothing, and the heat is like an oven! It must have been very depressing for the soldiers to live here."

"Everything depends on the man, on the way he approaches life," I answered. "Our soldier was well inured to this climate, and brought so much humor into life that he often was as happy living in a desert as in a town. The desert did not depress him too much. Around the tents and huts he planted flowers and lush castor plants. The military camps were gradually becoming oases."

"But the sick soldiers were not able to move about. Their lives must have been a torture," said Janek.

"They had entertainment—movies, radio, books, newspapers, talks, conversation, games. Some of the convalescents became home-bred Egyptologists. They would walk through the desert looking for ancient scarabs or figurines of deities. Some hoped to become famous by discovering a sarcophagus."

The children began to complain about the unbearable heat. "I wouldn't want to stay here even for a day," sighed little Janka.

"It is true," I said, "the heat of the day hurts, but God has sweetened the life of the desert dwellers by giving them crisp, cool nights. Some sick soldiers could go out for evening walks and watch brightly lit mansions sailing through the darkness—some of them three stories high."

"Eh, I think you're kidding, Father," said Frania.

"Stupid!" jeered Zosia, "Father speaks the truth. Don't you know what kind of 'brightly lit mansions' sail through the desert? They are the ships on the canal, and at night they must look like palaces from the thousand and one nights."

Stefka noticed a herd of camels resting near the town and asked, "Did our soldiers ride camels from the railway station near the Canal to the hospital?"

I explained that our soldiers were brought to the hospital in military cars. It did happen, though, that returning from excursions to Port Said, Cairo, Alexandria, or ancient Thebes, they had to take the hackney coaches parked near the railway station. These rides were often wildly funny. At the sight of a potential customer a coach driver would literally push his horse's nostrils close to the client's nose and noisily extol the beast. "Good Churchill horse!" "Bismark horse!" "Charoszyj horse!" The most persistent driver having won, the coach would begin its crazy dance along the road. The horse would run as if demented, urged on by the Polish swear words that the Arabs had learned from the military. And if the coach reached the hospital still on four wheels, and the old jade still willing to pull it, the trip was considered a happy one.

At night we sailed past a monument to Ferdinand de Lesseps, builder of the Canal, with a beautiful Latin inscription "Aperire terram gentibus" ("To open the earth to the nations"), and docked at Port Said. Instantly the ship was surrounded by nimble little boats of Arabian vendors calling out "Hi! Signore! Hi! Signorina! Do you speak English, French, German, Italian? Hi!" They were peddling Egyptian cigarettes, purses, rugs, shoes made of snake or crocodile leather, mats, garlands made of sea shells, and other trinkets. The vendor would hoist his goods to the deck in a little basket suspended from a rope dropped from the ship, and the buyer would deposit his money in the basket. The children enjoyed watching this bazaar brokenly reflected in the water, and the agile Arabs, who fought with an oar for a spot close to the ship and out-shouted each other praising their goods. The children could later use the few foreign words they picked up during the transaction, but the commotion did almost blot out the skyline of the town just emerging from the darkness in a swarm of lights.

The next day we admired the peace and beauty of the navy-blue Mediterranean Sea, and later on, the misty, grey peaks of Crete. The youngsters were given a tour of the ship and saw the giant machines in the engine room, the captain's bridge, and the navigational instruments.

In the meantime our group began to be uneasy about the two elderly persons, not known to us, who had joined our transport when we left Africa. On the orders of the IRO official, Mr. Lorriman, these two—Mr. Joseph Walczak and Mme. Waclawa Szyszko—had replaced the person most respected and loved by the children who was to have sailed with us, Mr. Jacob Hoffman, a teacher. The two substitutes, allegedly going to Canada, began deliberately to foment rebellion among the girls and boys against Mrs. Grosicki and me, stating that shortly they would be taking over the care of the orphans. Walczak often photographed the children, but no one ever saw these pictures. We suspected that the two were in the service of the Communists, but so far we had no grounds for such suspicions. Our first stop-over in Italy was at Brindisi. During our twelve hours there, the local bishop, DePhillipis, having been notified by the Vatican, visited us with a few priests, a few nuns, and some ladies from Catholic Action. Among the priests was a Pole, young but already known world wide as a Biblicist, Rev. Tadeusz Milik. He greeted us warmly on behalf of the Holy Father and assured us that the fate of the orphans was very close to the Pope's heart; the children were given candy and holy pictures. This visit raised our spirits, for feeling strange and unsure, we had been dreading the moment we would have to leave the ship.

We were to have landed in Venice, but we had to come ashore in Bari, depressed to be greeted by rain and the indifference of the local IRO officials. We suffered our first wave of nostalgia for Africa. At seven o'clock in the evening we boarded a train for Salerno, near Naples, all of us packed into the two dirty, smokey cars assigned to the whole group. With a few boys I found a spot on the platform between the two carriages and we lay there on our coats. There was no water in the toilets, and we could get drinking water only at the stations and only by asking a policeman for it. We were forbidden to get off the train. It ran across the Apennine Peninsula through the cold night, rushing into a tunnel every so often. During the long, sleepless hours we were all troubled by presentiments of evil. The next day, exhausted and depressed, we were oblivious to the beautiful Italian countryside. Twelve o'clock noon was striking when we passed through the gates of another camp.

33

The Children's Camp in Salerno

It was June 24, 1949, when we arrived at the Children's Center, called "The IRO Center," in Salerno. The camp was a complex of corrugated sheet metal buildings, the so-called barrels, lined up in rows along the famous beach where on the 8th of September, 1943, the American army had landed.

About 150 yards from the barracks was the murmuring sea. To the north, between the greenish wall of the mountains and Salerno Bay, stretched the panorama of the city of Salerno, adorned with palms and stone pines. Still farther north, nesting on the walls of rocks among the mountains, were the picturesque tourist towns Amalfi and Ravello. Here and there on a peak were the ruins of an old castle. Between Salerno Bay and Naples Bay, bathed in sea foam, was Capri, the little island with its famous blue grotto. Toward the south sprawled the green lowland of the shore. A more picturesque stopover for the children could not be imagined. No wonder it was here they wished to stay the longest.

The inhabitants of the camp were a mosaic of nationalities: Yugoslavs, Serbs, Slovaks, Czechs, Germans, Italians, Ukranians, Albanians, and Jews. The Polish group was distinctive in being the most cohesive and best organized.

Just as we expected, and despite the assurances of the IRO in Africa, we found the camp poorly equipped and somewhat neglected. Though energetic and helpful, the management was not always capable of handling the multi-lingual herd, among whom was no shortage of morally corrupt youth.

We occupied nineteen sleeping blocks, all provided with the necessary utensils, brushes, and pails. The camp management greeted with satisfaction our efforts to introduce order and establish a daily routine. Mrs. Grosicki, with the help of the girls, attained this goal in record time. The huts soon shone with cleanliness, along the walls even rows of beds covered with neat blankets from Africa and here and there an embroidered tapestry or a colorful cushion.

The daily program resembled that of a boy scout camp. We began the day with reveille, common prayer, and calisthenics; and the rest of the day, including swimming and beach games, was governed by rules. Lifeguards, organized by the older boys, ensured safety on the beach. Mrs. Grosicki reorganized the procedure for showering by separating the adults of either sex from the children, dividing them into groups according to age, and assigning certain hours for each group. Orderly duties in the dining hall, in the huts, and in the shops were performed by our youngsters, and the older boys enlisted in the camp police force.

Food was plentiful, though it did not always suit the tastes of the Polish children because it was prepared in Yugoslavian style. Having inadequate supplies of fats and jams, we opened our own stocks; and we bought fruit from orchards in the area since we had received no allocation.

Nobody was able to foresee how long we might stay in Salerno, and the children, after only a few days with nothing they had to do, were already beginning to get into mischief. We therefore decided to organize a temporary school. The difficulties were enormous. We had no teachers, textbooks, furnishings, or teaching aids. But the problems were solved one by one. Two ladies and the two most advanced high-school girls volunteered to teach, and I joined them. The IRO brought in benches and blackboards from their stores in Rome. We taught religion, Polish, English, geography, history, and mathematics, preparing our lectures entirely from memory. Some of the boys enrolled in courses organized by the camp authorities in cabinet making and agricultural and commercial studies. Some of the girls took sewing and embroidery, with the help of the two sewing machines we had brought from Africa. Impressed by our instinct for orgnization, the camp authorities requested us to take into our classes children of other nationalities, thus far prowling the camp unsupervised. The Italian director of the IRO children's department, Mme. Damiani, cooperated with us devotedly. With the reserve fund of our group we bought the materials for embroidery, sewing utensils, phonograph records, paper, and all other essentials. A small theatre in the camp served during the day for gatherings and lessons and in the evenings, for dances and games; on Sunday it became a chapel for the whole camp.

At the request of the IRO authorities, all the ethnic groups staged a variety program in this theatre. Only our group came well prepared, in colorful costumes and with a rich program. They received such an ovation that they had to repeat some of their numbers. They were even invited to appear in the local theatre.

Despite all these activities, however, it was difficult to discipline the children. They knew that they were staying in Salerno only temporarily; the sea and the beach enticed them, and the sun was making them lazy. Their learning progressed very slowly. This was nothing, however, compared with the problem caused by the group of older girls who had already caused us worry aboard the ship. Thoughtless as they were, they were quite willing to associate with brazen, aggressive men without principle or conscience. Once we had to ask the Italian carabinieri to intervene and kick the unruly Albanians out of the camp. Later on, our own boys organized guard duty to prevent undesirable characters from approaching our girls. Once one of the boys on duty caught three of them, splashed them with paint, and threw them out.

The boys always found eager audiences for their stories about Africa. They boasted about their courage, showed off their Swahili, described native customs, and stretched the truth a bit in recounting their adventures with big game. Their amazed listeners were likely to learn that each boy went about in Africa loaded with firearms, that all Negroes are over six feet tall, that cobras spit into the eyes of evil people. One credulous person was even ready to believe that an elephant is made entirely of ivory.

In spite of a few problems, then, we were spending, on the whole, beautiful days beside Salerno's silvery bay. There remained, of course, our long-standing fear of what the Communists might be planning. It was, then, with great relief that we received word of a new three-person Guardianship Committee formed in Rome and invested with all the powers of the former in Tengeru. The head of the new committee, Mr. Emeryk Hutten-Czapski, visited us frequently from then on.

Relieved to be protected at least in this way, we began to think about touring the area, especially its monuments of antiquity. One excursion took us by automobile to nearby Paestum with its ruins of an ancient Greek colony dating from 650-600 B.C. This town, originally called Poseidonea, although devastated again and again by invaders such as the Saracens in the ninth century A.D., survived until the fifteenth century, when it was stricken by malaria and had to be abandoned. The children, knowing at first hand all about malaria, listened with emotion to this story.

What has survived the assaults of invaders, plague, and time in Paestum is three large Doric temples still remarkably well preserved. The one devoted to Poseidon, ancient god of the seas, is among the best preserved of ancient Greek temples. The large blocks of stone still rest on their columns, though now overgrown with moss and grass. The roof caved in long ago, but the later Roman road, paved with large slabs of stone, still fends off the weeds. Against the yellow-grey background of the ruins, this land, once praised by Virgil and other Roman poets for its roses, today shows only the sad cypress.

On other excursions to neighboring villages, we saw the German wartime fortifications, visited humble little village churches, and viewed a beautifully kept military cemetery where, flooded with flowers, far from their homeland, rest the sons of the land of freedom, the United States of America, fallen in the assault on the beaches of Salerno. A few times we visited Salerno itself, a city known in the middle ages for its advanced medical science. We prayed at the grave of the great revolutionary Pope, Saint Gregory VII, who died here in exile because of his love for justice and his hatred of violence, and visited the tomb of Saint Matthew the Apostle. Always, the Italians treated us most cordially.

We had planned other excursions—to the Isle of Capri, to Naples, and to Monte Cassino, captured during the war by the Second Polish Army Corps commanded by General Anders. And our greatest wish was to get to Rome for a special audience with the Holy Father, who, according to Undersecretary of State Monsignor Giovanni Battista Montini, often asked how the Polish orphans were getting along in Salerno.

But the appearance of Communists in the camp made these trips impossible.

34

The Abduction of the Murawski Sisters

One of the objectives of the organizations for aiding war refugees (first UNRRA, 1943-1947, then IRO, 1947-1952, both operating within the framework of the United Nations Organization) was to encourage and facilitate their repatriation.

While UNRRA was at the helm, the Communists established strong influences within it, and the repatriation officials sent out by the Communist governments to the refugee camps in Western Europe terrorized the refugees and pressured them in various ways to accept repatriation. Some of these unfortunate refugees preferred to commit suicide rather than submit to Communist governments, but thousands did return by force, among them children and young people. The UNRRA children's centres were often managed by Communist agents.

The subsequent refugee organization, the IRO, mirrors the change within the United Nations Organization in relation to Russia and her satellites. The activity of this new organization was not aimed at forcing the refugees, even young people over sixteen, to be repatriated; and for children under sixteen, the IRO conducted thorough investigations to determine whether their close relatives were alive and if so, where they were residing. If the family was found, and if it formally requested the return of its children, the IRO reunited the family.

Polish orphans in India, New Zealand, Mexico, and Africa had avoided the terror applied by repatriation officers during the first post-war years to refugees in Austria and East Germany. They also avoided compulsory repatriation. Nonetheless, they were subjected to endless examinations and registrations to establish their orphanhood and their reason for refusing repatriation. These multiple reviews did cause a certain number of half-orphans and children with parents in Poland to return home. But the legal guardians of the other children tried to save them from being forced to return home and be brought up in the spirit of atheistic Communism.

The investigations conducted by the repatriation officials often terrified the children so much that they did not know what they were being quizzed about. Some of them were as afraid of the IRO officials as they had been of the Soviet officials; and some officials over-reached their authority and forced the children to make up stories about fictitious relatives in Poland.

The IRO had assured the Guardianship Committee, before we left Africa, that when they reached Europe the children would no longer be bothered by such investigations. Yet soon after our "domestication" in the Salerno camp, two self-styled repatriation officers, a Mr. Chrysz and a Mme. Babinski, arrived from the British Occupational Zone in Germany—a fact suspicious in itself because the central office of the IRO in Italy surely had their own personnel for such purposes. They were, however, officials of the IRO; and we decided that since our presence during the "reviews" of the children could be interpreted as a lack of confidence in the IRO, we should not insist on it. The newcomers were busy with their "reviews" for days. When the children confided to us that both officials had advised them to return home, describing their recent visit to Poland and their delight with everything there, we did not react. "Poland is expanding," the two said to the children, "and needs young energies. Nobody needs to fear anything. A great career is awaiting a young person there." Such temptations brought no results. Deep within the children's souls remained an instinctive fear of everything Communist; they needed no more indoctrination as to what Communism is all about than their sufferings in Russia.

Only two sisters requested repatriation, twenty-year-old Czeslawa and thirteen-year-old Bronislawa Murawski. Their mother in Poland, fearing that her daughters, while still in Africa, might go on endlessly globetrotting, had asked them to return to Poland. A few other children with a father or mother in Poland had letters from them consenting to their remaining abroad if they had a chance to be educated and to better themselves. Only parents who knew the meaning of Communist exile and imprisonment could have made such a sacrifice.

The Murawski sisters left Salerno for Cinecitta, a temporary camp near Rome, in the company of a Canadian IRO official, Miss Irene Pagé. Very much to our amazement, the girls returned after six days, having given up the idea of returning to Poland. They told us why.

When they arrived in Rome, the Polish embassy called Czeslawa in for an interview. The officials started questioning her about the African camps: Where in Africa had she been? How many Poles were originally there and how many remained? How many children had there been in the orphanage, and how many were there now? Were the majority under sixteen or over? Were the children well-mannered? How about their moral standards? Had their superiors in the orphanage or their teachers at school ever said anything bad about Poland? Had they counseled the children not to return to Poland? Were Mrs. Grosicki and the priest Krolikowski advising them not to return? Did she know of a person who could be trusted to approach the children cleverly and persuade them to return to Poland? What were the living conditions in Africa, and now in Salerno? Were the children poorly provided for? About how long might it take to get approval to go to Canada, and who was going to take care of the children there? What African port had they sailed from and on which ship? What port had they landed in? How many IRO people were in Salerno, and were they advising the children not to return to their fatherland? What percentage of grown-ups remained in Africa, and what did they intend to do? Why did the Murawski sisters wish to go to Poland?

During the interrogation the embassy officials repeatedly urged Czeslawa not to be afraid, to tell the truth without hiding anything because if she didn't, she would suffer since both sisters now belonged to them. While Czeslawa answered their questions, the officers communicated with each other by winking or smiling ironically.

It so happened that a few days afterward, while Czeslawa was still in Rome with Miss Pagé, Bronislawa was abducted to the embassy without anyone's permission or knowledge. When her disappearance caused a commotion in Cinecitta, the camp officials notified the police. Found and brought back to camp, the young girl told the officials that she had been asked strange questions that she was not always able to answer. Then for the first time, realizing what had happened, she began to be afraid. Czeslawa, uneasy after her own visit to the embassy, suffered still greater anxiety and confided in Miss Pagé that she was afraid to return to Poland. The IRO official helped both girls return to Salerno the night before they were to leave for Poland, their luggage already on its way there.

The Communist daily *Zycie Warszawy* gave the following version of the two sisters' story:

> The Murawski sisters, whose repatriation was demanded by their mother living in Poland, managed to outwit the watchfulness of the "noble London guardians" and of the IRO camp authorities and luckily reached the embassy of the Polish Republic in Rome, begging with tears in their eyes that they be repatriated to Poland. But when they returned from the embassy to the camp, the "noble guardians" took care of the girls so "eagerly" that the Murawski sisters had no chance to stick their nose outside the camp. Afterwards the IRO authorities officially notified the Polish Republic's embassy that the Murawski sisters declined repatriation.
>
> The desire to return to one's own country? The desire to return to one's mother? This, in the camps of IRO, is punishable in the highest degree! We emphasize, while at it, that out of 150 Polish children, kidnapped by the IRO, quite a few have one or both parents and other relatives in Poland, as was established by the Polish Red Cross and . . . IRO itself.

Meanwhile the Murawski sisters' mother in Poland was called to the administrative office of her village time after time and was finally forced to sign the following statement: "My life's greatest desire is that my beloved daughters finally return to the homeland after long wanderings . . ." A Communist publication *Repatriant*, dated August 20, 1949, commented on this affair, and the whole orphanage matter: "Polish society would have felt it a rank injustice if the Polish children had not been able to return to their homeland." *Repatriant* did not mention why the Polish children happened to be wandering in the first place. Nor did the Communist press disclose, much less elaborate on, the fact that the mother, in Russian exile with young children and herself fighting death from hunger and typhoid fever, had had to make that tragic decision to part with her children when they had the opportunity to escape to Persia. Only by a miracle had she avoided death and returned to Poland when so many thousands of other Poles, both grown-ups and children, had never had that good fortune.

35

Members of the Polish Communist Embassy in the Camp

Of course we could not know the Communists' plan for their campaign to take the children away from us, but it was obvious that they would do everything in their power. The affair of the Murawski sisters had been warning enough, and we sensed Communist intrigue everywhere. Through third persons working for the IRO, they attempted to win the cooperation of us guardians; when that failed, they tried to get rid of me by offering me an easy exit with luxurious accommodations from Italy to the country I wished to settle in. They then sought to undermine our authority and to replace us with Walczak and Szyszko. They spread rumors throughout the Salerno camp that this pair was going to take over the management of the orphans and provide them with a more comfortable existence. Needless to say, all these shameful tricks failed. Yet on the one day I traveled to Rome to attend to orphanage business and meet my superior, Father General Beda Hess of the Fanciscan Fathers Conventual, I received the disturbing news that members of the Warsaw regime embassy in Rome, having been invited by the IRO, intended to visit Salerno to meet the children. To reach the camp before they did, I had to cut short my visit and catch the night train.

Monsignor Walerian Meysztowicz, a member of the Guardianship Committee, introduced me to a Canadian lady, Miss Dorothy Sullivan, who had come from Germany as a representative of the American and Canadian Episcopate. Her assignment was to save the Catholic war orphans in Europe. Of Irish origin and rather militant, she announced a plan to accelerate the children's departure for Canada and thereby remove them from the reach of the Communists. Soon we were cordially welcoming her to the camp. Representatives of the children dressed in ethnic costumes gave her a bouquet of white and red roses and two letters of thanks, one for the Archbishop of Montreal, Joseph Charbonneau, who was willing to be legally responsible for our children in Canada, and the other for Miss Sullivan herself.

She acquainted us with the steps already taken to secure Canadian entry visas and even offered hope for the physically handicapped, whose applications had been rejected by the Federal Government of Canada. Having had several years of experience in child rescue operations, she sought to bring to Italy a Canadian Immigration Commission. With the steno pool of the IRO in Naples ready at a moment's notice to prepare the documents, the work could proceed rapidly without interruption. According to Miss Sullivan's optimistic calculations, our group should be able to sail for Canada within a few days aboard a ship leaving from Naples. The children's joy at this prospect defied description. But, alas, they were to experience yet another trial of terror. Much to our sorrow, Miss Sullivan was unexpectedly recalled to Rome by IRO authorities so that her presence in the camp would not upset the Communists from the embassy, who were to arrive on the 29th of July.

Two days after the enthusiastic reception for Miss Sullivan, we had to stand eye to eye with representatives of the Warsaw government: Embassy Counselor Alexander Koltonski, Major Jozef Dobrowolski (rumor had it that this name had been used by other Communists working for the embassy), and a secretary, Mrs. Krystyna Zglinska. They were accompanied by IRO officials: Colonel Woodcock from Rome, Miss Pagé of the Child Welfare Agency, Mrs. Damiani, Mr. Lenth, Mr. Lapema, a lawyer, and Mr. Martynowicz, second in command of the camp. The Communists displayed a deceptive kind of courtesy and kindliness—all except Major Dobrowolski, whose aggressiveness and air of self-assurance made us suspect that he was the political officer and director of the mission, responsible for its success.

At first the delegation tried to win sympathy and trust. They emphasized the fact that, though divided by conflicting views, we were, nevertheless, linked by our common origin. Major Dobrowolski chose me as his intermediary, avoiding Mrs. Grosicki, who had recognized him as a former second lieutenant from Lwow.

Soon all of us—Communist delegates, IRO officials, Mrs. Grosicki and I—entered the recreation hall where the children were already seated. I opened the meeting by introducing the visitors, explaining that they had come hoping to speak with each child separately, if possible, though no one would be forced to talk.

The embassy counselor spoke next. His brief, well composed address tallied with what I had said. He neither advocated repatriation nor scared the children; he only expressed his desire to meet with each one privately. But Major Dobrowolski, clearly unhappy with the counselor's talk, started on a note of pathos: "Poland is resurrected and alive!" (Smirks from the children, noted by the speaker.) "Maybe some of you don't believe it, but it is so!" (Again the smiles.) "Poland sends greetings to you, especially to the boys! From the whole army, the infantry, the airforce, the navy . . ." Throughout the rest of his speech he aimed to instill in his audience of children nostalgia for their homeland. Noticeably discouraged, however, by the children's indifference, he soon began to stammer, became confused, and eventually stopped.

The meeting lasted perhaps a quarter of an hour. After that the members of the embassy, the IRO officials, Mrs. Grosicki and I went to the Welfare Office to await the children willing to talk with the Communists. In the meantime the boys had to be dissuaded from wrecking the embassy cars; such an act would of course compromise the educators and harm the cause of rescuing the children.

Not one child came to the Welfare Office. The Communists began to get nervous. At that point I spoke to the children, urging the older ones to pluck up their courage and speak out: "If you don't want to go back to Poland, at least tell the Communists why!" Not one of the boys would volunteer, but two brave senior girls finally did. Counselor Koltonski asked for their names, surnames, and ages, which part of Poland they came from, where their parents were, what relatives they had living, with whom they corresponded in Poland, whether they had any brothers or sisters with them. The girls said they had no country to return to because Eastern Poland, their homeland, had been incorporated into Russia and their parents had died in the Siberian taiga. Of course, they would not return to a Poland governed by the Russians. The counselor replied that he had papers to prove that one of the girls had an uncle in Poland, but she replied that the uncle had emigrated to the United States just after the First World War. Unable to establish any other hold on the girls, the counselor tried to touch sentimental chords: "Maybe there is someone in Poland whom you knew in Africa? Just give us the address and we will deliver a food parcel. Maybe you need prayer books, rosaries, medallions? Give us your names and we will send them to you."

One girl answered that all of the children were provided with those items. During this conversation, noting that the embassy secretary was recording the girls' personal data, I protested: "You may register only those who wish to return to Poland. Any other kind of registraiton is absolutely pointless."

"But we have an order from the government. These children legally belong to the government and to the Polish nation. To care for these children is the duty of the government," interjected Counselor Koltonski.

Major Dobrowolski came to his aid: "The children do not decide for themselves. This is done by their legal guardian in this case, the Warsaw government. Who has given you power over the children?"

"Mister Koltonski spoke a moment ago saying that we are divided by differing political views. We have different views indeed: we do not recognize the Communist government," was my answer.

As the exchange of opinions grew more and more tense, the Counselor tried to prevent an explosion by interceding: "So, the priest does not allow the registration?"

"No."

"That is a different story," said the Counselor, with a threat in his voice. "In view of the priest's objections, do not continue recording," he added, turning to the secretary.

Mrs. Grosicki remarked pointedly: "If the children had wished to return to Poland, they would have done so before. When we were in Africa, a few of them went back to Poland upon being summoned by their fathers, mothers, or other relatives; the rest decided to emigrate to Canada or to Great Britain. So it is no wonder that they do not come now."

The Communist representatives asked the IRO's permission to come to the camp the next day, hoping that the children would have thought things over and would want to speak to them. And perhaps the guardians would not be so intractable. Though expressing doubt that the children would change their minds, the IRO consented. We parted in a state of great agitation. Mr. Koltonski left a handful of Polish newspapers; Major

Dobrowolski was boiling with anger. The children were standing in a group, a few steps away, eager to learn what the older girls had told the Communists.

The visit announced for the next day did not materialize: giving up their struggle for the souls of the children, the Communist delegates returned to Rome. But the calm that followed was anything but reassuring. We were positive that the Communists would not let the matter rest, but would try other means to exercise their "rights."

Meanwhile, the same night, I had another visit. At 1:30 A.M. there was a knock at my door, and I opened it on a most unexpected visitor, Prelate Walerian Meysztowicz from Rome. I hastily pulled on my pants, tossed my jacket over my shoulders and walked with him out beyond the camp to the highway. There we strolled arm in arm as I gave him an account of the Communists' visit. Although shaking with cold, I felt a deep warmth within my soul. Under the circumstances, the Prelate's visit was boosting my morale miraculously. I felt a new energy and a renewed faith in victory. In his own way the Prelate was honoring me as does a general who visits a soldier on guard duty at an important sector of the front line. I was so overwhelmed by this visit that I forgot to ask Monsignor Meysztowicz how he had got to Salerno. He quizzed me himself: "Guess who brought me here!"

I couldn't even guess. The Prelate pointed to a car hidden under the trees and as I jumped toward it, I saw, sitting there and smiling, Miss Dorothy Sullivan. I was overjoyed. This furtive, dangerous night trip from Rome to find out how we had fared in our encounter with the Communists suddenly recalled to my mind the words of this brave woman who, back in Rome, had raised her arms high and declared: "I will fight!"

After they had left, I was much too excited to sleep, and I felt ashamed to be resting while those two had no rest. In my imagination I was rushing with them toward the Eternal City, longing to guess from their smiles and their heartening words what plans they were making to rescue the children. Later, during the day, I saw again, in my imagination, the Monsignor standing in the middle of the road, in shabby clothes without a hat, holding a frayed briefcase under his arm. He had been smiling, and his smile had emanated kindliness, succor, and strength.

Around noon, while we were still feeling very nervous about another Communist visit, another person, Sister Celina Bednarski, a member of the Sisters of the Holy Family of Nazareth, beloved by us all and well remembered by the children from Rongai as their teacher. With her was a very young Italian nun who could speak Polish, and they had brought two huge packets of candies, chocolates, and cakes, as well as objects of religious devotion blessed by the Holy Father. Surrounded by the children, talking and laughing with them, they sat on the beach under an umbrella. It seemed to us that ever since the visit of the Communists, everyone was wishing us well. All of the inhabitants of the camp—Czechs, Slovaks, Croats, Slovenians, Serbs, Rumanians, Russians—they all loved the Polish children so much that they shared with them their miseries and their joys.

36

Escape to Germany

When the Communists gave up the idea of paying us another visit, Miss Sullivan, fearing some diplomatic ploy on their part, accelerated her efforts to obtain visas. A new project was born: to fly the children from Naples to Canada via New York City. However, other new developments were taking place.

At 6:00 P.M. on August 1, the IRO summoned Mrs. Grosicki and me to Salerno for an immediate consultation. The very suddenness of our trip made the children anxious. To make matters worse, a rumor began to circulate in the camp that the next day, at 8:00 A.M., the Polish children were to be sent to Germany. In despair they besieged the only educator in the camp, Mrs. Krystyna Czerniacki, pleading for an explanation. She was amazed. She was aware of the rumor, and guessed why we had been summoned, but could not reveal her suspicions to the children. Seeing their despair, she tried to reassure them, asking them not to believe rumors but wait patiently until we returned.

In the meantime, in a hotel in Salerno, we were holding a very important conference. The IRO revealed that the Communists had sent a sharply worded note to the Italian government demanding that they be given control over all Polish orphans currently living in Italian territory. The government, being a member of the IRO, could have rejected these demands by simply stating that the case of the Polish children was an international matter, that the children were in Italy only temporarily, and that they were being cared for by the IRO, an organ of the United Nations Organization. The Italian government, however, was anxious to avoid friction with Warsaw, especially since Moscow stood behind it. Advised about the note, the IRO saw no other solution than to transfer the orphans to Germany, to Bremen in particular since this city and its port constituted an American enclave within the British Occupational Zone. They assured us there would be no danger of Communist interference there.

The IRO presented us a plan they had already worked out for our escape to Germany. We were to return to the camp and order a general packing-up to be completed by dawn. In the morning, under the pretext of an excursion or a move to another camp, we would load children and baggage into buses and heavy trucks and take them to Bagnoli, near Naples, to a special train, which would carry them directly to Bremen.

Having been disappointed so many times before, we were skeptical about this adventurous scheme. In Africa they had assured us solemnly that no repatriation commission, and above all no Communists, would have access to the children, that the children would have better educational conditions in Salerno, that the camp would be more adequatly equipped than the Tengeru orphanage. None of this came about. Could we believe the loquacious, overly courteous counselors? Could we risk the fate of 150 children? What if this were a ruse to transport the children via Germany to Poland?

On the other hand, the IRO could be on the level this time. Wasn't it better to accept this plan before the Italian carabinieri surrounded the camp and forced the children onto a train bound directly for Poland? Uncertainty tugged at us.

We were relieved, then, when Mr. Emeryk Hutten-Czapski, representative of the Guardianship Committee in Rome, appeared in Salerno. In his opinion the only sensible thing to do under the circumstances was to accept the plan. We decided to leave for Bremen and so informed the IRO authorities.

When we returned to the camp at 9:00 P.M. the children ran from their barracks and surrounded our car. In dead, frightened silence, they moved with us into the theatre hall.

Mr. Hutten-Czapski addressed them on our behalf. In carefully chosen words, he confirmed the rumor that had so tormented them a few hours earlier. Now they were frightened by the fact that while Mr. Czapski spoke we said nothing, and assumed from our silence that they were to be returned to Poland. Would Mrs. Grosicki and Father Krolikowski be going with them? they wanted to know. Only when Mr. Czapski assured them that we would, did their faces brighten. Their enthusiastic applause shattered the silent night, and our eyes filled with tears.

The children back in their huts to begin packing, Mrs. Grosicki and I discussed details of the departure. Alone there, away from our orphans, we had a failure of nerve and burst out crying like children.

In the meantime, the boys were helping the girls rope up their bundles. Common sufferings and recent anxieties had bonded them even more strongly into one family. Some of them, still apprehensive, were at first unwilling to do any packing, and one group of boys discussed a plan to run away and work for Italian farmers; but they all later packed up with the others.

At three o'clock in the morning, Mr. Czapski came back to tell us that the Guardianship Committee still feared for the safety of the children in Germany because there were no guarantees of any sort anywhere. We were so confused that we found it impossible to deliberate. Finally we woke the commanding officer and informed him that we would not leave until we had received some guarantee of safety for the children. He looked at us as if we were crazy. Since the IRO was even then preparing the road and railway transportation, he wondered if we realized the consequences of such an irresponsible decision.

Later that morning when the IRO officials from Rome and Naples arrived and were told that we refused to leave, they were most irritated and placed all responsibility on me. They reminded us all once again that any delay would give the Communists an advantage. The children, they said, must be removed from Italian territory before the government could reply to Warsaw's demands. When they also protested that our refusal to move would entail extraordinary expenses for the IRO, I replied that no cost could compare with the value of 150 children. In any case, I maintained, we would have to have some guarantee that the children would be safe in Germany.

The situation became extremely tense. In those few hours we lost weight, we aged; this must have been the worst day of our lives. But all of the inhabitants of the camp, irrespective of nationality, lived through those horrible hours with us: they cried, they begged us not to give in, not to believe the beautiful promises. It occurred to us to seek shelter for the whole group of orphans on the neutral ground of Vatican City, where the children could not be touched; but such a move could cause still greater international complications, and the idea was rejected.

Feeling utterly helpless, Mrs. Krystyna Czerniacka sent out despairing dispatches calling for help. We were counting on assistance from Africa, and rightly so, for our message alerted all residents at Tengeru. The IRO representative there, Mrs. Rule, unable to contact the central office in Nairobi, went there with Zenon Wierzbinski, the parish priest, and a former member of the Guardianship Committee, to radio IRO headquarters in Geneva. The IRO was terrified by the threat of the inhabitants of the Tengeru camp to burn down the whole settlement if any harm came to the children.

Meanwhile the situation in Italy developed quickly. "The orphanage has left Salerno and is on its way to Bremen," the IRO headquarters told Africa, to mollify the people at Tengeru. In fact, we did leave for Bremen surprisingly soon. From the Director of the Italian Section of the IRO, Admiral Mantz of the Guardianship Committee, we had obtained a written guarantee that no repatriation commission would have access to the children, that they would be treated as applicants for Canadian visas, that besides their guardians, the children would be accompanied by a delegate of the Vatican, who would remain with them in Germany until they left for Canada. The Guardianship Committee also ensured the removal from the transport of Walczak and Szyszko, both of them now even more strongly suspected of cooperation with the Communists.

The orphanage left Salerno according to the previously arranged plan after a one-day delay. With a twelve-car train at our disposal, we were comfortably accommodated. In Rome, to the great joy of everyone, Monsignor Walerian Meysztowicz joined us as the Vatican delegate; and we were seen off at the station by the Ambassador to the Vatican, Dr. Kazimierz Papee, Mr. Hutten-Czapski, and a group of other Poles. Also traveling with us were the two Canadian ladies, Miss Dorothy Sullivan and Miss Irene Pagé. The train stopped for a long time at the Brenner Pass, and again at Innsbruck, amid the snowcapped Alps. Otherwise, it rushed nonstop to Bremen, taking us farther and farther from sunny Italy and into a Germany shrouded in leaden clouds.

Soon we were in Bremen. The train was shunted to a side track, and from a car in the distance a few persons rushed toward us. The children, who had been glued to the windows, jumped back as if burned and called out: "Please, Madame! Please, Father! That bad man is here at the station! We saw him rubbing his hands to greet us. He called out, 'Children, you are going to Poland, right?' " We could not believe our eyes. Right at the door of the car stood that despicable repatriation officer from Salerno. Could the IRO have deceived us? We tried to calm the frightened children, telling them that nothing could happen to them here; but this unpleasant encounter could only mean that the battle for the children had entered a new phase, that the escape to Germany had not solved the problem.

"Where are Walczak and Szyszko?" asked the Communist officer. Informed that they were not in the transport, he shouted in amazement: "That is impossible!" Obviously not believing "those trained liars," as he had called the children back in Salerno, he went to the next car and again asked for Mrs. Szyszko and Mr. Walczak. One of the girls answered quietly, "Do not get excited, Sir. They traveled with us, but got lost at one of the stations."

He guessed at once that the girl was taunting him, and stalked to his automobile trailed by his retinue. But the look on his face seemed to be saying, "We will square off again!"

37

Only the Battlefield Has Changed

The escape of the orphanage to Germany caused a fury in the Communist camp. It seemed that the children's departure for Canada would be "an international scandal." According to an article in *Zycie Warszawy (Warsaw Life)* headlined "Kidnappers on an International Scale," Mrs. Grosicki and I were "the representatives of the London government," "the emissaries of August Zaleski," the President, and "slave traders of the modern era." This paper predicted what fate the children could expect in Canada: "The dazzling careers of white Negroes, cheap slaves of those noble Canadian industrialists who keep their hired Polish girls locked in even after working hours."

The author of this article distorted the truth even further. According to him, members of the Warsaw embassy had "with a brazen arrogance" been refused admission to the camp in Salerno. In his eyes the IRO was nothing but an agency of the American State Department, whose apparent objective was to keep refugees from returning to their homelands and thus provide capitalists with cheap labor. "The representatives of Poland, the USSR, and other truly democratic countries [sic] have on many occasions unmasked the reactionary character of IRO," but this "last outrage," sending the children to Canada, was "something infinitely horrible, a violation of human feelings, of international law, and of the IRO statute itself." He also reviled the Italian government as having perpetrated a "monstrous outrage" and as incapable of "respecting international treaties on their own territory."

Radio stations in Poland called for the children to be handed over to the Warsaw regime, and appealed to the orphans to return home. The League of Women, representing one and a half million members, "unanimously" voted for a resolution protesting the "abduction" of the children to Canada. According to newspaper reports, all municipal offices, the offices of the State Repatriation Department, and of the Polish Red Cross, as well as government Ministries, were receiving daily hundreds of letters inquiring whether this child or that were among "those kidnapped." Later on, from Polish emigrés, I learned that many Poles, sensitive to the orphans' fate, believed the Communists' lies.

Again a tempest was raging above the children's heads, and it would not subside for a moment until their ship left Europe for Canada twenty-five days later.

The Communists tried through their sympathizers in the IRO to have the orphans transferred to the famous children's camp in Bad Aibling, Bavaria. Had this maneuver succeeded, Mrs. Grosicki and I would have been replaced by the educational personnel of "Bad Aibling Village," and the children would sooner or later have been taken to Poland.

In Bremen our orphans were housed in a transit camp called Tirpitz, in barracks dating from the Nazi regime. When a man with IRO credentials began cruising the area and snooping around, I reminded him of the IRO's written guarantee that no repatriation officer would be allowed to approach the orphans and asked Poles from the Watchguard Companies to keep an eye on him. In their eagerness they nearly arrested him one day as he came near the children.

Other people sent by the Communists tried to get to them, among them an IRO representative from Warsaw, a Polish-American who was organizing a trip to Poland for foreign tourists, and a correspondent for a Warsaw newspaper. Even more puzzling was the presence of a young Russian Orthodox minister who, because of his cunning and his incessant mobility, seemed to be an NKVD officer in disguise. The Communists never neglected an opportunity to gain control of the children. They even used the services of Catholics working for the IRO, including some in its highest echelons in Geneva, priests and laymen, all unfamiliar with Communism and its methods.

Some IRO moves, though without ill intent, would have been disastrous to the cause of the children. For example, the IRO wanted to give all boys and girls over sixteen the status of displaced persons, which would have required them to appear individually before the immigration commission of an interested country, to sign an employment contract, and to depart one by one for the place assigned. We were aware that even before they could receive a visa, they would suffer from moral and physical neglect, as had thousands of other refugees who for years had been kept waiting for their papers. The alumni of the African orphanages were too young to handle this kind of adversity; it was certainly not for this that we had brought them here. Fortunately the plan was abandoned.

All the while Miss Sullivan and Monsignor Meysztowicz worked tirelessly, late into the night, preparing lengthy telegrams and radiograms for Archbishop Charbonneau in Canada, seeking Canadian visas for the whole group.[1] At first Miss Sulli-

---

1. The texts of the telegrams collected by Prelate Meysztowicz were deposited in the archives of the Polish Embassy at the Vatican. Our own correspondence from Europe to the Guardianship Committee in Africa, and also all documents pertaining to the activity of the committee, were deposited by Mr. Jacob Hoffman in the Historical Institute of General Sikorski in London.

van lived in the camp, close to the children; but when she noticed that telegrams addressed to her were being opened and read, she moved to a hotel. The Monsignor shared a room with me. Often before bed-time he would pace the floor with his brisk military step (at one time he had been a cavalry captain), talking about current affairs. Although often tired, he was always in good humor. The relentless battle against the Communists did not daunt him. He had always, he said, loved a fight: "There is only one difference. When one was younger, one did not feel the enemy's blows as painfully as now. When we get older, each dirty trick hurts."

One day Father Krasocki and Mr. Geppert, a priest and a teacher from the refugee camp near Bremerhaven, visited our camp, bringing huge suitcases of clothing, underwear, and footwear, and forty German marks as gifts for the orphans from their countrymen. They had heard from somewhere that our orphans were "almost naked" and had taken up a collection. We were stunned by their visit. Children almost naked? What non-sense! Their outfits were more than adequate and brand new. It was the refugees in German camps who were, by comparison, poverty-stricken. Even before the suitcases were opened we guessed that they contained only poor, used clothing, though we were touched by the kind generosity they represented. But how had these good people been so misinformed?

I took the guests on a tour of the dormitories to show them the "riches" of our orphans. Beside each bed hung a few new dresses, not counting others locked away in the heavy luggage. Who could have spread such a false story? As it turned out, the culprit was one of our own girls, who had hoped to get money from the kind-hearted people she was corresponding with. Since our visitors were unwilling to take the gifts back for fear of the reproaches of the duped donors, the clothes were given to the poor refugees in our camp.

After a time the medical board began examining the children to establish who was qualified for admission to Canada. The examinations were conducted in a revolting manner, and a number of children were rejected—some suspected of tuberculosis, others of venereal disease, still others because they were crippled, and two boys adjudged mentally retarded. "If the Communists didn't manage to split the group, then the physicians will," we would say bitterly. In addition to everything else, we now had the new worry of what to do about the children who would have to remain in Europe.

Eventually, thanks to the indefatigable endeavors of Miss Sullivan, Monsignor Meysztowicz, and Archbishop Charbonneau, came the joyous news from Ottawa that the Canadian government had granted 150 visas, to be issued at the discretion of the Canadian consul and his medical staff. Now the problem was to make sure that the maximum number of children could take advantage of them. Miss Sullivan fought like a lioness for each orphan, for the paralyzed Frania, for Bronia with the curvature of the spine, for limping Wladek and deaf-mute Bolek, for the retarded Manius and Wiktor. Lame Wladek had impressed Miss Sullivan most of all, for as we were loading up for our trip he had insisted on carrying heavy bundles for his friends, perspiring but persisting until the job was done.

When nine tubercular children were rejected, Miss Sullivan cabled the American Bishops Committee National Catholic Welfare Council for financial assistance to have them treated in Switzerland. Because of the Communists, it would be too risky to leave them in Germany. Assured of ten thousand dollars for a start, she decided to go to Switzerland to find a suitable sanitarium.

Three girls, crystal-pure, were deemed by the doctors, on the basis of a blood analysis, to be infected with venereal disease. Since the girls had not heard of such infections, they could not understand the questions the doctors asked; but when, later on, they realized what they were suspected of, they cried bitterly. Further blood tests and particularly embarrassing investigations were a veritable torture to them for almost three weeks until, at Mrs. Grosicki's insistence, the doctors did gynecological examinations and established the incongruity of their suspicions. Not familiar with tropical diseases, they had overlooked the well established fact that a number of them, especially malaria, often produce reactions similar to those of venereal disease.

As a result of our efforts, 123 children, including the crippled ones, were granted visas, signed by kind Mr. Phillip Bird, acting consul attached to the Canadian Mission in Europe. Only twenty-four orphans were to remain in Germany for any reason. Mrs. Grosicki, with a small group of children, including her own five-year-old Nena, newly adopted, was to go to England. Thus the main body of orphans was ready to leave for Canada on

August 29, only a few days after their visas had been issued.

But our troubles were still not over: I, the manager and guardian of the group, was refused a Canadian visa, and the Polish Red Cross once again assailed the IRO Headquarters in Geneva in an attempt to keep the orphans from leaving.

38

Intrigue and Strategy

The IRO authorities, in spite of their written guarantees, invited the Polish Communists to the camp in Tirpitz to convince them that the orphans had freely, without pressure or coercion, elected to go to Canada. The invitation extended to the Polish Red Cross was not accepted; instead its members presented a set of demands: to be given a list of all the Polish children by name, and all documents pertaining to each individual child. They also demanded that the departure for Canada be canceled and the care of all the children under eighteen be transferred to the Warsaw government.

When the IRO rejected the demand for the children's documents on the ground that it would violate IRO statutes, the Communists tried to obtain them by theft; but their agent, who broke into the record office during the night, was scared off by the German cleaning woman.

As for the problem of my visa, the medical board had disqualified me for immigration because they had found traces of the pneumonia I had suffered in Russia. Actually this was only a ploy to hinder my departure. Not bothering themselves with how the group would be managed if I could not go with them, the IRO informed me that to get permission to enter Canada, I would have to procure an affidavit from a sponsor in Canada who would guarantee my maintenance there.

It was clear that these difficulties created artificially at each step were meant to separate me from the group. Since Mrs. Grosicki was going to England, I was the only one to be "liquidated." The Communist agents detailed to the orphans' affairs believed that, with the help of their sympathizers in the IRO, they would manage to get rid of me eventually. Indeed, it would be impossible for me to obtain the desired document in the three days remaining before we were to leave. This time the Communists were so sure of their triumph that they openly spread rumors about having me replaced by Mrs. Szyszko and Mr. Walczak, who would presumably "liberate" the children from their "abductors" and lead them in ostentatious triumph into the care of the Communist government in Poland.

But Miss Sullivan and Monsignor Meysztowicz were not to be outdone. They got in touch at once with Archbishop Charbonneau and requested him to urge the Canadian Government to wire me a special visa like the ones granted to the orphans. He instantly had Father G. E. Brosseau, Director of the Catholic Association for Aid for Immigrants, fly to Ottawa to make the request. The unconditional visa arrived, and I now had to report to the medical board and the Canadian Consul, then attend to my other affairs by the date the children were to sail. Since the team of Canadian officials had been moved to Fallingbostel, a considerable distance from Bremen, my friends in the IRO loaned me a jeep and a German driver, and I set out with one of my charges, Ludwik Burek.

Leaving Bremen in the early morning, we rode along the famous freeway to Hamburg. In Fallingbostel, in another transit refugee camp, were hundreds of refugees lined up in front of the labor recruiting offices, telling each other about the exacting requirements for visas. Single people, in perfect health, were the only ones who had a really good chance of being allowed to emigrate. I learned that out of three hundred candidates for jobs in the mines only one hundred were hired. Were I to remain in the line-up I could not even dream about getting a visa in one day. Some people had been waiting for weeks. There was only one thing to do: braving the violent babel of protests from refugees of a dozen nationalities, I plunged to the head of the line and entered the Consul's office along with the rightful occupant of that position. I was counting on the Consul's giving me priority, and he did. After hearing me out, however, he explained that applicants came to him only in the final stages, for his signature on the visa. But he was very kind and gave me a "safe conduct" that would get me into every office without waiting in line. Even so, the examinations had not been completed by noon, and I had to send the driver back to Tirpitz because his permit was fast expiring. About five o'clock the lines in front of the offices gradually disappeared and the offices closed. A half-hour later, I rushed breathlessly to the Consul's office with a handful of documents to get his precious signature and seal, hardly daring to hope that he would still be there. But to my great relief, the kind man, sure that I would come back, was waiting patiently with his secretary. At that moment, fairly trembling with exhaustion, I felt like the luckiest man in the world.

Ludwik and I rushed to the railway station only to learn that no train would leave till morning. Since the station was locked up at 11 p.m., we spent part of the night walking back and forth to keep warm. Finally we jumped over the railway fence and slept on the train side-tracked for the morning run to Bremen. Everyone rejoiced when Ludwik and I returned to camp with the visa all signed and sealed. But just then a telegram came from the IRO in Geneva, ordering Mrs. Grosicki to England via Holland immediately. This we considered a contemptible thing to do, to take her away from the orphans only two days before they were to leave for Canada and thus deprive her of the joy of seeing them off and savoring the success of our long fight for them. Since she had not yet obtained her English visa, Mrs. Grosicki defied the order. Then came more telegrams from Geneva, announcing that three other persons, unknown to us, would be arriving from Italy to travel with the children.

On the eve of the sailing we arranged a farewell party for our friends, especially Mrs. Grosicki. The boys and girls assembled in the officers' mess, along with Miss Dorothy Sullivan, Monsignor Meysztowicz, and Miss Eileen Eagan, a well-known American journalist with the Agency Press. The orphans were in a doleful mood, sad at parting with the dear guardian who had been like a mother to them since their early childhood. The girls seemed to age, almost to shrivel, as they wept, and though the boys tried to hide their feelings, many of them cried too, unmindful of the jeers of the little group that had been attached to ours as we left Africa. Mrs. Grosicki's words stuck in her throat as she said goodbye to those homeless children who needed only a loving father and mother. As a token of gratitude for his efforts in saving the children from repatriation, Monsignor Meysztowicz was presented an album of all the children's photographs. (After we had gone, Miss Sullivan was also rewarded: for the great merit of her work in saving the Polish children she was decorated with the medal of the "Polonia Restituta" Order.)

The next day, August 29, we took our sorrows, our anxieties, and our heartfelt gratitude to God at Holy Mass, the last I said in Europe. We were just over 400 kilometres from Poland, from which ten years earlier the Soviet Communists had deported those children, along with their parents; and now, as if in mockery, the Polish Communists were trying to take them back by force to subject them to the same kind of government.

We left from Bremerhaven by train on a dull, drizzly day. Gathered at the pier was a crowd of the children's friends: Monsignors Meysztowicz, Bernas, Lubowiecki, and Father Gorny; Mrs. Grosicki, Miss Sullivan, Miss Pagé, and Miss Eagan; Mr. Hutten-Czapski, Mr. Potocki, and a few others. A short distance away stood a group of Communist agents and sympathizers.

As the children boarded the IRO transport USAT *General Stuart Heinzelman*, I was detained at the gang-plank. The fact that I had the same visa as the children caused a bit of amazement. A few sensation-seeking reporters boarded the ship, and one, showing me a newspaper clipping about the "abduction" of the children, demanded an explanation. Another, a Ukrainian, inquired whether any Ukrainian children were in the group, as he had allegedly recognized in ten-year-old Magdzia a girl he had known in Poland. On learning that Magdzia had been an infant in her mother's arms when she was deported to Siberia, he left.

Standing at the ship's rail, we looked at our friends on the pier. We were short of words and could only smile at them tenderly to tell them how grateful we were for all their help and loving care.

An hour had passed since we boarded the ship; the gang-plank was up; the ship was ready to sail. What was holding us back? We noticed some anxiety among our friends. Miss Sullivan was certain we were dealing with the devil himself!

As we learned later, the captain was waiting for three additional passengers: Mme. Szyszko, Mr. Walczak, and a third person unknown. The Communists, counting on my being left behind with no visa, had obtained Canadian visas for them and flown them from Italy to assume the management of the orphans. It is difficult to imagine what would have happened if these known troublemakers had been on the ship with us. They would have stirred up trouble and disobedience among the young people and our battle would only have been transported across the Atlantic.

However, the devil, for all his cunning, had overlooked one

important maneuver: to alert the director of the Bremen airport that these special passengers would be arriving and to order him to transport them to the ship instantly. As it was, the would-be managers of our group were detained at the airport for several hours, and our captain, after waiting two hours, decided they were not coming and ordered the ship to sail.

As the anchor rattled up and we began moving, our children burst into our national anthem "Jeszcze Polska nie zginela poki my zyjemy!" (As long as we live, Poland has not perished.) But there was no enthusiasm on the ship as the silhouettes of our friends on shore grew smaller and smaller and finally disappeared in the grey mist.

PART FOUR

In Canada

39

On the Banks of the Saint Lawrence

The USAT *General Stuart Heintzelman* was making its eighteenth trip for the IRO, distributing refugees for resettlement all over the world but especially to the most hospitable countries, Australia, Argentina, Venezuela, Brazil, Chile, USA and Canada. Since the majority of the refugees were former inmates of Hitler's concentration camps, most of them spoke German.

Our children, as if through some premeditated malice, were dispersed all over the ship. Both the boys and the girls, who until now had lived together as one family, were assigned to dormitories among refugees of various ages, religions, and mores. This treatment damaged them psychologically. Nor did the ship's officers acknowledge me either as a priest or as the leader of the group. I was assigned a bed in the center of the dormitory, surrounded by people of all sorts, among them gamblers, drunkards, and derelicts. The lights were on day and night; and the noisy conversations and raucous shouting went on till early dawn. I spent the larger part of every night on deck.

To arrange games or talks for the children, to maintain even a semblance of order and discipline among them was impossible under these conditions, especially since I could not find them all. Finally, after I protested sharply, the IRO did assign the boys and girls to separate dormitories, away from the grown-ups. This change had a good effect on the habits of everyone aboard ship. The children so impressed everybody with their self-discipline and the cleanliness of their dormitories and washrooms that the orderly officers kept holding them up as an example to the others.

As we got closer and closer to North America, our anxieties grew. We wondered what reception we would have and what our fate would be. Having wandered across Asia, Africa, and Europe, we were now seeking a new life on a fourth continent. The children had acquired their ideas of Canada from a few American books, but primarily from films. They had heard about America as the land of progress, where economic expansion enabled the average man to attain a standard of life unknown anywhere else. They thought of it as a land of opportunity, immense energy, millions of cars, powerful machinery, enormous factories, and glamorous film stars. All this excited them. But at the same time it made them uneasy. What shape would their lives take in this new country? They would have to adjust to new people and new modes of life; learning French would not be easy either; and all that strangeness around them. . . . They were, in fact, so apprehensive that not once during the seven-day voyage did they ask about Indians and cowboys or Wild West adventures, topics that had always fired their imagination.

Just as a precaution, I made lists of candidates for employment, for continued education, and for adoption by families. Two-thirds of the children, the ones in the intermediate age group, opted for further education; the eighteen-year-olds were eager to go to work and start an independent life; the nine and ten-year-olds thought they were ready for adoption.

On September 7 we disembarked at the port of Halifax. The crowd of reporters were not allowed near us. The Canadian authorities, not having had direct contact with the Communists, were obviously more afraid of possible Communist reporters than we were. We were greeted on behalf of Archbishop Charbonneau by Father G. E. Brosseau, who had helped with my visa only ten days before. On the train to Contrecoeur a village about thirty miles north of Montreal, we met French nuns from the congregation of the Soeurs de Notre Dame du Bon Conseil, who kept exchanging glances with the children. The children did not know French at all and had had so little acquaintance with English that they could hardly understand a word. But the tension soon dissolved, for children always respond readily to those who offer friendship. When Abbé Brosseau surprised them by speaking very good Polish and urged them to sing, their alliance with the Canadians was sealed. Our girls were tireless singers, and their repertoire of hymns, ballads, and merry three-part songs seemed inexhaustible. Father Brosseau, repaying them in kind, taught them the French folk song “Alouette, Gentille Alouette!” They threw themselves enthusiastically into its gestures and repetitions and soon had it learned. All the while they were being treated to sandwiches, chocolates, ice cream, and fruit by the Sisters of Our Lady of Good Counsel.

We did not miss this opportunity to look at our new country. It was at first somewhat disappointing. While our new Canadian friends were cordial and kind, their land appeared terrifyingly bare. We were traveling across Eastern Canada, supposedly well populated, but even the steppe and the African jungle had seemed less deserted. The fields around the buildings were not cultivated, and though parts of the landscape resembled areas of Poland, we were remembering that early autumn in Poland is all silver and gold with the wheat almost ready for harvesting, fragrant orchards, cattle serenely mooing—all of nature poised to thank God for His beneficence. We were surprised at the wooden houses that seemed designed to last only a short time, maybe for the span of one generation, certainly not like the houses in Europe meant to stand "forever." The youngsters mocked them as "boxes," maintaining that one match would burn them down.

We were headed for Drummondville, a small town some fifty miles north of Montreal. After a tasty dinner there in the recreation room of the Soeurs de Notre Dame du Bon Conseil, we were driven in deluxe buses to Contrecoeur, a summer resort on the broad Saint Lawrence River. Both of these moves were designed to avoid interference from the Communists, who were supposedly waiting for us with gifts and candy at the railway station in Montreal; but they soon learned where we were and at once began sending in their arrogant and persistent agents.

In Contrecoeur the boys were assigned to the summer camp of the Freres du Sacré Coeur, Saint Vincent, and the girls to that of the Soeurs de Notre Dame du Bon Conseil, Saint Hyacinth, a few miles away. Soon after we arrived, we had a lovely surprise: Archbishop Charbonneau himself came to pay us a visit. From the first moment, we recognized in him a man of refinement and kindliness. Another distinguished guest was a minister of the Polish Government-In-Exile, Mr. Waclaw Babinski, and his wife.

Our two months in Contrecoeur were a rest period after the tension in Europe and the disturbing voyage. Archbishop Charbonneau assigned Father Jean Caron to take care of the orphans with Father Jacques Laramee as his temporary assistant. Of totally different temperaments, they complemented each other perfectly, and the youngsters loved them both: the first for his uncommon tenderness and warm heart; the second for his inexhaustible humor and radiant disposition. The priests and nuns were eager to get to know the children, their shortcomings as well as their good qualities. Particularly interested in individual character traits, they carefully studied their behavior and often consulted with me about their attitudes.

Both homes were soon resounding with carefree merriment from morning till night. Our children quickly discovered in Canada what they had found so attractive in Africa—a feeling of freedom and the grandeur of nature extolled in the cowboy ballads they played and sang constantly. In the nearby woods the boys found a perfect place to play cowboys and Indians. Long before they realized that American and Canadian children played with toy guns, they were arming themselves laboriously with make-believe weapons, taking Redskins as prisoners, tying them to the stake, smoking the peace pipe, and doing war dances.

Interest in the orphans grew, and the Canadians soon learned to love them for their vivacity and sincerity. The story of their tragic experiences began to be known and stirred up much sympathy. In the papers, especially in Montreal, long, detailed accounts of the children's odyssey appeared, along with photographs. The radio station in Sorel, the nearest large town, interviewed me on the air to highlight the children's adventures; groups of young French people from there came to teach the girls folk dances of old Quebec; and the Brothers of the Sacred Heart Academy in Sorel offered to accept thirty boys right away. Bundles of letters began arriving with requests for the orphans offered for adoption, and many people sent generous donations; apparently under the impression that the children had only recently come from Russia and had suffered severe deprivation in Africa, the Canadians showered me with proofs of their sympathy. Indeed, the interest shown by Canadians in general was so great that I began to fear that it might reinforce the attitude of some of the children that "everything is due us."

Management of the St. Hyacinth Centre was taken over by the nuns with the assistance of our girls, and at the St. Vincent Home, the older boys were managing on their own. Our own limping Wladzio, acquainted with Chinese, Hindu, and African cuisine, took care of all matters culinary. Besides cooking, he understood politics and was an able story-teller, so he always had a circle of admiring listeners around him.

Steeling ourselves for our first Canadian winter, which we feared would be hard on us after our many years in tropical climates, we almost failed to notice that a fabulously beautiful autumn had arrived.

40

Placing Children in Boarding Schools

The lovely autumn, so exotic to us, lasted for a long, leisurely while, but winter was just around the corner, and after two months in Contrecoeur we left that hospitable place. The boys were transferred to historic Châteauguay on Lake St. Louis, to the property of J. E. McComber, a Montreal furrier and a great friend of ours; the girls went to the home of the Soeurs de Notre Dame du Bon Conseil in Pointe Claire, a suburb of Montreal on the opposite shore.

These two youth centers formed an "operational base" for the management personnel. There we discussed with our charges the work available and the working conditions, and did counseling about the choice of trade schools. We taught basic French and I gave talks on the history and geography of Canada, emphasizing current social conditions. From here we also made trips to Montreal and to provincial towns seeking employment for the grown-up members of the group and locating schools that would give the younger ones free board and education, primarily those operated by French Catholic religious congregations. Everywhere we were received cordially, with a smile and a friendly "Bienvenue" expressing the fervent belief that the reception of orphans is a particular blessing of God. This atmosphere of kindliness was, to a certain extent, the result of Archbishop Charbonneau's ardent appeal to the faithful of the Archdiocese a few months before we arrived, an appeal to help those rescued from concentration camps and now deprived of their homeland and citizenship rights, and for the thousands of war orphans who had never known the sweetness of family life.

The Archbishop set the example for his flock by his own active Christian love. Our first Christmas Eve in Canada, his Excellency met and dined with the whole group at the Soeurs de Notre Dame du Bon Conseil Centre in Montreal. He was deeply moved as he witnessed the Polish custom of sharing the wafer, "oplatek," symbolic of the brotherly love commanded by Christ during the Last Supper; he was touched as he listened to the Polish carols, and he looked at the children's glad faces with fatherly affection. The Archbishop's immense kindness was always apparent whenever we needed his help or even a personal sacrifice. And he always inquired about "his children's" well-being.

"His children" suffered a severe blow when, in 1950, the Archbishop had to give up his office because of poor health. It is difficult to describe our grief. Shortly before he left Montreal, on his name day, a group of our children went to the archiepiscopal palace to offer our thanks and good wishes. Janek Mazur, who had already made substantial progress in French, expressed our deep gratitude, and the girls presented him flowers. He welcomed the children as graciously as ever, treated them with candies and smiled kindly at all of them; but we noticed signs of great fatigue in his face, and his hands shook.

The newly nominated Archbishop of Montreal, later the Cardinal His Eminence Paul-Emil Léger, continued his predecessor's kind interest in the children, their education and upbringing. In September, 1950, he assigned Father Marcel Dostaler to assist Father Caron, now chaplain of the rehabilitation school; Father Jacques Laramee had left us a few months earlier.

The allocation of children to various schools was not without some minor tragedies. The group instinctively fought against being separated from each other, and the very thought of a totally strange environment without an understanding guardian nearby naturally made them anxious and frightened. This anxiety itself had already predisposed the orphans against their Canadian surroundings. To help keep up their spirits, therefore, we placed at least two of them in each school.

But even that did not always work. For example, two boys, both thirteen, were assigned to Rawdon, some forty miles northwest of Montreal. After a few days the principal telephoned us that the boys were crying day and night, would not associate with the other boys, and refused to eat. Moreover, nobody at the school could speak Polish. Father Caron and I went to see them. In vain we tried to persuade them to make an effort to get through this first difficult period; in vain we assured them they would soon get used to the new place and the new people. Choking with tears, they clung to us, and as we were about to leave even tried to jump into our car. "For drying up their tears" Father Caron gave each of them a dollar. They took the money and quieted down, but with suspicious suddenness. I strongly suspected they would use the money for bus tickets back to Châteauguay. And so they did.

Taking advantage of a break between classes, the boys evaded the teachers on duty and disappeared. The police were alerted; we were terrified because in the mountains around Rawdon winter had begun and the boys were wearing only light clothing, nor did they know the road or the language, and they had no food. It was not until late in the evening of the next day that they appeared at Châteauguay. They told us they had not eaten for forty-eight hours. To elude the authorities they had not taken a bus but had walked most of the day and the whole night, hiding in the woods whenever a car approached. Finally they had taken a bus the rest of the way to Montreal and there had caught the one to Châteauguay. Needless to say, their desperate, courageous escape from school made them heroes to other boys who would later on resist with fierce determination any attempt to separate them from the group.

To explain to the Canadians what they considered strange behavioral and psychological reactions in our children, I delivered talks in almost every school—about forty of them—about the children's suffering in Russia and during their years of globetrotting. Everywhere we met compassion, understanding, and the desire to help.

From time to time I wrote mimeographed letters to the children in boarding schools, lonesome for their pals, trying to help them overcome their purely emotional prejudice against their new environment. I would tell them about their friends' scholastic progress and the whereabouts of other members of our family in schools or with Canadian foster parents. An excerpt from one of these letters reflects some of the nostalgia, sadness, breakdown, and rebellion the children were going through, and our incessant worry and difficulty:

> All of you have surely heard the sad news about our Father and Guardian, Archbishop Charbonneau, an irreparable loss to us. It seems to us that it is our natural father who has died. Just think of his kindliness toward us. What a beautiful lesson of evangelical mercy he has given to the world and to us. When he took you under his care, he did not reckon how many thousands of dollars it would cost to maintain you and educate you. Such material concerns were not important to him. He was following the voice

of his conscience and of his heart. When he decided to take care of you, he did not know how you look, how intelligent you are, how well-mannered. He accepted you because you were in need, because you are the children of God. He accepted you all equally—the intelligent, the less bright, the gentle, and the rough. And now he has gone because he did not consider what a burden he was taking upon himself in his willingness to help everybody. He did not sleep well for months, we are told. Remember him in your prayers. Receive Holy Communion for him, offer for him the merits of the Holy Mass. May the kind Lord reward his work and his toil. . . .

At school and in your boarding house be good, obedient, and hard-working. Do not by bad behavior, disobedience, or laziness create problems, because that way you would lose your reputation and thus the sympathy and love that everybody has for you. Such love may cool if you do not give of yourself—your heart, strength, health, ability, and time; you will receive instead indifference, disrespect, or—what is worse—contempt. Just think about it. Wouldn't people give up on you? Give them your smiles, your thanks; win the hearts of your superiors and your friends the Canadians through your gratitude and acts of kindness. Remember that the more you get into people's hearts, the easier and more joyful your life will be. Even if one of your present guardians is moved, whether Father Caron or I, you will be able to continue your schooling, provided you earn for yourself the love and confidence of your superiors and teachers.

Live peacefully with each other in brotherly love, because all eyes are on you, newcomers from across the ocean. By your behavior, your good points and bad, the Canadian people will form their opinion of the whole Polish nation. You are ambassadors of our homeland. Through your own cultural development you can help our oppressed country.

Have due respect for the Canadians. They will understand you, for they are themselves immigrants or descendants of immigrants. From the moment you disembarked, they have not once treated you as foreigners but as New Canadians. Once you complete your education you will have the same opportunities as native-born Canadians. You will have a chance to occupy high positions. It is very different in other countries where foreign birth is a kind of a stigma degrading the newcomer forever to second-class citizenship or worse. Most Canadians in the province of Quebec are Catholics like ourselves, and thus we have much in common with them. Do not weaken these bonds of friendship. . . .

From time to time our thoughts strayed to Switzerland, where in the Pro Juventute Sanitorium in Davos Platz the nine of our orphans suspected of having tuberculosis were being kept under observation. (Other children detained in Bremen as we were leaving Germany had since joined us in Contrecoeur.) The youngest, Wanda Cyran, a rather pugnacious nine-year-old, wrote us what was happening there:

> It is pleasant here, but sad because we do not understand any language. . . . I am playing with everybody very nicely and do not fight. We spent Christmas happily with Miss Sullivan. I got ten gifts: a doll, a record player, in a box a little rosary blessed by the Holy Father, a ball, a comb for the doll, a brush for the doll's hair, although the hair is not real . . . a tiny mirror, two soap dishes with soap, various games and candies. We go for walks, watch sports, go climbing in the mountains, and go to town. The boys push us into the snow and we push them. After walks we go to school and learn English. . . . We are all feeling well, and the doctor said that for sure we will be going to Canada in February, because those spots that we have (on our lungs) are from malaria, and the doctor said that we will be going to Canada with cheeks as round as doughnuts. Goodbye! Wanda
> P.S. I am sending a photograph of the town of Davos.

The little group, including the resolute Wanda, finally joined us in May, 1950. Not one of them was actively tubercular; they had only traces of calcification from diseases they had suffered in Russia.

The last one to join us was thirteen-year-old Stas. While in Italy, Stas had had the good fortune to be received by the Holy Father Pius XII in a private audience, along with children of other nationalities, all in the care of Miss Sullivan. The Pope, deeply touched by their tragedy, must have recalled that our group, because we had left Italy so hurriedly, had missed the scheduled audience; he suddenly turned and asked whether any Polish children were present. Stas, all alone, approached the Pope, who stretched his arms over him and said, "This child, and all the other innocent Polish children who have suffered through Communism, I bless!"

41

The Communists Appeal to the United Nations Organization

During our first months in Canada, the Communists tried once again to disturb our peace. Three of our thirteen-year-olds were living in the boarding house of the Sisters of the Holy Cross in Montreal. One Sunday afternoon they were invited for tea by the mother of one of their classmates, the wife of the Czechoslovakian consul. One of the orphans was Bronia Murawski, the one who, with her sister, had been abducted to the Polish Communist embassy in Rome. Grateful that the Polish youngsters had attracted some attention, the unsuspecting nuns allowed them to accept the invitation.

The consul's wife treated the girls warmly and eventually asked them to sit on the carpet at her feet; then she began to quiz them about how they happened to be in Canada: Why hadn't they gone back to their own country? Was anyone coercing them to remain here? How did they imagine their future in a strange country? She was, she said, shocked by the "scandalous abduction" of the girls to Canada, undoubtedly against their will. She offered to help. All they had to do was make it known that they wanted to return to Poland. Without taking part in the conversation, only observing the reactions of the girls, the consul stood behind his wife, waiting attentively for their answers. The girls were terrified and their replies stiff and mumbled; they also had difficulty not showing the fury they felt for the host and hostess who had received them so cordially. Back at the boarding house, the girls called me and recounted the whole episode.

On another occasion at a public gathering in Windsor, Ontario, just opposite Detroit, a female Polish Communist agent accused the IRO, Canada, and the United States of violating international treaties and infringing on the children's rights by "abducting" them to Canada. Two of our alumni, then working in Windsor as auto mechanics, happened to be at the meeting and jumped up to protest such calumnies. They themselves, they declared, were proof that she was lying, for they had settled and were working right there in Windsor, 600 miles from Montreal, and were doing very well. Thus belied by the orphans themselves the agent sat down amid the jeers of the audience.

One day I had a few telephone calls allegedly from a correspondent for the *Toronto Star Daily* asking me for an interview regarding the life of the orphans in Canada, and for permission to take photographs of their schools and places of employment. When I telephoned the newspaper office I learned that no one on their staff had been given such an assignment.

These attempts of the Communists to get at us did not worry us seriously, for they were nothing in comparison with their persecution of us in Africa and Europe. The ineffectiveness of their maneuvers, however, finally caused them to take their grievances straight to the Security Council of the United Nations Organization at Lake Success. Their delegates, Henryk Altman, Mme. Fryderyka Kalinowski, and Tadeusz Zebrowski, accused the IRO, Italy, the United States, Great Britain, and Canada of having conspired long ago in the "abduction" and having calculated its execution right down to the minutest detail. Their documents, however, made no reference to the real abduction of the children to Russia by the Bolsheviks in 1940, when they had been deported not to protect them from the threat of war on Polish territory but to destroy a part of the Polish nation. Delegate Zebrowski presented the matter quite differently. According to him the children had been evacuated from war-threatened territories for their own good, and when the war spread to Russia, she had magnanimously permitted them to be transferred to Persia then to Tanganyika, to improve their living conditions, "according to the UNRRA plan, for the duration of the war, with the proviso that upon cessation of war activities, they be returned to Poland. Meanwhile," complained the delegate, "they stayed in Africa for four years after the war. No Polish mission was able to contact them. No step was taken to have them sent back to Poland. And here, suddenly in August, 1949, the IRO transferred them to Italy!"[1]

He and the other delegates claimed falsely that despite the Polish government's official protest and diplomatic intervention at the British, Italian, and General Headquarters of the IRO, the

1. 4-ème Session de l'Assemblée Générale, 3-ème Commission, 264 Séance, 2 Dec. 1949.

children were completely isolated from Polish repatriation officers. They again brought up the affair of the Murawski sisters, still maintaining with patent falsehood that the girls, having been summoned by their mother, escaped from our Salerno camp to the Polish Communist embassy in Rome to request help to return to Poland. (They did not bother to explain why, then, the sisters returned by themselves to our camp.) Said Delegate Zebrowski, "During the children's stay in Italy, they were in the care of a certain Polish priest hostile to his country's government. He accompanied them on their journey to Halifax. The plot to have them abducted into Canada was completed then." He even maintained that I had not told the children where they were going, basing this false accusation on an article drawn from an interview with me in the Montreal *La Presse* of September 10, 1949. (When I re-read the article, I found some inaccuracies but nothing about my not having told the children where they were going. Indeed, the word "Canada" had been on their lips all the time, and even while we were still in Salerno, they were conveying their thanks through the Canadian Miss Sullivan to Archbishop Charbonneau for his readiness to welcome them to Canada.)

The delegate of the puppet White Russian Republic, Afanassy Stepanenko, supported the accusations of the Polish delegation by pointing out that in Yalta the three great powers had accepted the principle that all victims of fascist tyranny should be repatriated as soon as possible. He praised Russia as the only nation to adhere scrupulously to her obligations in this regard, having repatriated over one million citizens of Western Allied States, while hundreds of Soviet citizens had not been returned from the territories occupied by Western powers. Stepanenko saw in this the ill will of the West. The problem of the refugees should have been resolved long before, but the Western Allies, in order to obtain a cheap labor force, had created it artificially and were now artificially maintaining it. The IRO had become the agency of those states and their propagandist, enticing the refugees into their capitalistic paradise, where they would be bitterly disappointed. Now, with the Polish nation gagged and unable to speak for itself, those whose hands were stained with Polish blood purported to speak for it before the Tribunal of the United Nations, and there was no one to protest the atrocious crime the Communists had perpetrated against hundreds of thousands of Polish youngsters.

But at least the Communists' charges against Canada and the IRO were refuted. The Canadian delegate, Senator Mme. Cairine Wilson of Ottawa, denied the accusations and stated that the Communist government in Warsaw was apparently incapable of either perceiving or appreciating the sincerity of her government's humanitarian gesture. As for their complaints, she suggested that they be referred to the IRO, the organization most competent in such matters.

The Polish delegate Mme. Kalinowski then inquired, "If the Canadian government were guided by humanitarian motives, why did it object to Polish authorities meeting with the Polish children? For what reason were girls locked up in the cloister of the Sisters of Notre Dame du Bon Conseil? Poland had never recruited Canadians for work, nor had she ever abducted Canadian children to Poland. Poland sought no quarrel with Canada."

During the UNO Board session afterwards Mr. J. D. Kingsley, Director of the IRO in Geneva, strongly rebuffed the Communists.[2] He pointed out that a major problem of refugees was the current instability of life in all its aspects—social, economic, and political. The IRO's objective was not only to repatriate people, but also to help them settle in other countries if they wished. Over seven million refugees and deportees, 80% of the total, had been repatriated before the IRO was created; this is why such an insignificant percentage of current refugees were willing to return to their home countries. If they had wanted to return, they could have done so several years before.

Rejecting the Communist arguments that the IRO was not helping refugees to repatriate, he supplied statistics to prove that they had been strongly urged to return to their native countries. He pointed out that in June, 1949, the IRO had distributed in refugee camps in Germany 113,807 publications from East European countries and had shown films supplied by the Polish consulates depicting life in post-war Poland.

---

2. 4-ème Session de l'Assemblée Générale, 3-ème Commission, 259 Séance, 10 Nov. 1949.

As for the Polish orphans, Director Kingsley went on, a majority of them were sixteen years old and were therefore, by IRO statutes, to be regarded as adults. Seventeen of the twenty-four orphans under thirteen years of age had an older brother or sister, and of the twenty-three half-orphans with father or mother living, sixteen were at least sixteen years old and also had an older brother or sister.

The IRO, he noted, had tried to arrange a meeting between Polish authorities and the children. While they were in Bremen, just prior to leaving for Canada, the IRO had made such a proposal to the Polish Red Cross, and not for the first time; but the Polish Red Cross had stipulated that, before such a meeting, they must be given a list of the orphans. The matter of supplying their governments with lists of refugees had been discussed within the IRO several times, and their official policy had always been not to release such lists. The Polish Red Cross had then refused to meet with the children. Under the circumstances, the IRO had accepted the magnanimous offer of the Catholic hierarchy of Canada.

Mr. Kingsley assured the government in Warsaw that he was still willing to cooperate with them regarding the repatriation of the children under sixteen who were not accompanied by an older brother or sister and whose father or mother was alive. He also pointed out that in its brief period of activity, the IRO had repatriated 66,000 deportees and refugees, half of them Poles.

To these explanations the Polish delegates had little reply and apparently gave up on our orphans as a lost cause. But had it not been for the fact that the Western Allied Governments had collected ample proof, since the end of the war, of what Communism is and what is the true situation in Poland, these children would have been forced back to Poland against their will and that of their guardians.

42

The Lights and Shadows of Social Integration

I had hoped that by constant contact with their Canadian contemporaries at school our young people would become spirittually acclimated to their new environment before moving on to a hard life of work and duties.

Father Caron, Father Dostaler, and the Soeurs de Notre Dame du Bon Conseil Congregation brought up a matter important to us all: the maintenance of our Polish identity. We were given to understand that Canada wished not to assimilate the children but to integrate them. "Assimilation," as they understood it, was the total absorption of an immigrant into an alien environment, causing his ethnic traits and native culture to disappear, while "integration" was a uniting of the foreigner, his ethnic identity intact, with his adoptive country, whose culture and environment would enrich him. Even a superficial knowledge of the history of Poland reveals that any attempt at forcible assimilation of her people, known for their love of freedom and their attachment to tradition, would have failed.

Canadians of French origin readily understood our fears of assimilation because for many years they themselves had had to fight against absorption by the Anglo-Saxon element. The congregations which educated and provided for our orphans did not object to their retaining their Polish identity. Against the background of Canadian life, our national traits became, in fact, rather attractive to Canadian young people, evoking their interest in Poland itself.

While encouraging our youngsters to learn Canadian ways, the nuns promoted their interest in the history and language of Poland, pointing out that, because of the war, the Polish nation had lost many educated people. When Poland regained her freedom, the children would return there and, thanks to Canada, help rebuild her. Actually, by following national, religious, and family traditions, the children maintained their Polish ethnic spirit whenever they got together for festivities, weekends, and vacations. Many of them read with keen interest Polish books, periodicals, and newspapers. Father Dostaler carried in his car a modest circulating library and a handful of Polish papers, and the girls were provided with a library of a few hundred volumes at the Polish center managed by the nuns.

Tired of their unsettled life, however, our youngsters had no intention of staying in school any longer than necessary. Since they longed for independence, only a few enrolled in schools offering a general education program; most of them opted for technical schools, the boys to develop manual or mechanical skills, the girls to be trained in nursing or commercial studies.

At first many of the girls chose the "Ecoles Ménagères," training schools for domestic management. Popular then in Quebec, these schools taught religion, psychology, infant care, practical nursing, cooking, and home decorating, to prepare young girls to become housewives and mothers. For girls who have an anchor at home until they marry, such schools may have been ideal. But not for our orphan-exiles. Completing such a program would give them only one possibility for making their own way—domestic service, becoming "domestiques"; and this kind of work is generally unpopular among immigrant girls, who believe that their employer, as a rule, tries to exploit them, finding some pretext to pay them very low wages—their lack of experience, a physical inadequacy, or even the inclination of the European girl to "let too many dollars go to her head."

Two "Ecoles Ménagères" in the outskirts of Montreal showed a total lack of understanding of child psychology, as well as of the progress of the social sciences particularly with regard to war orphans. One group of girls wrote to us:

> We are feeling very bad, and we would like to change schools . . . We believed that after the first festivities the management would, according to their promise, change our education program, but it is not true. We are, more than before, engaged in the kitchen for almost all day—and what good is this to us? We do not feel at all that we are in school. We do not even attend the French language classes. They tell us that we shall learn through practice, in conversation at dishwashing. But we will not know the grammar nor the written language. What good is there for us in this? We wanted to telephone you, but we are not allowed to. Later on, under the pretext of going to buy candy, we left the boarding house in order to phone you from a restaurant, but they sent a group of girls who spied on us and did not let us get near the telephone.

Some of the girls who did complete the course in domestic management later asked to be sent to commercial schools for a chance to earn their living at a different job.

The orphans spent most of the year in boarding houses, often far from Montreal, which became the focal point of our life after the centers at Châteauguay and Pointe Claire were closed. The network of sixty-two schools accommodating our children covered hundreds of square miles, only twenty-two in Montreal itself. The very size of this area, as large as Poland, made our work extremely difficult, especially at first when we had to make frequent visits to lonesome children who found it hard to adjust. Our job was further complicated by our multifarious responsibilities: clothing, transportation, medical care, hospital calls, correspondence of all kinds, arrangements for holiday gatherings, and the continuing search for Polish homes where the orphans could spend festive seasons and vacations with a family. Merely looking for new schools and arranging a summer camp program, we averaged over 500 miles a week. By the end of the first year the French priests had used up three cars, and we found that our intense efforts were using up ourselves also.

Our day started at five and did not end until midnight. Our mode of life was irregular: we had to be ready for emergency calls from our charges and school principals; we ate without appetite most often at roadside inns, often content with a soft drink and a chocolate bar. The more energy we expended, the more nervous tension built up in us; and we got so little sleep that our eyelids became heavy with fatigue and words stuck in our dried-out throats. Yet all this weariness we had to camouflage with a smile, a bit of cheerful conversation, or a compliment. We lived in a car: we ate, meditated, said our breviary aloud (with the help of a loudspeaker installed by Father Dostaler), and discussed educational problems, as we drove mile after mile. Of course we spent hours repairing the car, and our gypsy life held other unpleasant surprises. Once in a blizzard, when every signpost was covered with snow and we had taken a wrong turn, some farmers in the area had to pull us out of the snow drifts with horses. A few times during the summer, when Father Dostaler would feel himself going to sleep at the steering wheel, he would have to pull over and take a nap at the side of the road.

The fact that the orphans were attending schools as completely equipped as those for Canadian children helped alleviate their inferiority complex. They had dictionaries, fountain pens, atlases, skates, and hockey sticks, and the girls in the nursing course had wristwatches with the red second dial. The very large majority took to learning enthusiastically. For many of them French posed the greatest difficulty; the boys in the trade schools, for example, worked vigorously in the shops but objected to classroom lessons in French. We tried to explain that though French is difficult, it is not impossible to learn; that it was not the English but the French-speaking Canadians who had taken us in; that their schools were the only ones we could go to; that language is only an instrument for acquiring knowledge, and it is that knowledge that counts. But since not everyone was convinced by our arguments, we finally gave all the children the opportunity to learn both official languages, French and English. In time all the language difficulties were overcome, and our children eventually excelled in their classes, even surpassing some of their Canadian classmates.

Some, however, lost interest in education altogether and dropped out because of this language problem, as well as the difficulty of resuming an education so often interrupted in the past. This pained us deeply, and they became a considerable problem for us: too young to get jobs, too impatient to stay in school. After a while some of them did make the effort to return to school and learn a trade, but others led a lazy life, playing cards, smoking, going to movies, but finding no real satisfaction in life. On the contrary, they gradually became aware of the precious time and talent they were wasting and grew even more frustrated. For this they would blame their superiors, unwilling to admit that they had driven themselves into this blind alley.

Some older boys, who had avoided the initial difficulties at school and gone directly to work, began to regret it now, realizing that learning is necessary in a technological age. The more intelligent tried to upgrade themselves all at once, ineptly and in vain. One of them, for instance, bought an *Encyclopaedia Britannica*, believing that he could teach himself wisdom. Another, distrustful of his elders and very conceited at that, hoped to solve life's problems by studying philosophy from a textbook. Still another, an introvert who tried to solve his personal problems by learning psychology on his own, only aggravated those problems. Some tried, in vain, to make careers in boxing, wrestling, or hockey to earn more than those who had completed their education.

Many of the orphans who dropped out of school after one or

two years derived some advantage from even their incomplete education. They got to know French and learned some kind of trade to give them a better start in life; and some had already developed, through their varied experiences, a natural inclination toward certain technical occupations.

We kept hoping that all of our orphans would enrich themselves by their experiences, increase their knowledge, and live useful, joyful lives in profitable occupations. It was painful for us, then, to watch the failure of young men who wanted to be somebody but did not have the internal strength to overcome their weaknesses and lacked faith in the good advice of their elders. But it was hard to blame them: they were defeated at least partly by the forces that had, not so long ago, threatened to destroy them utterly—exile in Russia, loss of parents, life in refugee camps.

43

The Problem of Adoption

At the time our ship had approached the shores of Canada, Montreal newspapers notified their readers of the possibility that the orphans would be offered for adoption. When we arrived, letters began pouring in to our office from well-to-do Canadians earnestly requesting interviews. Although our location was kept secret, a few applicants even came to Contrecoeur. But, alas, except for entrusting a few children to Polish families, we were unable to comply with other requests for many reasons.

The youngest children were already nine years old, and all of them were developed beyond their years mentally and psychologically. Keenly aware that they were orphans, most of them would not have been able to consider even the best of guardians as parents. Most of the children had already entered adolescence, when guidance is difficult even in the best of circumstances. To deal with any of our charges at this stage required a sensitivity to his or her emotional history. Their hypersensitivity, sudden outbursts, long-suppressed fears, and troubled memories all argued against adoption. Nor could the ethnic aspect be ignored. The whole atmosphere of their childhood, in India or Africa, had been truly Polish, and they were so deeply attached to their Polishness that it was impossible to place them in French or English homes.

All who met them were struck by their uncommonly early maturity. Ten-year-old Wladzio may serve as an example. When he first arrived at the home of a Polish family with whom he was to spend his vacation, they found him taciturn and uncommunicative. He thought that what they talked about was meaningless: why talk about nothing? At bedtime, in the room he shared with Janek, his hosts' son, he became talkative. Willingly and in detail he began to describe his experiences. He did not remember anything about Russia because there he was just an infant, but while he was attending school in Africa a lady brought him photographs of his parents. He did not know why he had not asked her what she knew about them or how she happened to have their pictures; maybe he had been too young to think about it. He never met the lady again, but he still preserved in the bottom of his trunk these precious mementos of his parents. Each night, alone with Janek, Wladzio told endless tales about Africa while Janek's parents, sitting in the adjoining room, listened with awe. They confessed to me later, "What we heard from Wladzio is simply astounding. It made us feel that we were the little children listening to a grown-up."

We did arrange for five girls and one boy to visit Polish families with a view to adoption. Only three of the girls were adopted: Bogusia, Stasia, and Magdzia. Bogusia, uncommonly captivating in manner and appearance, was born for adoption. An African couple had been eager to take her and were forever bringing her flowers and goodies; an Italian officer on board the S.S. *Gerusalemme*, and later on a baroness in Salerno, asked to become her guardian. But Bogusia would not dream of being separated from the group. Finally here in Canada she did agree to be adopted by a prosperous contractor and his wife. Stasia fell in love at once with her adoptive mother, and in a short time became very nearly like her in mentality and even in appearance. Today one can hardly believe that they are not natural mother and daughter. Magdzia was everybody's favorite. Her mother was in Poland, and her older brother and sister in an orphanage in Canada; but the kind mother, knowing that it might be years before she could be reunited with her children, consented to let nine-year-old Magdzia be adopted by a Polish family in the United States, to assure her little one of the warmth of home and family and the chance for an education. Magdzia was aware that everyone loved her, including me. (Before she left she stood on tiptoe to see "whether the priest is crying.") Her lively intelligence was matched by her kindness, the dominant trait of her character. Her dream was to become a medical assistant, following the examples of her brother Janek, a medical student, and her sister Kazia, a registered nurse.

The other children offered for adoption returned to the group. Krysia's adoptive parents admitted that they were helpless in the face of her specific nature as a war orphan, which demanded much more knowledge of psychology than they had. Wanda, a little girl with a rich, talented nature, had to be taken back, even though she was inclined to stay with the family. She did not grasp the moody ineptitude of the adoptive mother until a sudden, unprovoked incident made her realize it. In a fit of temper, the woman had ordered her to take off the dress and shoes they had given her and put on her modest African clothes.

Andrew, a lively, pugnacious, and aggressive nine-year-old, visited a Polish family in Cowansville for a trial period; but because of his temperament it was not successful. On his way with Father Caron and me to visit another family, he told us what had happened. His prospective new mother was exceedingly loving, and he had been determined to take advantage of that. He longed to replace her own son in her heart and thought he had a good chance to succeed because her natural son, his own age, was ungrateful, lazy, and disobedient. The fight for priority had been long and fierce, but in the end Andrew had lost. "I did everything I could to get her to love me best," he confessed, "but she still loved that good-for-nothing more than me."

In his second home, with a noble, elderly, childless couple, Andrew was still unable to take root. His new guardians' temperaments were diametrically opposed to his, and he felt constrained, asphyxiated; he longed for his own companions. But though subdued when he was with his foster parents, he managed to regain his vitality by visiting his friends often; and by the time he reached manhood and enlisted in the Canadian Army he had become so attached to the old folks that he spent every leave with them.

Even for the majority of the boys and girls who could not be considered for adoption, we still wanted to provide an experience of family life, if only during holidays and vacations. Going from door to door in the Polish sections, we searched for host families. Thus we managed to introduce almost all of the orphans who were in school to Polish families, and a few, at their own request, to French ones. If a child had problems adjusting to one family, we would find another. Our fear that the adolescent orphans might find it difficult to adjust to strange people was justified. After seven years in Canada, about a hundred of them visited Canadian families of their choice from time to time, but less than ten kept up a steady contact.

Bazyli, for example, felt his best in the company of his contemporaries with whom he shared the same mentality, the same psychological complexes, and so many of the same experiences. Among them he was talkative, open, and happy, but with a stranger he would become shy and embarrassed. The family to whom we introduced him gave him a most cordial welcome and were very proud of their young cosmopolitan guest. Since they had many relatives, they were always taking him visiting on Sundays and holidays, and we hoped he would form a firm bond with them. But one day Bazyli left their house and did not return. The worried family, feeling responsible, started a frantic search for him and telephoned me. Where to look for the boy if not among his African friends? I thought. There indeed was Bazyli. "They were," he said, "carting me around to show me off to their relatives like an African monkey!" After that he refused to be introduced to any other families.

Wanda, the plucky little girl who had stayed behind in Switzerland, now eleven and with us in Canada, was scheduled to visit a certain family for the first time at Christmas. The thought of it brought flushes of happiness and delight to her pale face. "Is this a good family?" she asked in a serious tone of voice. Her very manner of greeting her substitute parents encouraged us to hope that they would establish a strong attachment between them. Unaware of her own charm, which radiated from her goodness rather than her appearance, Wanda captivated their hearts. The large black eyes in her freckled face sparkled with intelligence, and through her unhealthy complexion shone the seriousness of a mature person and a healthy, natural good humor. One Sunday she called me and, in a voice timid and subdued by great emotion, said bluntly, "Please, Father, I am not going to stay here. This is a bad family."

"Oh, Wanda!" I said, "You can't judge people by your first impressions. Try to compose yourself."

"They do not go to church," complained Wanda, "and they won't let me go. When I woke up, I noticed it was time for Holy Mass. I woke the lady up, and she just turned over and said angrily, 'Go to sleep! That is what vacations are for. You have worked enough at school; now is the time to rest!' No, please, Father, I will not stay. Please, come and take me away from here!" After fruitless attempts to drag the family to Holy Mass, Wanda wanted to sneak out of the house and look for the church, but she was afraid of getting lost in the large town. In the end, their permission for her to go to church, their occasional gifts, the luxurious accommodation and the good cuisine were all useless. The little girl had ceased to care for these people once and for all.

For some of the orphans, used to a tumultuous life with a crowd of their contemporaries, the hopeless emptiness in some homes was insufferable, especially those where there were no other children. Although they had not the haziest idea of how to handle a child, some childless couples would ask for an orphan. The children all feared dull, self-centered people, and luxurious surroundings made no impression on them. Merry and carefree, they would rather sleep on a hard bench or on the floor and, as they used to say, cover themselves with a newspaper than in a soft bed under eiderdown in a loveless home.

Some of them encountered a very restrictive atmosphere, sometimes unbearably so. They were not allowed to open the blinds while reading because the drapes might fade, or use the armchairs because the springs would sag; they could remove the covers from the furniture only when visitors were coming. Such homes were mere show pieces on display for company, and a drape was more precious than a child's eyesight.

Twelve-year-old Bogna was overjoyed at the thought that as soon as she arrived in Canada she would be taken care of by an uncle living near Ottawa. Her dream was quickly realized, but just as quickly faded. We suspected that the family rejected her because she had a curvature of the spine and perhaps feared she might become a burden on them. Bogna came back to the orphanage.

Mila, after four years in a Canadian school, was finally granted her turn on the American immigration quota and allowed to join relatives in the United States. She had several of them in different locations, but she landed on a dull, remote farm in Minnesota. She wrote:

> My relatives are very good to me; they bought me many things, but what of it? I'm homesick for Canada. . . . Since I was a child I have lived with children, but here I am alone. My only friend is a large dog that never leaves my side. Please believe me, I shall never forget you, Father, and our group. I will admit confidentially that when I read your letter, I cried and cried. . . .

Unable to bear such isolation, Mila went south to Biloxi, Mississippi, hoping that among new relatives she would find an environment more suitable to a young person. But here too she found only elderly people. She planned to run away, alerting us in a letter: "If anything should happen—which God forbid!—I hope that you, Father, will allow me to return to the group in Canada." But instead, she moved again, this time to try living with a cousin in Cleveland. Shortly after, though so very young, she married.

One very sad case was that of fourteen-year-old Danuta, who had gone to live with an uncle in Alberta in Western Canada. For a long time we had no news from her, but when it came, it was like a bolt of lightning: her uncle wanted to send her back to Poland under escort. We could not imagine why, because she was a good, quiet girl. We demanded that she be returned immediately. When Father Caron and I met her at the Montreal railway station, the sight of her shocked us: her messy hair glittered with brilliantine and her face was provocatively painted. Although she was still a child, her appearance and behavior made us realize what had become of her. We learned that her uncle, ignoring our requests, had ridiculed the idea of sending her to school and told her to go to work on the ground that "in the Wild West" one did not have to know much to make a living. She had worked at many jobs, mostly in restaurants, with no one to care for her. Before her eyes had opened a new, corrupt world. In her innocence she either could not see or did not want to acknowledge that it was leading her to disaster. She was returned to us time and again, but we could not keep her in school. She always went to work, attracted by the delusion of a cheap glamor. Even when she eventually became pregnant and was evicted for not paying her rent, we still tried to help her; but she was finally lost to us completely, without a trace.

We suffered a few other painful losses. Two boys slipped away into the silent world of insanity. Mikolaj fell into a deep melancholy and developed suicidal tendencies. Physically well developed and handsome, he had been studying with a few friends in the technical school in Cap de la Madeleine and boarding with the kind Brothers of the Most Sacred Heart. They informed us that his behavior was becoming very strange. In a fit of incomprehensible fury, he would break equipment, insist that his name was being repeated constantly on the radio and in the newspapers, and speak about being persecuted by mysterious voices day and night. The other boy, Romek, had been the pride of the whole group, for, though perhaps too quiet and introverted, he had great scientific ambitions and phenomenal abilities bordering on genius. In a matter of months he had mastered English and French, and had acquired on his own a vast and accurate knowledge of history. But suddenly he asked to be switched from education to the hardest physical labor. At first we surmised that he felt embarrassed about accepting help for his studies and preferred to earn his own money. It turned out, however, to be only the first indication of a serious mental disease, soon followed by others. The psychiatrist described Romek's behavior as a "departure from reality." "Il s'en va (He's going away)," he said.

In other children we noted some psychological deviations, but none so tragic. One little girl complained of pains around her heart. Though she underwent medical and psychological examinations, the doctors could find no pathological problem and believed that she might have a very acute form of nostalgia for her homeland. After some time the pains went away.

The Canadian orphanage did live through two deeply felt tragedies: Stefania Kraus died of cancer, and a year later, during a severe heat wave in Montreal, her brother Wladyslaw drowned, leaving only the two youngest members of the family, Jozefa and Jozef. The path of exile for the Kraus family had begun in 1940 in Podole, where they had had to leave in the hands of the Russians their small holding already marked with graves; two more graves were dug in Persia for the mother and one child; and the father lies buried in the jungles of Uganda. Stefania and Wladek rest beside each other in a grave offered by Father Dostaler's family. No one could have guessed that such an apparently healthy, strong girl as Stefania, so full of charm, was carrying within herself the disease that was to end her life within three years of her coming to Canada. Perhaps God had permitted this beautiful young life to become an offering for the souls of others. Stefania must have been thinking about this when she wrote to an acquaintance just before her death: "Ted, I am offering myself to God, who has visited this suffering upon me. The world is so sinful today that there have to be some who are willing to suffer for all." Stefania gave her virginal life to God in her twenty-second year on the feast of Our Lady of Sorrows. Just before her coffin was closed, her brother Wladek arrived broken-hearted and in less than a year, almost on the anniversary of her death, he too died. With his death, Jozefa and Jozef became orphans again because Stefania had been their mother and Wladek their father.

44

Choosing Vocations

Time did not stand still, and our charges were quickly approaching the moment of their release from our care. Matured so early by their many trials, they readily deemed themselves well enough fledged to stretch their wings, especially those who were bored with orphanage life and now regarded it as a kind of prison. They felt an urgent, sometimes drastic, desire for independence. A few, not even waiting to complete their studies, just ran away, fearing that, since they were minors, their superiors would restrain them. Even in the face of disaster, these orphans severed their ties with their friends and guardians, and were too ashamed to return. The "escape" of one adolescent girl from a Montreal school was engineered by friends who had begun living on their own. Most of the girls wanted to marry and raise families as if to compensate for their own orphanhood, and at times they courted the boys very obviously, even inflicted themselves on them. Their behavior reflected, of course, the influence of an environment which seemed to encourage early indulgence: all around them Canadian and American girls of their own ages had, from early adolescence, been spending most of their time with boyfriends.

But despite occasional youthful vagaries, our orphans were saved from misery by their solid principles and a certain amount of experience. The Polish girls proved more prudent than some of their Canadian peers in refusing to base their hope of happiness on romantic notions or experimental indulgence. They would have nothing to do with licentious boys and drunkards, but sought to bring to their husbands moral values that would make their marriages durable and their families wholesome.

In keeping with their pragmatic outlook on life, the girls most often found their husbands among Polish Army Combatants, veterans hardened by life in exile or at the front. The girls brought up in Africa enjoyed the excellent reputation of being level-headed and morally healthy. Although in their contacts with other young people they were often too relaxed and naive because of their lack of social experience, Providence saved them from unfortunate marriages. Sincerely and ardently they shared burdens and worries, courage and joy with their young husbands and brought as a dowry their faith in a better tomorrow.

Just as parents glory in the sight of their children happily married, so we, their guardians, rejoiced to share in the matrimonial plans of our girls and boys. Before they became engaged, most of them brought their chosen ones to meet us, to ensure that we approved. The wedding celebrations were most often arranged in the French Centre or in the convent home for girls run by the Polish nuns. The festivities were merry affairs, but also solemn and dignified, something akin to a national celebration. And no wonder! Here was the nucleus of Polish life being renewed; and it was deeply significant that, if either of the newlyweds had parents or relatives still in Poland, they sent blessings, holy wishes, and of course advice from the homeland.

At the wedding of Kazia Mazur, a nurse, her new husband, Tadek, amidst a solemn silence read a letter from his parents in Poland. It was a beautiful and inspiring message from what seemed to us a different world. Though written in that enslaved country, it mirrored the indomitable spirit of the whole nation, oppressed but not subdued, pure, noble, dignified, unchanged by Communist usurpation with its godless mores. A Pole has a deep reverence for family life, as his religion teaches him to have, and he can never be made to deviate from it by any pressures or persecution. In this he reflects the immutable spirit of his country. To his new daughter-in-law, Tadek's father wrote:

> Everything passes in this world, the memory of oaths, ardent words, fond embraces. Only the true devotion of souls will never be obliterated, souls recognized and chosen from all others on

> the long road that all humanity must tread. When the wife is the loyal companion, the home forms itself around her. Had she only the stars above her head, the grass under her feet, and a glow worm for a hearth, the real home would be where she is, wherever her gentleness radiates its warmth upon the loved ones, who otherwise would be homeless. This is her domain, and as far as her authority reaches, everything should go straight forward. To perform such a task she must be thoroughly and unwaveringly good and resistant to corruption.
>
> She would be wise not to grow above her husband, but never to trip at his side, wise not with the wisdom of an emotion-free soul, but with the controlled sweetness of a serene and careful partner adjusting to daily needs.

And to his son he wrote:

> The man ought to offer his wife the gift of his pure soul, young and vigorous health, and the ardor of his strong spirit. The happiness should be composed of the purest elements. To be happy one has to win human friendship, earn the respect of others, build a family and establish an abode of peace and tranquility. This you must keep safe from exterior harms, from foolish fears, and from internal conflicts. Never give in to discouragement or to idleness; never be afraid of adversity; be noble, tenacious, and brave. Do not expect from life more than life can give. Take from life all of its precious joys. Accept with submission its unavoidable sorrows, disappointments, and sufferings in order to transform them into the wisdom of experience and awareness. Dear son of ours, love your young spouse, Kazia, with all your heart and soul. Carry her close to your heart; give her warmth, pleasure, and comfort, and you will be at peace. And she will grow close to you, until you become one spiritual unit.

So far, almost all the orphaned girls and a majority of the orphaned boys have married and have from one to three children. Five of the marriages were between classmates.

Three of our young ladies chose the religious life. Stasia Kunicki and Rozia Szwab entered the Order of the Felician Sisters of Toronto, where they work in pastoral services and teach in the Polish Saturday schools. Stasia, who spent her early school days with the Sisters of Providence, remembers the incident that led to her vocation: On her way to class one day, hurrying through a hallway for the use of elderly patients, she noticed a frail old woman standing motionless. She may be thinking about death, thought Stasia, may even be praying for it. Just then one of the sisters approached the lady and tenderly, as a mother would her child, caressed the mournful face. Instantly the woman's eyes brightened and she seemed to Stasia like a different person. "I learned then," said Stasia, "that even the most insignificant gesture lovingly rendered a fellow human being has great value. . . ."

The third, Stasia Kacpura, entered the Order of the Sisters of the Resurrection in Montreal and is now Sister Superior of St. Hubert Convent there. Her own former superior, writing of her election to that office, described in Stasia the fulfillment of capabilities, the complete fruition of self that we had always devoutly wished for all our children:

> Above everything else she is a good human being . . . with no airs about her although she is so highly gifted for so many kinds of work. She fulfills God's will. . . . So far she has accomplished many renovations, while assuring that everything else is properly attended to. For many years now, Sister has given excellent service to our parish of the Virgin Mary of Czestochowa, as she is also a fine catechist, as well as a music, dancing, and singing teacher. She produces top-quality theatrical performances. Father Pastor appreciates most her work with the little children.

Few of our charges can be said to have realized such a multiplicity of satisfactions in their vocations, nor can we take all the credit for those who have. Nevertheless, in their own homes with their own children, or in the convent entrusted with the care of someone else's children, they found that time did heal some of the wounds of those cruel days in Russia.

45

Tribulations

Characteristic of our charges was their great vitality. In games they were indefatigable, and in work too—if it took their fancy. But their long and early experience of forced labor in Russia had regrettably distorted their view of work as one of man's most honorable duties. They had learned to see work as slavery, performed under threat strictly for the advantage of the hated state. Their understandable reaction was, whenever possible, to avoid hard work.

The disruption of their schooling while the camps were being closed and they were being moved from one country to another tended to make them even more indifferent to work. In Africa, where rescued Poles were sent for prolonged periods of convalescence, the young people had observed that these adults welcomed the benefits of social aid and enjoyed their leisure. By the time they began to graduate from Canadian schools, their desire for employment had nothing to do in their minds with readiness to accept responsibility. On the contrary, they still considered the superiors of the orphanage responsible for their maintenance and comfort, and thought that all their earnings should serve their own needs. So the period prior to their eventual change of attitude abounded in dramatic tension.

Clever at designing plots to avoid work, one particular group would so arrange it that some of them could be on the job while the others loafed around the Centre pretending to have lost their jobs. (Lying was another habit they had developed in Russia, where it was sometimes the only way to stay alive.) This they did in rotation to prevent the orphanage from being closed down.

At first, those who were earning regular wages spent every cent on their own pleasure, using the approach they had learned as child-refugees in Russia: live from day to day and don't worry about tomorrow because tomorrow will take care of itself. Since, however, they also happened to have learned that sharing everything one has is the height of brotherly love, the lazy took advantage of the industrious, most often when the latter was absent. This habit of communal ownership made it difficult for us: if we wanted to force a boy to go to work by refusing him the price of something he needed, he just "borrowed" from one of his friends and refused to budge.

For some boys their first encounter with the world of work was disastrous. They were not met with the kindliness they had expected: jeers, rebuffs, reprimands, and tricks became their daily bread. To make matters worse, as unemployment increased, so did prejudice against immigrants, especially among Canadians of French origin, who saw the newcomers taking bread out of their mouths. They were further irritated by our boys' unwillingness to learn French because English was more commonly used. Although the boys worked capably and industriously, spats occurred; and being very sensitive, they were terribly hurt when French co-workers would taunt them: "When are you going back to your own country? The war is over. What are you waiting for?" These men knew well that the young Poles were in Canada because they had lost their homeland, their families, and their freedom. "After all, Communism can't be so horrible if millions of people can stand it, you damned Polacks!" Such taunting drove our boys to distraction. They would return to the orphanage miserable and disheartened, and some began to criticize the political system in Canada in ways that would have been endorsed by Communists; for example, that Canada was under the capitalist yoke, exploiting the working masses. Such outbursts caused two of the boys to be fired. Perhaps someone was feeding them such slogans, for a malcontent is always the best object of Communist propaganda.

We sorely needed experts in adolescent psychology, especially those familiar with the problems of refugees. In spite of our best intentions, we guardians—there were only two of us—found ourselves inadequate in this moral crisis. We tried to persuade the boys that antagonism toward immigrants comes from ignorance and narrow-mindedness, that the ugliness they had experienced was from a very insignificant segment of French-Canadian society, that they should try all the harder to gain the high level of recognition and respect already achieved by some of their own countrymen. But one group of boys in particular flaunted their misgivings about human goodness and their increasing grudge against their advisors, and turned complete cynics. During religious discussions, they would bring up the possibility that a war would break out and end their misfortunes. Their attitudes began affecting other boys, and some even stopped coming to church.

Yet these same boys were filled with a sickening terror at the thought of breaking all ties with the orphanage. The time was coming inexorably. We had reminded them year after year that they should carefully organize their lives, make friends, and become independent so that they would be able to make the transition without shock. But they clung all the more convulsively to the orphanage, daring to leave good jobs for a couple of weeks or months, or a whole summer, because their younger friends were on vacation from school. One year, almost every employed boy pulled this trick. After all, they thought, who had a better right? And besides, what were the orphanage and priest for if not to take care of them?

Some boys did save money, and some were highly respected at

work for their honesty, their industry, their ability, and their good behavior. But even many of these, sadly enough, still harbored a deep regret for having refused the opportunity for an education; and though they had achieved independence, they still felt the old need to come back to our nest.

46

Christian Caritas

"Out of the blood of countless mothers and innocent children there rises toward heaven a mournful, painful outcry on behalf of a beloved country, POLAND, who through her faith in the Church and her magnificent contributions to civilization, has indelibly recorded her name on the pages of history, and now merits the humane and brotherly compassion of the world." Thus the Holy Father Pius XII in his 1939 encyclical *Summi Pontificatus* appealed for compassion and help for Polish mothers and children; and his appeal found a deep emotional response in the kind hearts of people around the world.

Shortly after the outbreak of World War II, more than eight million Poles found themselves expatriated—almost a third of the twenty-seven million refugees from Europe alone. One Pole out of every four was a refugee. The free world was faced with the problem of finding them shelter and employment. Within its service agencies and charitable societies dormant emotions began to awaken—a feeling of general brotherhood, a compassion for the homeless, the disinherited, the persecuted. The trend toward the unification of humanity began to take a quite different form from that envisioned by the Nazis and the Communists, who aimed at forcing an artificial unity by enslaving minds. A crusade of mercy began on a scale unheard of before in history, to be carried on by international organizations representing the governments of various nations as well as by long-established private groups, both secular and religious. Among these the Catholic Church, through its hierarchy in the Vatican and in each nation, occupied a leading position. This revivified compassion not only brought help, comfort, and hope to the suffering but became at the same time a prayer for God's mercy on all of mankind.

When the Polish children left Russia in 1942, representatives of the American CRS-NCWC (Catholic Relief Service-National Catholic Welfare Conference) stood by their side and helped them in the Middle East, India, and Africa right up to the time the last of them left for their adoptive countries. The CRS-NCWC amalgamates all Catholics in the United States and incorporates workers from all walks of life: the Catholic Press, the worlds of science, labor, and social services; even Congressmen and Senators. The CRS-NCWC cooperated during the war with other American government-approved organizations and the Catholic organizations of forty-four other countries.[1]

Because great masses of Polish refugees had been dispersed throughout twenty-three countries, the CRS-NCWC created a Polish Section with Monsignor A. Wycislo as its director. With gifts from the Catholic League, an arm of Polish parishes, and from the Polish Council, this Polish Section rendered invaluable aid to the CRS-NCWC. It was able to supply the refugees with thousands of tons of clothing, food, and medicine and, attached to the front-line units of the Polish Army, operated flying canteens and tea rooms. In the refugee camps the CRS-NCWC fully equipped shelters for the aged, sanatoria, hospitals, medical centers, operating rooms and medical laboratories. For children and young people, the CRS-NCWC outfitted recreation halls for games and sports, libraries, reading rooms, scout dens, music classes, and laboratories for physics and chemistry. The Directorate of the Polish Section established a total of 176 branches in refugee centers, operated by at least 354 workers, the majority of them volunteers. From August, 1945, to November, 1959, the CRS-NCWC shipped to the Polish Caritas Organization in Poland food, medicine, and clothing valued at over ten million dollars.

---

1. CRS-NCWC (Catholic Relief Services-National Catholic Welfare Conference)

CRS has operated under the aegis of NCWC as a separate legal entity since 1943 to cope with war rehabilitation problems overseas. Each year since its founding CRS, relying for its resources on the Catholic people of the United States, has channeled hundreds of millions of dollars of food, clothing, and medicine to needy people all over the world. In addition to the basic relief program, CRS is directing its resources to technical assistance and community development in many countries to meet the changing needs of the people. CRS is subject to the Administrative Board of NCWC, which is an "agency of the Archbishops and Bishops of the United States to organize, unify, and coordinate Catholic activities for the general welfare of the Church." It was founded in 1917 with secretariat headquarters in Washington, D.C. *New Catholic Encyclopedia*, McGraw-Hill Book Co., New York, 1967, vol. 10, pp. 225-228.

Among American Catholics whose dedication to the care of refugees will remain forever in the grateful memory of the Polish nation were Prelate Wycislo and his assistant, Attorney Jozef Wnukowski. Often closely observed by refugees, they were known to have extended their energies well beyond the limits of duty. For three years Mr. Wnukowski tirelessly toured the Polish camps in Africa, a devotion which twice almost cost him his life, once in an automobile accident, once in a bout of cerebral malaria.

Great charitable achievements are, as a rule, made by quiet, self-effacing heroes. In the ranks of the CRS-NCWC was such a hero. Maria Kedzierski, a young American of Polish origin, worked in its New York City branch office and was responsible for the preparation of parcels for thousands of anonymous refugees in Africa, India, and the Middle East. Though she never saw them or their misery, she always enclosed extra packages—little treats besides the usual: fabrics, musical instruments, medical preparations, sporting goods, books, and toys. She worked at her post day and night. But not even that was enough for Maria. She applied for permission to go to India or Africa to be closer to the Polish children but was turned down because of her poor health. Strange are the ways of God, however. It was in New York that Maria lived the last tragic day of her young life, working as usual when an American bomber crashed into the Empire State Building where the NCWC office was located, and she died in the fire. Polish refugees in Africa, grateful for Maria's work, named a convalescent home in Morogoro for her.

The protector of the Polish refugees, Archbishop Gawlina, very aptly called the CRS-NCWC activity "a help from heaven," and after its campaign in Italy under General Anders, the Second Polish Army issued a commemorative stamp honoring the organization. From their first contacts with Americans, the Polish refugees never failed to notice the American regard for greatness: their heroes in song, in story, and in reality were always larger than life, and their tributes to historic statesmen were monumental. Now their compassion proved to be equally large-scale.

When the Polish children first arrived in Canada, the total burden of keeping and educating them was taken over by Archbishop Charbonneau; a year and a half later, by the Canadian Episcopate, whose charitable institution is The Canadian Catholic Conference. This organization, supporting its work by donations from all Canadian Catholics, paid for the maintenance of a centre for the boys and girls, board and room for students, tuition fees (when they were not waived), school supplies, food, clothing, footwear, medical care, transportation, and entertainment. The expenses of the orphanage ran into thousands of dollars. Had it not been for the unstinted charity of conventual congregations and secular benefactors, the cost would have been several times greater. That the children had come to Canada in compliance with the wish of the Holy Father did much to open people's hearts to them everywhere. Though their initial generosity waned somewhat as donors grew tired of such long-term assistance and were discouraged by the ingratitude of some orphans, many congregations, with patience and a deep faith, unceasingly bore the burden of caring for them.

Despite their own poverty, the Sisters of the Congregation of Providence never refused to accept our girls, and those of the Congregation of the Holy Names of Jesus and Mary gave many of them complete trade-school training. Schools operated by nuns from the Congregations of the Presentation of Mary and of Notre Dame helped to educate others. The ladies who operated the Excelsior Business College in Montreal amazed us by enthusiastically welcoming our girls, in the belief that the presence of an orphan brings a particular blessing from God. The gracious charity of these nuns and lay women was entirely in the spirit of the great French matrons Jeanne Mance, Blessed Marguerite Bourgeois, Blessed Marguerite d'Youville, and others, whose noble work had laid the foundation for such deeds of compassion in Canada.

The Congregation of the Brothers of Charity rendered an extraordinary service to our boys when we first arrived. As an immediate accommodation for them, Frère Jacques, Director of the Rehabilitation Institution in Montreal, offered the use of St. Vincent School facilities: the swimming pool, playground, drill hall, projection room, ice rink, and equipment such as bicycles, balls, and roller skates. Thanks to the kindness of the Brothers, all the boys, even the working ones, could take their meals in the Institute's kitchen for only fifty cents a day and also were welcome to use the medical aid center and the employment office.

The kind-hearted Fathers of Assumption College and Brothers of the Congregation of St. Viateur, in their schools in Rawdon and Berthierville, provided full secondary education for a few of our charges. Even when fire gutted a school and boarding house in Berthierville and the Brothers had to limit the number of applicants, they took in two of our boys as non-paying boarders.

At Christmas and Eastertime, various Polish organizations in Canada and the United States sent gifts of money to help pay for the festivities. In providing for the youngsters' celebrations, the donors "shared" the traditional Polish wafer (oplatek) and blessed Easter egg (święcone) with their orphaned kinsmen.

Besides help from organized groups, we received many kindnesses from individuals. The furrier Mr. J. E. McComber loaned his summer cottage in Châteauguay for the use of our boys, and later two buildings in Montreal for our orphanage center. Moreover, two of our boys enjoyed his family's hospitality during vacations. Mr. Gerard Tardiff, a Notary Public from Pointe Claire, gave us permission to use Dowker Island in Lake St. Louis as long as the orphanage existed. On this charming island, later named after St. Hedwig (Jadwiga), partly forest, partly pasture, we were free to use a large home with a wide, glass-enclosed veranda. Another noble benefactor who became very dear to us was the humble, hard-working, very capable physician, Noel Verschelden, who for a number of years treated our orphans without payment.

The most valuable services were rendered day after day by two devout Canadian priests, Father Jean Caron and Father Marcel Dostaler. The axiom usually applied to zealous priests, "C'est un homme mangé (He is a driven man)," perfectly suited these two. After both learned to speak Polish well, their toilsome labors on our behalf ate up their energies.

Father Caron was the embodiment of goodness of heart; it radiated from his every word and gesture. His fatherly kindness toward children bordered on weakness, but he would rather have sinned by being too soft than by being too stern. Whatever character flaws he found in some of the orphans he attributed to the brutal treatment they had endured. Nothing shook his certainty that the wounds still unhealed in their young souls required, more than anything else, the balm of tenderness. Their sufferings and problems were the sole object of his interest. At one time, having been urged to spend a few days' respite in France, he arrived in Paris only to find that he had no interest whatever in its historic sites and did not even get off the train except to return to Canada. For him the only meaningful history was that being made in the souls of the younger generation, his orphans in particular. He loved his daily classroom contacts with them, and the kayak trips, the hunting, fishing, and tenting excursions that made them momentarily oblivious of the abrasions of their past. He would seclude himself for hours of meditation and then return to shower his charges with affectionate attention.

Father Dostaler's athletic build and great physical strength earned him the nickname "Tarzan." His huge frame, over six feet tall, contained a generous nature and an unusual aptitude for technical and mechanical pursuits. The orphans' admiration for him became boundless when we began the summer camp programs. On Dowker Island, with no electricity, we felt like a bunch of Robinson Crusoes in need of a Friday; in Father Dostaler we had one. He installed not only a generator to supply electricity but also a private telephone line, using an underwater cable to link the island with the mainland. With deceptive ease, while carrying out his many other responsibilities, he taught the orphans to water ski, play volleyball, use their new cameras, and manage row boats and the motorboat in their summer paradise.

Because Father Dostaler could not tolerate laxity, he met stubborn resistance from those youngsters who regarded all favors as their due. But he remained adamant in his decisions, and though he spared neither time nor money on the children who were industrious and obedient, at the same time he dealt strictly with the wastrels who tried to take advantage of his charity. Spiteful, then, they would commandeer boats for hours, break the oars on "pirate raids," hurl tomahawks into the trunks of the beautiful island trees, steal food, and damage equipment. Father Dostaler was remarkably just and did not relax the strictness of his discipline. How much goodness he instilled into the lives of these boys and girls only time will tell.

Though of course thousands of anonymous contributors to charitable organizations also sustained our homeless youngsters, Father Caron and Father Dostaler were the two whose charity most touched their souls. Even those who had to grow in gratitude do not forget them; and in each of the children—and in me—is indelibly inscribed the memory of these two exceptional personalities.

47

Stolen Childhood

Living with war orphans kept us constantly aware of the enormity of their deprivation. Observing and dealing with its effects drove us to an absolute condemnation of everything in the world that causes families to disintegrate. It is a statistical fact that among infants deprived of their mothers' love and the security of their fathers' presence, the mortality rate is very high even though they are provided all of the material elements for their development. Like a plant without the warmth and light of the sun, a child withers without its parents' love; and those who do live through infancy generally become insecure, often unhappy adults.

The strength and flexibility of the family have made it the most successful unit in the world. The ideal family, through the parents' love and common sense, inculcates habits of order, respect for authority, regard for the rights of others, a spirit of sacrifice, a sense of responsibility, and, above all, a sense of security.

The great majority of our children never experienced or could remember one trace of that kind of love. In caring for them we tried always to keep in mind this unique irreparable harm they had suffered. Naturally, during their long, homeless wandering, they gravitated toward us and fought for our favor; but we seemed able only to try our best to balance individual desires against group needs. There could be no question of favoritism; but in their unsatisfied longing for love, the orphans never gave up striving for signs of special sympathy and affection. To their inmost sorrows and fears, none of our logical responses could ever replace a mother's brief, wordless caress. And each implied rejection, each slight suggestion of indifference to their mood left its scar.

Every age level had its own demands that required different kinds of supervision, and the children's problems seemed to multiply with each successive stage. Every single day we discovered new proof that nothing could ever supplant the love and support of a family in their lives. That void began to be felt most acutely in Canada during their adolescence. Determined to be independent, each one went through the ordeal alone though suffering the embarrassment of needing help. Many a tear dampened a boarding-house pillow when there was no sympathetic, Polish-speaking friend nearby to share the anxieties of that disturbing period.

Charity and compassion came naturally to our orphans, but a few of the first teenagers, unable to cope with their frustrations, slipped into an obsessive egoism "because no one else is thinking of me." Meddlesomeness became their right to acquire information; laziness, their right to rest; envy, rivalry; wastefulness, a manifestation of power. Their days were full of contradictions. Even while experiencing painful disillusionments in their own relationships, they could be oblivious to the feelings of others, unconsciously intense and volatile, uncouth and over-polite, bafflingly silent and abrasively glib. Since they were scattered all over the Province of Quebec, I could not help them, and there seemed to be no other adult they could so readily communicate with.

In Africa they had been treated with deliberate care as the victims of an outrage against their native country, but here in Canada those in their teens discovered both at school and at work that the term "orphan" carried a stigma setting them apart from their peers. They began to be ashamed of their orphanhood and to dislike being called orphans. Once one of them whom I was admonishing for improper behavior protested, "Don't you know, Father, that we're different from other kids? We never had any family life!"

Some few of the older teenagers were offensively ungrateful. Unlike children who have come to appreciate the struggles of their hard-working parents, these youngsters took for granted the help of the thousands of Canadian Catholics who regularly contributed to their welfare through church collections. And they thought nothing of the sacrifices being made by their immediate benefactors. Another few disdained the accepted forms of courtesy as superfluous and restrictive. In greeting others, they would not take off their caps, remove their cigarettes, or even take their hands out of their pockets. Some resorted to drinking to drown their perplexities and achieve a "spiritual equilibrium." Shy, confused, and unsociable, they needed somehow to justify themselves at this time when they did not seem to matter to anyone else.

Their very contempt for the establishment and its obligations and restrictions kept these young people from facing reality. For years they preferred to cling to their few friends who felt the same way, the girls self-conscious and wistful, the boys touchy and insecure. Why should they change their ways? To emulate the manners of well-bred people would divest them of their joy in life. Besides, certain forms of courtesy were not becoming to boys from Africa.

It was not surprising that some failed to appreciate the clean, carpeted, tastefully furnished meeting halls, not to mention the neat Canadian homes into which they were so cordially welcomed. The style of life they had grown accustomed to in their abnormal living conditions in Russia and Africa were having an all but indelible effect: in Russia they had been abandoned, and in Africa they had lived in grass huts without flooring, toilets, sinks, or even simple furnishings. Some of the boys were careless with their cigarette ashes and they often turned carefully planned activity into horseplay: more than once in their rough-and-tumble joshing they accidentally knocked a hole in a wall with an elbow or a chair. After games at one host school, the custodian said that he had had to shovel out about a bushel of their tracked-in dirt. In private homes they would use straight chairs as rockers, sofa cushions for pillow fights, staircases for scuffles, and the telephone for private debates. In their own living quarters they left clothing, books, and playing cards wherever they fell, and since they disliked sitting on chairs, their beds were always in a state of rumpled disarray.

Actually these young people were neither vengeful nor malicious. Having seriously upset a teacher or a benefactor, they would behave as if nothing had happened, entirely unmindful of the effect of their impropriety. Unconsciously, without understanding its origin, they were coping with the trauma of their stolen childhood. Tadek writes an anguished apology:

> When a boy becomes a man, he begins to think about his life. I was disrespectful. Forgive me. I could have been a better person but I let outside trends influence me.

Bolek speaks from northern Canada of an unrealized hunger for the "tranquility of order":

> Do not interpret my silence as a forgetting of my benefactors. I did not write earlier because at times I did not know where to go, what to eat, when to sleep, or what to do with myself.

How much they needed a home whose homes had been stolen from them! In their souls, overwhelmed by personal sorrow and chronic suffering, always lurked an awareness of that outrageous theft. They had been torn from homes that breathed the very spirit of Polish tradition. For the rest of their lives they would resent this displacement. They found forgiveness inconceivable. Often we had entreated them to summon up Christian love for their Russian enemy, but they always responded as did this young woman:

> There is something great in this idea, but it is a challenge almost impossible to carry out. Each time I think about it, I envision someone known to me for his goodness; then I picture one of the Russians I encountered in Siberia. How could I love them equally? All I can afford is not to feel hatred. Even to imagine loving such an enemy is hard! Please do not wonder at my attitude. I can afford only indifference. That is, I do not wish them evil. . . .

They left us, then, one by one, with wounds still unhealed. There was still a deep sadness in their faces, fear and restlessness in their eyes. They were truly comfortable only with those who had been their comrades in Russia and Africa.

Even as they moved from adolescence to young adulthood, they were already dimly aware that "childhood is the whole of life," that "this nebula of childhood holds in abeyance all the sorrows still to be, all the terrors, all the secret tears." They were still pilgrims trudging the fog-bound roads of a foreign world. They were living proof that the childhood they were bidding farewell to "stays with us till the end."[1]

---

1. *Mémoirs Intérieurs*, Francois Mauriac. Copyright 1960, by Farrar, Straus & Cudahy, New York.

Epilogue

All those thousands of children, once termed "criminal" by the Communist code and deported to Russia, bear subconsciously the scars of inhuman degradation and the harm inflicted by the political injustice of the free world's indifference to the rape of Poland, for whose liberation six million of her countrymen died.

Their suffering has been assuaged and recompensed in part by their adoption into new fatherlands—Australia, New Zealand, Argentina, England, the United States, Canada—and their acquisition of new cultural values. The three girls who became nuns exemplify the benevolence of heart eventually achieved by most of the members of that orphaned group that landed on Canadian shores.

Almost all of them completed their secondary education. A few became dentists, physicians, civil engineers, and registered nurses. Most of the boys are welders, lathe operators, auto mechanics, radio and television technicians. Several have risen to supervisory positions in the textile industry. One, highly skilled in the construction of diesel engines, helped build the St. Lawrence Seaway. Another worked as a draftsman in the planning of Toronto's Metro transit system.

Wanderers at heart, some find it hard to give up their dreams of returning to the Africa of their childhood. They are like men sitting on packed suitcases looking for the right horizon. For all of them the orphanage with its camp society had been the embodiment of Poland, and to leave it was to succumb to a lifelong nostalgia for Poland, a longing that no amount of success in Canada could diminish. Aniela reflects their sentiments:

> At times I seek within myself the cause of this unnameable ache and I find the answer. This is a yearning for the lost homeland that thought and heart fly out to. Oh! How I bless the Polish literature classes! You may wonder, Father, that I, having been just a little girl at the time of leaving Poland, can still remember her. Yet I can hardly thwart my longings. There in Poland remain my family nest, my town. . . .

Reunions over the years have helped to gratify these deep hungers of the heart. From Hamilton, St. Catherine, and Kitchener, from Windsor and London, from Winnipeg, Edmonton, and Vancouver, have come husbands, wives, children, and I their guardian to relive the pleasant moments of our odyssey. So close are we in spirit that our relationship has the permanence of true family ties.

At the reunion of 1969 the children were favored by the unexpected presence of Karol Cardinal Wojtyla, Archbishop of Cracow, now Pope John Paul II, who was then visiting Canadian Polonia. Passing through Montreal and learning that the reunion of the Polish orphans was under way, he insisted his schedule be rearranged so that he could meet, cheer and bless them.

In a cemetery in Leicester, England, is the grave of Mrs. Eugenia Grosicki, beloved mother and teacher, whose zealous care inspired her Polish orphan children to inscribe their love on her tombstone:

Guardian of Polish Orphans in Russia and East Africa
Polish Activist
Served God and Fatherland
Alumni and Friends from USA, Canada, and England

Measuring the long miles of their exile in psychological suffering but also in spiritual growth, remembering the selfishness but also the charity, the corruption but also the nobility they met along the way, most of these survivors agree that their path led through at least as much joy as sorrow, as much goodness as evil, as much tranquility as conflict. Many of today's children could envy them that.

The great reward of their former guardians is the conviction that almost every one has emerged from the ordeal realizing that adversities did strengthen their spirit and that those who managed to preserve from their stolen childhood a deep faith, a childlike wonder and a sense of humor have triumphed over the bitterness that might have destroyed them and the malignancy of those who conspired against them.

Appendix A

Additional Accounts of the Orphans

Some orphans of the East African Refugee Camp, to whom this part of the book is particularly dedicated, recorded their recollections of what they had experienced before settling down in hospitable Canada. The four accounts given here represent the untold stories of thousands of their young compatriots who were made to suffer only because they were children of Poland.

I

Casimir Majewski, now a textile supervisor and director of the Polish Radio Program in Milford, Connecticut, U.S.A., remembers:

> On the 10th of February, 1940, I was barely ten years old. The snow had been falling incessantly since morning . . . My father had gone before dawn to inspect the tree felling in the nearby forest where he had worked as a forester for a number of years. Mother, as usual, was working in the house; my elder brother had gone to school, but I had not got ready yet.
>
> Suddenly Soviet soldiers surrounded our home, and two NKVD agents entered. Right away they started searching the house. My father hurried from the forest and then patiently waited for them to finish. Finally one of the agents announced that within forty minutes we had to leave. There was no chance of packing everything in such a short time, and we managed to take with us only some clothing and some food.
>
> After two hours of travel by sleds we arrived at the railway station, where thousands of people were already waiting beside a long freight train. Later on, in the evening, we were loaded into one of the cars. The train started at dawn, and we traveled in locked cars northeasterly under the supervision of the NKVD.
>
> At long last, on the 3rd of March, we stopped at a small railway station amid the Siberian forests. It was from here that the approximately five thousand of us were to be organized into groups of three hundred families and taken to nearby settlements. Each settlement consisted of long, low buildings, all of

them supervised by NKVD agents. We were assigned to settlement number 152, located in the region of Topcheeka in Altai Land.

All persons above twelve years of age were ordered to report for work the very next day. Mother, along with other women, had to remove the snow a few metres deep among the pines which were to be felled by the men. Such work lasted till spring. For the first few days the Siberian winter did not bother us very much. Soon, however, the food we had brought from Poland was nearly gone, and life became much more difficult. . . . For the whole settlement there was only one well, and soap was not available in the store. A few families were assigned to one room; because of the filth, vermin multiplied rapidly. Now it was not only hunger that gnawed at us but also lice and bedbugs.

When the snow disappeared at the beginning of June, the work changed. The men made incisions in the trunks of the pine trees, using special knives, and the women went with pails to gather the resin oozing out. To reach the "norm" one had to fill forty pails a day, and that was not easy because the resin oozed out slowly. Mother received 120 rubles a month for her work, and one kilogram of bread cost 15 rubles. Father, who was carting barrels of resin to one area, earned the same wages. Usually by the middle of the month there was no money to buy bread, which often was not available in the store anyway. In order to stay alive, my parents sold to the Russian officials all the clothes we had brought from Poland.

At the beginning of 1941 there was nothing else left for sale, and then we really began to feel the hunger. For weeks on end there was no bread in the store. The people ate mostly mushrooms and orach, the liquid found in the tiny pouches of a small shrub. Dysentery broke out. At first it was mostly the elderly who died, then more often the young people. In one settlement, out of three hundred families, fifty persons died.

When in June of 1941 the Soviet-German war broke out, the Polish people in the settlements had hopes that they would soon be freed, but the NKVD treated us the same as before, even after the pact was signed between the Polish government in London and the Soviet government regarding the release of all Poles in Siberian prisons. By October we had all heard that the pact had been signed in July, so we began openly to demand freedom. . . . But it was not till November that we were allowed to leave the settlement. I shall never forget this day when, hungry but overjoyed, carrying our little bundles on our backs, we walked the twenty-five miles to the nearest railway station.

For a whole week we had to wait for the train (a freight train, of course). But we were lucky enough to find room in some barracks to shelter ourselves from the cold. Many other Poles could not find any shelter, and froze while waiting under the open sky.

When at long last we left for the southern parts of Soviet Asia, nobody knew for sure how far we were to go or where we should get off. . . . The journey was long and, because we were crowded like cattle into our car, exhausting. Near Novosibirsk the train stopped at a small station. Obviously there was no hunger in this part of Russia because the local people brought potatoes for sale. They were bought out immediately. Father bought as many as our pot would hold, and Mother made a fire right beside the train to cook them, as did other women. Suddenly the train started, leaving behind a hundred women standing beside their fires. So my mother was stranded in an unknown station with a pot of half-cooked potatoes, while we, all crying, went on with our father. Miraculously, however, after two days of separation, our mother rejoined us at the station in Novosibirsk. It was a great joy because in Russia, when people get lost they sometimes stay lost for years.

Finally we came into the vicinity of Tashkent in Uzbekistan, and a few days later alighted at the Amu-Daria River and embarked on barges for Kazakhstan. This river journey was even more exhausting than the train trip from Siberia. For days and nights we could only sit on our lice-infested bundles. Every once in a while somebody would die. After five days we reached a landing stage and from there were transported to the neighboring kolkhozes, to work on the cotton harvest. We had been on these collective farms only two days when suddenly, like lightning, came the news that on the other side of the river the Polish Army was being formed. At once we headed back to Uzbekistan without any regard as to what might be awaiting us there. In fact, although we met Polish soldiers here and there, we civilians, including women and children, were told to go back and work on the collectives.

So again we landed at the farm and lived in a stable shared with the donkeys. In February, 1942, an epidemic of typhoid fever broke out. First my brother got sick, then our mother, then I myself. Our father had already joined the Polish Army, but we did not know where he was. To this day, no trace of him has been found. Thank God, our mother recovered as did the two of us boys, but we were terribly weak and could barely stand on our feet. Wanting to save us at all costs, our mother left us alone on the farm and walked ten miles to the nearest Polish Army detachment looking for work. One of the non-commissioned officers gave her a job in the military hospital. She returned after three days to the collective farm and brought us some bread she had gotten from soldiers sick with typhoid or dysentery. We satisfied our hunger, my brother and I, but we also contracted dysentery. Mother took us away from the kolkhoz and placed us in the Polish military hospital. I recovered quickly, but my brother was confined to bed with a high fever for two weeks. In this hospital alone, twenty or thirty soldiers were dying every day and were buried in common graves. But thanks to our mother's care, my brother and I were saved from death. . . .

II

Zoska Matusiewicz had lived in Poland through six springs, in the primeval forest near Bialystok, where her father was a senior forester. This period of life remained in her memory as a picture of fragrant springtime. But eternal winter, as she remembered it, soon followed.

She has a vivid memory of the arrest and the order to leave their home. She does not care to think about it. In one freight car, on plank beds, ten large families were crowded together. Since there was no toilet except for an unscreened pail in the center of the car, they would not, out of shyness, relieve themselves till night.

The winter was severe with much snow and many icicles, which did, however, provide water for washing and drinking. Zoska and her father were released from this prison-car after a one-month journey. They landed beyond the Urals, in Novosibirsk, almost five thousand kilometers from home.

Everything in the new location was alien to them. Nobody here attempted to show any kindness; nobody asked why they had been deported to the taiga. The natives feared the NKVD as much as the Poles did.

They lived collectively, with other families, in a large, bedbug-infested barracks with no furniture. The cold, the hunger, the atrocious living conditions were lesser evils. But worse ones soon came:

> Daddy worked on construction and died after a certain time. After him my younger sister Julia died. Daddy's death was the greatest misfortune, because with it we had lost our guardian.

After being liberated the family landed in Russian Central Asia, about fifty kilometers from Buchara on the kolhoz "Stalin." "We ate," writes Zoska,

> whatever was available—a horse, a dog, a turtle, linseed cake, various roots. We worked picking cotton and harvesting onions. . . . Typhoid and dysentery broke out . . . the hospitals had no room for the sick . . . the people died like flies.

In the general plague Zoska's remaining family began gradually to descend into the grave. The first to go was Stach, the oldest, dead of typhoid fever. Nobody in the family was at his side when he died in the hospital. At first he wrote letters to his people, but soon the correspondence ceased. The family deluded themselves that Stach would return. "We waited," writes Zoska, "from day to day; we thought that he wanted to give us a pleasant surprise by appearing suddenly. But he never returned."

After a certain time the whole family came down with various diseases, except young Edward. In a hospital near Buchara, Zoska was separated from her mother, who died a week later, as Zoska learned only by accident. Looking out of the hospital window she saw an arba (a tall, two- or four-wheeled cart with a moving axle) loaded with a pile of corpses of those who had died of typhoid, all covered with bedsheets. The little girl had a premonition. Determinedly she began to inquire about her mother. The women in the ward where her mother had been treated confirmed that she had died.

Throughout her illness Zoska did not have any news about her two elder sisters. When the time came for her to leave the hospital, cured, she had no idea where to go. She had no mother, no home. Her youngest brother was somewhere on the collective farm, but she did not have his address; besides, who was going to take her there? While she was feeling thus desolate, a Polish soldier happened to visit his relatives in the hospital, and seven-year-old Zoska approached him and asked him to take her away from there.

In that way she found herself in a Polish orphanage in Buchara. There she met two other girls with the same surname as hers. Questioned by the supervisors as to whether she had two sisters, she answered "yes," but she did not know anything about them. The depositions of the three girls were correlated. Yes, these were her natural sisters, but Zoska did not recognize them at all, so changed were they by their illnesses. The sisters did not return to health somehow and looked poorer every day, so Zoska took them under her special care. Despite her efforts, both died.

Zoska was again all alone. She often thought about her brother. Had he been able to stay alive, alone among the strange people? Was he able to protect himself against hunger and disease? Would she ever see him again? It was so hard to be left alone in this world. . . .

III

Stasia Kunicka lived constantly in fear that she might unwittingly wrong or hurt someone. This fear may have commenced when, at the age of ten, the greatest harm befell her.

> How often do I recall the times of my childhood in Poland! This period remains sacred in my memory. I had my parents, whom I loved very much; I had brothers and sisters, and everything that I needed in life. Never afterwards was I so happy! But it did not last long. . . . And now our experiences in Russia. . . . With regard to my own personal ones, they commenced somewhat earlier, because that was before the war, in August of 1938; for the whole family it was the beginning of sad experiences, for that was when my beloved mother died. Her death was the worst moment in my life. . . . However, the kind Lord knows what He is doing. Later on, in Russia, seeing the dying mothers buried somewhere in the steppes of Kazakhstan, we thanked God for having taken our mother a bit earlier.
>
> There came now horrible times for all Poles: the war, the Bolsheviks in Poland, the arrests, the deportations into the depths of Russia.
>
> The second date that sticks in my memory is April 9, 1940, when Daddy was arrested, and then April 13, when we were all deported to Russia. I could not describe everything, but it was terrible, horrendous, barbaric. Terrible were the NKVD officers and the Ukrainians who took our daddy away, leaving us total orphans. Barbaric was their driving us from our own home, and the deportation to Russia to suffer hunger and to toil in inhuman labor. . . . Did we pack up? No, we never intended to leave our place. But nobody reckoned with our wishes. We had to leave everything behind. . . .
>
> The militia, while taking us, used all sorts of lies, among them that they were going to reunite us with Daddy. To this day it is not known what happened to him. They took four of us for deportation, my two elder sisters, my younger brother, and me. The fifth, my oldest brother, fearing that he might share our father's fate, hid before our arrest and stayed in Poland.
>
> The journey lasted over two weeks. The Russians inspected our freight car every day and counted the people in case anyone got lost. With the most crude and offensive language, they slandered Poland, but quickly ran away when the women asked for food for their children. . . .
>
> Our journey ended in the steppes of Kazakhstan. There we lived for almost two years. For a change we were greeted by dark-complexioned Kazakhs, with whips in their hands. It was the first time in my life I had ever seen such people. We lived in barracks, with eighteen families, and slept on plank beds.

Only faith in God and the hope of a better tomorrow kept us going. We waited for a change in our fate, but not all of us lasted that long. Many died of typhoid fever and other infectious diseases. Filth was everywhere. The women made large bricks out of mud, the so-called samans. Later on, even the ten-year-olds were forced to work, weeding millet fields, poisoning gophers, and gathering manure which, when dried, was used as fuel.

Winter brought the greatest hunger, and the cold was unendurable. The water in the barracks froze. There was no fuel. And yet we managed to overcome everything. The Lord watched over us always and everywhere.

Release finally came. Everybody was anxious to leave that hell as soon as possible, to get to some place where there was no Soviet Communist government. Not everyone got out.

IV

Krysia Michniak also returned in memory to the steppes of Kazakhstan, though it was not easy for her.

At the time she was deported her family consisted of a grandmother, over eighty years old, her mother, and her two sisters, Felicja and Bogna. Felicja was twelve; Bogna, five. Their father was not with them; he "was already wasting away in a Soviet prison."

The girls remembered that in the spring the steppes turned into an ocean of grasses and flowers; but the winter brought only horror.

In Kazakhstan Krysia's mother found work in a garment factory. Being still only thirty, and looking even younger, she was soon courted by a local Russian who wanted to marry her. Whenever she told him she had to be faithful to her imprisoned husband, he persecuted her, made her life miserable, and threatened her with revenge. Once he tied her up and put a gag in her mouth; but fortunately, the daughters arrived at that moment and he had to restrain himself. The mother regarded it as the Russian's revenge that she was transferred to construction work, lifting and carrying heavy unfired bricks. This work was beyond her strength, and she had a heart attack. Twelve-year-old Felicja helped her a bit, while Krysia looked after the pigs.

The mother began to be tormented by forebodings and nightmares. She dreamed once that she was on a very tall tower and could not get down to her children. The dream came true during the very severe winter, when the cold wind penetrated to the marrow of the bones and the snowstorm so blanketed the world that one could not see two steps ahead and could get lost even near one's own lodgings. The mother had some urgent work to do for the factory, so when the other women left early because of the snowstorm, she remained to finish the job.

The girls waited patiently, but the later it got, the more anxious they became. They tried to dismiss their thoughts. "Mother is sure to come back," they told themselves; "she could not leave us alone—something has held her up at work, and then the snowstorm blocked her way, and she may be waiting somewhere at the neighbors'. . . ." Later on, they remembered that in the morning their mother had had a premonition and had been afraid to go to work, but that the Russians had chased her out. The girls became more and more worried. In the howling wind they thought they heard their mother calling for help and knocking at the window. They opened it and looked out but, apart from the white cloud, could see nothing. They left the window ajar, kept the light on as a guide, and prayed all night.

When dawn came the neighbors began to dig paths near the hut. But the search was futile. The children learned from a worker who had left the factory with their mother that on the way home he had found shelter in a haystack, but their mother had decided to go on, to buy bread.

Felicja returned from her own search with frostbitten feet. By the time the third day had passed with no trace of their mother, the girls began to lose hope. Finally the local baker, a Russian, was ploughing through the snow with the girls, his dog nosing on ahead, when suddenly the dog trotted back with a piece of frozen bread in its mouth. They found the corpse of the mother only a few yards from the barracks. In the blinding storm she must have circled many times just beyond the door step.

Although the authorities did not want to return the body to the children, they fought for a last visit with their mother and took care of the funeral themselves. There are no forests in Kazakhstan so they could not get a coffin, but they did find some boards for which they bartered some of their mother's clothing. Only Felicja went to the cemetery; it was too cold for the younger ones.

"All that winter," remembered Krysia, "Granny had lain on her cot, not knowing anything; whether from old age or hardships, she had become like a sick child. Shortly after mother's burial, she died." The girls' uncle from Soviet-occupied Poland, having learned about their orphanhood, tried to take them home from Russia and even pre-paid their passage, just as he was instructed to do by the local NKVD. Instead, the Communist "guardians" had them deported to Semipalatinsk and separated them. It was from this new exile that Polish soldiers rescued them and took them to an orphanage after the "amnesty."

Appendix B

In Other Parts of the World

Palestine and Egypt

Many young Poles who escaped from Soviet Russia journeyed in properly organized transports to countries other than Africa. Some had begun their elementary and secondary education while still in Russia. The Polish Army of General Anders, preparing in Iraq for its D-Day in Italy, desired to keep for its para-military schools these youngsters soon to be eligible for military service. Enrolled in schools in Palestine and Egypt were approximately 3,000 boys and 500 girls, 14 to 18 years old. The boys, called *junaks*, resourceful young men, and the girls, called *mlodsze* and *starsze ochotniczki*, junior and senior volunteers, would form reserve cadres of officers in technical and medical services.

These boys and girls were transferred from Russia to Persia by steamboat and railway and by heavy trucks through the desert of the Middle East—Iraq and Transjordan, with a longer stopover near Bagdad on the artificial Lake Habaniya. The first of the *junaks* arrived in Palestine in May, the *ochotniczki* in August, 1942.

Here the school system was modified and improved. Military authorities detached qualified officers as teachers and a good number of very young soldiers as students. Also enrolled were other young people who had managed to get to the Middle East by routes other than Russia.

Junaks who had been initially grouped in a locality called Bashit, along with some of the *ochotniczki* from Rehovot, were later sent to schools scattered all over Palestine and Egypt. Near

Haifa, in Kiriat Mockin, was the second technical school with both elementary and secondary levels. In Nazareth the *junaks'* school was located in quarters of the Salesian Fathers, at Christ the Youth Basilica, and the *mlodsze ochotniczki*'s school at the Basilica of the Annunciation of the Most Blessed Virgin Mary. In the Judean mountain town of Ain Karim, not far from Jerusalem, were the secondary school and the lyceum or liberal arts school established for girls who were not enlisted in the Army.

Near Tel Aviv were technical schools, and in Bayt-Nabala an elementary and a secondary school, which was also the fifth *junak* technical school. These had access to the British Military Workshops, the largest in the Middle East. Near the Egyptian border was the second *junak* technical school.

The Cadets School, training approximately seven hundred students, was located first in Quastina, later in Barbara, Palestine. In Barbara also were elementary and secondary schools with a general education program; the lyceum, which emphasized the humanities; and a technical school specializing in road building.

In Egypt there were three colleges: the Communications College in Mena, near the pyramids; the Air Force College in Heliopolis near Cairo; and the 1st Technical College in Tel-el-Kebir, organized from a disbanded school in Rafah, its enrollment increased by the liquidation of schools in Mena and Heliopolis. In 1946-47, a secondary technical school was operating here also, with nearly one thousand students. A group of *junaks* assigned to naval and airforce training was sent to Great Britain. For the *mlodsze ochotniczki*, besides the lyceums with their liberal arts programs, secondary schools were established for training in commerce, business administration, elementary school teaching, and fashion design. These varied curricula and their administration reflect the gigantic effort made by the Poles to provide attractive educational opportunities for their exiled youngsters.

All the schools had state credentials, and the quality of their education, according to experts, equalled that of pre-war schools in Poland, although now attained under incomparably greater difficulties. The British authorities always had a very favorable opinion of the quality of education in the *junak* schools. The teaching staff was selected with the greatest care. Military authorities never objected to detaching properly qualified people to work in the schools, even though in wartime conditions the choice must have been limited—all the more so since the Army conducted secondary as well as post-school courses for their men wherever the Polish Army was deployed, as for example in Italy and Iraq.

The command of the *junak* schools in Palestine evolved a statute for both *Junak* and *Mlodsze Ochotniczki* Schools which was approved by the Ministry of Religion and Public Enlightenment of the Polish Government in London. This Ministry's Mission in the Middle East undertook to print textbooks, and the military provided funds for libraries and school aids. The professors simplified their students' work by photocopying their lectures. The Polish Branch of the YMCA published for the young people a weekly paper called *Junak*. Learning progressed well despite the peculiar circumstances, such as clashes between the so-called "scholastic" cadres of educators and the "militaristic" faction of regular army officers assigned to the schools as commandants.

As for the teen-agers, they rushed to the schools, impelled by a strong desire to learn, attracted by the good organization and maintenance of the system as well as by the charm of the military uniform. They were overjoyed that, despite exile and war, they could continue their education and acquire the technical skills necessary for working in their homeland. By introducing lessons that could be compressed into a seven-month school year, the teachers managed, within the first two years of the program, to make up for the long lapse in learning. In subsequent years the school terms were of normal duration.

All school centres provided for lively cultural activity and entertainment. In Tel-el-Kebir, the *junaks* built an amphitheatre accommodating a few hundred people where concerts, variety shows, celebrations of all sorts, and theatrical productions took place. Exhibitions arranged by the schools attracted large crowds. The scouting movement, aided by chaplains and teachers, was developing steadily. Sightseeing tours were organized to give the school children a chance to tour Palestine with its holy places and Egypt with its magnificent monuments and relics of that ancient civilization. All these activities, with their joyous excitement, helped relieve and quicken the young people's imaginations, so long burdened by the heavy memory of a most painful childhood.

The schools for the *junaks* and the *ochotniczki* were transferred, toward the end of 1947, to Great Britain. Here they were assigned their own camps and operated for a full year with their whole apparatus, their teachers and administrators. After that, when the British began to liquidate the camps, most of the students were transferred to Polish schools organized in Great Britain by the Polish Education Committee; some others enrolled in the British Air Force trade schools.

As the data indicate, the children who found themselves in the Middle East, cared for by the Polish Army, were not disappointed in these guardians, who had been so close to them in their tender years. In those schools established or administered by the military, some thousands of youngsters obtained practical knowledge of trades; others completed the education which had been interrupted by their deportation to Russia.

India

Well over 2,000 children and as many grown-ups—almost 5,000 Polish people—found shelter in India, which was one of the first countries to offer hospitality to them for the duration of the war.

The Polish "colony" in Bombay, settled there for years (see Chapter XI), had stirred up concern for the Polish children dying of hunger and disease in Central Asia; and gradually their concern reached prosperous and influential circles of India. In April, 1942, they managed, with food, medicine, and clothing supplied by the Red Cross, to remove 160 Polish orphans from Russia, along with educational personnel.

To provide for those orphans, 4,000 rupees were collected spontaneously, the beginning of the "Polish Children's Fund" in India. Help was also given by the Red Cross, the Government of India, and the local British authorities. Gifts, often anonymous, came in from all parts of the country.

In September of 1942, 220 more orphans arrived, and in December, another 250. These came in trucks through Ashabad, Meshed, Zahidan, and Nok-Kundi (on Indian territory) to Bombay. The first children who arrived were accommodated in Bandra, a suburb of Bombay, where a twenty-eight-room villa, with a garden and verandas looking out on the sea, was rented for them and they were assured maximum comfort and care.

Medical examinations carried out immediately showed avitaminosis in the majority of the children, hence a greatly reduced immunity to disease. An intensive nutritional program was begun at once. The weakest children, and those in danger of pulmonary disease, were selected for special treatment. The healthier ones, though they commenced schooling, were given as much rest as possible.

After a three months' stay in Bandra, the orphans were transferred to a settlement especially built for them in Balachadi, one more properly described as an educational establishment. Subsequent groups of orphans made this their new home.

The Balachadi facility was built on ten acres of cactus-covered desert overlooking the Cutch Bay in the Duchy of Nawagar, approximately eighteen miles from Jamnagar, the capital. On this rocky foundation the barracks were built in the native style, covered with loose-fitting shingles, without ceilings, and with clay floors.

After Bandra this accommodation seemed very primitive, but it brought joy as the long-awaited permanent shelter; and it offered warmth and peace without hunger. But most important, there was no fear that the former tormentor was too close. If the refugees had any kind of anxiety, it was the fear of how the change of climate would affect them and of tropical diseases, particularly malaria. But though every evening their guardians anxiously watched the clouds of mosquitoes attacking the settlement, the children did not bother their heads with that.

The anxiety was justified. In November of 1942, eighty percent of the children contracted malaria. Greatly perturbed, the Government of India sent to Balachadi the Deputy Director of the Institute for Matters Related to Malaria, who examined the area and undertook energetic preventive measures. In this he was greatly assisted by a Polish doctor delegated by the Army, and by the superintendent of the settlement, Rev. Francis Pluta, who demanded that the children and the personnel strictly adhere to all anti-malaria regulations. After months of stubborn struggle, the percentage of malaria cases dropped to only twenty-five.

The choice of Balachadi as a location for the Educational Establishment was influenced primarily by the very kind attitude of the owner of the site, Maharaja Jam Saheb and his wife, residing in Jamnagar. "The Polish children are not orphans any longer," he said; "I will be their father." He showed them so much kindness that the children spoke of him as "our maharaja" or as "babu" (in Gujarati, "father").

To have a maharaja as an adoptive father meant even more to our children than the prospect of material possessions. His very title increased their chance of seeing the legendary wonder of life in India. Unfolding before their eyes was a world known to them until now only from fairy tales. Jam Saheb was in fact a very modern maharaja, given to magnanimous gestures, as becomes an exotic ruler. He remembered to provide variety for the children, inviting them to his palace and often visiting the settlement.

Except for that, life here was spartan. The superintendent introduced stern regulations which were strictly observed not only by the personnel but also by the children. They discovered that in this matter there was to be no fooling around: though Rev. Francis Pluta cared for his charges like a father, he could also, like a father, be strict. This discipline did not impede, but rather encouraged, the family atmosphere of the Establishment, and the children could develop in it quite normally. This atmosphere was encouraged also by the "babu" himself.

The children had cordial friends as well. First in their hearts was the Polish chauffeur, Dajek, himself a globe-trotter since the first World War, a man who had had fantastic adventures but whose soul longed incessantly for his home village near Lublin. With all his heart he became firmly attached to the little wanderers. He felt happy when they laughed, and he spent all his earnings for their entertainment. The American troops stationed not too far away also brought a few surprises. One Christmas, when already the lighted tree and the puppet show had caused great rejoicing, two camels loaded with Christmas gifts appeared in Balachadi, thanks to those American friends. The theater produced more than puppet shows; from time to time the children gave their own performances. Games in the recreation hall also brightened their lives.

But learning was their first priority. In Balachadi, where the younger children were a majority, a full elementary school was organized, as well as one secondary class. The children who qualified for higher grades were directed to another Polish settlement formed in India, or to British Catholic convents. Some of the school-age girls completed sewing and knitting courses.

The orphanage was maintained by the Council of Indian Princes under the government's guidance. For the expense of maintaining and educating one child, one rupee (about thirty cents) per day was allotted. Later on the allotment was raised to a rupee and a half.

India's climate often bothered the children: now too much sun, now too much humidity. During the time of heat the best relief was a splash in the Arabian Sea, only half a mile from the settlement. Thanks to strict dietary hygiene and good habits of work and rest, there were no epidemics. Because they had been scrupulously acclimated, the children also avoided the many dangers of contact with scorpions, venomous snakes, and other reptiles. The young bodies recovered quickly. Even though malaria caused much worry, and many neighboring Hindu children died, the settlement avoided major losses. The camp lost only two children in four years: eight-year-old Peter, whose heart was so ruined in Russia that nothing could save him, and Bolek J., who drowned in an accident.

The Educational Establishment in Balachadi existed for over four years. Toward the end of 1946, when it was liquidated, some of the children went back to Poland, summoned by a mother or a father who was found there; others enrolled in convents or other schools in the United States. The remainder of the children were transferred to an educational centre in Valivade, India.

Maharaja Jam Saheb bade a heartfelt farewell to the children: "For the four years of your stay here I have never heard any complaints or grievances against you. We all enjoyed your stay with us. . . ."

Now living in Canada, Msgr. Francis Pluta fondly remembers his former charges:

> In my thoughts I see you often, all together, and each one of you separately. I see you through the screen of the incessantly pouring monsoon, and through the sweltering heat of the tropical sky; I see you at parties in the palaces of the maharaja, our friend; I see you among mud huts of the neighboring peasants, always kind, always smiling; I see scenes of crane hunting, the gazelles, the snakes; I hear the mournful howling of hungry jackals; I hear the ebb and flow of the ocean; I see the flat mirror of the lake, and the palms growing on the rocky soil, watered by the salty water; I hear your melodious voices through the creaking sounds of our water well's windmill. In each recollection there return to me the Polish Children's Camps in Balachadi and in Jamnagar, India, with their rows of primitive mud huts and barracks, and in the distance the red-and-white flag fluttering on a tall flag pole, proud symbol of freedom, symbol of Poland, recreated in miniature by our own effort on hospitable foreign soil.

Other transports of Poles reached India by sea, departing from the Persian port of Pahlevi and landing at the Indian port of Karachi, now in Pakistan.

A large transit camp in Karachi was always overcrowded with grown-ups and children awaiting further transportation, to Africa and Mexico. A total of 22,000 Poles went through this camp. Initially, in December, 1942, it was located in an old Hindu quarter of the city, later on some twelve miles outside, where it became known as "the Country Club." Trucks brought new arrivals directly from the port, and their first impressions of India were registered here. They were not the best ones. All around were desert sands sweltering in the heat, not one tree, only dust-covered cacti, sudden gusts of wind blowing sand in the eyes, and the merciless sun, difficult to bear for those who had spent so long a time in the Siberian cold. On a hill stood a small chapel, and on a wide plateau many long tents where one could hear the howling of jackals.

As nasty as in Balachadi, the climate of Karachi favored the spreading of tropical diseases, especially malaria, against which we fought arduously. The children suffered the most. Yet despite those difficulties and despite the casual character of each group's stopover, the children continued to be taught, and they were offered theatre, choirs, recreation-hall activities and movies.

The transit camp in Karachi was the only refugee camp in India still under direct British care. The camp's commandant, Major Allan, devoted heart and soul to helping the Polish refugees. A kind fate had given him two dedicated co-workers, Governor Sindu and his wife, Lady Dow; and the District Commander, General Hind, earned the children's most loving memory.

British and American soldiers stationed in the Karachi area tried very often to brighten the lives of the children with a film show or a trip to town, and small gifts, remembering that these were the orphans of their Polish comrades-in-arms.

Refugee transports, arriving in India for the duration of the war, stopped over in Karachi only for short periods. After a few days' rest the refugees were directed to a camp in Malir, not far from Karachi, equally desert-like but with military buildings rather than tents. The people were fed in a communal kitchen. Here the desert sands clogged the eyes, nose, and mouth much more fiercely than in Karachi. There were no trees or flowers, but an abundance of scorpions and "forty-legs," a kind of venomous insect. The refugees were to stay here for a few months while a settlement was built for them in Dekana, close to the Portuguese Goa. Again, without regard to the shortness of their stay, the teaching program for the children went on: schools were organized, as well as recreational activities, talks, lectures, and biweekly "live newspapers", that is, news related orally.

The first transport, led by Captain Wladyslaw Jagiellowicz, left Malir for Valivade, the new Polish settlement, in June, 1943. The new arrivals at once undertook to organize activities. The remainder of the people in Malir were moved in groups throughout 1943, as accommodations were completed.

Valivade differed from the other camps. Here there were no prickly bushes or cacti; here there were trees—not dwarfed ones—but real trees with rich crowns and green leaves. Though the settlement itself was not thickly forested, nearby was a road lined with trees on both sides: huge trees with grotesquely twisted limbs, often aglow with swarms of fireflies. Over the gently rolling countryside the abundant greenery rested the eyes, weary of looking at nothing but desert sands.

Another important change awaited the Polish families in Valivade. Their communal barracks life was coming to an end, and family life was about to commence, each family in its own quarters. These quarters consisted of two rooms and a kitchen equipped with modest furniture and the necessary utensils. The dwellings were constructed in long blocks built of thick mats, each with its own stone skirting. They were covered with red shingles, and, since they had no ceilings, the shingles got so hot in the sun that by noon the temperature inside would become unbearably high. The floors were made of clay, again according to local practice, so that they could be spread with cattle manure as a safeguard against ants and other nasty insects. But everything seemed bearable in return for the privilege of having separate quarters, a substitute for the lost home in Poland, and for the hope of returning to conditions in which the people could again live and bring up their children according to their ways.

In next to no time, colorful flower beds appeared in front of the blocks, and green vines grew over the verandas. The settlement began to look beautiful, and its appearance reminded the youngsters that although they had, in Soviet Russia, grown accustomed to living in filth without order or harmony, there were other, more human forms of daily existence, easily attained with a bit of goodwill. A significant example of this truth was the church quickly built in the settlement by the collective effort and contributions of the exiles. Above the entrance they placed the inscription: "Boze zbaw Polski (O Lord, save Poland)."

Valivade's population, initially about 4,000 persons, grew to 5,000 after the camps in Karachi and in Balachadi were liquidated. They were mostly families of Polish soldiers and officers who had rushed straight from Soviet prisons, labor camps, and exile into the ranks of the Polish Army being organized in Russia. Some of their wives, children, and aged parents had managed to escape with the Army to Persia and then India. There were only a few men in the settlement. Apart from those detached from the Army for various important functions, these were men unsuited for military service because of age, health, or total physical disability. The children without mothers had their own educational centre, which cared for 410 of them, in addition to some orphans from Balachadi who arrived later.

In Polish law, a child is an orphan when one parent dies. In Valivade were total orphans, semi-orphans, even non-orphans separated from their parents by a variety of circumstances. For example, some children who had been deported to Russia from summer camps had a father in the Army and a mother in Russia, or a father in a prisoner-of-war camp and a mother in Poland. Some of them were reunited with their parents after the war; many were not.

Though not all of the orphans needed extraordinary care, no efforts were spared to give them what they did need. They were well fed, with plenty of fruit, and the frail ones had a special diet. The centre's kitchen was under constant medical supervision. All girls past school age lived in a special boarding house. The most serious problem was with the adolescent boys, a problem all the more acute because of the shortage of male teachers and, especially, parents.

The educational centre tried to provide the youngsters with as much recreation as its limited facilities permitted: it had its own drama, orchestra, choir, and gymnasium programs. The children could also attend shows and concerts in the theatre. There were twenty-four school and post-school sports teams, with a few physical education instructors and an adequate number of playgrounds. Official basketball and volleyball competitions were arranged, sometimes with Indian teams. The church, the school, and scouting exerted their beneficial influences on both total orphans and those who, by God's grace, had their mothers with them.

Nine sightseeing tours were organized, some by car, some on bicycles. Though time and means were in short supply, the country was so interesting that it seemed essential to travel as much as possible. It was the Boy and Girl Scouts who probably got to know the area best. Scout troops were gradually organized in the schools, the movement being helped greatly by the arrival of two Polish scouting instructors delegated by the Army, another proof of its concern for the young people. The scouting ranks grew fast. By October of 1943, there were 803 Boy and Girl Scouts, and within a few years nearly one thousand. The scouts camped in many places such as Panhalu in the beautiful rolling countryside. The grown-ups left the settlement rather rarely, and then to go no farther than the nearest town of Kolhapur, because they did not know the language, were bewildered by the strangeness of the environment, and lacked funds. Only very few groups of people, especially young people, managed to visit the most interesting places that attest to the ancient, unique culture of India.

From the very beginning of settlement life in Valivade, school attendance was a respected duty, strictly observed. Because the small children were most numerous, three elementary schools were organized, each with a separate kindergarten. Within a short time secondary schools were also organized with a general educational program, a lyceum for preparing school teachers, a secondary school for commercial studies, and an agricultural school with its own experimental farm. A handyman's shop for the Boy Scouts, at first open only during vacation periods, gradually became a school for extracurricular lessons in technical skills. The teaching team was very large. The fact that around one-fourth of Valivade's adults had had secondary or higher education facilitated the organization of continuing education courses, and a variety of recreation-hall programs. Eight halls were established in various parts of the settlement, and they were well equipped. Besides basic course in English, the sciences, and nursing, the schools offered training for laboratory technicians, typists, typesetters, bee keepers, chauffeurs, telegraph operators, and beauticians, as well as continuous lessons in sewing, knitting, weaving, and fashion design. As well as dispelling the growing belief that the settlement dwellers were becoming lazy, the courses proved that teaching and learning can be accomplished even under adverse conditions.

There was a general trend toward work in Valivade. Having no chance to earn money outside the settlement, the refugees seized on any form of occupation inside it. Besides the Indian shops, Polish shops began to appear, offering their profits for the settlement's cultural and educational activities. Valivade now had a cooperative store, a canteen, and workshops in nursing, cabinet-making, brick-laying, shoemaking, weaving, the fashion industry, doll-making, and handicrafts. It had its own barbershop, its own confectionery, and even its own printing shop where the Polish weekly *Polak w Indiach (The Pole in India)* was printed. Though not large, these establishments did attest to the inhabitants' vigor, all the more so because most of the women also had children and households to take care of, and the climate made any work very difficult. One's energy is soon exhausted when the temperature is 100° Fahrenheit. The situation only worsened during the monsoon season from June to September, when streams of rain poured down incessantly, to become clouds of hot steam.

This humid heat and tropical diseases were the chief difficulties during our stay in India. Attacks of malaria frequently disorganized school work, though not to the same extent as in Balachadi, and the amoeba was also troublesome. This time again the Army came to the rescue with eight Polish doctors and a pharmacist. A 200-bed hospital with an outpatient clinic, a pharmacy, and a medical laboratory were established. Cases requiring surgery were directed to Bombay, where a Polish hospital was organized under the auspices of the Polish Red Cross. People with pulmonary problems—and there were many of them in India—were sent to a sanatorium in the hills at Pangehani, 4,000 feet above sea level. In the summer of 1943, another Polish centre in India was established together with a post-hospital convalescence depot for both grown-ups and children. This centre operated a kitchen which distributed meals cooked in the Polish way to patients in the sanatorium who could not get used to Indian cuisine.

Some of the weaker children remained in Pangehani for long periods, and so a school using the team teaching method was formed there. The patients also had their own Polish pediatrician, a reading room, and entertainment. A few villas were at the disposal of the centre, all located in the picturesque valleys of the so-called Table-Landau, where the children began to recover quickly. As time passed, the number of the sick and frail who used these facilities grew to an average of two hundred.

There were other advantages of having a Polish centre in Pangehani; it became a family home of sorts for the girls sent to the local British convent and for the boys in the local boys' school. Here they were able to spend their days off in a Polish environment, something they had often longed for.

Some youngsters, when they graduated from the Valivade schools, were sent to others: some to convent training schools in Mount Abu, Sangor, or Bombay; some girls to the Art School and the Commercial School in Bombay; thirty-seven boys to Naval Training Centres in Great Britain; and thirty-one boys, financed by the National Catholic Welfare Council, to theological seminaries in the United States.

Although the sojourn of the Poles in India was intended to last only till the end of the war, the Valivade settlement continued to exist for a few years afterwards. It participated in the joyous celebration of India's Day of Independence and later in the general mourning following the assassination of Mahatma Gandhi. However, the settlement shrank from day to day as transports left, one after another. Military families joined their men, discharged from the Army, in England. Some of the children returned to Poland at the request of parents who survived. Some of the more mature young people emigrated to the United States for university training, or to enter monasteries or seminaries; some went to Australia, where they found employment; and some to other countries of the free world.

The orphans who did not have anywhere to go, especially those too young to undertake physical work, those most desolate, and those most in need of motherly love, caused the greatest anxiety. For the time being they remained at Valivade, sharing the fate of the 600-odd others "without attachment," who were not accepted for travel to Great Britain or to other countries because of poor health or advanced age. They did not want to return to Poland, now rapidly being turned into a Communist country, since they had already experienced the "blessings" of the Communist system; nor did they want to go to camps in Germany, though such proposals were being made by the International Refugee Organization. Eventually, in the summer of 1948, it was decided to send them, together with the orphans, to refugee camps still existing in East Africa. The last small group remaining in Valivade left soon afterwards for Lebanon.

Mexico

In addition to Palestine and India, Mexico was the third country to which the Polish children traveled after the stop-over in Persia. The Polish Government-in-Exile in London had endeavored to have them accepted by the United States, where for a number of generations millions of citizens of Polish extraction had already made sacrifices for people from their homeland. But, alas, the honeymoon between the United States and Russia at the time did not favor such plans. Offer shelter to Polish children thrown out of their homes by the Soviet ally? No, the Soviets might not like it. The presence of those children in the States would be most embarrassing.

In the face of this, President Roosevelt facilitated the settlement of the troublesome guests in Mexico, where the presence of these victims of Soviet barbarism would attract less attention. On the strength of a pact between the Mexican Government and General W. Sikorski, 20,000 Poles were to be sent there from Persia.

The refugees landed in Mexico in two groups, in July and November, 1943. The first transport brought the children with parents; the second brought the orphanage, for a total of 1,586 persons, half of them children. After that, Mexico admitted no more refugees.

The two-month voyage led from the Gulf of Persia by way of Bombay to Australia, and from there to California. The newcomers were settled in the colony of Santa Rosa near the township of Leon in the province of Guanajuato in Central Mexico. They were assigned to farm buildings and a derelict flour mill, gloomy and humid. Later on, thanks to their own efforts, the camp assumed a better appearance. The Poles leveled an area for playgrounds, built two swimming pools, and started a garden 2,600 square metres large, with several garden plots to be taken care of by the children themselves.

Over seven hundred children soon began attending schools in which classes were taught in Polish and Spanish. The Trade School offered three courses: dental technology, artistic silversmithing, and tailoring. Fifty students completed the dental technology course. In laboratories also at the secondary level, many young people were engaged in animal husbandry and horticulture. In 1944 the orphanage was taken over by Polish nuns, Felician Sisters from Chicago, who, because of Mexican legal restrictions, had to wear ordinary civilian clothes.

Among the orphans were 88 whose parents had died in Russia, 177 who had parents but were separated from them, and 11 whose parents were in Poland. Seventy-two children had lost their mothers in Russia but had fathers in the Army in the Middle East; the parents of 94 remained in Russia. The Polish Government-in-Exile paid for the maintenance of the camp, aided by the Polish American Council and the American "Caritas," known as the National Catholic Welfare Council. The refugees were not allowed to leave the camp in search of employment. The children, however, using the bus offered by the NCWC, made frequent sightseeing tours.

When the war ended, the welfare of the Polish children in Mexico deteriorated markedly. The secondary school was disbanded under the pretext that it was not preparing the students for practical life. Pressed by the Soviets and the Warsaw regime, the American Embassy began dismantling the Santa Rosa camp. A number of mothers with children emigrated to Canada, to Argentina, and to Great Britain; one group of students was accepted at Cambridge Springs College in the United States but was dismissed not long afterwards. Polish families in the United States offered shelter to the orphans from Santa Rosa, but their stay was not long either. After the camp was finally closed in 1947, a shelter was provided in Mexico City for the forty Polish children remaining, and they were provided for by the NCWC and the Polish Council of America. Since the local people were kindly disposed toward the shelter, it was maintained until 1952.

New Zealand

The children who went to Mexico unknowingly rendered a favor to their little peers who remained in Persia, by accidentally causing the gates of hospitality to open on the tranquil, charming island of New Zealand.

This is what happened: In June, 1943, the ship carrying the

Polish children to Mexico docked in the harbor of Wellington to replenish its supplies. At that time an official of the Red Cross, a Polish lady, happened to be at the quay. Seeing the miserable, emaciated little creatures, she began talking with them. Having learned about the sad turns of their fate, she alerted Mrs. Peter Frazer, the wife of New Zealand's Prime Minister, and informed her that in Persia there still remained thousands of Polish children in just as deplorable a condition as those heading for Mexico. Thanks to the extraordinary kindness of the Prime Minister and his wife, and of Archbishop Thomas O'Shea of Wellington, the government of New Zealand immediately sent to the Polish government in London an offer of New Zealand's hospitality for the Polish children.

As a result of this invitation, 736 children, four to fifteen years of age, mostly orphans, left Isfahan to go via Ahwaz to Basra, and from there to Bombay, where they boarded an American ship, the *SS General Randall*, that was returning New Zealand and Australian troops. After a lengthy voyage over mined waters, the ship called at Wellington on November 1, 1944. The children were accompanied by 105 grown-ups, the educational and service staffs, among them two nuns from the Order of Ursuline Sisters.

New Zealand made the occasion a manifestation of great cordiality. A documentary film was produced showing the scene of welcome and the close-cropped heads of the children cuddling confidently with the soldiers. Schools and social organizations came out with banners to greet the guests, the children were showered with flowers and kissed, and toasts were raised in honor of Poland.

Wellington City charmed the newcomers with its uncommon beauty. The multicolored houses scattered over the hills, the sensible planning of the city, the masses of greenery and flowers—all of it seemed unreal after the bleakness of the Soviet Union. The city oozed tranquility. There was no nervous rush, none of the noise or hubbub of the big cities of Europe. At this time of the year even the ocean murmured languidly, never revealing how formidable it can be in its wintertime of June and July. And such a mild climate! No wonder both of the islands forming New Zealand looked to the refugees like two precious emeralds.

The older children wanted right away to check their new location on their maps. Here was the country to come to! On some occasion, in one of their classes, they had learned that the island to the north abounds in geysers, hot springs, salt-water lakes, and the like, while the one to the south resembles Switzerland with its mountains and its rugged shores akin to the Norwegian fiords. What a bewitching variety! This was a far cry from the taiga and the desert.

The New Zealanders noticed with amazement that nothing gave their little guests so much joy as the luxuriant abundance of green, puffy grass to run and frolic on. The Polish grown-ups were struck with admiration by impressive technical progress, the comfort of the homes, the pleasant mode of life. The national economy was thriving, and social legislation, especially concerning child welfare, was on a very high level. Everything seemed to indicate that the children would be happy here.

The government of New Zealand was generous toward them. It assigned for their maintenance an annual budget of $70,000. In the course of a parliamentary debate, one of the members of the Legislature maintained that this sum would not be enough: "Assure the well-being of the Polish children to such an extent," he urged, "that they will never want to leave our country."

The children were accommodated in a place called Pahiatua, not far from Wellington, in a camp perfectly organized and well supplied by the New Zealand Army. The buildings belonged to the military; the educational and service staffs were composed exclusively of Poles. On a flagpole fluttered the flags of New Zealand and Poland, side by side.

The New Zealanders called the Pahiatua camp "Little Poland," and rightly so because here the Polish language was spoken and Polish national customs and mores were observed. English was the secondary language. The whole educational system—kindergartens, elementary and secondary schools with the general educational program, and the trade courses—was intended to prepare the children for life and work in Poland, where all who could were to return. The New Zealanders, although eager to adopt all the children, understood the intentions of the Polish authorities and did not interfere.

The educational standard in the Polish schools was acknowledged by New Zealanders to be high, but they believed that the Polish school system deprived the student of initiative and constrained his self-development, not allowing him room to become self-confident.

They were amused by some of the children's manners, acquired at home or imitated from the soldiers. The boys would take off their caps while greeting someone, bow and click their heels when shaking hands; the girls would curtsy and kiss the hands of the elderly ladies. It did not escape the New Zealanders' attention, however, that the children showed large gaps in their upbringing. In a normally functioning society proper upbringing is acquired almost automatically by good example; but our children had had too many bad examples during their exile and their globe-trotting not to have evolved their own brand of ethics among themselves. To correct bad behavior at school or the infringement of official regulations, especially by the older children, required constant watchfulness on the part of the school staff.

The end of the war brought about the complete sell-out of all Poland to Kremlin oppression—an unexpected blow to Poles dispersed throughout the world. The matter of returning home suddenly ceased to be taken for granted. How could one return to such a Poland?

Even before the end of the war, foreseeing that recognition of the legal Polish government in London would probably be withdrawn, Consul General Dr. K. A. Wodzicki, in cooperation with the Polish authorities in London, arranged to form the Guardianship Council for the Polish Children in New Zealand. The Council, composed of three New Zealanders and five Poles, was approved by the Highest Court of New Zealand in May, 1945. Under the Presidency of Dr. J. P. Kavanagh, Bishop of Dunedin, the Council took care of 644 children, 424 orphans and 220 with parents outside New Zealand.

From that time on the general trend of life in the Pahiatua camp changed significantly. Their education began to prepare them for life in New Zealand. The teaching of English was intensified, though the elementary school was still in the hands of Polish teachers. The secondary school with its general educational program was liquidated. When they reached adolescence, young people, tempted by easy work and high wages, took jobs. The younger students were transferred to the country's high schools on both islands. In predominantly Protestant New Zealand, the state schools are non-denominational, but the Polish Catholic children were given the opportunity to enter private Catholic schools and were accommodated in boarding houses. In Wellington, three Polish boarding houses were opened, two for boys, one for girls; they were run by Ursuline Sisters, whose team was increased by three nuns brought in from France and six others from the Pahiatua camp.

In 1947 and again in 1948, the Warsaw regime demanded that the children be returned to Poland, but the New Zealand government refused, arguing that the children were the responsibility of the Guardianship Council. Young persons past eighteen years of age were offered the choice of going back to Poland at the country's expense or of remaining there permanently. Not one of them chose to return. Significantly enough, of the forty-nine who had already gone back, ten were taken by their mothers returning to Poland, and the other thirty-nine returned to New Zealand at the request of their parents living in Poland. Their requests were in most cases notarized by the local parish priest.

The Pahiatua camp and the male boarding houses in Wellington no longer exist. The elementary school was liquidated in 1949, and only a boarding house for females remained, under the Ursuline Sisters' management, giving shelter to fifty-two girls working or still studying. Its superior was Sister Monica Aleksandrowicz, who for many years had meritoriously served in the Pahiatua Camp. This boarding house now has the character of a Polish Centre, where former alumni of the nuns often gather, spending their time in communal prayer, conversation, games, and singing. The nuns take care to maintain the Polish spirit among the young ones.

In 1955 the alumni of the Pahiatua camp held a rally to commemorate the tenth anniversary of their stay in New Zealand. New Zealanders also participated, among them the representative of their government, Minister Corbett, and Reverend Monsignor McRae of the Archbishopric in Wellington. Holy Mass, opening the three-day rally, was said by the rector of the Polish Catholic Mission in Wellington, Rev. Dr. Leon Plater. The former refugees expressed their gratitude for the hospitality they had received and for the very kind attitude of New Zealand society toward them. New Zealanders looked with justifiable pride at the fruits of their humanitarian effort, fruits which had matured through endeavors of their government, the educators, the Ursuline Sisters, and the children themselves. The proud results were confirmed by statistics showing that a large percentage of the alumni had completed trade schools or acquired a university education. One of them, A. Zak, won a scholarship for further study at Indiana University in the United States, specializing in aeronautical engineering. The following occupations had attracted the Polish youngsters most: architecture, agriculture, nursing, laboratory work, office work, auto mechanics, metallurgy, and electronics. Many boys chose cabinet-making, and many girls chose work in the fashion industry. Seven of them opted for convent life. By 1956 over two hundred Pahiatua alumni had married, and from these marriages over three hundred infants had been born. The number of marriages was continuing to grow.

The youngest orphans were assured free education until they could complete secondary school. Students over twenty-one years old still received assistance, with the proviso that they contribute to their own upkeep from their earnings during vacations. Apart from that, the government paid all of the youngsters' travel expenses whether to Poland or to another country they wished to settle in. The government also maintained the handicapped, taking care of them in a most humanitarian manner. One girl, for example, partly paralyzed after ten years of hospital treatment including all sorts of therapy and several unsuccessful operations, was assured not only subsistence but also education by correspondence in a special institution where she was designated for employment. She lived in the boarding house run by the Ursuline Sisters, had two wheelchairs of her own and a radio; her room was furnished in such a way that she could move around freely in her wheelchair.

The government of New Zealand had come to the aid of the Polish children just when they needed it most. This was not a casual favor, not just a kind gesture, but a genuine long-term commitment fulfilled to the last detail. On retiring from office, Prime Minister Frazer asked his successor to treat the problem of the Polish children with no less care than he himself had. New Zealand gave the Polish children the best care possible, believing that they owed it to those little exiles who had been deprived of everything.

Lebanon

Lebanon was another country where the Polish children in Persia sought shelter. The Poles who went to Lebanon were those who had stayed in Persia the longest, to the end of 1945 and the beginning of 1946.

This resettlement started with the departure of young people to begin university studies in Beirut. Most of their families went with them. By the time the last group of Poles from Persia landed in Lebanon, their number had grown to approximately five thousand, half of them young adults and children. The young people concentrated in Beirut around two universities, the French St. Joseph's University, operated by the Jesuit Fathers, and the American university. During the 1946-47 term, these universities enrolled 250 Polish students of both sexes.

Mothers with children were located in small Lebanese towns and villages such as Ghazir, Ajaltown, Baabdat, Beit-Chebab, Roumy, and Zouk-el-Micael, among the quiet, industrious population of the Catholic rite known as Maronite Christians. In these villages, partly hidden in the gentle hillsides, the Poles occupied cozy little stone houses scattered over craggy rocks in the valleys and on the hillsides which had been abandoned by natives emigrating to the United States to make a fortune and then return to their homeland. The local Maronite parish priests offered the Poles the use of their churches, and the newly ordained young Polish priests from St. Joseph's University in Beirut often said Mass there. In the Polish families the mothers looked after their households, cared for their children, and did handwork, mostly embroidery. In Ghazir, for instance, the women made beautiful chasubles for the newly ordained priests.

Lebanon's landscape, its mild climate, and the beautiful location acted soothingly upon the children, shielding their eyes from the cruel pictures of their recent past. From the mountain area where the Poles lived, a magnificent view opened upon a chain of green mountain peaks blooming with stone-pine forest, here and there shining with bald patches of whitish rock. The highest peak in Lebanon, the Sannin, attracted the eyes with its phantasmagoria of sun rays reflected from the scattered snow. Among the rocky precipices frothed and roared mountain streams from which the hard-working highlander would drain off water into his garden, stretching down the slopes in terraces guarded by stone dikes. Sheep and goats grazed in the mountain pastures. The hillsides, gradually falling toward the sea, displayed a variety of trees—olive, lemon, orange, banana—as well as many vineyards. From the distance Beirut was enchanting with the whiteness of its little homes and the redness of its roofs covered with Marseille shingles. No wonder the Arabic poets used to compare Beirut to a beautiful princess who, while resting wistfully on the seashore, supports her elbow on a cushion of lush greenery. Along the seashore quiet little bays lay dreaming, the sun-silvered waves withdrawing from their shores and running into the distance for a rendezvous with the horizon.

This small, charming, quiet corner of the world was paradise for the Polish children and young people. Health conditions were ideal, social services good. In return for all the benefits, the children were expected to study diligently. Learning in Lebanon had the spiritual patronage of the great Polish poet, Juliusz Slowacki, who in 1837 during his journey to the East spent three months here in Beit-Chasz-Bau near the mountain township of Ghazir in the retreat of an Armenian Catholic monastery, and subsequently in Beirut, where he wrote his "Anhelli." He was then a political emigre, just like the Poles who now were enjoying Lebanon's hospitality. Touched by this contact with the great poet, the Poles placed a memorial plaque in three languages on the wall of the monastery where he had stayed.

The people of Lebanon, cordial by nature, had great sympathy for the Poles. This feeling dated back to the time when, in the mid-nineteenth century, the Polish Dragoons, in the service of Turkey, were garrisoned here. (As is well known, Turkey dominated this beautiful land for over three centuries.) When in 1860 the Druze Moslems committed a heinous slaughter of the Christian population in Lebanon, France and Great Britain intervened, with the result that Turkey promised to nominate only Christian governors for Lebanon and to maintain garrisons composed only of Christians.

One of those Christian governors was a Pole, W. A. Czaykowski, otherwise known as Muzaffer Pasha, son of Michael, the famous Sadyk-Pasha, creator of the 2nd Regiment of the Ottoman Dragoons, composed of three thousand Polish soldiers. He played an important and memorable role in the history of Lebanon. The officers commanding the regiment were Polish Catholics, Stefan Gosciminski, called here Tufay-Bey, and Ludwik Sas-Monasterski, whose descendants live in Lebanon to this day.

This former link with the history of Lebanon eased the way for the refugees. Even during the Second World War, in 1940 and 1941, thousands of armed Polish soldiers had crossed the border into Romania and had gone on to Syria. There in Homs was formed the embryo of the Polish Armed Forces in the Middle East, later to be known as the Brygada Karpacka, the Carpathian

Brigade, who covered themselves with glory in the battles in North Africa.

Very memorable services had also been rendered to Lebanon by the well-remembered Pole, Father Maximilian Ryllo, 1802-1848, apostolic delegate to the Middle East, known in Arabic as "Abuna Mansur (Our Father Conqueror)." In 1836 he initiated and organized the so-called "Collegium Asiaticum," which eventually became St. Joseph's University in Beirut. Thanks to his merits the Jesuits cordially received the Polish youth for university studies.

Lebanon's new guests thus had predecessors of considerable stature. This fact not only imposed on them a moral obligation but also fired their imagination and spurred them on to become more closely acquainted with this country, part of the former homeland of the Phoenicians and a land which, because of its location and its beauty, has for ages attracted conquerors, poets, and men of learning.

Getting acquainted was not difficult, for various reasons. The status of the refugees in Lebanon was not that of people in a restricted camp life. On the contrary, the Polish guests, scattered in many locations, intermingled with the native Lebanese; and the country's small area, with only one and a half million inhabitants, made it very easy to move around. Picnics and outings were not as difficult or as expensive as in India. Everything here was within easy reach. The young people discovered with amazement that, in Lebanon, history speaks to one everywhere, that the days of antiquity seem as fresh as yesterday. Each trip to Beirut, for instance, reminded them that it was the ancient Berytos, recorded on the tablets of the Pharaoh Amenofis IV, and the city of Roman days famous for the teaching of law and the manufacture of silk. It was here that St. Louis stopped during the Crusades.

Just as it was the greatest pleasure for the younger children to submerge themselves in the luscious grass of New Zealand, without danger from venomous snakes, so with the same abandon did the older young Poles inhale Lebanon's atmosphere, so full of antiquities. For example, what an amount of history they encountered, in, say, Djebal (Phoenician Gebal), the Greek "Byblos" ("Book"), so named because paper was manufactured here, one of the oldest cities in the world, which existed even before the fall of Troy.

Lebanon's history could almost be learned from its many

inscriptions on rocks in a multitude of languages—Egyptian, Assyrian, Greek, Latin, French, and English—in the narrow passageway between the mountains and the sea. On the tall mountain walls, which require considerable skill to climb, are still preserved the polished rock-mirrors which in ancient days told the Phoenicians of the arrival of their deity, the Sun, rising behind the Anti-Lebanon mountains. The ruins of Roman temples in the Bekaa valley in Baalbek seem like modern history in comparison with such relics of the ancient Phoenicians.

Here one follows the traces of antiquity all the more eagerly because of the enchanting natural beauty. The young people liked to travel to Djoune, situated on a charming bay yet hidden among the mountains that form a natural amphitheatre. Here rises heavenward the gigantic statue of Notre Dame du Liban overlooking the town. They made outings to the valley of Bekaa, where, in Bikfaya, Father Maximilian Ryllo placed a miraculous picture of the Virgin Mary; they visited the Jesuit astronomical observatory, a winery in Ksara, and the summer residence of the Jesuits in Tanail, where the Polish clerics spent their yearly vacations.

Lebanon's charm is always very much alive and is reflected in the Bible stories depicting some of its famous settlements and the everlasting cedars of Lebanon, symbol of a country which, although conquered many times in the past, now wants to remain independent and free.

The Lebanese government was very friendly toward the Polish guests and wanted to help them settle on farms in the large, desert-like valley of Bekaa between Lebanon and Anti-Lebanon, where plans for an effective irrigation system were being prepared. Before leaving this charming country, the Poles left in Ghazir monastery a memorial plaque with the image of the Most Blessed Virgin Mary of Ostrabrama as an expression of gratitude to God for His care over them and for the hospitality offered by the Lebanese people. Today, their memories return fondly to Lebanon, the small country with the big heart.